Why Not Same-Sex Marriage

Why Not Same-Sex Marriage

A MANUAL FOR DEFENDING MARRIAGE AGAINST RADICAL DECONSTRUCTION

Daniel Heimbach

TRUSTED
BOOKS
A DIVISION OF DEEP RIVER BOOKS

Trusted Books is an imprint of Deep River Books. The views expressed or implied in this work are those of the author. To learn more about Deep River Books, go online to www.DeepRiverBooks.com.

Scripture is taken from the following versions:

Scripture references marked ESV are taken from *The Holy Bible: English Standard Version*, copyright © 2001, Wheaton: Good News Publishers. Used by permission. All rights reserved.

Scripture references marked NIV are taken from the *Holy Bible, New International Version*®, *NIV*®. Copyright © 1973, 1978, 1984 by Biblica, Inc.™ Used by permission of Zondervan. All rights reserved worldwide. www.zondervan.com

Scripture references marked NKJV are taken from the *New King James Version*. Copyright © 1982 by Thomas Nelson, Inc. Used by permission. All rights reserved.

The stories titled "I Thought Change Was Impossible" and "I Didn't Much Like Being a Girl" are published with permission of their authors.

The essay titled "Destroying Marriage by Deconstruction" first appeared by the title "Deconstructing the Family" in *The Religion & Society Report* (October/November, 2005) and is revised and republished with permission.

The essay titled "How the Mental Health Associations Misrepresent Science" first appeared by the title "The Trojan Couch" in *NARTH Conference Reports*, 2005, and is revised and republished with permission.

ISBN 13: 978-1-63269-276-4
Library of Congress Catalog Card Number: 2013913338

*Never
have Americans
faced a challenge so
severe as the one raised by
the present movement to
deconstruct the one
institution without
which no society
can survive.*

*Never
have Americans
faced a challenge so
severe as the one raised by
the present movement to
deconstruct the one
institution without
which no society
can survive.*

CONTENTS

Part II: For Further Consideration

It makes sense to
continue a practice that all societies
everywhere have practiced for all time,
especially when it is so obviously connected with
social continuity and survival. But it makes
no sense to remove what has given that
practice coherence just to pacify
desires that are incompatible with
that coherence.

INTRODUCTION

NOTHING IS MORE controversial these days than arguing over same-sex marriage. Other controversies exist, but no issue strikes as deeply, as close to home, or affects what everyone considers to be essential so drastically as the one that is currently threatening to deconstruct and destroy the framework of the institution that is without a doubt the most necessary to human flourishing. We live in times when the news is filled with one alarming crisis after another. Global warming, worldwide economic collapse, terrorist attacks, drug cartels, collapsing governments, revolutions, wide-scale corruption, massacres, persecution, tsunamis, droughts, floods, and earthquakes occupy the front page one day only to be replaced by another crisis the next. My belief is that the same-sex marriage debate should not only be deemed a *crisis* but is indeed the *most threatening* of the many crises we face.

Of course, not everyone agrees with this. Some do not agree because they are so preoccupied with other things that nothing else matters—their attention is focused elsewhere. Others do not agree because they do not know what is going on—they are not fully informed. But there are some who dispute the critical nature of this issue not because they deem it insignificant or are uninformed but because they comprehend its enormity and do not want others to realize what is happening. This group knows great changes are at stake and fear that if word gets out others will prevent them. In other words, people in this category desire enormous changes to occur and are afraid average people will oppose them if they find out the real stakes.

For those in this last category, denying the crisis nature of same-sex marriage is a ploy for easing general acceptance of the sort of change they think most people would try to stop if they knew what was happening. In this book, I will give those not following the controversy a better understanding of what is going on. I will do this by responding clearly and directly to 101 arguments currently being used by individuals to change popular thinking in ways meant to deaden their reaction to something terribly bad.

What this book addresses not only is important but timely. Polls show that Americans are equally divided on the issue of same-sex marriage. But this state is fluid. Opinions have been changing and are changing rather rapidly. They are not what they were just a few years ago, and they are not what they will be very soon. Popular attitudes are shifting toward acquiescence and outright preference. But shifting whims do not make redefining something as important as marriage either right or necessary. There was a time when slavery was so accepted as to be thought impossible to resist, but people of conviction spoke up. They challenged what was culturally popular, made a clear and compelling case against slavery based on enduring truth and the common good, and ultimately won the day. That can happen again.

Polls suggest that soon more Americans will favor same-sex marriage than oppose it, but we must not become discouraged. Rather, we must challenge the aura of inevitability because these polls are not giving a true measure of how people think or will vote on the issue. In truth, people rarely tell pollsters what they think or will do at the ballot box, especially when pressed to reveal convictions they think will be criticized. Americans are not yet as closely divided on same-sex marriage as some recent polling suggests. A more reliable and useful measure of where Americans stand these days can be seen in the fact that nearly every time the issue has been put to a popular vote, it has been soundly rejected—usually by 2-to-1 margins.

In this book, I stand on what is actually true. I rely on what is objectively the case as opposed to what people merely feel or desire. Without name-calling, shifting blame, or disparaging personal character, facts are allowed to speak for themselves.

When it comes to the rise and fall of political power, enormous pressures can distort the truth unless firmly resisted. Truth is the first casualty in political contests where one or both sides rely chiefly on emotion, on making good impressions, and on grabbing favorable attention at all costs. When this occurs, contests degenerate into emotional rhetoric severed from objective reality. Opponents are blackened beyond recognition, and champions become larger than life. This book enters a fray in which both sides are passionate, but it does so clinging to objective reality while resisting mischaracterization and distortion. It addresses an emotional issue with dispassion, fairness, and respect for those who may disagree.

Lies only work when not refuted. When exposed, lies not only collapse but end up diminishing the credibility and influence of those who employ them. Today, statements contrary to fact are being slung in the controversy over same-sex marriage. We must realize that when it comes to the nature, meaning, and structure of universal marriage over time, there is one—and only one—objectively real state of things. Objective truth regarding the nature, meaning, and structure of marriage as a social institution (worldwide and for all time) is not a question of personal feeling, choice, or opinion, but is a matter of *facts*. The fact is that those now proposing same-sex marriage are disputing something real. They oppose and are trying to deconstruct an institution that exists now and has existed throughout human history. We must decide who is telling the truth and who is not based on that reality—not based on something we imagine but based on something we already know is well proven by billions of our ancestors.

In this book, I dispute, challenge, and push back against many false claims used these days to sway popular opinion toward favoring same-sex marriage. I do this simply by exposing these claims for what they are. I employ truth to reveal how arguments favoring same-sex marriage consist of nothing more than distortion, inconsistency, misrepresentation, mischaracterization, contradiction, irrationality, and, sometimes plain nonsense. Of course, those favoring same-sex marriage will claim the reverse. Fair enough. This only means readers must think and decide for themselves which side is most credible. I am confident that those who do will soon realize that what they read here does, indeed, fit the facts.

The issue of same-sex marriage is both daunting and enormous. This is so not only because it is an issue that matters to everyone everywhere, but also because it is terribly complex. It is political, social, moral, scientific, legal, and religious; it concerns justice, equality, fairness, and the common good; and it affects social stability, social cohesion, social strength, social endurance, and social survival. While we should address every false argument for same-sex marriage in its own right, we should not forget that particular arguments are linked to a larger picture. Removing one argument affects others—often many—and redefining the most basic and essential of social institutions threatens every other social institution, not just itself.

This means there is great danger in supposing the same-sex marriage debate can be reduced to one simple component—such as what motivates individuals to marry, or how some opposite-sex couples are infertile or choose to have no children, or how children raised by same-sex couples lack married parents, or how a same-sex couple feels compared to opposite-sex couples. Such issues matter privately to those concerned, but they have little importance compared to the value of maintaining essential social institutions, or to the public interest in having governments secure the common good. Private feelings, motivations, and experiences matter privately but have nothing to do with the public value of assuring intergenerational social survival.

When arguments are made that subordinate something as essential to the common good as guarding the procreational structure of marriage to something as irrelevant to the common good as personal feelings, they fall into a category of reasoning that logicians call *Reductio ab Absurdum*. In other words, they reduce reasoning to absurdity. Generally speaking, all arguments for same-sex marriage fall into this category, because it is absurd to affirm how a few people feel by doing something that harms everyone in major ways—destabilizing society and causing civilization to collapse in the process. It is logically absurd to sacrifice a critically important public good for something of no public value or significance. It is logically absurd to threaten something on which everyone in the human family depends merely to favor something non-essential to the human family.

Finally, I designed this book to be used not only to convince the undecided of the social necessity of keeping the nature, meaning, and structure of civil marriage from being radically deconstructed, but also to serve as a resource for those taking up this important cause. It is my goal that those who defend marriage will use this book as a reference manual to quickly and effectively respond to various strategies of attack when the issue of same-sex marriage comes up in family conversations, or is questioned by their neighbors, or is discussed at corporate board meetings, or is contested in the courts, or is made the focus of public debate and policy decision-making. When decisions must be made and votes must be cast, there is seldom time to think things through—but these moments of crisis are not the time to wing it and hope for the best. This book offers readers the benefit of having already "thought things through" by providing responses to opposing arguments that are both accessible and to the point.

It is my hope this book will serve that purpose well, because marriage is well worth preserving and defending.

It is
absurd to
compare causing the
collapse of civilization with
enhancing how a few people feel
about themselves. It is absurd to sacrifice
an essential public good for something entirely
private. It is absurd to sacrifice
something so terribly important
to everyone just to achieve
something so trivial it
affects almost
no one.

INDEX OF ARGUMENTS GIVEN FOR ALLOWING SAME-SEX MARRIAGE

(That Deny Marriage Has Any Fixed Structure)

INDEX OF REFUTATIONS FOR ALLOWING SAME-SEX MARRIAGE

(That Defend the Current Structure of Marriage)

Refutations Regarding Constitutional Law

Refutations Regarding Morality and Ethics

Refutations Regarding God and Theology

PART I

Gracious Answers to Arguments You Hear

*Trying
to separate
what marriage means
from sex is like trying
to separate what a
car means from
transportation.*

Arguments 1–11

Gracious Answers to Arguments Regarding the Nature of Marriage

*Marriage is
the institution on which social
survival most depends, but same-sex
marriage deinstitutionalizes the institution
by removing its structure. Feelings are not
structure, and no institution can be
structured, much less survive,
on nothing more than feelings.*

REGARDING THE NATURE OF MARRIAGE

(Arguments 1–11)

1

You May Hear Proponents Argue ...

SAME-SEX MARRIAGE SHOULD be allowed because it only concerns homosexuals and does not affect others. Allowing same-sex marriage affects no one but homosexuals and has nothing to do with anyone else. For this reason, people should either support gay marriage or just mind their own business. Civility, good manners, and common decency all require that those with no direct interest in same-sex marriage get out of the way and stop making things harder for others. If people do not have the common decency to stop interfering, then others should just ignore what they say. Same-sex marriage should be approved because opponents have no valid stake in resisting it.

You Can *Graciously Refute* This By Saying ...

Everyone in society has a valid stake in opposing same-sex marriage because marriage is the centerpiece of our entire social structure. When we remove the gender-based structure of civil marriage, it turns marriage into something with no structure at all—and doing so harms everyone by deconstructing and thereby destroying the one institution without which our society cannot survive. While singles and same-sex couples can feed children and take them to school, no society can endure if it does not encourage men and women to become parents who raise children of their own.

Furthermore, removing the gender-based structure of marriage harms everyone because (1) it changes marriage into something that merely affirms adult appetites and has nothing to do with having children; (2) it no longer compels father-mother pairs to set aside individual or couple-related goals in order to do what is best for having and raising children; and (3) it leads to fewer children learning to respect, expect, or even desire pursuing procreationally structured marriage.

As the example of Scandinavia demonstrates, once society removes the gender-based structure of publically supported marriage, it results in that society's general loss of interest in getting married at all. Allowing same-sex marriages will encourage more and more people to regard marriage as nothing more than a way to affirm adult appetites, which will lead to fewer adults deciding to sacrifice their interests for the sake of children. This is a bad thing for children, and it is bad for society as a whole.

The Truth Is …

Same-sex marriage is wrong because it undermines public interest in favoring relationships required to perpetuate the race.

References and Further Reading

For an example of this argument, see Tod Lindberg, "Husbands and Wives: What Gay Marriage Won't Change," *Weekly Standard* (August 2, 2004), pp. 27-29.

Maggie Gallagher and Joshua K. Baker, "Demand for Same-Sex Marriage: Evidence from the United States, Canada, and Europe," *Policy Brief*, Institute for Marriage and Public Policy, 3/1 (April 26, 2006).

Maggie Gallagher, "Normal Marriage: Two Views," *Marriage and Same-Sex Unions: A Debate*, ed. Lynn Wardle, Mark Strasser, William Duncan, and David Coolidge (Westport, CT: Praeger, 2003), pp. 13-24.

Maggie Gallagher, "(How) Will Gay Marriage Weaken Marriage as a Social Institution: A Reply to Andrew Koppelman," *University of Saint Thomas Law Journal*, 2/1 (Fall 2004), pp. 33-70.

Kerry Jacoby, "You Call This 'Respect'?" *American Thinker* (October 01, 2009), accessible at http://www.americanthinker.com/2009/10/you_call_this_respect.html. Jacoby notes that the gay lobby "wouldn't want [same-sex marriage] if it didn't have a more public effect…. The goal of the gay rights lobby is, and always has been, to change society and force it to accept their 'lifestyle choice' as a legal and moral equivalent to traditional, heterosexual marriage."

Robert P. George and Jean Bethke Elshtain, eds., *The Meaning of Marriage: Family, State, Market, and Morals* (Dallas, TX: Spence Publishing, 2006).

Glenn T. Stanton and Bill Maier, *Why Marriage Matters: Reasons to Believe in Marriage in Postmodern Society* (Colorado Springs, CO: Pinion Press, 1997).

William C. Duncan, "The State Interest in Marriage," *Ave Maria Law Review*, 2/1 (Spring 2004), pp. 153-182.

Timothy Dailey, "Comparing the Lifestyles of Homosexual Couples to Married Couples," published by *Family Research Council* (April 29, 2004), accessible at http://www.frc.org/get.cfm?i=IS04C02.

Anthropologist Claude Lévi-Strauss shows that procreationally structured marriage is not necessarily or uniquely religious but rather should be categorized as a universally practiced "social institution with a biological foundation." See Claude Lévi-Strauss, "Introduction," in *A History of the Family*, by André Burguière (Cambridge, MA: Harvard University Press, 1996), p. 5. Lévi-Strauss also observes that marriage is everywhere structured as "a union, more or less durable, but socially approved, of two individuals of opposite sexes who establish a household and bear and raise children." He says this marital form is found "to be a practically universal phenomenon, present in every type of society." See Claude Lévi-Strauss, *The View from Afar* (New York: Basic Books, 1985), pp. 40-41.

2

You May Hear Proponents Argue ...

Same-sex marriage should be allowed because marriage has become nothing more than a way of affirming deeply held emotional commitments. Marriage in our modern culture has become nothing more than a way for people to confer social approval for forming deeply held emotional, financial, and psychological bonds between individuals. Homosexuals are identical in this respect to heterosexuals, thus there is no public basis for treating homosexuals differently from heterosexuals. For this reason, the state should extend the public approval that marriage confers to all persons who share deeply held personal bonds—whether those bonds are homosexual or heterosexual.

You Can *Graciously Refute* This By Saying ...

Most of the same-sex couples now demanding freedom to marry view marriage in terms of what one homosexual theorist calls "an intensified form of coming out." In other words, what these couples really want is to redefine marriage by changing how marriage is structured—all as a way of forcing others to approve how they choose to behave. Instead of accepting the institution of marriage as it currently exists, they want to change what getting married *means* for everyone who wants to get married. Rather than adjusting their own personal goals and behaviors to deserve the sort of social approval that goes with being married, they want to force others to approve their personal goals and behaviors by changing what getting married means.

In this way, proponents of same-sex marriage advocate changing the meaning and institutional structure of marriage to get others to validate how they satisfy private desires. They really have no respect for the way historic marriage has been structured to serve the public interest in favoring the common good of procreation. In addition, as they ignore legitimate public interest in favoring procreation, they wrongly claim that marriage never was—or is no longer—intrinsically procreative. In truth, the public interest in favoring and supporting the procreational structure of marriage has never changed, and it continues to be as strong as ever. This strong and legitimate public interest has nothing to do with validating or affirming private feelings, but only with getting biological fathers and mothers to cooperate in raising their own children and, as a result, to secure the intergenerational survival of society as a whole.

The Truth Is ...

Same-sex marriage is wrong because it uses marriage to reach a goal that is incompatible with the structure of marriage as a social institution.

References and Further Reading

Theodore Olson and David Boies used this argument to try to persuade a federal court to invalidate California's Proposition 8, which banned same-sex marriage in the state. See Theodore B. Olson, "The Conservative Case for Gay Marriage: Why Same-Sex Marriage Is an American Value," *Newsweek* (January 18, 2010), pp. 48-54.

Maggie Gallagher and Joshua K. Baker, "Demand for Same-Sex Marriage: Evidence from the United States, Canada, and Europe," *Policy Brief*, Institute for Marriage and Public Policy (IMAPP), 3/1 (April 26, 2006).

Maggie Gallagher, "Normal Marriage: Two Views," in *Marriage and Same-Sex Unions: A Debate*, ed. Lynn Wardle, Mark Strasser, William Duncan, and David Coolidge (Westport, CT: Praeger, 2003), pp. 13-24.

Maggie Gallagher, "What Marriage Is For: Children Need Mothers and Fathers," *Weekly Standard* (August 4/August 11, 2003), pp. 22-25.

Timothy Dailey, "Comparing the Lifestyles of Homosexual Couples to Married Couples," published by *Family Research Council* (April 29, 2004), accessible at http://www.frc.org/get.cfm?i=IS04C02.

Robert P. George and Jean Bethke Elshtain, eds., *The Meaning of Marriage: Family, State, Market, and Morals* (Dallas, TX: Spence Publishing, 2006).

Glenn T. Stanton and Bill Maier, *Marriage on Trial: The Case Against Same-Sex Marriage and Parenting* (Downers Grove, IL: InterVarsity Press, 2004).

David Popenoe, *Disturbing the Nest: Family Change and Decline in Modern Societies* (Edison, NJ: Transaction, 1988).

For examples of gay social revolutionaries admitting they are using same-sex marriage as a way to completely abolish the institution of marriage, see Thomas B. Stoddard, "Why Gay People Should Seek the Right to Marry," chapter 35 in *Families in the US: Kinship and Domestic Politics*, ed. Karen V. Hansen (Philadelphia, PA: Temple University Press, 1998); Richard D. Mohr, *A More Perfect Union: Why Straight America Must Stand Up for Gay Rights* (Boston, MA: Beacon, 1994); Gretchen A. Stiers, *From This Day Forward: Commitment, Marriage, and Family in Lesbian and Gay Relationships* (New York: St. Martin's Press, 1999); Michelangelo Signorile, "Bridal Wave," *Out* (December/January 1994); "Sociologist Says Gay Marriage Does Threaten Established Order and That's Good," *Ascribe Law News Service* (November 16, 2003); and Margaret Gullette, "The New Case for Marriage," *American Prospect* (March 1, 2004).

3

You May Hear Proponents Argue …

Same-sex marriage should be allowed because it increases the general level of respect for marriage. Expanding the options for couples who want to marry raises the value of marriage as a whole by increasing the number of people in society who favor marriage over non-marriage. Allowing same-sex marriage will increase people's regard for marriage in the same way that allowing racially mixed marriage has increased social regard for marriage as a whole. In this way, allowing same-sex marriages is a great way to raise respect for marriage among more people throughout society.

You Can *Graciously Refute* This By Saying …

The problem with this argument is that legalizing same-sex marriage radically redefines marriage in a way that *lessens*—not *increases*—the public's general regard for marriage as a social institution. It does this in three ways.

First, it redefines marriage by shifting the significance of marriage away from something that is socially necessary toward something that is only a matter of personal preference, away from something fixed toward something that is transitory, and away from something that serves others to something that only satisfies the self.

Second, same-sex marriage opens the door to marriages being based on satisfying every sexual desire imaginable. The more the institution of marriage incorporates, the less difference there is between marriage and non-marriage. The less difference there is between marriage and non-marriage, the less people will value getting married at all. Marriage that includes everything is worth nothing. *20% of Vermont*

Third, while mixed-race marriages increased social regard for marriage, it did so by strengthening respect for procreation, bridging the male-female divide, and uniting fathers with mothers to raise children. Same-sex marriage will only lower the public's regard for marriage by deconstructing these same three values and reconceiving marriage in a manner that erodes the welfare of future generations.

Homosexual activist Michelangelo Signorile admits that legalizing same-sex marriage will destroy marriage. He notes that it is the gay lobby's goal to "fight for same-sex marriage … and then, once granted, [to] redefine the institution completely … not as a way of adhering to society's moral codes but rather to debunk America and radically alter an archaic institution."

The Truth Is …

Same-sex marriage is wrong because it reduces marriage to nothing special by confusing marriage with non-marriage.

References and Further Reading

For an example of this argument, see Michelangelo Signorile, "Bridal Wave," *Out* (December/January 1994), p. 161.

Mollie Ziegler Hemingway, "Same-Sex, Different Marriage: Many of Those Who Want Marriage Equality Do Not Want Fidelity," *Christianity Today* (May 18, 2010), accessible at http://www. christianitytoday.com/ct/2010/may/11.52.html.

Daniel R. Heimbach, "Deconstructing the Family," *Religion and Society Report*, 22/7 (October/November 2005), p. 112.

Stanley Kurtz, "The End of Marriage in Scandinavia: The 'Conservative Case' for Same-Sex Marriage Collapses," *Weekly Standard* (February 2, 2004), pp. 26-33.

Stanley Kurtz, "Beyond Gay Marriage: The Road to Polyamory," *Weekly Standard* (August 4/August 11, 2003), pp. 26-33.

Stanley Kurtz, "Here Comes the Brides: Plural Marriage Is Waiting in the Wings," *Weekly Standard* (December 26, 2005), pp. 19-27.

David Popenoe, *Disturbing the Nest: Family Change and Decline in Modern Societies* (Edison, NJ: Transaction, 1988).

Maggie Gallagher, "Normal Marriage: Two Views," in *Marriage and Same-Sex Unions: A Debate,* ed. Lynn Wardle, Mark Strasser, William Duncan, and David Coolidge (Westport, CT: Praeger, 2003), pp. 13-24.

Maggie Gallagher, "What Marriage Is For: Children Need Mothers and Fathers," *Weekly Standard* (August 4/August 11, 2003), pp. 22-25.

Maggie Gallagher, "(How) Will Gay Marriage Weaken Marriage as a Social Institution: A Reply to Andrew Koppelman," *University of Saint Thomas Law Journal,* 2/1 (Fall 2004), pp. 33-70.

Robert P. George and Jean Bethke Elshtain, eds., *The Meaning of Marriage: Family, State, Market, and Morals* (Dallas, TX: Spence Publishing, 2006).

Carle Zimmerman, *Family and Civilization* (Wilmington, DE: ISI Books, 2008).

Glenn T. Stanton and Bill Maier, *Marriage on Trial: The Case Against Same-Sex Marriage and Parenting* (Downers Grove, IL: InterVarsity Press, 2004).

4

You May Hear Proponents Argue ...

Same-sex marriage should be allowed because it aligns the practice of marriage with human nature. There have always been homosexuals, and homosexuals are certainly as fully human as heterosexuals. Variations in sexual attraction come from differently oriented desires that are as natural for homosexuals as opposite-sex attraction is for heterosexuals. Marriage should not conflict with human nature but support it, and for this reason limiting marriage to opposite-sex partners is both unnatural and inhuman. Marriage will never align with human nature until every person is allowed to marry a partner to whom he or she is most naturally attracted.

You Can *Graciously Refute* This By Saying ...

While it is true that human marriage should align with human nature, proponents of this argument are wrong because they assume different human natures, when really there is only one human nature shared by everyone. This commonly shared human nature does not vary from individual to individual; it is something we all share and not something that changes or is affected by personal feelings, desires, preferences, or self-interpretations. There simply is no such thing as one version of human nature for homosexuals and a different version for others. People share it the same way, regardless of differences.

Human nature cannot be affected by feelings, desires, preferences, or self-interpretations because these things always differ and change over time. Nothing defined by such things can be true of everyone, in the same way, all the time. Commonly shared human nature in relation to sex is not a matter of preferences, feelings, or desires, but rather connects to the way human bodies function to

human nature in sex = propogation of species.

propagate the species. In other words, it is hardwired to the way human bodies naturally "fit" when procreating, regardless of what the human partners happen to choose, enjoy, or even like.

Only male-female unions align with this commonly shared human nature in relation to sexual activity, and only marriage between a man and a woman supports this commonality as an institution. The drive to legalize same-sex marriage is really a Trojan horse that, on closer inspection, is meant not to protect a threatened minority, but rather to entrench in law the notion that gender is essentially a social construct. This idea is based not in the natural order, but in arbitrary acts of human self-interpretation.

The Truth Is …

Same-sex marriage is wrong because it does not align with human nature in relation to sex.

References and Further Reading

For an example of this argument see Matthew Ridley, *The Red Queen: Sex and the Evolution of Human Nature* (New York: Macmillan, 1994), and Tod Lindberg, "Husbands and Wives: What Gay Marriage Won't Change," *Weekly Standard* (August 2, 2004), pp. 27-29.

Fred Mann, *Human Nature in Marriage* (Washington, DC: National Council of Catholic Men, 1948).

Robert P. George and Jean Bethke Elshtain, eds., *The Meaning of Marriage: Family, State, Market, and Morals* (Dallas, TX: Spence Publishing, 2006).

Sherif Girgis, Robert P. George, and Ryan T. Anderson, "What Is Marriage?" *Harvard Journal of Law and Public Policy*, 34/1 (Winter 2011), pp. 245-287.

Sherif Girgis, Ryan T. Anderson, and Robert P. George, "Marriage: Merely a Social Construct?" *Public Discourse: Ethics, Law and the Common Good* (December 29, 2010), accessible at http://www.thepublicdiscourse.com.

Sherif Girgis, Ryan T. Anderson, and Robert P. George, "Does Marriage, or Anything, Have Essential Properties?" *Public Discourse: Ethics, Law and the Common Good* (January 12, 2011), accessible at http://www.thepublicdiscourse.com.

For arguments on disputing the normal view of marriage, see Maggie Gallagher, "Normal Marriage: Two Views," in *Marriage and Same-Sex Unions: A Debate*, ed. Lynn Wardle, Mark Strasser, William Duncan, and David Coolidge (Westport, CT: Praeger, 2003), pp. 13-24.

Maggie Gallagher, "(How) Will Gay Marriage Weaken Marriage as a Social Institution," *University of Saint Thomas Law Journal*, 2/1 (Fall 2004), pp. 33-70.

Douglas Farrow, "Blurring Sexual Boundaries," *First Things*, 211 (March 2011), pp. 17-19.

For arguments on how legalizing same-sex marriage will align marriage to homosexual categories and not align homosexuals to what marriage is now, see Lawrence Auster, "The Extreme Radicalism of Homosexual 'Marriage," *View from the Right* (June 2, 2008), accessible at http://www.amnation.com/vfr/archives/010723.html.

Oliver O'Donovan notes that "the either-or of biological maleness and femaleness to which the human race is bound is not a meaningless or oppressive condition of nature." See Oliver O'Donovan, *Transsexualism and Christian Marriage* (Bramcote, UK: Grove Books, 1982), p. 7.

5

You May Hear Proponents Argue …

Same-sex marriage should be allowed because it enhances respect for the religious value of marriage. Although religion deals with matters beyond the sphere of government, the public's general respect for marriage is strengthened when religion and law are aligned. For many people, respect for marriage follows governmental recognition. When a government refuses to recognize that a marriage is blessed by religion, it lessens people's respect for the religious value of marriage in general. Denying same-sex marriage thus prevents governments from affirming that all marriages are blessed by religion, which only serves to erode society's general regard for marriage as a whole.

You Can *Graciously Refute* This By Saying …

Proponents of this argument praise the religious value of marriage when a religious group permits or approves more than is recognized under civil law, but not when a religious group permits or approves less. In this way, they rely on a level of rational inconsistency in which they reject religious thinking when it aligns with keeping marriage law the way it has always been, but approves religious thinking when it aligns with changing marriage in a manner that has no significant history in either religious or civil terms.

What this reveals is that those who are making this argument are only using it as a tactic for getting what they want, regardless of consistency. In other words, it reveals that their interest in legalizing same-sex marriage is more about using the debate to gain public acceptance of their beliefs—that homosexual behavior is good and normal. It is more a method for forcing society to normalize homosexuality than it is about increasing general respect for the value of marriage—whether religious or not. By appealing to religion only when it suits their agenda, those who use this argument actually show more disrespect than honor for the sanctity of marriage.

Proponents of this argument are attempting either to separate civil marriage from everything religious, or to align marriage law with anything a religious group happens to allow. Instead, laws and public policies in relation to marriage as a social institution should simply focus on serving the legitimate, well-grounded public interest in supporting the common good of bridging the male-female divide. These laws and policies should encourage procreation and compelling fathers and mothers to cooperate in raising their own children.

The Truth Is …

Same-sex marriage is wrong because it devalues maintaining the structure of marriage as a social and religious institution.

References and Further Reading

For examples of gay social revolutionaries admitting they are using same-sex marriage as a way to completely abolish the institution of marriage, see Thomas B. Stoddard, "Why Gay People Should Seek the Right to Marry," chapter 35 in *Families in the US: Kinship and Domestic Politics*, ed. Karen V. Hansen (Philadelphia, PA: Temple University Press, 1998); Richard D. Mohr, *A More Perfect Union: Why Straight America Must Stand Up for Gay Rights* (Boston, MA: Beacon, 1994); Gretchen A. Stiers, *From This Day Forward: Commitment, Marriage, and Family in Lesbian and Gay Relationships* (New York: St. Martin's Press, 1999); Michelangelo Signorile, "Bridal Wave," *Out* (December/January 1994); "Sociologist Says Gay Marriage Does Threaten Established Order and That's Good," *Ascribe Law News Service*

(November 16, 2003); and Margaret Gullette, "The New Case for Marriage," *American Prospect* (March 1, 2004).

Douglas Laycock, Anthony Picarello, and Robin Wilson, eds., *Same-Sex Marriage and Religious Liberty: Emerging Conflicts* (New York: Rowman and Littlefield, 2008).

Maggie Gallagher, "Banned in Boston: The Coming Conflict Between Same-Sex Marriage and Religious Liberty," *The Weekly Standard* (May 15, 2006), pp. 20-26.

Marc D. Stern, "Liberty v. Equality; Equality v. Liberty," *Northwestern Journal of Law and Social Policy*, 5/2 (Fall 2010), pp. 307-317, accessible at http://acadia.law.northwestern.edu/journals/njlsp/v5/n2/5/5Stern.pdf.

Mary Ann Glendon, "For Better or for Worse?" *Wall Street Journal* (February. 25, 2004), p. A14, accessible at http://www.catholic-fidelity.com/for-better-or-for-worse-by-mary-ann-glendon/.

Tom Strode, "Scholars: 'Gay Marriage' Will Cause Church-State Clashes," *Baptist Press* (June 2006), accessible at http://www.bpnews.net/printerfriendly.asp?ID=23383.

Emily Donohue, "Same-Sex Marriage Would Have Disastrous Effects on Churches," *Rhode Island Catholic* (March 13, 2008), accessible at http://www.thericatholic.com/news/detail.html?subid=968.

M.V. Lee Badgett, *When Gay People Get Married: What Happens When Societies Legalize Same-Sex Marriage* (New York: New York University Press, 2009).

For how the U.S. Constitution will be interpreted to deny any religious exception should resisting homosexual normalization be classified in the same legal category as racial discrimination, see Chai R. Feldblum, "Moral Conflict and Liberty; Gay Rights and Religion," *Brooklyn Law Review*, 72/1 (2006), pp. 61-123.

6

You May Hear Proponents Argue …

Same-sex marriage should be allowed because it reduces the number of marriages ending in divorce. Denying same-sex marriage forces homosexuals to marry partners to whom they are not sexually attracted, which only increases the number of marriages ending in divorce. Homosexuals understand that the strength of a marriage requires both partners to be honest about their sexual attraction and that allowing extramarital outlets enable marriages to last longer. Allowing same-sex marriage will thus reduce the number of failed marriages by allowing homosexuals to form stronger marital bonds and by treating marriage in a more flexible way for everyone.

You Can *Graciously Refute* This By Saying …

Proponents of this argument are more concerned with forcing social approval of homosexual sex than they are with honestly trying to reduce the number of failed marriages. It is ridiculous to imagine that homosexuals would be forced to marry partners they do not find attractive. This idea would make sense if—and only if—homosexuals believed in saving sex for marriage and limiting sex to marriage, which simply is not the case.

While marriage is a form of sexual relationship, it is not meant for any form at all. It is wrong to think that marriage as a social institution is structured merely as a way to gratify whatever desires one happens to have, or that the public interest in favoring marriage concerns nothing more than affirming private appetites, or that everyone is entitled to marry whatever partner he or she thinks pleasing, or that homosexuals are getting married for access to partners they do not find sexually attractive. It is also incredibly

foolish to imagine that any marriage can be made stronger and longer lasting by detaching sexual fidelity from marital commitment.

In reality, allowing same-sex marriage will weaken and
destabilize all marriages by completely overturning the way
society treats sex and marriage. It will upset the public's value
of sex in marriage by centralizing the importance of individual
gratification and marginalizing the importance of sexual fidelity and
procreation. It will redirect public support away from disciplining
personal appetites for the sake of having and raising responsible
citizens toward indulging personal appetites regardless of marital
commitment, duties, or responsibilities.

The Truth Is …

*Same-sex marriage is wrong because it destabilizes marriage by
removing what gives marriage institutional structure.*

References and Further Reading

Stanley Kurtz, "The End of Marriage in Scandinavia: The
    'Conservative Case' for Same-Sex Marriage Collapses," *Weekly
    Standard* (February 2, 2004), pp. 26-33.
Stanley Kurtz, "Beyond Gay Marriage: The Road to Polyamory,"
    Weekly Standard (August 4/August 11, 2003), pp. 26-33.
Stanley Kurtz, "Here Comes the Brides: Plural Marriage Is Waiting
    in the Wings," *Weekly Standard* (December 26, 2005), pp. 19-27.
David Popenoe, *Disturbing the Nest: Family Change and Decline in
    Modern Societies* (Edison, NJ: Transaction, 1988).
Mathew D. Staver, *Same-Sex Marriage: Putting Every Household at
    Risk* (Nashville, TN: Broadman and Holman, 2004).
Timothy Dailey, "Comparing the Lifestyles of Homosexual
    Couples to Married Couples," published by *Family Research
    Council* (April 29, 2004), accessible at http://www.frc.org/get.
    cfm?i=IS04C02.

Maggie Gallagher, "Normal Marriage: Two Views," in *Marriage and Same-Sex Unions: A Debate*, ed. Lynn Wardle, Mark Strasser, William Duncan, and David Coolidge (Westport, CT: Praeger, 2003), pp. 13-24.

Maggie Gallagher, "What Marriage Is For: Children Need Mothers and Fathers," *Weekly Standard* (August 4/August 11, 2003), pp. 22-25.

Maggie Gallagher, "(How) Will Gay Marriage Weaken Marriage as a Social Institution: A Reply to Andrew Koppelman," *University of Saint Thomas Law Journal*, 2/1 (Fall 2004), pp. 33-70.

Maggie Gallagher, "The Case Against Same-Sex Marriage," in *Debating Same-Sex Marriage* (New York: Oxford University Press, 2012), pp. 91-178.

Robert P. George and Jean Bethke Elshtain, eds., *The Meaning of Marriage: Family, State, Market, and Morals* (Dallas, TX: Spence Publishing, 2006).

Carle Zimmerman, *Family and Civilization* (Wilmington, DE: ISI Books, 2008).

Glenn T. Stanton and Bill Maier, *Marriage on Trial: The Case Against Same-Sex Marriage and Parenting* (Downers Grove, IL: InterVarsity Press, 2004).

7

You May Hear Proponents Argue ...

Same-sex marriage should be allowed because the ability to have children is not essential to the nature of marriage. The only reason for denying marriage to homosexuals is their inability to procreate. However, this inability to have children has never kept infertile heterosexuals from getting married, and it has never been used to disqualify anyone from getting married except homosexuals. While society used to link marriage to procreation, it now makes no connection at all. Today, marriage is considered to be one thing and having children something else. Parents have children regardless of marriage, and society treats marriage as something recreational, not procreational.

You Can *Graciously Refute* This By Saying ...

Denying that procreation is a primary function of marriage is like denying that a primary function of a car is to drive. A car will still be a car even if it is left in a garage and never driven anywhere, but denying a car is *designed* or *structured* for driving changes what a *car* means by turning it into something entirely different. While it is true that marriages can exist without children, severing procreation from the marital structure turns marriage into non-marriage.

Proponents of this argument confuse the *form* (a non-varying structure) of marriage as a social institution with an *accident* (a non-structural variation) in how some couples perform. They use an accidental similarity (infertility) to justify a formal equality (that same-sex and opposite-sex couples are no different). They wrongly reject a formal difference (procreational and non-procreational forms are not the same) as just an accident (that it makes no formal difference). However, the way marriage is structured as a social institution requires a male-female form in order to procreate, whether the couple is fertile or not. Changing marriage to include same-sex couples alters its formal structure so that what passes for *marriage* is not procreational at all.

In the end, proponents of this argument reduce procreation to something *accidental* (not inherent to the marital form) and leave marriage with no fixed structure and no public value in justifying its institutional support. In reality, the public interest in marriage is in supporting the importance of generational replacement to societal continuity. Severing the marital form from procreation threatens not only the existence of marriage as a social institution but also the survival of society itself.

The Truth Is …

Same-sex marriage is wrong because it threatens the survival of a society by severing procreation from how marriage is structured.

References and Further Reading

Maggie Gallagher, "Normal Marriage: Two Views," in *Marriage and Same-Sex Unions: A Debate*, ed. Lynn Wardle, Mark Strasser, William Duncan, and David Coolidge (Westport, CT: Praeger, 2003), pp. 13-24.

Maggie Gallagher, "What Marriage Is For: Children Need Mothers and Fathers," *Weekly Standard* (August 4/August 11, 2003), pp. 22-25.

Maggie Gallagher, "(How) Will Gay Marriage Weaken Marriage as a Social Institution: A Reply to Andrew Koppelman," *University of Saint Thomas Law Journal*, 2/1 (Fall 2004), pp. 33-70.

Maggie Gallagher and Joshua K. Baker, "Do Moms and Dads Matter? Evidence from the Social Sciences on Family Structure and the Best Interests of the Child," 4/161, *Margins* (2004), pp. 161-180.

Patrick Lee, Robert P. George, and Gerard V. Bradley, "Marriage and Procreation: The Intrinsic Connection," *Public Discourse:*

Ethics, Law and the Common Good (March 28, 2011), accessible at http://www.thepublicdiscourse.com.

Sherif Girgis, Robert P. George, and Ryan T. Anderson, "What Is Marriage?" *Harvard Journal of Law and Public Policy*, 34/1 (Winter 2011), pp. 245-287.

Robert P. George and Jean Bethke Elshtain, eds., *The Meaning of Marriage: Family, State, Market, and Morals* (Dallas: Spence Publishing, 2006).

Carle Zimmerman, *Family and Civilization* (Wilmington, DE: ISI Books, 2008).

Glenn T. Stanton and Bill Maier, *Why Marriage Matters: Reasons to Believe in Marriage in Postmodern Society* (Colorado Springs, CO: Pinion Press, 1997).

Glenn T. Stanton and Bill Maier, *Marriage on Trial: The Case Against Same-Sex Marriage and Parenting* (Downers Grove, IL: InterVarsity Press, 2004).

David Popenoe, *Disturbing the Nest: Family Change and Decline in Modern Societies* (Edison, NJ: Transaction, 1988).

Mathew D. Staver, *Same-Sex Marriage: Putting Every Household at Risk* (Nashville, TN: Broadman and Holman, 2004).

Stanley Kurtz, "Beyond Gay Marriage: The Road to Polyamory," *Weekly Standard* (August 4/August 11, 2003), pp. 26-33.

8

You May Hear Proponents Argue ...

Same-sex marriage should be allowed because marriage is about love, and homosexuals love each other as much as heterosexuals. Marriage is for couples in love and is the way in which people express approval for the love the partners declare to one another. It is how society affirms the decisions lovers make to care for each other through good times and bad. Love is not limited by sexual orientation, and homosexual partners love each other as sincerely as heterosexual partners. Love defines marriage. Allowing same-sex lovers to marry is thus consistent with the purpose of marriage and should not be restricted.

You Can *Graciously Refute* This By Saying ...

Proponents of this argument confuse a valued, though not absolutely essential, motive for mate selection with what qualifies marriage as a social institution. A marriage certainly is more enjoyable for the participants when it incorporates how they feel about one another and how they desire to treat one another. But a marriage still is real (and continues to exist) when the participants do not like one another and even when they treat each other badly.

While love leads couples to get married and helps them stay married, it does not define what marriage is as a social institution. Love makes the participants in a marriage feel worthwhile, but the love they feel for each other is not what warrants the public interest in affirming that marriage. This interest is based in how the marriage moves individuals toward bridging the male-female divide, how it favors procreation, and how it disciplines the participants' appetites in order to have and raise children.

If what qualifies marriage for social affirmation shifts from favoring procreation to satisfying private feelings, marriage will lose its structure and will soon cease to be any sort of institution at all. It is similar to redefining books as no longer being limited to something people read, but being anything anyone enjoys in any way at all. While many people enjoy reading, changing the definition of a book destroys what makes a book a *book* and not a walk in the park. Basing public marriage on private sentiment leads to redefining it as any kind of relationship between any number of people and between any sorts of partners—even nonhuman. The logic of basing marriage on sentiment is already leading to human partners requesting marriage to animals.

The Truth Is ...

Same-sex marriage is wrong because it confuses sentiment with what structures marriage as a social institution.

References and Further Reading

William C. Duncan, "The State Interest in Marriage," *Ave Maria Law Review,* 2/1 (Spring 2004), pp. 153-182.

Maggie Gallagher, "Normal Marriage: Two Views," in *Marriage and Same-Sex Unions: A Debate*, ed. Lynn Wardle, Mark Strasser, William Duncan, and David Coolidge (Westport, CT: Praeger, 2003), pp. 13-24.

Maggie Gallagher, "What Marriage Is For: Children Need Mothers and Fathers," *Weekly Standard* (August 4/August 11, 2003), pp. 22-25.

Robert P. George and Jean Bethke Elshtain, eds., *The Meaning of Marriage: Family, State, Market, and Morals* (Dallas, TX: Spence Publishing, 2006).

Sherif Girgis, Robert P. George, and Ryan T. Anderson, "What Is Marriage?" *Harvard Journal of Law and Public Policy*, 34/1 (Winter 2011), pp. 245-287.

Stanley Kurtz, "Beyond Gay Marriage: The Road to Polyamory," *Weekly Standard* (August 4/August 11, 2003), pp. 26-33.

Stanley Kurtz, "Here Comes the Brides: Plural Marriage Is Waiting in the Wings," *Weekly Standard* (December 26, 2005), pp. 19-27.

For how accepting this argument would justify sex and marriage with animals, see Peter Singer, "Heavy Petting," accessible at http://www.Nerve.com (March 12, 2001); Midas Dekkers, *Dearest Pet: On Bestiality* (London: Verso, 1994); Barbara Sumner Burstyn, "The Love That Dare Not Bark Its Name," *Men's News Daily* (April 29, 2002), accessible at http://www. mensnewsdaily.com/archive/a-b/burstyn/burstyn042902.htm; and Arthur Weinreb, "And They Call It Puppy Love," *Canada Free Press* (July 22, 2002), accessible at www.canadafreepress. com/2002/weinreb72202.htm.

For examples of gay social revolutionaries admitting they are using same-sex marriage as a way to completely abolish the institution of marriage, see Thomas B. Stoddard, "Why Gay People Should Seek the Right to Marry," chapter 35 in *Families in the US: Kinship and Domestic Politics*, ed. Karen V. Hansen (Philadelphia, PA: Temple University Press, 1998); Richard D. Mohr, *A More Perfect Union: Why Straight America Must Stand Up for Gay Rights* (Boston, MA: Beacon, 1994); Gretchen A. Stiers, *From This Day Forward: Commitment, Marriage, and Family in Lesbian and Gay Relationships* (New York: St. Martin's Press, 1999); Michelangelo Signorile, "Bridal Wave," *Out* (December/ January 1994); "Sociologist Says Gay Marriage Does Threaten Established Order and That's Good," *Ascribe Law News Service* (November 16, 2003); and Margaret Gullette, "The New Case for Marriage," *American Prospect* (March 1, 2004).

9

You May Hear Proponents Argue …

Same-sex marriage should be allowed because marriage is not necessarily connected with sex. Because people can marry and stay married without having any sex at all, there is no reason for restricting socially approved civil marriage to one form of sex over others. Marriage is not about how people have sex, but only about how society distributes benefits to people committed to loving and caring relationships. Marriage is about people bonding for relational security. The social interest in marriage concerns nothing more than supporting the commitments people make to care for each other—none of which has anything to do with how people have sex.

You Can *Graciously Refute* This By Saying …

In this argument, the proponents of same-sex marriage try to separate things that cannot be separated. Trying to separate marriage from sex is like trying to separate driving from what it means to be a car. You can try thinking that way, but what it leads to is not a real car no matter how many people you get to go along with calling it a *car*. The kind of change involved is not the sort that just embellishes or enhances what you start with, but rather is the sort of change that replaces one thing with something quite different.

What this argument really does is to make comparisons after confusing marriage with friendship. And, while marriage and friendship work very nicely together, they are not the exact same thing and can exist perfectly well completely separate from each other. People can be friends without being married, and people can be married without being friends. It is also the case that friendship is not something defined by sex. But marriage is defined sexually and cannot be marriage otherwise. Marriage is not just any sort of friendship unrelated to sex and suggesting otherwise is preposterous. A friendship is not necessarily sexual, but a marriage is always structured in sexual terms whether a particular married couple ever has sex or not.

The undeniable connection linking marriage to sex is seen two ways. It is seen publically in how the main value of marriage to society is found in the way it supports procreation. And it is seen privately in the way nearly every spouse still expects his or her married partner to be sexually faithful whether still having sex with each other or not. If that was not so, sexual infidelity would not still be the number one reason for divorce.

Proponents of this argument are trying to separate things in marriage that cannot be separated. As previously noted, you can call anything a *car*, but if it doesn't drive a person from one place to the next, it is not a real car—regardless of how many people you can get to believe it is. Taking sex out of marriage is not the sort of change that just embellishes or enhances what marriage was in the beginning, but replaces it with something quite different.

What proponents of this argument are actually doing is making comparisons after confusing marriage with friendship. While marriage and friendship work nicely together, they are not the exact same thing, and they can exist perfectly well when completely separated from each other. People can be friends without being married, and people can be married without being friends. It is also the case that friendship is not something defined by sex, while marriage is—and actually cannot be defined as *marriage* otherwise.

The idea that marriage is any sort of friendship unrelated to sex is preposterous. A friendship is not necessarily sexual, but a marriage is always structured in sexual terms, whether a particular married couple ever has sex or not. This undeniable connection between marriage and sex can be seen two ways: (1) publically, in how the main value of marriage to society is found in the way it supports procreation; and (2) privately, in the way nearly every spouse believes his or her married partner should be sexually faithful, whether or not the couple is having sex with each other. If that were not so, sexual infidelity would not be the number one reason for divorce .

The Truth Is ...

Same-sex marriage is wrong because it severs sex from marriage and treats marriage as nothing more than friendship.

References and Further Reading

Theodore Olson and David Boies used this argument to try to persuade a federal court to invalidate California's Proposition 8, which banned same-sex marriage in the state. See Theodore B. Olson, "The Conservative Case for Gay Marriage: Why Same-Sex Marriage Is an American Value," *Newsweek* (January 18, 2010), pp. 48-54.

Maggie Gallagher, "Normal Marriage: Two Views," in *Marriage and Same-Sex Unions: A Debate,* ed. Lynn Wardle, Mark Strasser, William Duncan, and David Coolidge (Westport, CT: Praeger, 2003), pp. 13-24.

Maggie Gallagher, "What Marriage Is For: Children Need Mothers and Fathers," *Weekly Standard* (August 4/August 11, 2003), pp. 22-25.

Maggie Gallagher, "(How) Will Gay Marriage Weaken Marriage as a Social Institution: A Reply to Andrew Koppelman," *University of Saint Thomas Law Journal,* 2/1 (Fall 2004), pp. 33-70.

Robert P. George and Jean Bethke Elshtain, eds., *The Meaning of Marriage: Family, State, Market, and Morals* (Dallas, TX: Spence Publishing, 2006).

Sherif Girgis, Robert P. George, and Ryan T. Anderson, "What Is Marriage?" *Harvard Journal of Law and Public Policy,* 34/1 (Winter 2011), pp. 245-287.

David Popenoe, *Disturbing the Nest: Family Change and Decline in Modern Societies* (Edison, NJ: Transaction, 1988).

Carle Zimmerman, *Family and Civilization* (Wilmington, DE: ISI Books, 2008).

Glenn T. Stanton and Bill Maier, *Marriage on Trial: The Case Against Same-Sex Marriage and Parenting* (Downers Grove, IL: InterVarsity Press, 2004).

Douglas Farrow, "Blurring Sexual Boundaries," *First Things*, 211 (March 2011), pp. 17-19.

Mathew D. Staver, *Same-Sex Marriage: Putting Every Household at Risk* (Nashville, TN: Broadman and Holman, 2004).

Stanley Kurtz, "Beyond Gay Marriage: The Road to Polyamory," *Weekly Standard* (August 4/August 11, 2003), pp. 26-33.

Stanley Kurtz, "Here Comes the Brides: Plural Marriage Is Waiting in the Wings," *Weekly Standard* (December 26, 2005), pp. 19-27.

10

You May Hear Proponents Argue ...

Same-sex marriage should be allowed because it will save marriage from the mess heterosexuals have caused. Heterosexuals have caused the mess marriage is in today, so who are they to criticize homosexuals for trying to make marriage stronger and better? It is time for society to try a different path. Heterosexuals are out of answers, so society should consider what homosexuals know about forming strong marriage relationships. Allowing same-sex marriage will save marriage by giving homosexuals a chance to show how much better it can be when it is based on sexual attraction and mutual affection.

You Can *Graciously Refute* This By Saying ...

It is true that nearly half of all heterosexual marriages now end in divorce. But this also means that about half do not—and that rate of success is much higher if you focus on the older rather than the younger population. Furthermore, while the divorce rate is bad, it does not mean that heterosexuals have no idea how marriages succeed. Proponents of this argument are being myopic because they are ignoring history and arbitrarily assuming that the marital success of previous generations is irrelevant or not worth restoring. Yet why should centuries of marital success be ignored just because marital stability has declined in the current generation?

Good sense dictates that we blame what has occurred recently, not what has worked for centuries. The recent drop in marital success shows that young people are being influenced by destructive ideas that earlier generations did not accept. It is sadly ironic that proponents of this argument are themselves generating the very problem they would allegedly *fix* by continuing to perpetuate the idea causing the marriage crisis in the first place. They want to change the reason for socially approved marriage from limiting selfish appetites in favor of assuming responsibility to have and raise children to the socially destructive idea of assessing the public value of marriage by determining how it gratifies individual feelings and desires.

It is this very idea that most troubles marriage today, and same-sex marriage will make it worse, not better. Under homosexual terms, marriage will be no stronger than feelings of private satisfaction. It will cease to be an authoritative pro-child institution in which people are encouraged to endure regardless of how their feelings fluctuate.

The Truth Is …

Same-sex marriage is wrong because giving feelings priority over form and commitment will make the marriage crisis worse instead of better.

References and Further Reading

Daniel R. Heimbach, "Deconstructing the Family," *Religion and Society Report*, 22/7 (October/November 2005), pp. 1-12.

Maggie Gallagher, "Normal Marriage: Two Views," in *Marriage and Same-Sex Unions: A Debate*, ed. Lynn Wardle, Mark Strasser, William Duncan, and David Coolidge (Westport, CT: Praeger, 2003), pp. 13-24.

Maggie Gallagher, "(How) Will Gay Marriage Weaken Marriage as a Social Institution: A Reply to Andrew Koppelman," *University of Saint Thomas Law Journal*, 2/1 (Fall 2004), pp. 33-70.

Timothy Dailey, "Comparing the Lifestyles of Homosexual Couples to Married Couples," published by *Family Research Council* (April 29, 2004), accessible at http://www.frc.org/get.cfm?i=IS04C02.

Robert P. George and Jean Bethke Elshtain, eds., *The Meaning of Marriage: Family, State, Market, and Morals* (Dallas, TX: Spence Publishing, 2006).

Carle Zimmerman, *Family and Civilization* (Wilmington, DE: ISI Books, 2008).

Glenn T. Stanton and Bill Maier, *Marriage on Trial: The Case Against Same-Sex Marriage and Parenting* (Downers Grove, IL: InterVarsity Press, 2004).

David Popenoe, *Disturbing the Nest: Family Change and Decline in Modern Societies* (Edison, NJ: Transaction, 1988).

For examples of gay social revolutionaries admitting they are using same-sex marriage as a way to completely abolish the institution of marriage, see Thomas B. Stoddard, "Why Gay People Should Seek the Right to Marry," chapter 35 in *Families in the US: Kinship and Domestic Politics*, ed. Karen V. Hansen (Philadelphia, PA: Temple University Press, 1998); Richard D. Mohr, *A More Perfect Union: Why Straight America Must Stand Up for Gay Rights* (Boston, MA: Beacon, 1994); Gretchen A. Stiers, *From This Day Forward: Commitment, Marriage, and Family in Lesbian and Gay Relationships* (New York: St. Martin's Press, 1999); Michelangelo Signorile, "Bridal Wave," *Out* (December/January 1994); "Sociologist Says Gay Marriage Does Threaten Established Order and That's Good," *Ascribe Law News Service* (November 16, 2003); and Margaret Gullette, "The New Case for Marriage," *American Prospect* (March 1, 2004).

Mathew D. Staver, *Same-Sex Marriage: Putting Every Household at Risk* (Nashville, TN: Broadman and Holman, 2004).

11

You May Hear Proponents Argue …

Same-sex marriage should be allowed because marriage is a social construct that people can change and redefine however they please. Marriage is nothing more than a social arrangement made up in ancient times to suit people's needs and has no relevance for today. Each generation chooses to accept or modify marriage to suit their particular situation. Marriage has no inherent structure and can be changed in any way that people desire. Most of what has been tried in the past has had horrific outcomes. We should avoid what did not work and focus on what makes sense now—basing marriage on mutual caring regardless of sexual preference.

Marriage precedes culture - creates culture.

You Can *Graciously Refute* This By Saying …

While it is true that some marital practices have changed with culture and over time, the procreational structure of marriage as a social institution has never changed. The institutional structure of marriage precedes culture, because the existence of society and culture depends on the prior existence of marriage—not the other way around. Every civilization throughout history has recognized the procreational structure of marriage in bridging the male-female divide. This structure does not vary, because marriage is essentially a complementary pro-child institution that is able to transmit life beyond present existence, extend social commitments beyond the span of individual life, and ensure that fathers and mothers raise children together.

Proponents of this argument make two serious mistakes. First, they wrongly assume that homosexual identity is fixed, when in fact that identity changes all the time. Second, they wrongly believe that the procreational structure of marriage changes, when it never does. Jeffery Satinover, a scientific expert on the study of homosexuality, reports that since 1994, "The most common natural course for a young person who develops a 'homosexual identity' is for it to spontaneously disappear unless that person is discouraged or interfered with by extraneous factors."

The structure of marriage has always been about keeping mothers and fathers together long enough to raise their own biological children. Everything else is secondary. Pretending otherwise will only ruin the one institution that is most needed to assure the survival of a society.

The Truth Is ...

Same-sex marriage is wrong because the procreational structure of marriage cannot be removed without destroying marriage.

References and Further Reading

For an example of this argument, see John Borneman and Laurie Kain Hart, "An Elastic Institution," *Washington Post* (April 14, 2004), accessible at http://www.aaanet.org/press/min_borneman_4-15–04.htm; and Gabriel Arana, "Redefining Marriage," *The American Prospect* (January 21, 2011), accessible at http://prospect.org/cs/articles?article=redefining_marriage.

Jeffrey Satinover, "The Trojan Couch: How the Mental Health Associations Misrepresent Science," *Conference Reports 2005*, National Association for Research and Therapy of Homosexuals, accessible at http://www.narth.com/docs/thetrojancouchsatinover.

Daniel R. Heimbach, "Deconstructing the Family," *Religion and Society Report*, 22/7 (October/November 2005), pp. 1-12.

Maggie Gallagher, "(How) Will Gay Marriage Weaken Marriage as a Social Institution: A Reply to Andrew Koppelman," *University of Saint Thomas Law Journal*, 2/1 (Fall 2004), pp. 33-70.

Sherif Girgis, Ryan T. Anderson, and Robert P. George, "Marriage: Merely a Social Construct?" *Public Discourse: Ethics, Law and the Common Good* (December 29, 2010), accessible at http://www.thepublicdiscourse.com.

Anthropologist Claude Lévi-Strauss shows that procreationally structured marriage is not necessarily or uniquely religious but rather should be categorized as a universally practiced "social institution with a biological foundation." See Claude Lévi-Strauss, "Introduction," in *A History of the Family*, by André Burguière (Cambridge, MA: Harvard University Press, 1996), p. 5. Lévi-Strauss also observes that marriage is everywhere structured as "a union, more or less durable, but socially approved, of two individuals of opposite sexes who establish a household and bear and raise children." He says this marital form is found "to be a practically universal phenomenon, present in every type of society." See Claude Lévi-Strauss, *The View from Afar* (New York: Basic Books, 1985), pp. 40-41.

For examples of gay social revolutionaries admitting they are using same-sex marriage as a way to completely abolish the institution of marriage, see Thomas B. Stoddard, "Why Gay People Should Seek the Right to Marry," chapter 35 in *Families in the US: Kinship and Domestic Politics*, ed. Karen V. Hansen (Philadelphia, PA: Temple University Press, 1998); Richard D. Mohr, *A More Perfect Union: Why Straight America Must Stand Up for Gay Rights* (Boston, MA: Beacon, 1994); Gretchen A. Stiers, *From This Day Forward: Commitment, Marriage, and Family in Lesbian and Gay Relationships* (New York: St. Martin's Press, 1999); Michelangelo Signorile, "Bridal Wave," *Out* (December/January 1994); and "Sociologist Says Gay Marriage Does Threaten Established Order and That's Good," *Ascribe Law News Service* (November 16, 2003).

Arguments 12 – 20

Gracious Answers to Arguments Regarding Children and Families

*Children need
reliable parents, and they are
more likely to be abandoned
by adults who think marriage
is more about satisfying
adult appetites than about
what children most need.*

REGARDING CHILDREN AND FAMILIES

(Arguments 12–20)

12

You May Hear Proponents Argue …

*S*AME-SEX MARRIAGE SHOULD *be allowed because it promotes family values.* Denying same-sex marriage only serves to condemn family values. Marriage is uniquely good for promoting the strength and stability of families, and by encouraging couples to marry, a society recognizes and supports the value of people making family commitments. Denying marriage to same-sex couples will not stop homosexuals from starting families, but it will keep others from recognizing and supporting the value of those families. Allowing same-sex marriage will promote family values by giving the benefit of marriage to all individuals, not just those who happen to conform to a single model.

You Can *Graciously Refute* This By Saying …

This argument is like saying that just because some children get to school without wheels, wheels should be optional on school buses. Children can be raised without a father or mother, but that does not justify the idea that marriage as a social institution has no necessary structure, that living with both a father and mother makes no real difference to children, or that society has no stake in favoring and encouraging families to form along lines that everyone knows is best for raising well-adjusted children.

Scientists all over the world overwhelmingly agree that healthy, successful, well-adjusted children are most likely to come from families in which both a biological father and mother are present. Procreationally structured marriage is the best way a society has to get men and women to bear and raise their own children. Family structure matters to children, and the optimal family structure for them to thrive is one in which they live with their biological parents.

All reliable parenting research shows that children raised by homosexuals are more likely to experience sexual confusion, be exposed to greater health risks, initiate sexual activity at earlier ages, and suffer mental health problems. Studies that claim to show otherwise all contain critical flaws. Same-sex marriage diminishes the value of children by treating marriage as a way for adults to satisfy their feelings instead of providing what is best for their children. In same-sex marriages, the children are more likely to be abandoned by the adults who think that marriage is more about satisfying themselves than doing what is best for having and raising children.

The Truth Is …

Same-sex marriage is wrong because it interferes with promoting the family structure best suited for having and raising children.

References and Further Reading

Theodore Olson and David Boies used this argument to try to persuade a federal court to invalidate California's Proposition 8, which banned same-sex marriage in the state. See Theodore

B. Olson, "The Conservative Case for Gay Marriage: Why Same-Sex Marriage Is an American Value," *Newsweek* (January 18, 2010), pp. 48-54.

Mark Regnerus, "How Different Are the Adult Children of Parents Who Have Same-Sex Relationships? Findings from the New Family Structures Study," *Social Science Research*, 41 (2012), pp. 752-770.

Robert Lerner and Althea Nagia, *No Basis: What the Studies Don't Tell Us About Same-Sex Parenting*, Marriage Law Project (Washington, DC, January 2001).

Mary Parke, "Are Married Parents Really Better for Children: What Research Says About the Effects of Family Structure on Child Well-Being," Center for Law and Public Policy, *Policy Brief #3* (May 2003), pp. 1,6.

Maggie Gallagher and Joshua K. Baker, "Do Moms and Dads Matter? Evidence from the Social Sciences on Family Structure and the Best Interests of the Child," 4/161, *Margins* (2004), pp. 161-180.

"Homosexual Parenting: Is It Time for Change?" *American College of Pediatricians* (January 22, 2004), accessible at http://www.acpeds.org/index.cgi?cat=10005andart=50andBISKIT=http://www.acpeds.org/Homosexual-Parenting-Is-It-Time-For-Change.html.

Jeanne Hilton and Esther Devall, "Comparison of Parenting and Children's Behavior in Single-Mother, Single-Father, and Intact Families," *Journal of Divorce and Remarriage*, 29/3-4 (1998), pp. 23-54.

Elizabeth Thompson, Thomas Hanson, and Sara McLanahan, "Family Structure and Child Well-Being," *Social Forces*, 73/1 (September 1994), pp. 221-242.

Barbara Schneider, Allison Atteberry and Alfred Owens, *Family Matters: Family Structure and Child Outcomes* (Birmingham, AL: Alabama Policy Institute, 2005), available at http://www.alabamapolicyinstitute.org/pdf/currentfamily.

Fiona Tasker and Susan Golombok, "Do Parents Influence the Sexual Orientation of Their Children?" *Developmental Psychology*, 32/1 (January 1996), pp. 3-11.

Judith Stacey and Timothy J. Biblarz, "(How) Does the Sexual Orientation of Parents Matter," *American Sociological Review*, 66/2 (April 2001), pp. 159-183.

13

You May Hear Proponents Argue ...

Same-sex marriage should be allowed because it strengthens family bonding. Marriage is the commonly shared social ritual in which relatives and friends of the couple gather to openly recognize and affirm the formation and addition of new branches to the family tree. It is the officially recognized and socially approved mechanism for generating new family units and connecting them to old ones. It also is the best means a society has for making sure new family attachments will endure for as long as possible. Denying marriage to same-sex couples keeps homosexuals from adding new families to existing family trees and does not serve the societal goal of helping ensure families endure.

You Can *Graciously Refute* This By Saying ...

Proponents of this argument deny that it is best for children to have both a father and mother, and they pretend that the most important factor in a family is making the adults happy. This is like denying the fact that heat is best for cooking a turkey and pretending that nothing matters in making a good meal than having a good time in the kitchen. As things now stand, nothing prevents homosexuals from getting married and forming families like everyone else other than their refusal to marry a person of the opposite sex.

Same-sex marriage is bad for family integrity and for children because it removes the procreative form that structures marriage as a social institution, which, in turn, removes what is most responsible for getting adults to control their appetites for the purpose of having and raising children. Pretending that marriage is for nothing more than satisfying adult sexual attractions threatens the couple's fulfillment of family duties that are critical to raising well-adjusted children. Denying the procreational form of marriage as a social institution elevates adult passions over what is best for children and makes temporary pleasure more important than family obligations. This hinders the couple's interest in agreeing to long-term marriage and family commitments by making cohabitation seem a less costly way to fulfill the same desires.

Looking again at the example of Scandinavia, the legalization of same-sex marriage in that region has only served to worsen family formation, stability, and endurance. Not only have few same-sex couples chosen to marry since it became legal, but the change has weakened marriage and family attitudes throughout that society. The already high rates of family dissolution and non-married parenting have shot up, and the rate at which people marry (if at all) has dropped.

The Truth Is ...

Same-sex marriage is wrong because it makes cohabitation seem preferable to a couple over accepting the long-term responsibility of raising and caring for children.

References and Further Reading

For an example of this argument, see Barbara Ehrenreich, "How Banning Gay Marriage Will Destroy the Family," *Barbara's Blog*, accessible at http://ehrenreich.blogs.com/barbaras_blog/2006/06/how_banning_gay.html.

For information on how homosexual partnerships are more prone to dissolution, see David McWhirter and Andrew Mattison, *The Male Couple: How Relationships Develop* (Englewood Cliffs, NJ: Prentice-Hall, 1984), pp. 252-253; Marcel Saghir and Eli Robins, *Male and Female Homosexuality* (Baltimore, MD: Williams and Wilkins, 1973), p. 225; Letitia Anne Peplau and

Hortensia Amaro, "Understanding Lesbian Relationships," in W. Paul, J. D. Weinrich, J. C. Gonsiorek and M. E. Hotvedt, eds., *Homosexuality: Social, Psychological, and Biological Issues* (Beverly Hills, CA: Sage, 1982), pp. 233-248; and Michael Pollak, "Male Homosexuality," in Philippe Aries and André Bejin, eds., *Western Sexuality: Practice and Precept in Past and Present Times* (New York: Blackwell, 1985), pp. 124-125.

Loren Marks, "Same-Sex Parenting and Children's Outcomes: A Closer Examination of the American Psychological Association's Brief of Lesbian and Gay Parenting," *Social Science Research*, 41 (2012), pp. 735-751.

Stanley Kurtz, "The End of Marriage in Scandinavia: The 'Conservative Case' for Same-Sex Marriage Collapses," *Weekly Standard* (February 2, 2004), pp. 26-33.

David Popenoe, *Disturbing the Nest: Family Change and Decline in Modern Societies* (Edison, NJ: Transaction, 1988).

Maggie Gallagher and Joshua K. Baker, "Do Moms and Dads Matter? Evidence from the Social Sciences on Family Structure and the Best Interests of the Child," 4/161, *Margins* (2004), pp. 161-180.

Patricia Morgan, *Children as Trophies? Examining the Evidence on Same-Sex Parenting* (Newcastle upon Tyne, UK: Christian Institute, 2002).

Carle C. Zimmerman, *Family and Civilization* (Wilmington, DE: ISI Books, 2008).

Joseph Daniel Unwin, *Sex and Culture* (London: Oxford University Press, 1934).

Joseph Daniel Unwin, *Sexual Regulations and Cultural Behavior: An Address Delivered Before the Medical Section of the British Psychological Society* (London: Oxford University Press, 1935).

14

You May Hear Proponents Argue ...

Same-sex marriage should be allowed because it respects the religious meaning of family life. The government does not define the religious meaning of family life. However, both religion and government affect social attitudes, including the level of respect people feel toward marriage and family life. While marriage laws are secular, it is nevertheless true that people's respect for marriage and family increases when religion and government work together. The failure of government to recognize same-sex marriages blessed by religion threatens social respect for, and cooperation with, the role of religion in supporting families that are dependent on those marriages.

You Can *Graciously Refute* This By Saying ...

Proponents of this argument are correct in saying that civil government should respect the religious meaning of family life. However, this does not mean that the government should recognize, much less support, any action by any religion regardless of how it affects families. Civil government has a secular interest in favoring family life, but this does not come from the interest it has in respecting and protecting religious practices and teachings. The government's secular interest is limited to supporting the *public value* of families as it relates to social strength, and this interest does not extend to meeting the religious, psychological, or emotional needs of individuals.

A government has no legitimate public interest in adding civil recognition to religious practices that are irrelevant or contrary to the overall good of strengthening social order. To this end, no government can pretend that changing the public structure of marriage in ways that deny the essential importance of heterosexual union, or in ways that change the public structure of family as being necessarily childless, does not result in loss for society.

The public's value of raising well-adjusted children is met when marriage results in forming families in which biological fathers and mothers raise children and when all other arrangements are treated as contingent, exceptional, and less complete. Conversely, the public's value of raising well-adjusted citizens is threatened when marriage and family are structured in other ways. Maintaining the procreational structure of civil marriage as a social institution does not interfere with religious freedom to practice marriage in other ways, as long as those other ways do not threaten the common good.

The Truth Is …

Same-sex marriage is wrong because religion does not override the public's duty to favor fathers staying with mothers to raise their own children.

References and Further Reading

Douglas Laycock, Anthony Picarello and Robin Wilson, eds., *Same-Sex Marriage and Religious Liberty: Emerging Conflicts* (New York: Rowman and Littlefield, 2008).

Maggie Gallagher, "Banned in Boston: The Coming Conflict Between Same-Sex Marriage and Religious Liberty," *The Weekly Standard* (May 15, 2006), pp. 20-26.

Clyde Haberman, "When Conscience and the New Marriage Law Collide," *The New York Times*, November 10, 2011, accessible at http://cityroom.blogs.nytimes.com/2011/07/18/when-conscience-and-the-new-marriage-law-collide/.

Robin F. Wilson, "Same-Sex Marriage and Religious Liberty: Life after Prop 8," 14 NEXUS 101 (2009), accessible at http://

heinonline.org/HOL/LandingPage?collection=journalsandhan
dle=hein.journals/nex14anddiv=14andid=andpage=.

Katie Zezima, "Obey Same-Sex Marriage Law, Officials Told," *New York Times* (April 26, 2004), p. A15.

John Jalsevac, "U.S. Christian Camp Loses Tax-Exempt Status over Same-Sex Civil-Union Ceremony," *LifeSiteNews* (September 19, 2007), accessible at http://www.lifesite.net/ldn/2007/sep/07091902.html. Jalsevac reported that the New Jersey Department of Environmental Protection revoked the tax-exemption of a Methodist ministry after it refused to allow a same-sex couple to use its boardwalk pavilion for their civil commitment ceremony.

Mary Ann Glendon, "For Better or for Worse?" *Wall Street Journal* (February. 25, 2004), p. A14, accessible at http://www.catholic-fidelity.com/for-better-or-for-worse-by-mary-ann-glendon/.

Tom Strode, "Scholars: 'Gay Marriage' Will Cause Church-State Clashes," *Baptist Press* (June 2006), accessible at http://www.bpnews.net/printerfriendly.asp?ID=23383.

Emily Donohue, "Same-Sex Marriage Would Have Disastrous Effects on Churches," *Rhode Island Catholic* (March 13, 2008), accessible at http://www.thericatholic.com/news/detail.html?sub_id=968.

M.V. Lee Badgett, *When Gay People Get Married: What Happens When Societies Legalize Same-Sex Marriage* (New York: New York University Press, 2009).

For how the U.S. Constitution will be interpreted to deny allowing any religious exception should rejecting homosexual normalization be classified in the same legal category as racial discrimination, see Chai R. Feldblum, "Moral Conflict and Liberty; Gay Rights and Religion," *Brooklyn Law Review*, 72/1 (2006), pp. 61-123.

15

You May Hear Proponents Argue …

Same-sex marriage should be allowed because the way in which people have sex has nothing to do with raising children. Nurturing children has nothing to do with sex, and what parents do in the bedroom has nothing to do with raising children. Raising children is not a matter of biology but of love and provision, and a strong family life is not a matter of fertility but caring. It does not matter what parents do in the bedroom as long as they nurture their children with love. This can be seen in the fact that when it comes to parenting, the infertility of same-sex partners is no different from the infertility of heterosexual parents. Both homosexual and heterosexual parents provide the same care, and in neither case does sexual attraction have any bearing on providing a good home.

You Can *Graciously Refute* This By Saying …

Proponents of this argument are incorrect in stating that the way people have sex has no bearing on childbearing and childrearing. Same-sex marriage destroys the essential structure of marriage—the one institution that is critical in assuring children are given the gift of being raised to maturity by their biological parents. In fact, the most important benefit to society that is derived from the procreational structure of marriage is that procreational pairs (a man and woman having sex) are supposed to share responsibility for raising the children they beget.

Even though some male-female couples are childless, and even though some children are adopted, the male-female structure of marriage as a publically affirmed social institution is essential to promoting the long-term shared commitment of biological parents to achieve the difficult task of raising their children to maturity.

Treating the social purpose of civil marriage as if it has more to do with indulging private sexual appetites than with having and raising children is a detriment to society and a detriment to children.

Pretending that the way in which people have sex is irrelevant to marriage destroys the power of marriage for keeping procreation linked to raising children. Moreover, the American College of Pediatrics notes good scientific evidence that shows children exposed to the homosexual lifestyle are "at increased risk for emotional, mental, and even physical harm." The organization warns that studies "that appear to indicate neutral to favorable results for homosexual parenting have critical flaws such as non-longitudinal design, inadequate sample size, biased sample selection, lack of proper controls, and failure to account for confounding variables."

The Truth Is ...

Same-sex marriage is wrong because it destroys the value and power of marriage for linking sex with having and raising children.

References and Further Reading

Barbara Schneider, Allison Atteberry, and Alfred Owens, *Family Matters: Family Structure and Child Outcomes* (Birmingham, AL: Alabama Policy Institute, 2005), available at http://www.alabamapolicyinstitute.org/pdf/currentfamily.

Maggie Gallagher and Joshua K. Baker, "Do Moms and Dads Matter? Evidence from the Social Sciences on Family Structure and the Best Interests of the Child," 4/161, *Margins* (2004), pp. 161-180.

Elizabeth Thompson, Thomas Hanson, and Sara McLanahan, "Family Structure and Child Well-Being," *Social Forces,* 73/1 (September 1994), pp. 221-242.

Dawn Stefanowicz, *Out from Under: The Impact of Homosexual Parenting* (Enumclaw, WA: Annotation Press, 2007).

Theo Sandfort, Ron de Graaf, Rob Bojl, and Paul Schnabel, "Same-Sex Sexual Behavior and Psychiatric Disorders," *Archives of General Psychiatry,* 58 (January 2001), pp. 85-91.

Loren Marks, "Same-Sex Parenting and Children's Outcomes: A Closer Examination of the American Psychological Association's Brief of Lesbian and Gay Parenting," *Social Science Research*, 41 (2012), pp. 735-751.

"Homosexual Parenting: Is It Time for Change?" *American College of Pediatricians* (January 22, 2004), accessible at http://www. acpeds.org/index.cgi?cat=10005andart=50andBISKIT=ht tp://www.acpeds.org/Homosexual-Parenting-Is-It-Time-For-Change.html.

Lettie Lockhart, et al., "Letting Out the Secret: Violence in Lesbian Relationships," *Journal of Interpersonal Violence*, 9/4 (December 1994), pp. 469-492.

Fiona Tasker and Susan Golombok, "Do Parents Influence the Sexual Orientation of Their Children?" *Developmental Psychology*, 32/1 (January 1996), pp. 3-11.

Judith Stacey and Timothy J. Biblarz, "(How) Does the Sexual Orientation of Parents Matter," *American Sociological Review,* 66/2 (April 2001), pp. 159-183.

Mary Parke, "Are Married Parents Really Better for Children: What Research Says About the Effects of Family Structure on Child Well-Being," Center for Law and Public Policy, *Policy Brief #3* (May 2003), pp. 1,6.

For how legalizing same-sex marriage will align marriage to homosexual categories and not align homosexuals to what marriage is now, see Lawrence Auster, "The Extreme Radicalism of Homosexual 'Marriage,'" *View from the Right* (June 2, 2008), accessible at http://www.amnation.com/vfr/archives/010723. html.

16

You May Hear Proponents Argue …

Same-sex marriage should be allowed because it does not change the way children perceive marriage. Marriage is one thing, and raising children is another. Marriage does not require children, and parenting no longer requires marriage. These days, marriage is about affirming the commitment of adults to each other, and parenting only concerns adults caring for children. When it comes to raising children, what matters is not whether the adults raising them are married, biologically related, or of opposite genders, but only whether they are loving and responsible. Same-sex marriage is compatible with doing what is best for children.

You Can *Graciously Refute* This By Saying …

While it is possible for couples to marry and not have children, and while it is possible for children to be adopted into a family, this does not mean that the structure of marriage as a social institution has no bearing on what is best for children. As it is, the long and universally recognized procreational structure of marriage is truly the best for raising well-adjusted children, and ignoring or denying this important connection is bad for children. Children do best when raised by their own biological fathers and mothers who are bound to each other by marriage. While other arrangements are possible, they are not nearly as good for children and should not be treated as normal.

Viewing marriage as normal and preferred when it encourages biological fathers and mothers to raise their children is like viewing cars in a way that treats driving as normal and preferred. A person may certainly sit or sleep in a car without driving it anywhere, but that does not change the fact that cars are designed for getting a person from one place to the next. A person can also get out and push a car from place to place, but that does not make the action as normal as using the car for transportation.

The problem with this argument is that viewing the institutional structure of what is normal in marriage to having and raising children cannot be denied for a few without denying it for all. Redesigning marriage to affirm homosexual sex destroys what is best for children by raising the value of adult satisfaction over the value of children. It also destroys what is best for children by weakening the very structure that compels biological parents to share the difficult task of raising children.

The Truth Is …

Same-sex marriage is wrong because it changes the view that marriage linked to parenthood is normal and not abnormal.

References and Further Reading

Theodore Olson and David Boies used this argument to try to persuade a federal court to invalidate California's Proposition 8, which banned same-sex marriage in the state. See Theodore B. Olson, "The Conservative Case for Gay Marriage: Why Same-Sex Marriage Is an American Value," *Newsweek* (January 18, 2010), pp. 48-54.

For how legalizing same-sex marriage will align marriage to homosexual categories and not align homosexuals to what marriage is now, see Lawrence Auster, "The Extreme Radicalism of Homosexual 'Marriage,'" *View from the Right* (June 2, 2008), accessible at http://www.amnation.com/vfr/archives/010723.html.

Maggie Gallagher, "What Marriage Is For: Children Need Mothers and Fathers," *Weekly Standard* (August 4/August 11, 2003), pp. 22-25.

Maggie Gallagher and Joshua K. Baker, "Do Moms and Dads Matter? Evidence from the Social Sciences on Family Structure and the Best Interests of the Child," 4/161, *Margins* (2004), pp. 161-180.

Loren Marks, "Same-Sex Parenting and Children's Outcomes: A Closer Examination of the American Psychological Association's Brief of Lesbian and Gay Parenting," *Social Science Research,* 41 (2012), pp. 735-751.

Mark Regnerus, "How Different Are the Adult Children of Parents Who Have Same-Sex Relationships? Findings from the New Family Structures Study," *Social Science Research,* 41 (2012), pp. 752-770.

Judith Stacey and Timothy J. Biblarz, "(How) Does the Sexual Orientation of Parents Matter," *American Sociological Review,* 66/2 (April 2001), pp. 159-183.

Marriage Rights for Homosexuals: Not the Best for Children: Critique of AAP Special Report," *American College of Pediatricians* (posted prior to January 22, 2004), accessible at http://www.acpeds.org/Marriage-Rights-for-Homosexual-Couples-Not-the-Best-for-Children.html.

Mary Parke, "Are Married Parents Really Better for Children: What Research Says About the Effects of Family Structure on Child Well-Being," Center for Law and Public Policy, Policy Brief #3 (May 2003), pp. 1,6.

Elizabeth Thompson, Thomas Hanson, and Sara McLanahan, "Family Structure and Child Well-Being," *Social Forces,* 73/1 (September 1994), pp. 221-242.

Barbara Schneider, Allison Atteberry and Alfred Owens, *Family Matters: Family Structure and Child Outcomes* (Birmingham, AL: Alabama Policy Institute, 2005), available at http://www.alabamapolicyinstitute.org/pdf/currentfamily.

17

You May Hear Proponents Argue …

Same-sex marriage should be allowed because children need married parents, not biological fathers and mothers. It is better for children to be raised by parents who are married than who are unmarried, and it makes no difference whether those parents are heterosexual or homosexual. The American Academy of Pediatrics (AAP) states there is ample evidence to show "there is no relationship between parent's sexual orientation and any measure of a child's emotional, psychological, and behavioral adjustment." It is more important to the best interests of children to have parents who are committed to each other in marriage than it is to have a biological father and mother.

You Can *Graciously Refute* This By Saying …

Proponents of this argument agree there is a link between marriage and childrearing, but they rely on poor science to justify removing the essential structure of marriage as a social institution. The American College of Pediatrics (ACP) strongly criticizes the AAP's endorsement of homosexual parenting because the so-called *evidence* it provides to justify its position comes from faulty research that lacks proper controls or fails to account for confounding variables.

In fact, all scientifically reliable childrearing studies indicate that having two heterosexual parents—a mother and father living together—makes a great difference in the emotional, psychological, and physical wellbeing of children. In addition, children raised by homosexual parents are more likely to experience mental problems, physical health problems, behavioral problems, sexual confusion problems, substance abuse, anxiety disorders, and suicidal ideation than children raised in heterosexual households.

Proponents of this argument depend on two unsustainable ideas: (1) that having both a mother and father makes no difference to the psychological, emotional, and physical wellbeing of children; and (2) that what does matter flows from the status parents are given by the state in relation to marriage law. Neither idea is sustained by reliable science, and both conflict with real life. Children will be adversely affected if marriage is changed in a manner that treats having both a father and mother as being something arbitrary, unnecessary, and not relevant.

The Truth Is ...

Same-sex marriage is wrong because it denies that children need both fathers and mothers and that they will face difficulties if either is lacking.

References and Further Reading

Maggie Gallagher, "What Marriage Is For: Children Need Mothers and Fathers," *Weekly Standard* (August 4/August 11, 2003), pp. 22-25.

Maggie Gallagher and Joshua K. Baker, "Do Moms and Dads Matter? Evidence from the Social Sciences on Family Structure and the Best Interests of the Child," 4/161, *Margins* (2004), pp. 161-180.

Mary Parke, "Are Married Parents Really Better for Children: What Research Says About the Effects of Family Structure on Child Well-Being," Center for Law and Public Policy, *Policy Brief #3* (May 2003), pp. 1,6.

Elizabeth Thompson, Thomas Hanson, and Sara McLanahan, "Family Structure and Child Well-Being," *Social Forces*, 73/1 (September 1994), pp. 221-242.

Barbara Schneider, Allison Atteberry, and Alfred Owens, *Family Matters: Family Structure and Child Outcomes* (Birmingham,

AL: Alabama Policy Institute, 2005), available at http://www. alabamapolicyinstitute.org/pdf/currentfamily.

Marriage Rights for Homosexuals: Not the Best for Children: Critique of AAP Special Report," *American College of Pediatricians* (posted prior to January 22, 2004), accessible at http://www. acpeds.org/Marriage-Rights-for-Homosexual-Couples-Not-the-Best-for-Children.html.

Robert Lerner and Althea Nagia, *No Basis: What the Studies Don't Tell Us About Same-Sex Parenting*, Marriage Law Project (Washington, DC, January 2001).

Mark Regnerus, "How Different Are the Adult Children of Parents Who Have Same-Sex Relationships? Findings from the New Family Structures Study," *Social Science Research*, 41 (2012), pp. 752-770.

Dawn Stefanowicz, *Out from Under: The Impact of Homosexual Parenting* (Enumclaw, WA: Annotation Press, 2007).

David Island and Patrick Letellier, *Men Who Beat the Men Who Love Them: Battered Gay Men and Domestic Violence* (New York: Haworth Press, 1991).

"Violence Between Intimates," *Bureau of Justice Statistics Selected Findings* (November 1, 1994), Bureau of Justice Statistics, Office of Justice Programs, U. S. Department of Justice. Washington, DC, accessible at http://bjs.ojp.usdoj.gov/index.cfm?ty=pbdetail andiid=804.

18

You May Hear Proponents Argue …

Same-sex marriage should be allowed because homosexuals raise children just as well as heterosexuals. The APA states that the wellbeing of children is "unrelated to parental and sexual orientation" and that research "provides no justification for discriminating against same-sex couples in marriage or in parenting." What matters for children is whether they have loving and responsible parents, not whether their parents are straight or gay. Heterosexual couples can get married, which strengthens family bonds; however, same-sex parents must raise children without that benefit. This is bad for children and for society as a whole.

You Can *Graciously Refute* This By Saying …

There is no objective or reliable scientific basis to sustain this claim. In fact, there is a great body of good psycho-social evidence to the contrary. As previously mentioned, the ACP opposes the APA's endorsement of homosexual parenting "because of its absence of evidence-based research and potential negative consequences for children." Children raised by homosexuals generally do *far worse* over a range of factors when compared to children raised by heterosexual fathers and mothers. This negative comparison is especially evident when measured against children who have been raised by their biological parents.

The APA's declaration was motivated by politics, not science, and the organization based its position on studies that used small and nonrepresentative convenience samples. The APA's findings went against all objectively reliable evidence and did not support the same general conclusions reached by other parenting studies. Drs. Robert Lerner and Althea Nagai evaluated forty-nine same-sex parenting studies, but they found *no basis* for concluding that children raised by homosexuals do as well as those raised by heterosexual couples.

In fact, Drs. Lerner and Nagai found that children raised by parents who engage in gay or lesbian relationships are at a *much greater risk* for gender confusion, suicide, depression, mood disorders, bipolar disorders, sexual promiscuity, out-of-wedlock pregnancy, and sexually transmitted diseases. Furthermore, these children are more likely to have trouble with the law, abuse drugs, be expelled, struggle with employment, die of maltreatment, and be sexually abused.

The Truth Is ...

Same-sex marriage is wrong because children do worse when raised by homosexual parents than by heterosexual parents.

References and Further Reading

For the APA's position, see "Resolution on Sexual Orientation, Parents, and Children," (adopted July 2004), accessible at http://www.apa.org/pi/lgbc/policy/parentschildren.

Robert Lerner and Althea Nagia, *No Basis: What the Studies Don't Tell Us About Same-Sex Parenting*, Marriage Law Project (Washington, DC, January 2001).

Marriage Rights for Homosexuals: Not the Best for Children: Critique of AAP Special Report," *American College of Pediatricians* (posted prior to January 22, 2004), accessible at http://www.acpeds.org/Marriage-Rights-for-Homosexual-Couples-Not-the-Best-for-Children.html.

"Homosexual Parenting: Is It Time for Change?" *American College of Pediatricians* (January 22, 2004), accessible at http://www.acpeds.org/index.cgi?cat=10005andart=50andBISKIT=http://www.acpeds.org/Homosexual-Parenting-Is-It-Time-For-Change.html.

Jeffrey Satinover, "The Trojan Couch: How the Mental Health Associations Misrepresent Science," *Conference Reports 2005*, National Association for Research and Therapy of Homosexuals, accessible at http://www.narth.com/docs/ thetrojancouchsatinover.

A. Dean Byrd, "When Activism Masquerades as Science," National Association for Research and Therapy of Homosexuals, accessible at http://www.narth.com/docs/masquerades (posted 2004, updated September 3, 2008).

Loren Marks, "Same-Sex Parenting and Children's Outcomes: A Closer Examination of the American Psychological Association's Brief of Lesbian and Gay Parenting," *Social Science Research,* 41 (2012), pp. 735-751.

Theo Sandfort, Ron de Graaf, Rob Bojl, and Paul Schnabel, "Same-Sex Sexual Behavior and Psychiatric Disorders," *Archives of General Psychiatry,* 58 (January 2001), pp. 85-91.

Patricia Morgan, *Children as Trophies? Examining the Evidence on Same-Sex Parenting* (Newcastle upon Tyne, UK: Christian Institute, 2002).

Elizabeth Thompson, Thomas Hanson, and Sara McLanahan, "Family Structure and Child Well-Being," *Social Forces,* 73/1 (September 1994), pp. 221-242.

For evidence showing that children needing both mothers and fathers, see Maggie Gallagher and Joshua K. Baker, "Do Moms and Dads Matter? Evidence from the Social Sciences on Family Structure and the Best Interests of the Child," 4/161, *Margins* (2004), pp. 161-180; and Maggie Gallagher, "What Marriage Is For: Children Need Mothers and Fathers," *Weekly Standard* (August 4/August 11, 2003), pp. 22-25.

19

You May Hear Proponents Argue …

Same-sex marriage should be allowed because homosexuals make better parents than biological mothers and fathers. Research reveals that homosexuals make better parents than heterosexuals and that children raised by homosexuals are better adjusted. Gay and lesbian couples cooperate more readily with others, so they make more attentive parents than heterosexuals. Children raised by homosexuals learn to be flexible and accepting of others, which makes them better future citizens than those who are raised to think everyone must be heterosexual. Same-sex marriage is thus a good thing for children, for families, and for society.

You Can *Graciously Refute* This By Saying …

Proponents of this argument rely on two false premises. First, they wrongly suppose that the psychological and emotional wellbeing of children derives primarily from legal recognition of the marital status of their parents. Second, they appeal to a number of politically motivated childrearing studies that suffer from a number of flaws, including non-longitudinal design, inadequate sample sizes, biased sample selections, lack of proper controls, and a failure to account for confounding variables and contrary results. The ACP says "it is appalling that a professional medical organization [such as the AAP and APA] could so recklessly champion [alleged] 'evidence' when none exists."

Few people deny that homosexual partnerships tend to be highly promiscuous (not sexually monogamous) and unstable (not enduring). In fact, the average homosexual relationship lasts no more than two to three years. For this reason, children raised in homosexual households are generally less secure than those raised in heterosexual households, and they are also more likely to suffer psychological problems that lead to major depression, conduct disorder, and substance abuse. In addition, because violence among homosexual partners is two to three times higher than among heterosexual partners, children living with homosexuals are also more vulnerable to physical harm.

The negative impact of children living with homosexuals is well documented. Based on this evidence, it is obvious that the motive and driving interest in legalizing same-sex marriage does not derive from a dedication to what will most benefit children. Rather, the motivation comes from the homosexual community's eagerness to coerce the public's endorsement of their lifestyle.

The Truth Is ...

Same-sex marriage is wrong because children do best when their mothers and fathers raise them, and they are put at risk by living in homosexual households.

References and Further Reading

For examples of advocates using this argument, see Alice Park, "Children of Lesbians May Do Better than Their Peers," *TIME* (June 7, 2010), accessible at http://www.time.com/time/printout/0,8816,1994480,00.html; and Dana Rudolph, "Gay Dads Also Better than Straight Parents?" *Change.org* (June 16, 2010), accessible at http://news.change.org/stories/gay-dads-also-better-than-straight-parents.

Mark Regnerus, "How Different Are the Adult Children of Parents Who Have Same-Sex Relationships? Findings from the New Family Structures Study," *Social Science Research*, 41 (2012), pp. 752-770.

Loren Marks, "Same-Sex Parenting and Children's Outcomes: A Closer Examination of the American Psychological Association's

Brief of Lesbian and Gay Parenting," *Social Science Research*, 41 (2012), pp. 735-751.

Robert Lerner and Althea Nagia, *No Basis: What the Studies Don't Tell Us About Same-Sex Parenting*, Marriage Law Project (Washington, DC, January 2001).

Mary Parke, "Are Married Parents Really Better for Children: What Research Says About the Effects of Family Structure on Child Well-Being," Center for Law and Public Policy, *Policy Brief #3* (May 2003), pp. 1,6.

David M. Fergusson, et al., "Is Sexual Orientation Related to Mental Health Problems and Suicidality In Young People?" *Archives of General Psychiatry*, 56 (October 1999), pp. 876-880.

Gwat Yong Lie and Sabrina Gentlewarrier, "Intimate Violence in Lesbian Relationships: Discussion of Survey Findings and Practice Implications," *Journal of Social Service Research*, 15/1-2 (1991), pp. 41-59.

David Island and Patrick Letellier, *Men Who Beat the Men Who Love Them: Battered Gay Men and Domestic Violence* (New York: Haworth Press, 1991).

Maggie Gallagher and Joshua K. Baker, "Do Moms and Dads Matter? Evidence from the Social Sciences on Family Structure and the Best Interests of the Child," 4/161, *Margins* (2004), pp. 161-180.

For evidence on how homosexual partnerships are more likely to dissolve than heterosexual partnerships, see D. McWhirter and A. Mattison, *The Male Couple: How Relationships Develop* (Englewood Cliffs, NJ: Prentice-Hall, 1984), pp. 252-253; and L. A. Peplau and H. Amaro, "Understanding Lesbian Relationships," in W. Paul, et al., eds., *Homosexuality: Social, Psychological, and Biological Issues* (Beverly Hills, CA: Sage, 1982), 233-248.

20

You May Hear Proponents Argue …

Same-sex marriage should be allowed because it is better for the children of homosexuals to have parents who are married than not married. It is good for children to have parents who are married. All children need a family environment that is stable and secure, and marriage helps to assure this. However, today thousands of children are being raised by homosexuals who cannot marry—even though those children need strong and stable families just as much as children raised by heterosexual couples. Allowing same-sex marriage will promote family stability through marriage to *all* children, regardless of the orientation of their parents, and will not limit these benefits to just the children of heterosexual parents.

You Can *Graciously Refute* This By Saying …

Proponents of this argument use misguided pity to get people to accept something that is bad for children everywhere, including children living with homosexuals. They propose removing the social support that favors the family structure best suited for children in order to give a small number of homosexuals a way of forcing others to condone their lifestyle. The number of children who live full time with homosexuals is less than 0.2% (two-tenths of 1%) of the total number of households. However, those making this argument would have the public abandon the significant child-benefitting reason society has for keeping marriage law as it is—and all for the sake of something that is not likely to help the children they call others to pity.

This argument is much like saying that because some children are homeless, we should change what *home* means to include any location on a street. We could then say no child was *homeless*, but only at the cost of doing more harm than good. Children living on the street would still be living on the street, and children living in houses would be less secure.

The best childrearing studies show that the psychological and emotional wellbeing of children depends more on being raised by both a father and mother (a heterosexual pair) than on the legal status of their parents' relationship (a married pair). Same-sex marriage will destroy what children most need—a mother and father—only to substitute something dubious and less important (having married parents regardless of gender). This will sacrifice what is best for children and substitute something marginal in its place that will help very few—if any at all.

The Truth Is …

Same-sex marriage is wrong because it assumes that having both a mother and father is irrelevant for children, which ends up being bad for children.

˙References and Further Reading

For an example of this argument, see Barbara Ehrenreich, "How Banning Gay Marriage Will Destroy the Family," *Barbara's Blog*, accessible at http://ehrenreich.blogs.com/barbaras_blog/2006/06/how_banning_gay.html.

Mary Parke, "Are Married Parents Really Better for Children: What Research Says About the Effects of Family Structure on Child Well-Being," Center for Law and Public Policy, *Policy Brief #3* (May 2003), pp. 1,6.

Maggie Gallagher and Joshua K. Baker, "Do Moms and Dads Matter? Evidence from the Social Sciences on Family Structure and the Best Interests of the Child," 4/161, *Margins* (2004), pp. 161-180.

Elizabeth Thompson, Thomas Hanson, and Sara McLanahan, "Family Structure and Child Well-Being," *Social Forces*, 73/1 (September 1994), pp. 221-242.

Barbara Schneider, Allison Atteberry, and Alfred Owens, *Family Matters: Family Structure and Child Outcomes* (Birmingham, AL: Alabama Policy Institute, 2005), available at http://www.alabamapolicyinstitute.org/pdf/currentfamily.

Dawn Stefanowicz, *Out from Under: The Impact of Homosexual Parenting* (Enumclaw, WA: Annotation Press, 2007).

Robert Lerner and Althea Nagia, *No Basis: What the Studies Don't Tell Us About Same-Sex Parenting*, Marriage Law Project (Washington, DC, January 2001).

Marriage Rights for Homosexuals: Not the Best for Children: Critique of AAP Special Report," *American College of Pediatricians* (posted prior to January 22, 2004), accessible at http://www.acpeds.org/Marriage-Rights-for-Homosexual-Couples-Not-the-Best-for-Children.html.

Patricia Morgan, *Children as Trophies? Examining the Evidence on Same-Sex Parenting* (Newcastle upon Tyne, UK: Christian Institute, 2002).

David M. Fergusson, et al., "Is Sexual Orientation Related to Mental Health Problems and Suicidality In Young People?" *Archives of General Psychiatry,* 56 (October 1999), pp. 876-880.

Mark Regnerus, "How Different Are the Adult Children of Parents Who Have Same-Sex Relationships? Findings from the New Family Structures Study," *Social Science Research*, 41 (2012), pp. 752-770.

Theo Sandfort, Ron de Graaf, Rob Bojl, and Paul Schnabel, "Same-Sex Sexual Behavior and Psychiatric Disorders," *Archives of General Psychiatry*, 58 (January 2001), pp. 85-91.

Arguments 21 – 28

Gracious Answers to Arguments Regarding Justice and Rights

It cannot
be right to redefine
legal marriage in a way that
creates the very wrong homosexuals
say must be fixed—but that does not
exist without first redefining
legal marriage to generate
the wrong they
want fixed.

REGARDING JUSTICE AND RIGHTS

(Arguments 21–28)

21

You May Hear Proponents Argue ...

SAME-SEX MARRIAGE SHOULD be allowed because justice requires treating homosexuals the same as everyone else. Civil marriage is not only a private matter, but also how society gives public approval and support to couples entering into committed relationships. In fact, the *only* reason for having legal marriages is to give approval and respect to couples entering into such relationships. For this reason, it is fundamentally unjust to offer public approval to some marriages but not to others. Homosexuals will never have equal justice under the law until they are allowed to marry like everyone else. Same-sex marriage will remove the injustice by treating homosexuals the same as others.

You Can *Graciously Refute* This By Saying ...

Proponents of this argument attempt to change the meaning of marriage and create a sense of injustice that does not exist without *purpose of marriage* [handwritten margin note]

changing what marriage means in the first place. They advocate that marriage has no intrinsic link to procreation and means nothing more than two people sharing a *committed relationship*. Thus, because homosexuals have the same committed relationships as heterosexuals, these couples must now be allowed to marry, just the same as heterosexuals.

This simply is not the case. Marriage is not—and has never been—just *any* sort of committed relationship that two people happen to choose. It is not simply a permission slip giving public approval to any sort of relation with anyone at all. Public recognition and approval of marriage is—and always has been—linked to the procreational structure of the institution. On the one hand, this institution favors restricting procreation to couples who are committed to staying together; on the other hand, it is committed to getting biological fathers and mothers to share responsibility for raising children. *cultural mandate* [handwritten note]

it is not public acceptance of "any" relationship [handwritten margin note]

No one has a right to marry any partner he or she happens to desire, regardless of how that union would relate to the social need of getting biological mothers and fathers to take responsibility for raising their own children, or how it would affect the procreational structure of marriage as an essential social institution. Nor does anyone have the right to change what marriage means in order to generate a legal inequity that does not exist without first changing what marriage means. It is unjust to turn something currently just into something unjust simply to create a legal basis for promoting homosexual desires.

The Truth Is ...

Same-sex marriage is wrong because it is unjust to change marriage to remove an inequity that would not exist before marriage was changed.

References and Further Reading

For an example of this argument, see Andrew Sullivan, "Frum on Marriage," *The Daily Dish*, accessible at http://AndrewSullivan. com (posted February 28, 2005). In making this argument, Sullivan claims that the only legitimate purpose of marriage law is to encourage "social support for relationships as such."

Theodore Olson and David Boies also used this argument to try to persuade a federal court to invalidate California's Proposition 8, which banned same-sex marriage in the state. See Theodore B. Olson, "The Conservative Case for Gay Marriage: Why Same-Sex Marriage Is an American Value," *Newsweek* (January 18, 2010), pp. 48-54.

For the weakening effect of legalizing same-sex marriage on marriage as a social institution, see David Blankenhorn, "Deinstitutionalizing Marriage?" chapter 6 in *The Future of Marriage* (New York: Encounter Books, 2007), pp. 127-169; Stanley Kurtz, "The End of Marriage in Scandinavia: The 'Conservative Case' for Same-Sex Marriage Collapses," *Weekly Standard* (February 2, 2004), pp. 26-33; and Maggie Gallagher, "(How) Will Gay Marriage Weaken Marriage as a Social Institution: A Reply to Andrew Koppelman," *University of Saint Thomas Law Journal*, 2/1 (Fall 2004), pp. 33-70.

For how abandoning the procreational structure of marriage threatens civilization, see Joseph Daniel Unwin, *Sex and Culture* (London: Oxford University Press, 1937); and Carle Zimmerman, *Family and Civilization* (Wilmington, DE: ISI Books, 2008).

Carson Holloway, "Same-Sex Marriage and the Death of Tradition," *First Things* (June 10, 2009), accessible at http://www.firstthings. com/onthesquare/2009/06/same-sex-marriage-and-the-deat.

Sherif Girgis, Robert P. George, and Ryan T. Anderson, "What Is Marriage?" *Harvard Journal of Law and Public Policy*, 34/1 (Winter 2011), pp. 245-287.

Maggie Gallagher, "Should Gay Marriage Be Legal? No," *ProCon. org* (May 22, 2009), accessible at http://gaymarriage.procon. org/view.answers.php?questionID=001607.

On disputing the normal view of marriage see Maggie Gallagher, "Normal Marriage: Two Views," in *Marriage and Same-Sex Unions: A Debate*, ed. Lynn Wardle, Mark Strasser, William Duncan, and David Coolidge (Westport, CT: Praeger, 2003), pp. 13-24.

For how legalizing same-sex marriage will align marriage to homosexual categories and not align homosexuals to what marriage is now, see Lawrence Auster, "The Extreme Radicalism of Homosexual 'Marriage,'" *View from the Right* (June 2, 2008), accessible at http://www.amnation.com/vfr/archives/010723. html.

22

You May Hear Proponents Argue …

Same-sex marriage should be allowed because human dignity requires all couples who love each other to marry. Marriage expresses social recognition and public respect for the human dignity of those uniting with each other at a deep level. All humans have equal human dignity and deserve the same degree of respect for their commitments. Equal regard for human dignity requires treating all attractions that lead couples to form deeply committed relationships the same, whether those relationships are homosexual or heterosexual. Same-sex marriage will correct the injustice of treating homosexuals with less human dignity than heterosexuals.

You Can *Graciously Refute* This By Saying …

It is impossible to redefine marriage in a way that addresses a person's human dignity and makes the heterosexual-homosexual difference irrelevant. Human dignity does not come from following whatever urges come along but from doing what it takes to keep impulses under control. In other words, human dignity has less to do with sensual experiences and more to do with being creatures who are able and responsible to keep desires checked within proper boundaries. *human dignity = keeping urges in check.*

Marriage does not involve approving whatever couples feel like doing. If a society has no public interest in favoring marriage other than to affirm whatever relational desires people have, it transforms marriage into something different than it has ever been. When it comes to the public value of marriage to society, a union of two men or two women can never be the same as the union of a man with a woman in marriage—regardless of how committed these other couples might be.

Thus, there can be no injustice, because along with the public interest of justifying laws favoring marriage as a social institution comes the public interest in connecting procreational sex with getting fathers and mothers to set aside their separate individual interests long enough to raise their own children. When it comes to promoting this essential social interest, opposite-sex relationships and same-sex relationships are not in the same category. Marriage law is justified as it is. It would be foolish and unjust to change these well-justified laws to *fix* a supposed equity problem that would not exist prior to changing what marriage means simply to generate the sort of inequity proponents say they want to fix.

The Truth Is …

Same-sex marriage is wrong because human dignity does not allow changing marriage into something irrelevant to having children.

References and Further Reading

Maggie Gallagher, "Normal Marriage: Two Views," in *Marriage and Same-Sex Unions: A Debate*, ed. Lynn Wardle, Mark Strasser, William Duncan, and David Coolidge (Westport, CT: Praeger, 2003), pp. 13-24.

Carson Holloway, "Same-Sex Marriage and the Death of Tradition," *First Things* (June 10, 2009), accessible at http://www.firstthings.com/onthesquare/2009/06/same-sex-marriage-and-the-deat.

William C. Duncan, "The State Interest in Marriage," *Ave Maria Law Review,* 2/1 (Spring 2004), pp. 153-182.

Sherif Girgis, Robert P. George, and Ryan T. Anderson, "What Is Marriage?" *Harvard Journal of Law and Public Policy*, 34/1 (Winter 2011), pp. 245-287.

Robert P. George, Ryan T. Anderson, and Sherif Girgis, "The Argument Against Gay Marriage: And Why It Doesn't Fail,"

Public Discourse: Ethics, Law and the Common Good (December 17, 2010), accessible at http://www.thepublicdiscourse. com.

Sherif Girgis, Ryan T. Anderson, and Robert P. George, "Marriage: Merely a Social Construct?" *Public Discourse: Ethics, Law and the Common Good* (December 29, 2010), accessible at http://www.thepublicdiscourse.com.

Sherif Girgis, Ryan T. Anderson, and Robert P. George, "Marriage: Real Bodily Union," *Public Discourse: Ethics, Law and the Common Good* (December 30, 2010), accessible at http://www.thepublicdiscourse.com.

Sherif Girgis, Ryan T. Anderson, and Robert P. George, "Marriage: No Avoiding the Central Question," *Public Discourse: Ethics, Law and the Common Good* (January 3, 2011), accessible at http://www.thepublicdiscourse.com.

Sherif Girgis, Ryan T. Anderson, and Robert P. George, "Does Marriage, or Anything, Have Essential Properties?" *Public Discourse: Ethics, Law and the Common Good* (January 12, 2011), accessible at http://www.thepublicdiscourse.com.

Patrick Lee, Robert P. George, and Gerard V. Bradley, "Marriage and Procreation: The Intrinsic Connection," *Public Discourse: Ethics, Law and the Common Good* (March 28, 2011), accessible at http://www.thepublicdiscourse.com.

Patrick Lee, Robert P. George, and Gerard V. Bradley, "Marriage and Procreation: Avoiding Bad Arguments," *Public Discourse: Ethics, Law and the Common Good* (March 30, 2011), accessible at http://www.thepublicdiscourse.com.

23

You May Hear Proponents Argue ...

Same-sex marriage should be allowed because marriage is a basic human right for both homosexuals and heterosexuals. Allowing gays to marry does not create a special right for gays—it only removes a barrier that denies gays access to a fundamental right to which they already are entitled as members of the human race. All humans have a fundamental right to marry a partner to whom they are sexually attracted, but homosexuals in America are denied this right. Extending this right to everyone except homosexuals is terribly inconsistent, terribly unfair, and terribly unjust. Allowing same-sex marriage will solve the problem.

You Can *Graciously Refute* This By Saying ...

The practical benefits given by law favoring marriage and family relationships—such as filing a joint tax return, Social Security surviving spouse payments, hospital visitation, and rights of inheritance—have never been to affirm just any committed relationship. People form many strong relational bonds with others—such as the bond between close friends, neighbors, classmates, roommates, or teammates—but these do not qualify for the special benefits associated with marriage.

In addition, not every sexual relationship qualifies as marriage either. For example, prostitutes have no right to inherit the property of their regular customers, and lap-dance patrons cannot list performers as dependents when they are filing their income tax forms. When it comes to what qualifies as marriage, the question is not whether a relationship is committed or sexual, but whether it fits the structure of marriage as a social institution. Same-sex relationships do not qualify because they do not fit the procreational structure of marriage. Whether the individuals involved in those relationships are *committed* or *sexual* has nothing to do with it.

Society does not recognize a person's universal right to marry whatever partner he or she happens to find attractive because the right to marry is intrinsically linked to the institution's procreational structure and interest in getting fathers and mothers to raise their own children. An individual's right to marry does not include a right to change marriage into something other than it currently is. Homosexuals already have a right to marry, just like everyone else. What they do not have is a right to redefine marriage in order to get everyone to affirm what they do sexually.

The Truth Is …

Same-sex marriage is wrong because no one has a right to marry whatever partner he or she happens to find attractive.

References and Further Reading

Theodore Olson and David Boies used this argument to try to persuade a federal court to invalidate California's Proposition 8, which banned same-sex marriage in the state. See Theodore B. Olson, "The Conservative Case for Gay Marriage: Why Same-Sex Marriage Is an American Value," *Newsweek* (January 18, 2010), pp. 48-54.

A good refutation of this argument is presented by the Hawaiian Supreme Court in *Baehr v. Lewin*, 74 Hawaii 645, 852 P.2d 44 (1993).

Maggie Gallagher, "Normal Marriage: Two Views," in *Marriage and Same-Sex Unions: A Debate*, ed. Lynn Wardle, Mark Strasser, William Duncan, and David Coolidge (Westport, CT: Praeger, 2003), pp. 13-24.

Maggie Gallagher, "The Case Against Same-Sex Marriage," chapter 3 in *Debating Same-Sex Marriage* (New York: Oxford University Press, 2012), pages 91-178.

For the weakening effect of legalizing same-sex marriage on marriage as a social institution, see David Blankenhorn, "Deinstitutionalizing Marriage?" chapter 6 in *The Future of Marriage* (New York: Encounter Books, 2007), pp. 127-169; Stanley Kurtz, "The End of Marriage in Scandinavia: The 'Conservative Case' for Same-Sex Marriage Collapses," *Weekly Standard* (February 2, 2004), pp. 26-33; and Maggie Gallagher, "(How) Will Gay Marriage Weaken Marriage as a Social Institution: A Reply to Andrew Koppelman," *University of Saint Thomas Law Journal*, 2/1 (Fall 2004), pp. 33-70.

For how abandoning the procreational structure of marriage threatens civilization, see Joseph Daniel Unwin, *Sex and Culture* (London: Oxford University Press, 1937); Joseph Daniel Unwin, *Sexual Regulations and Cultural Behavior: An Address Delivered Before the Medical Section of the British Psychological Society* (London: Oxford University Press, 1935); Carle Zimmerman, *Family and Civilization* (Wilmington, DE: ISI Books, 2008); Pitirim Sorokin, *The Crisis of Our Age* (Richmond, VA: Dutton, 1941); Pitirim Sorokin, *Social and Cultural Dynamics*, vol. 4 (Boston, MA: Porter Sargent, 1957); and Daniel Heimbach, "The Future Based on Science," in Daniel Heimbach, *True Sexual Morality* (Wheaton, IL: Crossway, 2004), pp. 345-348.

Patrick Lee, Robert P. George, and Gerard V. Bradley, "Marriage and Procreation: The Intrinsic Connection," *Public Discourse: Ethics, Law and the Common Good* (March 28, 2011), accessible at http://www.thepublicdiscourse.com.

Patrick Lee, Robert P. George, and Gerard V. Bradley, "Marriage and Procreation: Avoiding Bad Arguments," *Public Discourse: Ethics, Law and the Common Good* (March 30, 2011), accessible at http://www.thepublicdiscourse.com.

24

You May Hear Proponents Argue …

Same-sex marriage should be allowed because it is not fair for marriage law to favor one form of sexual attraction over another. Marriage law should treat human sexuality in a manner that does not prefer one form to another. Sexual attraction is a private matter that others cannot assess, and marriage simply offers public recognition and support to couples making relational commitments. Because sexual attraction can be homosexual or heterosexual, and because only those involved know the strength and quality of what draws them together, justice requires civil law to be neutral by permitting couples to marry without assessing what draws them together.

You Can *Graciously Refute* This By Saying …

Proponents of this argument presume the public has no interest in maintaining marriage laws except as a way to affirm whatever draws people together. If this argument were true, it would follow that (1) only those who are attracted to each other could verify their feelings, and (2) there would be no just basis for refusing to allow homosexuals to marry. Yet it is ridiculous to think there is no public interest in maintaining the procreational structure of marriage as a social institution, and it is foolish to think civil marriage has no purpose except to affirm whatever attractions people happen to have. If so, pedophiles would be allowed to marry children, necrophiles would be allowed to marry dead bodies, pornophiles would be allowed to marry pictures, and bestialphiles would be allowed to marry animals .

Proponents of this argument are actually redefining marriage in a way that makes *everything* marriage. In reality, society must make distinctions that exclude all sorts of sexual attractions from what marriage means. Society does so not by evaluating how anyone feels but by evaluating how relationships serve the public interest in keeping men and women together long enough to raise biological children.

Proponents of this argument confuse the public interest of supporting the procreational structure of marriage with satisfying people's private appetites, and in so doing, they deny that marriage has any institutional purpose or structure at all. In truth, just as the office of the President of the United States is greater than any person occupying that office, so the institution of marriage is greater than the particular people who get married. In both cases, the public reason for justifying the structure of the institution is completely different from what motivates people to participate or what satisfies those who do.

The Truth Is ...

Same-sex marriage is wrong because the public structure of marriage has nothing to do with affirming private attractions.

References and Further Reading

Theodore Olson and David Boies used this argument to try to persuade a federal court to invalidate California's Proposition 8, which banned same-sex marriage in the state. See Theodore B. Olson, "The Conservative Case for Gay Marriage: Why Same-Sex Marriage Is an American Value," *Newsweek* (January 18, 2010), pp. 48-54.

Robert P. George and Jean Bethke Elshtain, eds., *The Meaning of Marriage: Family, State, Market, and Morals* (Dallas, TX: Spence Publishing, 2006).

Sherif Girgis, Robert P. George, and Ryan T. Anderson, "What Is Marriage?" *Harvard Journal of Law and Public Policy*, 34/1 (Winter 2011), pp. 245-287.

Robert P. George, Ryan T. Anderson, and Sherif Girgis, "The Argument Against Gay Marriage: And Why It Doesn't Fail," *Public Discourse: Ethics, Law and the Common Good* (December 17, 2010), accessible at http://www.thepublicdiscourse. com.

Sherif Girgis, Ryan T. Anderson, and Robert P. George, "Marriage: Merely a Social Construct?" *Public Discourse: Ethics, Law and the Common Good* (December 29, 2010), accessible at http:// www.thepublicdiscourse.com.

Sherif Girgis, Ryan T. Anderson, and Robert P. George, "Marriage: Real Bodily Union," *Public Discourse: Ethics, Law and the Common Good* (December 30, 2010), accessible at http://www. thepublicdiscourse.com.

Sherif Girgis, Ryan T. Anderson, and Robert P. George, "Marriage: No Avoiding the Central Question," *Public Discourse: Ethics, Law and the Common Good* (January 3, 2011), accessible at http://www.thepublicdiscourse.com.

Sherif Girgis, Ryan T. Anderson, and Robert P. George, "Does Marriage, or Anything, Have Essential Properties?" *Public Discourse: Ethics, Law and the Common Good* (January 12, 2011), accessible at http://www.thepublicdiscourse.com.

Patrick Lee, Robert P. George, and Gerard V. Bradley, "Marriage and Procreation: The Intrinsic Connection," *Public Discourse: Ethics, Law and the Common Good* (March 28, 2011), accessible at http://www.thepublicdiscourse.com.

Patrick Lee, Robert P. George, and Gerard V. Bradley, "Marriage and Procreation: Avoiding Bad Arguments," *Public Discourse: Ethics, Law and the Common Good* (March 30, 2011), accessible at http://www.thepublicdiscourse.com.

William C. Duncan, "The State Interest in Marriage," *Ave Maria Law Review*, 2/1 (Spring 2004), pp. 153-182.

25

You May Hear Proponents Argue ...

Same-sex marriage should be allowed because it is not right to require everyone to conform to a single template for marriage. Limiting marriage to only uniting opposite-sex couples excludes other partnerships from participating in the supreme act of unifying love. Preventing gays from uniting in this way restricts human flourishing, which diminishes life for everyone, not just homosexuals. Marriage today has no fixed structure and only concerns affirming the value of human bonding without sexual limitations, so denying same-sex marriage is unjust. There is no reason for restricting marriage to just one form.

You Can *Graciously Refute* This By Saying ...

Proponents of this argument assume that marriage has become nothing more than a way of affirming undefined personal relationships that arise from any form of sexual attraction whatsoever. However, no society has ever held this view before, and the vast majority of Americans do not hold it today. To accept this view would require changing marriage into something different than it currently is to make marriage laws into weapons for getting rid of public social support for linking marriage to any form at all. This would make private satisfaction the reason for public interest in supporting marriage, rather than a private benefit that results from serving what truly justifies the public interest in supporting marriage—maintaining an institution structured to get fathers and mothers to cooperate long enough to raise biological children.

In truth, the only legitimate public reason for supporting marriage is to give children the fathers and mothers who made them. Public support of marriage is not given to satisfy adult appetites, maximize their sexual freedom, affirm any sort of sexual orienta-tion, or celebrate family diversity. Denying that marriage has any fixed structure destroys it as a coherent social institution, which harms everyone—including homosexuals.

Denying all fixed structure in marriage turns it into non-marriage, because when marriage includes everything, it is the same as everything else. In truth, legalizing same-sex marriage will not bring new types of couples into the institution historically affirmed as marriage. Instead, it will *abolish* the conjugal conception of marriage in law and public policy by *replacing* it with what actually is non-marriage, because that new form would be totally subjective and have no fixed structure at all.

The Truth Is …

Same-sex marriage is wrong because it is terribly unjust to abolish real marriage and pretend it is the same as non-marriage.

References and Further Reading

For examples of advocates using this argument, see Andrew Sullivan, *Virtually Normal* (New York: Random House, 1995), 203-204; and Jonathan Rauch, *Gay Marriage: Why It Is Good for Gays, Good for Straights, and Good for America* (New York: Times Books, 2004).

Robert P. George and Jean Bethke Elshtain, eds., *The Meaning of Marriage: Family, State, Market, and Morals* (Dallas, TX: Spence Publishing, 2006).

John Witte, Jr., "The Tradition of Traditional Marriage," in *Marriage and Same-Sex Unions: A Debate*, ed. Lynn Wardle, Mark Strasser, William Duncan, and David Coolidge (Westport, CT: Praeger, 2003), pp. 47-59.

Dan Cere, *The Future of Family Law: Law and the Marriage Crisis in North America* (New York: Institute for American Values,

2005), accessible at http://www.marriagedebate.com/pdf/ future_of_family_law.pdf.

William C. Duncan, "The State Interest in Marriage," *Ave Maria Law Review*, 2/1 (Spring 2004), pp. 153-182.

For the weakening effect of legalizing same-sex marriage on marriage as a social institution, see Stanley Kurtz, "The End of Marriage in Scandinavia: The 'Conservative Case' for Same-Sex Marriage Collapses," *Weekly Standard* (February 2, 2004), pp. 26-33; Maggie Gallagher, "Should Gay Marriage Be Legal? No," *ProCon.org* (May 22, 2009), accessible at http://gaymarriage. procon.org/view.answers.php?questionID=001607; and Maggie Gallagher, "(How) Will Gay Marriage Weaken Marriage as a Social Institution," *University of Saint Thomas Law Journal*, 2/1 (Fall 2004), pp. 33-70.

For how abandoning the procreational structure of marriage threatens civilization, see Joseph Daniel Unwin, *Sex and Culture* (London: Oxford University Press, 1937); Carle Zimmerman, *Family and Civilization* (Wilmington, DE: ISI Books, 2008); and Pitirim Sorokin, *Social and Cultural Dynamics*, vol. 4 (Boston, MA: Porter Sargent, 1957).

For how science has been misrepresented and politicized, see Jeffrey Satinover, "The Trojan Couch: How the Mental Health Associations Misrepresent Science," *Conference Reports 2005*, National Association for Research and Therapy of Homosexuals, accessible at http://www.narth.com/docs/thetrojancouch-satinover; Robert Lerner and Althea Nagia, *No Basis: What the Studies Don't Tell Us About Same-Sex Parenting*, Marriage Law Project (Washington, DC, January 2001); and A. Dean Byrd, "When Activism Masquerades as Science," National Association for Research and Therapy of Homosexuals, accessible at http:// www.narth.com/docs/masquerades (posted 2004, updated September 3, 2008).

26

You May Hear Proponents Argue …

Same-sex marriage should be allowed because denying it is the same as denying racial equality. Homosexuals are being denied the same rights under current laws that members of different races were denied under segregationist laws that prohibited interracial marriage. This discrimination is morally wrong because it places people in different categories for no reason other than to suppress the category by which they are classified. Just as there was found to be no compelling state interest that justified prohibiting interracial marriage, so there is no compelling state interest to justify denying marriage licenses to same-sex couples.

You Can *Graciously Refute* This By Saying …

Of course it is wrong for the law to treat items in the same category differently, which is what made laws against interracial marriage so bad. But opposing same-sex marriage is not the same as opposing laws restricting marriage by race. The public interest in justifying laws that affirm and protect procreational marriage is based on the need all societies have to get men and women to take responsibility for raising their own children. Many types of sexual partnering—such as polygamy, sex with children, and bestiality—do not qualify for marriage because they conflict with this public interest.

Limiting marriage to male-female couples is dissimilar to limiting marriage by race because: (1) interracial marriage *affirms* procreational responsibility, while same-sex marriage *redefines* marriage by denying it has any structure at all; (2) interracial marriage serves the public interest in getting biological fathers and mothers to raise their own children, while same-sex marriage serves no public interest; and (3) interracial marriage supports the procreative structure of marriage, while same-sex marriage does not protect the procreative structure of marriage as a social institution.

In fact, it is the proponents of same-sex marriage who are most similar to those who once opposed interracial marriage, because these advocates are also using marriage law to pursue socially harmful private passions that are unrelated to the institution itself. Likewise, opponents of gay marriage are similar to those who once championed interracial marriage, because they also are defending the institution against abuse that is driven by nothing more than private passions.

The Truth Is ...

Same-sex marriage is wrong because it unfairly mistreats and misuses marriage in the way racists used to oppose interracial marriage.

References and Further Reading

For examples of advocates using this argument, see Michelangelo Signorile, "Bridal Wave," *Out* (December/January 1994), p. 161; and Theodore Olson, "The Conservative Case for Gay Marriage," *Newsweek* (January 18, 2010), pp. 48-54.

Glenn T. Stanton and Bill Maier, "Isn't Banning Gay Marriage Just Like Banning Interracial Marriage?" in *Why Marriage Matters: Reasons to Believe in Marriage in Postmodern Society* (Colorado Springs, CO: Pinion Press, 1997), pp. 36-39.

In challenging this particular argument, Sherif Girgis, Robert George, and Ryan Anderson note that "antimiscegenation [opposing interracial marriage] was about whom to allow to marry, not what marriage was essentially about; and sex, unlike race, is rationally relevant to the latter question ... [in direct contrast], there is nothing unjustly discriminatory in marriage law's reliance on genuinely relevant distinctions."

See Sherif Girgis, Robert P. George, and Ryan T. Anderson, "What Is Marriage?" *Harvard Journal of Law and Public Policy*, 34/1 (Winter 2011), pp. 245-287.

For examples of gay social revolutionaries admitting they are using same-sex marriage as a way to completely abolish the institution of marriage, see Thomas B. Stoddard, "Why Gay People Should Seek the Right to Marry," chapter 35 in *Families in the US: Kinship and Domestic Politics*, ed. Karen V. Hansen (Philadelphia, PA: Temple University Press, 1998); Richard D. Mohr, *A More Perfect Union: Why Straight America Must Stand Up for Gay Rights* (Boston, MA: Beacon, 1994); Gretchen A. Stiers, *From This Day Forward: Commitment, Marriage, and Family in Lesbian and Gay Relationships* (New York: St. Martin's Press, 1999); Michelangelo Signorile, "Bridal Wave," *Out* (December/January 1994); "Sociologist Says Gay Marriage Does Threaten Established Order and That's Good," *Ascribe Law News Service* (November 16, 2003); and Margaret Gullette, "The New Case for Marriage," *American Prospect* (March 1, 2004).

Maggie Gallagher, "Normal Marriage: Two Views," in *Marriage and Same-Sex Unions: A Debate*, ed. Lynn Wardle, Mark Strasser, William Duncan, and David Coolidge (Westport, CT: Praeger, 2003), pp. 13-24.

Maggie Gallagher, "What Marriage Is For: Children Need Mothers and Fathers," *Weekly Standard* (August 4/August 11, 2003), pp. 22-25.

Maggie Gallagher, "(How) Will Gay Marriage Weaken Marriage as a Social Institution: A Reply to Andrew Koppelman," *University of Saint Thomas Law Journal*, 2/1 (Fall 2004), pp. 33-70.

William C. Duncan, "The State Interest in Marriage," *Ave Maria Law Review*, 2/1 (Spring 2004), pp. 153-182.

27

You May Hear Proponents Argue ...

Same-sex marriage should be allowed because justice requires all families to be treated the same in the eyes of the law. Americans must rethink what a family means. A family today should be defined by function, not by any fixed structure. All social units comprised of members who are deeply committed to caring for one another function as family units, and all such units should be treated the same under the law. Same-sex couples are functional family units; but without freedom to marry, they do not receive the same recognition and protection for their families as married couples. Same-sex marriage will correct this injustice by treating all families the same.

You Can *Graciously Refute* This By Saying ...

Proponents of this argument create the wrong they demand should be fixed. By changing the definition of a family to include *any* sort of committed relationship, they create an injustice. In fact, a family means far more than just a group of people committed to caring for one another. Members of fraternities, churches, and service groups care for one another, but this does not make them a family. Friends care for one another, but what makes a family is more than friendship. Schools, the armed services, and professional organizations care for individuals by providing discipline and instruction, but this also does not make them a family.

The way in which a family functions will vary with the circumstances, but what defines family structure always comes down to preserving what keeps children with their biological fathers and mothers. A family is not just a group associating together in any way they choose. For the same reasons, it is wrong to assume that what marriage means must adapt to whatever family means, because family structure derives from and cannot oppose the structure of marriage.

While society has a strong and legitimate public interest in preserving the procreational structure of marriage—which, in turn, preserves the procreational structure of family order—society has no legitimate public interest in preserving associations structured by nothing more than friendly feelings and private satisfaction. It is not just to change marriage law by pretending that all sexual partnerings are the same in relation to the only procreationally structured social institution that is able to assure social stability and intergenerational survival.

The Truth Is …

Same-sex marriage is wrong because there is nothing unjust about marriage to fix—and severing procreational sex from marriage would be unjust.

References and Further Reading

Governor Pat Quinn of Illinois made this claim when signing a civil unions bill. See Rex Huppke, "State Says They Can, So Same-Sex Couples Say 'I Do,'" *Chicago Tribune* (June 2, 2011). Also note that the organization promoting same-sex marriage in Minnesota calls itself, "Minnesotans United for All Families."

Theodore Olson and David Boies also used this argument to try to persuade a federal court to invalidate California's Proposition 8, which banned same-sex marriage in the state. See Theodore B. Olson, "The Conservative Case for Gay Marriage: Why Same-Sex Marriage Is an American Value," *Newsweek* (January 18, 2010), pp. 48-54.

For how legalizing same-sex marriage will align marriage to homosexual categories and not align homosexuals to what marriage is now, see Lawrence Auster, "The Extreme Radicalism of Homosexual 'Marriage,'" *View from the Right* (June 2, 2008), accessible at http://www.amnation.com/vfr/archives/010723. html.

Mary Parke, "Are Married Parents Really Better for Children: What Research Says About the Effects of Family Structure on Child Well-Being," Center for Law and Public Policy, *Policy Brief #3* (May 2003), pp. 1,6.

Robert Lerner and Althea Nagia, *No Basis: What the Studies Don't Tell Us About Same-Sex Parenting*, Marriage Law Project (Washington, DC, January 2001).

Patricia Morgan, *Children as Trophies? Examining the Evidence on Same-Sex Parenting* (Newcastle upon Tyne, UK: Christian Institute, 2002).

Elizabeth Thompson, Thomas Hanson, and Sara McLanahan, "Family Structure and Child Well-Being," *Social Forces,* 73/1 (September 1994), pp. 221-242.

Maggie Gallagher and Joshua K. Baker, "Do Moms and Dads Matter? Evidence from the Social Sciences on Family Structure and the Best Interests of the Child," 4/161, *Margins* (2004), pp. 161-180.

For how abandoning the procreational structure of marriage threatens civilization, see Joseph Daniel Unwin, *Sex and Culture* (London: Oxford University Press, 1937); Joseph Daniel Unwin, *Sexual Regulations and Cultural Behavior: An Address Delivered Before the Medical Section of the British Psychological Society* (London: Oxford University Press, 1935); Carle Zimmerman, *Family and Civilization* (Wilmington, DE: ISI Books, 2008); Pitirim Sorokin, *The Crisis of Our Age* (Richmond, VA: Dutton, 1941); Pitirim Sorokin, *Social and Cultural Dynamics,* vol. 4 (Boston, MA: Porter Sargent, 1957); and Daniel Heimbach, "The Future Based on Science," in Daniel Heimbach, *True Sexual Morality* (Wheaton, IL: Crossway, 2004), pp. 345-348.

28

You May Hear Proponents Argue …

Same-sex marriage should be allowed because it would remove prejudice and violent behavior toward homosexuals. Weddings today are repugnant heterosexual rituals that send a message condemning gay relationships as immoral, abnormal, and not worthy of respect. Denying same-sex marriage sanctions discrimination by sexual orientation and promotes the idea that gays deserve to be ridiculed, despised, and even beaten up or killed. Allowing gays to marry same-sex partners will change weddings from symbols of heterosexual oppression into symbols of approval and equality.

You Can Graciously Refute This By Saying …

Proponents of this argument reveal that they are more interested in using marriage to accomplish an agenda than they are to get married or serve the good of all. They ignore or deny the legitimate public reason for supporting marriage and focus instead on how a few individuals will privately benefit from changing what marriage means. The public interest in marriage is to support the single social institution historically and universally structured to get biological fathers and mothers to raise their own children.

Public interest in supporting marriage has nothing to do with respecting or disrespecting various ways of satisfying personal appetites. Changing what marriage law currently recognizes will not only approve the way in which gays satisfy their appetites but will also remove the institutional structure of marriage for everyone. Legalizing same-sex marriage will force law and public policy to redefine heterosexual marriage as a social institution to make it conform to same-sex relationships, not the other way around.

In fact, the evidence shows that homosexuals have no interest in becoming sexually exclusive and that once the structure of marriage is removed, gay interest in getting married evaporates. After Canada legalized same-sex marriage, there were few homosexuals who applied for licenses. Likewise, when Scandinavian countries allowed same-sex couples to marry, not only did homosexual interest in marriage never materialize, but heterosexual interest in marriage also began to erode. This is because deconstructing marriage based on sexual satisfaction erodes interest in sacrificing desires for the sake of having and raising children.

The Truth Is ...

Same-sex marriage is wrong because the truly justified public interest in marriage has nothing to do with affirming private appetites.

References and Further Reading

For examples of gay social revolutionaries admitting they are using same-sex marriage as a way to completely abolish the institution of marriage, see Thomas B. Stoddard, "Why Gay People Should Seek the Right to Marry," chapter 35 in *Families in the US: Kinship and Domestic Politics*, ed. Karen V. Hansen (Philadelphia, PA: Temple University Press, 1998); Richard D. Mohr, *A More Perfect Union: Why Straight America Must Stand Up for Gay Rights* (Boston, MA: Beacon, 1994); Gretchen A. Stiers, *From This Day Forward: Commitment, Marriage, and Family in Lesbian and Gay Relationships* (New York: St. Martin's Press, 1999); Michelangelo Signorile, "Bridal Wave," *Out* (December/January 1994); "Sociologist Says Gay Marriage Does Threaten Established Order and That's Good," *Ascribe Law News Service* (November 16, 2003); and Margaret Gullette, "The New Case for Marriage," *American Prospect* (March 1, 2004).

For how the science has been misrepresented and politicized, see Jeffrey Satinover, "The Trojan Couch: How the Mental Health Associations Misrepresent Science," *Conference Reports 2005*, National Association for Research and Therapy of Homosexuals, accessible at http://www.narth.com/docs/thetrojancouch-satinover; Robert Lerner and Althea Nagia, *No Basis: What the Studies Don't Tell Us About Same-Sex Parenting*, Marriage Law Project (Washington, DC, January 2001); and A. Dean Byrd, "When Activism Masquerades as Science," National Association for Research and Therapy of Homosexuals, accessible at http://www.narth.com/docs/masquerades (posted 2004, updated September 3, 2008).

For how legalizing same-sex marriage will align marriage to homosexual categories and not align homosexuals to what marriage is now, see Lawrence Auster, "The Extreme Radicalism of Homosexual 'Marriage,'" *View from the Right* (June 2, 2008), accessible at http://www.amnation.com/vfr/archives/010723.html.

Mollie Ziegler Hemingway, "Same-Sex, Different Marriage: Many of Those Who Want Marriage Equality Do Not Want Fidelity," *Christianity Today* (May 18, 2010), accessible at http://www.christianitytoday.com/ct/2010/may/11.52.html.

Sherif Girgis, Robert P. George, and Ryan T. Anderson, "What Is Marriage?" *Harvard Journal of Law and Public Policy*, 34/1 (Winter 2011), pp. 245-287.

Patrick Lee, Robert P. George, and Gerard V. Bradley, "Marriage and Procreation: The Intrinsic Connection," *Public Discourse: Ethics, Law and the Common Good* (March 28, 2011), accessible at http://www.thepublicdiscourse.com.

Patrick Lee, Robert P. George, and Gerard V. Bradley, "Marriage and Procreation: Avoiding Bad Arguments," *Public Discourse: Ethics, Law and the Common Good* (March 30, 2011), accessible at http://www.thepublicdiscourse.com.

Arguments 29 – 38

Gracious Answers to *Arguments Regarding* Reason and Philosophy

Legalizing
same-sex marriage
will introduce into law a
philosophy of institutional
deconstruction that—if
applied consistently—
will destroy every
institution
we have.

REGARDING REASON AND PHILOSOPHY

(Arguments 29–38)

29

You May Hear Proponents Argue …

*S*AME-SEX MARRIAGE SHOULD *be allowed because denying it promotes a philosophy that law should be used to protect the interests of certain groups.* There is no real difference between what society calls *normal* or *abnormal*. Laws only protect the self-interests of one group over others, and what laws exist only reflect which group is winning the power struggle. Limiting marriage to heterosexuals by law is an arbitrary social construct that advances the power of heterosexuals over homosexuals. Same-sex marriage will remove this arbitrary power advantage by making sexual orientation irrelevant to what counts for marriage in society.

You Can *Graciously Refute* This By Saying …

Proponents of this argument make a false charge that creates a false problem. This, in turn, leads to a false solution, which if pursued will cause serious problems in real life. The false charge comes from deconstructionist postmodern philosophy, which states that marriage has no fixed structure because there is no good reason for structuring any institution any way at all. Of course, that claim is false and terribly dangerous.

There is a good and legitimate public reason for favoring and protecting the procreational structure of marriage—getting biological fathers and mothers to share in the task of raising children. How a marriage functions varies with circumstances, but the institution is structured procreationally whether couples have children or not. Legitimate public interest in supporting the procreational structure of marriage has nothing to do with favoring the private interests of one group over others and everything to do with preserving the common good of social survival and stability.

Denying there is *any* good reason for structuring an institution in *any* way at all not only reduces marriage to non-marriage, but also destroys the structure of all other social institutions. This includes the institutions of family, law, justice, government, business, education, and religion. And, of course, there is an objectively significant difference between what is *normal* and *abnormal* when it comes to maintaining the public interest in preserving the single most important institution that affects social stability and survival.

The Truth Is …

Same-sex marriage is wrong because it promotes a philosophy that there is no good reason for supporting any institution at all.

References and Further Reading

For examples of advocates using this argument, see Franklin E. Kameny, "Deconstructing the Traditional Family," *The World and I* (October 1993), pp. 383-95; William Eskridge, *The Case for Same-Sex Marriage: From Sexual Liberty to Civilized Commitment* (New York: Free Press, 1996), p. 12; Andrew Koppelman, "The

Miscegenation Precedents," in *Same-Sex Marriage: A Reader*, ed. Andrew Sullivan (New York: Random House, 1997), pp. 335-342; the majority decision in *Goodrich v. Department of Public Health*, 798 N.E. 2d 941 (Massachusetts 2003); and Alan M. Dershowitz, "To Fix Gay Marriage, Government Should Quit the Marriage Business," *Los Angeles Times*, December 3, 2003. For examples of individuals developing and applying philosophical deconstructionism, see Michel Foucault, *Ethics, Subjectivity and Truth* (New York: New Press, 1997); Michel Foucault, *The History of Sexuality*, 3 volumes (London: Penguin, 1976–1998); Michel Foucault, *The History of Madness* (London: Routledge, 2006); Jacques Derrida, *A Derrida Reader: Between the Blinds*, ed. Peggy Kamuf (New York: Columbus University Press, 1991); Jacques Derrida, *Deconstruction and Philosophy: The Texts of Jacques Derrida*, ed. John Sallis (Chicago: University of Chicago Press, 1987); Jacques Derrida and John D. Caputo, *Deconstruction in a Nutshell: A Conversation with Jacques Derrida* (New York: Fordham University Press, 1997); Christopher Norris, *Deconstruction* (London: Routledge, 1991); and Franklin E. Kameny, "Deconstructing the Family," *The World and I* (Washington, DC: *The Washington Times*, October 1993), pp. 383-395. For examples of individuals exposing and criticizing philosophical deconstructionism, see Daniel R. Heimbach, "Deconstructing the Family," *Religion and Society Report*, 22/7 (October/November 2005), pp. 1-12; Stephen W. Melville, *Philosophy Beside Itself: On Deconstruction and Modernism* (Minneapolis, MN: University of Minnesota Press, 1986); Christopher I. Fynsk, "A Deceleration of Philosophy," *Diacritics*, 8/2 (Summer 1978), pp. 80-90; John M. Ellis, *Against Deconstructionism* (Princeton: Princeton University Press, 1989); Barbara Johnson, *The Wake of Deconstruction* (Oxford, UK: Blackwell, 1994); Christopher Norris, *Against Relativism: Philosophy of Science, Deconstruction, and Critical Theory* (Oxford, UK: Blackwell, 1997); and Scott Lash, "Postmodern Ethics: The Missing Ground," *Theory, Culture and Society*, 13/2 (May 1996), pp. 91-104.

Mary Bernstein confirms that same-sex marriage will change so much in law and public policy regarding the meaning of marriage that it poses "the ultimate threat to conservatively defined *family values* that view two parents of the opposite sex as necessary for a child's proper gender and sexual development." Mary Bernstein, "Gender, Queer Family Policies, and the Limits of Law," in *Queer Families, Queer Politics: Challenging Culture and the State*, ed. Mary Bernstein and Renate Reimann (New York: Columbia University Press, 2001), p. 433.

30

You May Hear Proponents Argue …

Same-sex marriage should be allowed because a reasoned argument should not be rejected for no good reason. Arguments against same-sex marriage are expressions of irrational prejudice. It is irrational to claim sterility disqualifies same-sex couples from getting married and then claim it does not disqualify others. If sterility truly mattered, then postmenopausal women should not be allowed to marry. Because no one objects to that, it shows that sterility is only being used against homosexuals to rationalize something irrational. Marriage today affirms the value of making relational commitments, and there is no rational reason for excluding homosexuals.

You Can *Graciously Refute* This By Saying …

This argument is itself irrational. One cannot quickly dismiss continuing to practice marriage as it has been practiced by all civilizations for all time and call that "irrational." Proponents of this argument wrongly assume that marriage has already become nothing more than a way of affirming relational commitments, regardless of procreation. However, that never has been sustained by any civilization before, and Americans do not as a whole accept it now. There is no good reason to replace what structures marriage as a social institution with something that has no structure at all.

The public interest in favoring marriage as a social institution is not a blank check to affirm *any* sort of relationship at all. There is indeed a rational reason for linking public interest in marriage with procreation—to get biological fathers and mothers to share the task of raising their own children. How individual marriages function varies with circumstances, and individual fertility is one of those circumstances, but the institution is structured procreationally whether particular couples are fertile or not.

The perfectly valid and rationally justified reason for maintaining the procreational structure of marriage as a social institution has nothing to do with fear or prejudice, and has everything to do with preserving social survival and stability. Denying that marriage is structured procreationally is irrational, because such a claim would destroy marriage as a coherent social institution, which in turn would harm everyone (including homosexuals). If what qualifies marriage for institutional affirmation shifts from favoring generational replacement to merely satisfying whatever desires people have, marriage will lose structure and cease to be an institution at all.

The Truth Is ...

Same-sex marriage is wrong because it is irrational to destroy the institutional social coherence of a coherent social institution.

References and Further Reading

For examples of advocates using this argument, see Theodore B. Olson, "The Conservative Case for Gay Marriage: Why Same-Sex Marriage Is an American Value," *Newsweek* (January 18, 2010), pp. 48-54; and Katha Pollitt, "Don't Say I Didn't Warn You," *Nation* 262 (April 29, 1996), accessible at http://www.questia.com/PM.qst?a=oandd=5002258944.

Nelson Lund, "The Case Against Boies-Olson: Wrong on the Law, and on Civilization," *National Review Online* (September 24, 2009), accessible at http://article.nationalreview.com/?q=MmI0NWU2ZTU4ZGJlNDUwYWZjNzI4MzFmZjYwMDA1MGY=.

Jeffrey Lord, "A Rebuttal to Theodore Olson," *American Spectator* (January 19, 2010), accessible at http://spectator.org/archives/2010/01/19/a-rebuttal-to-theodore-olson.

On the rationality of normal marriage, see Maggie Gallagher, "Normal Marriage: Two Views," in *Marriage and Same-Sex*

Unions: A Debate, ed. Lynn Wardle, Mark Strasser, William Duncan, and David Coolidge (Westport, CT: Praeger, 2003), pp. 13-24.

Sherif Girgis, Ryan T. Anderson, and Robert P. George, "Marriage: Merely a Social Construct?" *Public Discourse: Ethics, Law and the Common Good* (December 29, 2010), accessible at http://www.thepublicdiscourse.com.

Sherif Girgis, Ryan T. Anderson, and Robert P. George, "Does Marriage, or Anything, Have Essential Properties?" *Public Discourse: Ethics, Law and the Common Good* (January 12, 2011), accessible at http://www.thepublicdiscourse.com.

For examples of gay social revolutionaries admitting they are using same-sex marriage as a way to completely abolish the institution of marriage, see Thomas B. Stoddard, "Why Gay People Should Seek the Right to Marry," chapter 35 in *Families in the US: Kinship and Domestic Politics*, ed. Karen V. Hansen (Philadelphia, PA: Temple University Press, 1998); Richard D. Mohr, *A More Perfect Union: Why Straight America Must Stand Up for Gay Rights* (Boston, MA: Beacon, 1994); Gretchen A. Stiers, *From This Day Forward: Commitment, Marriage, and Family in Lesbian and Gay Relationships* (New York: St. Martin's Press, 1999); Michelangelo Signorile, "Bridal Wave," *Out* (December/January 1994); "Sociologist Says Gay Marriage Does Threaten Established Order and That's Good," *Ascribe Law News Service* (November 16, 2003); Margaret Gullette, "The New Case for Marriage," *American Prospect* (March 1, 2004); and Mary Bernstein, "Gender, Queer Family Policies, and the Limits of Law," in *Queer Families, Queer Politics: Challenging Culture and the State*, eds. Mary Bernstein and Renate Reimann (New York: Columbia University Press, 2001). Especially note what she says on page 433.

31

You May Hear Proponents Argue ...

Same-sex marriage should be allowed because it is no longer reasonable to believe that procreation is linked to marriage. In the past societies tied marriage to procreation, but most do not do so now. Today, human societies struggle to feed their existing population, so they no longer need to stress the need for people to have children. Procreation is no longer central to social welfare, and marriage has become more a way to affirm relationships than to assure reproduction. For this reason, there is no longer any good reason for limiting marriage to heterosexuals.

You Can *Graciously Refute* This By Saying ...

Proponents of this argument allege that while there was *once* a good reason for limiting marriage to male-female couples, that reason no longer exists. As feminist same-sex marriage proponent Katha Pollitt claims, "We are moving toward [being] a society in which the old forms of human relationships are being disrupted and reshaped, and sooner or later the law must accommodate that reality." However, there are at least three reasons why Pollitt and those who agree with her are wrong.

First, regardless of how anyone feels about the issue, procreation is no less essential to intergenerational survival now than it ever was before. *Every* society is just one generation away from extinction, and no society can afford to deny that generational replacement remains essential.

Second, legalizing same-sex marriage will inevitably redefine the institution completely. Removing the procreational structure of marriage will deconstruct marriage as a social institution by denying it has any structure at all, and this will destroy the structure of marriage for all people.

Third, proponents of this argument claim that marriage is already redefined in the way they want it to be, which is circular reasoning. Marriage has *not* already been so redefined, or else same-sex marriage proponents would have no reason to try to change existing marriage laws. Favoring procreation is still the only public reason for justifying civil interest in recognizing and supporting marriage. Marriage remains a structured social institution. Americans as a whole do not think that marriage is just some friends living together, or roommates who take care of each other, or teammates who bond and socialize together off the field.

The Truth Is …

Same-sex marriage is wrong because procreation remains the only reason why societies have a civil interest in supporting marriage.

References and Further Reading

Theodore Olson and David Boies used this argument to try to persuade a federal court to invalidate California's Proposition 8, which banned same-sex marriage in the state. See Theodore B. Olson, "The Conservative Case for Gay Marriage: Why Same-Sex Marriage Is an American Value," *Newsweek* (January 18, 2010), pp. 48-54. See also Katha Pollitt, "Don't Say I Didn't Warn You," *Nation* 262 (April 29, 1996), accessible at http://www.questia.com/PM.qst?a=oandd=5002258944.

Nelson Lund, "The Case Against Boies-Olson: Wrong on the Law, and on Civilization," *National Review Online* (September 24, 2009), accessible at http://article.nationalreview.com/?q=MmI 0NWU2ZTU4ZGJ1NDUwYWZjNzI4MzFmZjYwMDA1MGY=.

Jeffrey Lord, "A Rebuttal to Theodore Olson," *American Spectator* (January 19, 2010), accessible at http://spectator.org/archives/2010/01/19/a-rebuttal-to-theodore-olson.

Robert P. George and Jean Bethke Elshtain, eds., *The Meaning of Marriage: Family, State, Market, and Morals* (Dallas, TX: Spence Publishing, 2006).

Sherif Gergis, Robert P. George, and Ryan T. Anderson, "What Is Marriage?" *Harvard Journal of Law and Public Policy*, 34/1 (Winter 2011), pp. 245-287.

Maggie Gallagher, "Normal Marriage: Two Views," in *Marriage and Same-Sex Unions: A Debate*, ed. Lynn Wardle, Mark Strasser, William Duncan, and David Coolidge (Westport, CT: Praeger, 2003), pp. 13-24.

Maggie Gallagher, "What Marriage Is For: Children Need Mothers and Fathers," *Weekly Standard* (August 4/August 11, 2003), pp. 22-25.

Maggie Gallagher, "(How) Will Gay Marriage Weaken Marriage as a Social Institution: A Reply to Andrew Koppelman, *University of Saint Thomas Law Journal*, 2/1 (Fall 2004), pp. 33-70.

For how abandoning the procreational structure of marriage threatens civilization, see Joseph Daniel Unwin, *Sex and Culture* (London: Oxford University Press, 1937); Joseph Daniel Unwin, *Sexual Regulations and Cultural Behavior: An Address Delivered Before the Medical Section of the British Psychological Society* (London: Oxford University Press, 1935); Carle Zimmerman, *Family and Civilization* (Wilmington, DE: ISI Books, 2008); Pitirim Sorokin, *The Crisis of Our Age* (Richmond, VA: Dutton, 1941); Pitirim Sorokin, *Social and Cultural Dynamics*, vol. 4 (Boston, MA: Porter Sargent, 1957); Daniel R. Heimbach, "Deconstructing the Family," *Religion and Society Report*, 22/7 (October/November 2005), pp. 1-12; and Daniel Heimbach, "The Future Based on Science," in Daniel Heimbach, *True Sexual Morality* (Wheaton, IL: Crossway, 2004), pp. 345-348.

32

You May Hear Proponents Argue …

Same-sex marriage should be allowed because it represents the ideals on which America was founded. America was founded on the pursuit of liberty, equality, and justice for all, and it is un-American to abandon these ideals by denying gays the freedom to marry. We live in a country today that allows anything that is not expressly prohibited—not one that disallows anything not expressly permitted. So, in the absence of compelling reasons to the contrary, gays should be allowed to marry simply because they want to do so. Our national identity centers on the freedom of all to pursue personal happiness, which includes the happiness homosexuals can have by marrying same-sex partners.

You Can *Graciously Refute* This By Saying …

Our nation's founders were not utopian social engineers; they distinguished carefully between universal social norms and efforts to radically redefine all social institutions. They would have strongly defended the procreative structure of marriage and would have never treated it as a way to affirm whatever desires people have. The idea of a gay freedom right to marry is not in the same category as civil rights that have enriched our nation's history. Racial equality and universal suffrage are not similar to allowing individuals to redefine a public institution merely to affirm their own personal feelings.

Other civil rights movements in our nation have always affirmed the structure of institutions that were essential to the common good, but same-sex marriage threatens an essential institution by denying it has any fixed structure at all. Our nation only favors and protects individual liberty in ways that serve the general welfare. In this way, gays are confusing freedom to uphold our essential institutions with a license to redefine and destroy our most essential social institution. Homosexuals already have the same sort of freedom we all have to pursue happiness without harming the common good.

What gays do *not* have—and no Americans have—is the right to harm the common good by changing what marriage means by separating the institution from its procreational structure. Legalizing same-sex marriage will make *private* satisfaction the reason for *public* interest in civil marriage, rather than treating marriage as a private benefit that may or may not result from public regulation of the institution. That is a radical and most dangerous shift that our nation's founders would never have made.

The Truth Is …

Same-sex marriage is wrong because it is contrary to our nation's founding ideals as interpreted by our nation's founders themselves.

References and Further Reading

For examples of advocates using this argument, see Franklin E. Kameny, "Deconstructing the Traditional Family," *The World and I* (October 1993), pp. 388-389; Evan Wolfson, *Why Marriage Matters: America, Equality, and Gay People's Right to Marry* (New York: Simon and Schuster, 2004); and William Eskridge, *The Case for Same-Sex Marriage: From Sexual Liberty to Civilized Commitment* (New York: Free Press, 1996).

Theodore Olson and David Boies also used this argument to try to persuade a federal court to invalidate California's Proposition 8, which banned same-sex marriage in the state. See Theodore B. Olson, "The Conservative Case for Gay Marriage: Why Same-Sex Marriage Is an American Value," *Newsweek* (January 18, 2010), pp. 48-54.

Nelson Lund, "The Case Against Boies-Olson: Wrong on the Law, and on Civilization," *National Review Online* (September 24, 2009), accessible at http://article.nationalreview.com/?q=MmI 0NWU2ZTU4ZGJ1NDUwYWZjNzI4MzFmZjYwMDA1MGY=.

Jeffrey Lord, "A Rebuttal to Theodore Olson," *American Spectator* (January 19, 2010), accessible at http://spectator.org/ archives/2010/01/19/a-rebuttal-to-theodore-olson.

Jean Bethke Elshtain, "Against Gay Marriage," *Commonweal* (October 22, 1991).

Maggie Gallagher, "Normal Marriage: Two Views," in *Marriage and Same-Sex Unions: A Debate*, ed. Lynn Wardle, Mark Strasser, William Duncan, and David Coolidge (Westport, CT: Praeger, 2003), pp. 13-24.

Carson Holloway, "Same-Sex Marriage and the Death of Tradition," *First Things* (June 10, 2009), accessible at http://www.firstthings. com/onthesquare/2009/06/same-sex-marriage-and-the-deat.

John Witte, Jr., "The Tradition of Traditional Marriage," in *Marriage and Same-Sex Unions: A Debate*, ed. Lynn Wardle, Mark Strasser, William Duncan, and David Coolidge (Westport, CT: Praeger, 2003), pp. 47-59.

Sherif Gergis, Robert P. George, and Ryan T. Anderson, "What Is Marriage?" *Harvard Journal of Law and Public Policy*, 34/1 (Winter 2011), pp. 245-287.

Glenn T. Stanton and Bill Maier, "Isn't Banning Gay Marriage Just Like Banning Interracial Marriage?" in *Why Marriage Matters: Reasons to Believe in Marriage in Postmodern Society* (Colorado Springs, CO: Pinion Press, 1997), pp. 36-39.

William C. Duncan, "The State Interest in Marriage," *Ave Maria Law Review*, 2/1 (Spring 2004), pp. 153-182.

33

You May Hear Proponents Argue ...

Same-sex marriage should be allowed because it would force bigots to accept and affirm homosexuals. Resistance to same-sex marriage is based on nothing more than irrational fear and prejudice. Homophobia is not productive social policy; in fact, it only erodes it. Homophobia must be taken off the national agenda—by force, if necessary. Once the courts demand legal recognition of same-sex marriage, the opposition will fade, and gay marriage will be generally accepted. Human culture has been homophobic for millennia, and it is time to change all that by turning weddings from symbols of heterosexual oppression into symbols of equality and respect.

You Can *Graciously Refute* This By Saying ...

Proponents of this alleged "argument" really have no argument at all, because they are claiming nothing more than a judgment of others based on pure emotion—not reason. This argument is equivalent to saying, "I refuse to think and prefer using force." Approaching the same-sex marriage public policy debate in this manner only demonstrates that they have no real interest in marriage itself, or in getting gays to behave civilly, but are only interested in forcing others to validate the way a small minority likes having sex.

The public interest in supporting the institution of marriage does not come from irrational prejudices about gays or anyone else but from the legitimate stake society has in supporting the procreational structure of marriage. This legitimate stake has nothing to do with personal prejudice or with satisfying how anyone feels but with ensuring intergenerational survival by favoring procreationally structured relationships that get fathers and mothers to have and raise children.

Few homosexuals have any interest in limiting sex to one person or in aligning their behavior to what best suits children or even social survival. Once marriage is realigned in the manner the proponents of this argument would prefer, gay interest in marriage will evaporate just as it did when it was legalized in Scandinavian countries and in Canada. Weddings have never symbolized what some call *homosexual oppression* because they have never stood for any sort of private satisfaction, gay or otherwise. Weddings are not *private* events to affirm *private* feelings but are *public* events to affirm the *public* value of an institution structured to serve the common good of assuring social survival though generational replacement.

The Truth Is …

Same-sex marriage is wrong because it makes no sense to require anyone by law to affirm anything opposed to the common good.

References and Further Reading

Theodore Olson and David Boies used this argument to try to persuade a federal court to invalidate California's Proposition 8, which banned same-sex marriage in the state. See Theodore B. Olson, "The Conservative Case for Gay Marriage: Why Same-Sex Marriage Is an American Value," *Newsweek* (January 18, 2010), pp. 48-54.

Nelson Lund, "The Case Against Boies-Olson: Wrong on the Law, and on Civilization," *National Review Online* (September 24, 2009), accessible at http://article.nationalreview.com/?q=MmI 0NWU2ZTU4ZGJ1NDUwYWZjNzI4MzFmZjYwMDA1MGY=.

Jeffrey Lord, "A Rebuttal to Theodore Olson," *American Spectator* (January 19, 2010), accessible at http://spectator.org/ archives/2010/01/19/a-rebuttal-to-theodore-olson.

For gays having no interest in limiting sex to marriage, see Michelangelo Signorile, "Bridal Wave," *Out* (December/January

1994), p. 161; William Aaron, *Straight* (New York: Bantam Books, 1972), p. 208; Gretchen A. Stiers, *From This Day Forward: Commitment, Marriage, and Family in Lesbian and Gay Relationships* (New York: St. Martin's Press, 1999); and Mollie Ziegler Hemingway, "Same-Sex, Different Marriage: Many of Those Who Want Marriage Equality Do Not Want Fidelity," *Christianity Today* (May 18, 2010), accessible at http://www. christianitytoday.com/ct/2010/may/11.52.html.

Gretchen Stiers reveals (1) that few dedicated gay and lesbian couples actually expect that same-sex marriage will limit their own promiscuity, (2) that nearly half of these same couples openly despise straight marriage, and (3) that most homosexuals look on same-sex marriage as a strategy for subverting the institution from within. See Gretchen A. Stiers, *From This Day Forward: Commitment, Marriage, and Family in Lesbian and Gay Relationships* (New York: St. Martin's Press, 1999).

For how legalizing same-sex marriage will align marriage to homosexual categories and not align homosexuals to what marriage is now, see Lawrence Auster, "The Extreme Radicalism of Homosexual 'Marriage,'" *View from the Right* (June 2, 2008), accessible at http://www.amnation.com/vfr/archives/010723. html.

Maggie Gallagher, "What Marriage Is For: Children Need Mothers and Fathers," *Weekly Standard* (August 4/August 11, 2003), pp. 22-25.

Maggie Gallagher and Joshua K. Baker, "Demand for Same-Sex Marriage: Evidence from the United States, Canada, and Europe," *Policy Brief*, Institute for Marriage and Public Policy, 3/1 (April 26, 2006).

William C. Duncan, "The State Interest in Marriage," *Ave Maria Law Review*, 2/1 (Spring 2004), pp. 153-182.

34

You May Hear Proponents Argue …

Same-sex marriage should be allowed because it makes sense to have more options for marriage rather than less. More options for marriage will not lower interest in marriage any more than having more travel options will lower interest in traveling. Just as public education has not lowered the value of private education, neither will same-sex marriage lower the value of heterosexual marriage. If there is any impact at all, more options for marriage will lead to people finding ways for making marriage better, not worse. People are always looking for new and better options in politics, education, business and travel, so why not in how they arrange marriage as well?

You Can *Graciously Refute* This By Saying …

The idea that having more options always makes something better is only reasonable if (1) you start with something good in the first place, (2) what you have does not lose value when it is mixed with other things, and (3) what you add is similar to what you started with in the first place. Based on this, proponents of this argument make at least three unreasonable claims.

First, they wrongly assume that the good to be expanded is how marriage affirms sexual appetites. However, to do so would require changing the nature of marriage in a bad way, which would end up expanding a bad thing.

Second, they wrongly assume that because real marriage affirms heterosexual sex, realigning marriage to affirm *any* sort of sex would not erode the public respect and support for heterosexual marriage. This makes no sense if the public value of marriage is about getting couples to have and raise children and is not merely concerned with affirming whatever appetites people have that are unrelated to procreation.

Third, proponents of this argument assume relationships between same-sex pairs are in the same category as relationships uniting husband-wife pairs. However, same-sex pairs are not in the same relational category in regard to marriage as a social institution because the institution is structured to favor having and raising children and is not merely a way to affirm however people like to have sex.

In the end, it only makes sense to continue a practice that all societies everywhere have practiced for all time, especially when that practice so obviously connects with assuring social continuity and survival. Likewise, it makes no sense to remove what has given that practice coherence in order to pacify desires that are incompatible with that coherence.

The Truth Is ...

Same-sex marriage is wrong because it is irrational to mistake a procreational institution for a way to affirm sexual appetites.

References and Further Reading

Andrew Sullivan argues a similar point in *Virtually Normal* (New York: Random House, 1995), pp. 202-205.

On the rationality of normal marriage see Maggie Gallagher, "Normal Marriage: Two Views," in *Marriage and Same-Sex Unions: A Debate*, ed. Lynn Wardle, Mark Strasser, William Duncan, and David Coolidge (Westport, CT: Praeger, 2003), pp. 13-24.

Maggie Gallagher, "Should Gay Marriage Be Legal? No," *ProCon. org* (May 22, 2009), accessible at http://gaymarriage.procon. org/view.answers.php?questionID=001607.

John M. Finnis, "Law, Morality, and 'Sexual Orientation,'" *Notre Dame Law Review*, 69/5 (1994), pp. 1049-1076.

John M. Finnis, "Marriage: A Basic and Exigent Good," *The Monist* (July–October 2008), pp. 388-406.

John M. Finnis, "The Good of Marriage and the Morality of Sexual Relations: Some Philosophical and Historical Observations," *The American Journal of Jurisprudence*, 42 (1997), pp. 97-134.

Sherif Gergis, Robert P. George, and Ryan T. Anderson, "What Is Marriage?" *Harvard Journal of Law and Public Policy*, 34/1 (Winter 2011), pp. 245-287.

William C. Duncan, "The State Interest in Marriage," *Ave Maria Law Review*, 2/1 (Spring 2004), pp. 153-182.

For how legalizing same-sex marriage will align marriage to homosexual categories and not align homosexuals to what marriage is now, see Lawrence Auster, "The Extreme Radicalism of Homosexual 'Marriage,'" *View from the Right* (June 2, 2008), accessible at http://www.amnation.com/vfr/archives/010723.html.

Mary Bernstein confirms that same-sex marriage will change so much in law and public policy regarding the meaning of marriage that it poses "the ultimate threat to conservatively defined *family values* that view two parents of the opposite sex as necessary for a child's proper gender and sexual development." Mary Bernstein, "Gender, Queer Family Policies, and the Limits of Law," in *Queer Families, Queer Politics: Challenging Culture and the State*, ed. Mary Bernstein and Renate Reimann (New York: Columbia University Press, 2001), p. 433.

35

You May Hear Proponents Argue ...

Same-sex marriage should be allowed because opponents of same-sex marriage do not follow their own logic. Opponents of same-sex marriage cannot have it both ways. If they think allowing gays to marry would harm society, then they should be fighting a lot more homosexual behaviors than they currently are. However, if the activities of homosexuals outside of marriage do not harm society, then neither will same-sex marriage. Tolerating homosexuals and maintaining social strength are not exclusive. No one denies that homosexuals can be good citizens, and there is a huge discrepancy between agreeing that homosexuals can be good citizens and claiming that same-sex marriage will threaten society.

You Can *Graciously Refute* This By Saying ...

Legalizing same-sex marriage deinstitutionalizes marriage by denying it has any structure. This destroys marriage as a social institution by reducing it to nothing more than a way of affirming whatever desires people have. It makes everything *marriage*, and when everything becomes marriage, marriage becomes nothing special, existing marriages fall apart, and fewer people get married in the first place. When this inevitably spreads, society loses cohesion and collapses.

This is what occurred in the cultures of ancient Greece and Rome, and it will happen to America as well if we deinstitutionalize marriage by legalizing same-sex marriage. There is nothing inconsistent with not criminalizing homosexual behavior while affirming same-sex couples are in a different category as husbands and wives in relation to marriage. Deconstructing marriage deinstitutionalizes marriage; deinstitutionalizing marriage destroys marriage; and destroying marriage ultimately threatens the survival of society.

Legalizing same-sex marriage shatters the conventional definition of marriage. It moves society toward a homosexual vision of
utopian non-order in which all relational structures are declared
irrelevant in favor of allowing people to pursue their sexual
passions with no structural limits. Most homosexuals have less
interest in conforming their desires to what best suits society than
in conforming society to what best suits their desires. They have no
real interest in marriage itself and are only using deconstruction of
the institution to force everyone else to affirm in public what they do
in private—even at the cost of deinstitutionalizing the institution.

The Truth Is …

*Same-sex marriage is wrong because it is not logical to threaten social
survival merely to affirm whatever sexual desires people have.*

References and Further Reading

Theodore Olson and David Boies used this argument to try to
persuade a federal court to invalidate California's Proposition
8, which banned same-sex marriage in the state. See Theodore
B. Olson, "The Conservative Case for Gay Marriage: Why
Same-Sex Marriage Is an American Value," *Newsweek* (January
18, 2010), pp. 48-54.

Nelson Lund, "The Case Against Boies-Olson: Wrong on the Law,
and on Civilization," *National Review Online* (September 24,
2009), accessible at http://article.nationalreview.com/?q=MmI
0NWU2ZTU4ZGJ1NDUwYWZjNzI4MzFmZjYwMDA1MGY=.

Jeffrey Lord, "A Rebuttal to Theodore Olson," *American Spectator*
(January 19, 2010), accessible at http://spectator.org/
archives/2010/01/19/a-rebuttal-to-theodore-olson.

Stanley Kurtz, "The End of Marriage in Scandinavia: The
'Conservative Case' for Same-Sex Marriage Collapses," *Weekly
Standard* (February 2, 2004), pp. 26-33.

Sherif Gergis, Robert P. George, and Ryan T. Anderson, "What Is Marriage?" *Harvard Journal of Law and Public Policy*, 34/1 (Winter 2011), pp. 245-287.

For examples of individuals developing and applying philosophical deconstructionism, see Michel Foucault, *Ethics, Subjectivity and Truth* (New York: New Press, 1997); Michel Foucault, *The History of Sexuality*, 3 volumes (London: Penguin, 1976–1998); Michel Foucault, *The History of Madness* (London: Routledge, 2006); Jacques Derrida, *A Derrida Reader: Between the Blinds*, ed. Peggy Kamuf (New York: Columbus University Press, 1991); Jacques Derrida, *Deconstruction and Philosophy: The Texts of Jacques Derrida*, ed. John Sallis (Chicago: University of Chicago Press, 1987); Jacques Derrida and John D. Caputo, *Deconstruction in a Nutshell: A Conversation with Jacques Derrida* (New York: Fordham University Press, 1997); Christopher Norris, *Deconstruction* (London: Routledge, 1991); and Franklin E. Kameny, "Deconstructing the Family," *The World and I* (Washington, DC: *The Washington Times*, October 1993), pp. 383-395.

For examples of individuals exposing and criticizing philosophical deconstructionism, see Daniel R. Heimbach, "Deconstructing the Family," *Religion and Society Report*, 22/7 (October/ November 2005), pp. 1-12; Stephen W. Melville, *Philosophy Beside Itself: On Deconstruction and Modernism* (Minneapolis, MN: University of Minnesota Press, 1986); Christopher I. Fynsk, "A Decelebration of Philosophy," *Diacritics*, 8/2 (Summer 1978), pp. 80-90; John M. Ellis, *Against Deconstructionism* (Princeton: Princeton University Press, 1989); Barbara Johnson, *The Wake of Deconstruction* (Oxford, UK: Blackwell, 1994); Christopher Norris, *Against Relativism: Philosophy of Science, Deconstruction, and Critical Theory* (Oxford, UK: Blackwell, 1997); and Scott Lash, "Postmodern Ethics: The Missing Ground," *Theory, Culture and Society*, 13/2 (May 1996), pp. 91-104.

36

You May Hear Proponents Argue …

Same-sex marriage should be allowed because opposition depends on circular reasoning. Opponents criticize homosexuals for lacking sexual discipline but then stop them from participating in an institution that would improve their behavior. It is circular reasoning to oppose same-sex marriage while criticizing gay and lesbian partners for having sex outside marriage. Social approval of same-sex marriage will change homosexual behavior by encouraging homosexuals to limit sex to marriage. Denying same-sex marriage will give homosexuals no choice but to pursue sex outside of marriage. It is simply irrational to criticize homosexuals for promiscuity without giving them a chance to marry.

You Can *Graciously Refute* This By Saying …

This argument is neither fair nor logical because it presumes what it concludes. It basically says that something is true because it is true, which should persuade no one. There is nothing circular about taking gays at their word when they say they have no interest in restricting sex to one partner after getting married. There is also nothing circular about arguing that something with an objectively measurable structure (the procreational form of uniting a man with woman) is not the same as something that has no objectively measurable structure (the mere satisfaction of private feelings). For this reason, these different things require different treatment.

Proponents of this argument confuse what motivates some people to marry (sexual satisfaction) with what makes marriage a social institution (favoring procreational unions to encourage men and women to become mothers and fathers). They ignore the fact that same-sex couples can already marry privately any time they want, which shows they are not really seeking access to marriage for its own sake but are only using the institution to get everyone to affirm their private behavior in public. As political pundit Andrew Sullivan states, homosexuals as a whole do not want "to flatten out their varied and complicated lives into a single, moralistic model [of marriage]." This reveals that proponents of this argument are using circular logic themselves, because it is circular to criticize opponents for something that only makes sense after redefining marriage to allow same-sex marriage.

The Truth Is ...

Same-sex marriage is wrong because denying marriage has any fixed structure will never change the way homosexuals behave.

References and Further Reading

For Sullivan's quote, see Andrew Sullivan, *Virtually Normal* (New York: Random House, 1995), pp. 203-204.

For gays having no interest in limiting sex to marriage, see Michelangelo Signorile, "Bridal Wave," *Out* (December/January 1994), p. 161; William Aaron, *Straight* (New York: Bantam Books, 1972), p. 208; Gretchen A. Stiers, *From This Day Forward: Commitment, Marriage, and Family in Lesbian and Gay Relationships* (New York: St. Martin's Press, 1999); and Mollie Ziegler Hemingway, "Same-Sex, Different Marriage: Many of Those Who Want Marriage Equality Do Not Want Fidelity," *Christianity Today* (May 18, 2010), accessible at http://www.christianitytoday.com/ct/2010/may/11.52.html.

Gretchen Stiers reveals (1) that few dedicated gay and lesbian couples actually expect that same-sex marriage will limit their own promiscuity, (2) that nearly half of these same couples openly despise straight marriage, and (3) that most homosexuals look on same-sex marriage as a strategy for subverting the institution from within. See Gretchen A. Stiers, *From This Day Forward: Commitment, Marriage, and Family in Lesbian and Gay Relationships* (New York: St. Martin's Press, 1999).

For how legalizing same-sex marriage will align marriage to homosexual categories and not align homosexuals to what marriage is now, see Lawrence Auster, "The Extreme Radicalism of Homosexual 'Marriage,'" *View from the Right* (June 2, 2008), accessible at http://www.amnation.com/vfr/archives/010723.html.

For examples of gay social revolutionaries admitting they are using same-sex marriage as a way to completely abolish the institution of marriage, see Thomas B. Stoddard, "Why Gay People Should Seek the Right to Marry," chapter 35 in *Families in the US: Kinship and Domestic Politics*, ed. Karen V. Hansen (Philadelphia, PA: Temple University Press, 1998); Richard D. Mohr, *A More Perfect Union: Why Straight America Must Stand Up for Gay Rights* (Boston, MA: Beacon, 1994); Gretchen A. Stiers, *From This Day Forward: Commitment, Marriage, and Family in Lesbian and Gay Relationships* (New York: St. Martin's Press, 1999); Michelangelo Signorile, "Bridal Wave," *Out* (December/January 1994); "Sociologist Says Gay Marriage Does Threaten Established Order and That's Good," *Ascribe Law News Service* (November 16, 2003); Margaret Gullette, "The New Case for Marriage," *American Prospect* (March 1, 2004); and Mary Bernstein, "Gender, Queer Family Policies, and the Limits of Law," in *Queer Families, Queer Politics: Challenging Culture and the State*, ed. Mary Bernstein and Renate Reimann (New York: Columbia University Press, 2001). Especially note what she says on page 433.

Daniel R. Heimbach, "Deconstructing the Family," *Religion and Society Report*, 22/7 (October/November 2005), pp. 1-12.

37

You May Hear Proponents Argue …

Same-sex marriage should be allowed because it does not change the exclusive importance of heterosexual unions for species and social survival. It is possible to affirm the value of heterosexual unions for species and social survival while allowing gays to marry. Legalizing same-sex marriage would modify the *exclusivity* of heterosexual unions but not decrease their *centrality*. Affirming the centrality of procreational marriage is one thing, while requiring the exclusivity of procreational marriage is something else. Same-sex marriage can be allowed in a way that continues to affirm the centrality of heterosexual unions to social and species survival.

You Can *Graciously Refute* This By Saying …

Proponents of this argument accept that heterosexual marriage is *central* to assuring social survival while denying that it must be *exclusive*. They claim that it is not inconsistent to continue stressing the central importance of procreative marriage while allowing gays to marry. However, their idea is logically impossible because what is at stake is not a matter of *exclusivity* but of *deconstruction*. Allowing same-sex marriage is not a matter of *sharing* something that would stay the same but of *redefining* an institution in a way that changes it for all. It is not a matter of keeping marriage the same while adding more but of reducing the institution to non-marriage and supposing it can survive without structure.

The current drive for same-sex marriage in the United States comes from the philosophy of deconstruction developed and popularized by Michel Foucault and Jacques Derrida, which homosexuals embraced because it advocated destroying institutions by removing their structure. In truth, there is no coherent way to unite mutually incompatible things, and preserving the institutional structure of marriage cannot be united with denying it has any structure at all. Legalizing same-sex marriage deconstructs marriage.

If marriage law is changed to accommodate homosexuals, it will become impossible to recognize the social value of procreational over non-procreational relationships. Deinstitutionalizing marriage by deconstructing marriage destroys marriage and threatens social survival by turning marriage into non-marriage. As evidence of this fact, we find that since the time same-sex partnerships were approved in Scandinavia, the marriage rate has dropped for everyone while births out of wedlock have risen dramatically.

The Truth Is …

Same-sex marriage is wrong because it conflicts with the central importance of keeping marriage linked with social survival.

References and Further Reading

Theodore Olson and David Boies used this argument to try to persuade a federal court to invalidate California's Proposition 8, which banned same-sex marriage in the state. See Theodore B. Olson, "The Conservative Case for Gay Marriage: Why Same-Sex Marriage Is an American Value," *Newsweek* (January 18, 2010), pp. 48-54.

For a leading lesbian lawyer admitting there is room for compromise between the opposing views involved, see Chai R. Feldblum, "Moral Conflict and Liberty; Gay Rights and Religion," *Brooklyn Law Review*, 72/1 (2006), pp. 61-123.

For examples of individuals developing and applying philosophical deconstructionism, see Michel Foucault, *Ethics, Subjectivity and Truth* (New York: New Press, 1997); Michel Foucault, *The History of Sexuality*, 3 volumes (London: Penguin, 1976–1998);

Michel Foucault, *The History of Madness* (London: Routledge, 2006); Jacques Derrida, *A Derrida Reader: Between the Blinds*, ed. Peggy Kamuf (New York: Columbus University Press, 1991); Jacques Derrida, *Deconstruction and Philosophy: The Texts of Jacques Derrida*, ed. John Sallis (Chicago: University of Chicago Press, 1987); Jacques Derrida and John D. Caputo, *Deconstruction in a Nutshell: A Conversation with Jacques Derrida* (New York: Fordham University Press, 1997); Christopher Norris, *Deconstruction* (London: Routledge, 1991); and Franklin E. Kameny, "Deconstructing the Family," *The World and I* (Washington, DC: *The Washington Times*, October 1993), pp. 383-395.

For examples of individuals exposing and criticizing philosophical deconstructionism, see Daniel R. Heimbach, "Deconstructing the Family," *Religion and Society Report*, 22/7 (October/November 2005), pp. 1-12; Stephen W. Melville, *Philosophy Beside Itself: On Deconstruction and Modernism* (Minneapolis, MN: University of Minnesota Press, 1986); Christopher I. Fynsk, "A Decelebration of Philosophy," *Diacritics*, 8/2 (Summer 1978), pp. 80-90; John M. Ellis, *Against Deconstructionism* (Princeton: Princeton University Press, 1989); Barbara Johnson, *The Wake of Deconstruction* (Oxford, UK: Blackwell, 1994); Christopher Norris, *Against Relativism: Philosophy of Science, Deconstruction, and Critical Theory* (Oxford, UK: Blackwell, 1997); and Scott Lash, "Postmodern Ethics: The Missing Ground," *Theory, Culture and Society*, 13/2 (May 1996), pp. 91-104.

Stanley Kurtz, "The End of Marriage in Scandinavia: The 'Conservative Case' for Same-Sex Marriage Collapses," *Weekly Standard* (February 2, 2004), pp. 26-33.

Maggie Gallagher, "Normal Marriage: Two Views," in *Marriage and Same-Sex Unions: A Debate*, ed. Lynn Wardle, Mark Strasser, William Duncan, and David Coolidge (Westport, CT: Praeger, 2003), pp. 13-24.

Jeffrey Lord, "A Rebuttal to Theodore Olson," *American Spectator* (January 19, 2010), accessible at http://spectator.org/archives/2010/01/19/a-rebuttal-to-theodore-olson.

38

You May Hear Proponents Argue …

Same-sex marriage should be allowed because it aligns marital practice with what occurs in nature. Some people are naturally homosexual, while others are naturally heterosexual. Given this, opposite-sex marriage is as unnatural for homosexuals as same-sex marriage is for heterosexuals. The very nature of heterosexuals requires marriage to partners of the opposite sex, while the nature of homosexuals requires marriage to partners of the same sex. Limiting marriage to heterosexuals is not consistent with the nature of homosexuals; thus, the only logical way to align marital practice to the natural order of humanity is to allow gays to marry partners of the same-sex.

You Can *Graciously Refute* This By Saying …

Proponents of this argument are wrong for two reasons. First, they rely on a false philosophical view of nature and human nature. Second, they assume a false understanding of why societies have laws favoring and supporting marriage. There is only one human nature for the entire human race, not a whole range of natures. This means that nothing that varies from individual to individual can be inherent to the basic human nature shared by all.

Furthermore, the only legitimate interest the public has in justifying civilly enforced laws favoring and supporting marriage has nothing to do with affirming private feelings or individual satisfaction. This interest has only to do with helping to ensure the survival of society by getting men and women to sacrifice individual freedoms long enough to have and raise children of their own. Pretending human nature somehow varies from individual to individual according to feeling is like confusing a Jell-O mold with Jell-O, or confusing real birds with someone who feels "free as a bird." Sharing human nature in relation to sex is not a question of how individuals feel but with how human bodies are designed to reproduce.

Human bodies exist in one of two—and *only* two—dimorphic sexual forms: male or female. These forms are biologically ordered toward human reproduction, which, of course, means that only a male-female sexual union aligns with human nature in relation to biological reproduction. It also means the institution of marriage aligns with the sexual part of human nature only when a male human being unites with a female human being—not when partners of the same sex unite.

The Truth Is …

Same-sex marriage is wrong because it adopts a false view of marriage, nature, and human nature.

References and Further Reading

The homosexual community is actually quite torn over what to consider *natural* or *normal*. For examples of advocates using this argument, see Michael Warner, *The Trouble with Normal: Sex, Politics, and the Ethics of Queer Life* (Cambridge, MA: Harvard University Press, 1999); and Matthew Ridley, *The Red Queen: Sex and the Evolution of Human Nature* (New York: Macmillan, 1994).

For how legalizing same-sex marriage will align marriage to homosexual categories and not align homosexuals to what marriage is now, see Lawrence Auster, "The Extreme Radicalism of Homosexual 'Marriage,'" *View from the Right* (June 2, 2008), accessible at http://www.amnation.com/vfr/archives/010723.html.

Robert P. George and Jean Bethke Elshtain, eds., *The Meaning of Marriage: Family, State, Market, and Morals* (Dallas, TX: Spence Publishing, 2006).

Sherif Gergis, Robert P. George, and Ryan T. Anderson, "What Is Marriage?" *Harvard Journal of Law and Public Policy*, 34/1 (Winter 2011), pp. 245-287.

Maggie Gallagher, "What Marriage Is For: Children Need Mothers and Fathers," *Weekly Standard* (August 4/August 11, 2003), pp. 22-25.

Maggie Gallagher, "Normal Marriage: Two Views," in *Marriage and Same-Sex Unions: A Debate*, ed. Lynn Wardle, Mark Strasser, William Duncan, and David Coolidge (Westport, CT: Praeger, 2003), pp. 13-24.

Fred Mann, *Human Nature in Marriage* (Washington, DC: National Council of Catholic Men, 1948).

Douglas Farrow, "Blurring Sexual Boundaries," *First Things*, 211 (March 2011), pp. 17-19.

Glenn T. Stanton and Bill Maier, *Marriage on Trial: The Case Against Same-Sex Marriage and Parenting* (Downers Grove, IL: InterVarsity Press, 2004).

David Popenoe, *Disturbing the Nest: Family Change and Decline in Modern Societies* (Edison, NJ: Transaction, 1988).

Mathew D. Staver, *Same-Sex Marriage: Putting Every Household at Risk* (Nashville, TN: Broadman and Holman, 2004).

William C. Duncan, "The State Interest in Marriage," *Ave Maria Law Review*, 2/1 (Spring 2004), pp. 153-182.

Arguments 39 – 48

Gracious Answers to Arguments Regarding Society and Social Order

In the most
comprehensive study
of its kind, J. D. Unwin proved
there is a direct connection between
social support favoring male-female marriage
and the ability of societies to endure.
Americans can choose between
same-sex marriage
or survival, but
not both.

REGARDING SOCIETY AND SOCIAL ORDER

(Arguments 39–48)

39

You May Hear Proponents Argue ...

*S*AME-SEX MARRIAGE SHOULD *be allowed because it is a proven practice that poses no risk to society.* Same-sex marriage has been legal in Denmark since 1989, has been allowed in some form in other Scandinavian countries for nearly twenty years, and has been legal in Holland since 2001. These countries have not collapsed. The American Anthropological Association declares that research across cultures provides "no support whatsoever for the view that either civilization or viable social orders depend upon marriages as an exclusively heterosexual institution." For this reason, allowing a few same-sex couples to marry is not a risky social experiment.

You Can *Graciously Refute* This By Saying ...

Same-sex marriage deinstitutionalizes marriage by redefining it in a way that denies marriage has any fixed structure. Doing so destroys marriage as a social institution by reducing it to nothing more than a way of affirming whatever desires people possess. When *marriage* includes everything, it becomes nothing special. And when it becomes nothing special, fewer and fewer people see any reason to discipline their appetites in favor of having and raising well-adjusted children.

Such thinking is bad for society because it will cause society to lose social cohesion and eventually disintegrate. Deconstructing marriage to affirm homosexual desires thus threatens social survival by turning marriage into non-marriage. The evidence shows that since the time same-sex partnerships were approved in Scandinavia, the marriage rate has dropped for everyone, and the number of out-of-wedlock births has risen dramatically.

In the most comprehensive study of its kind, British anthropologist J. D. Unwin clearly proved that the strength and endurance of a society over time comes from guarding the procreational structure of marriage by limiting sex to one heterosexual partner for life. Even against his own initial expectations, Unwin found that there has never been any exception to the rule that when a society ceases doing this, it always weakens and collapses. This happened in ancient Greece and Rome, and it will happen to the United States as well if lawmakers legalize same-sex marriage. Even gay activist Michael Bronski readily admits this argument is false, because the same-sex marriage movement aims to "change society as we know it."

The Truth Is …

Same-sex marriage is wrong because it threatens the strength and survival of society and everything depending on it.

References and Further Reading

For examples of advocates using this argument, see "2004 AAA Statement on Marriage and the Family," American Anthropological Association, 2004, accessible at http://www. aaanet.org/issues/policy-advocacy/Statement-on-Marriage-and-the-Family; Eugene Volokh, "Same-Sex Marriage and Slippery Slopes," *Hofstra Law Review*, 33/3 (Spring 2005), pp. 1155-1201; Courtney Megan Cahill, "Same-Sex Marriage: Slippery Slope Rhetoric, and the Politics of Disgust: A Critical Perspective on Contemporary Family Discourse and the Incest Taboo," *Northwestern University Law Review*, 99/4 (2005), pp. 1543-1611; and Michael Bronski, "Beyond," *Z Magazine* (September 2006), accessible at http://www.zmag.org/viewArticle/13676.

For examples of gay social revolutionaries admitting they are using same-sex marriage as a way to completely abolish the institution of marriage, see Thomas B. Stoddard, "Why Gay People Should Seek the Right to Marry," chapter 35 in *Families in the US: Kinship and Domestic Politics*, ed. Karen V. Hansen (Philadelphia, PA: Temple University Press, 1998); Richard D. Mohr, *A More Perfect Union: Why Straight America Must Stand Up for Gay Rights* (Boston, MA: Beacon, 1994); Gretchen A. Stiers, *From This Day Forward: Commitment, Marriage, and Family in Lesbian and Gay Relationships* (New York: St. Martin's Press, 1999); Michelangelo Signorile, "Bridal Wave," *Out* (December/January 1994); "Sociologist Says Gay Marriage Does Threaten Established Order and That's Good," *Ascribe Law News Service* (November 16, 2003); and Margaret Gullette, "The New Case for Marriage," *American Prospect* (March 1, 2004).

Stanley Kurtz, "The End of Marriage in Scandinavia: The 'Conservative Case' for Same-Sex Marriage Collapses," *Weekly Standard* (February 2, 2004), pp. 26-33.

For how abandoning the procreational structure of marriage threatens civilization, see J. D. Unwin, *Sex and Culture* (London: Oxford University Press, 1937); J. D. Unwin, *Sexual Regulations and Cultural Behavior: An Address Delivered Before the Medical Section of the British Psychological Society* (London: Oxford University Press, 1935); Carle Zimmerman, *Family and Civilization* (Wilmington, DE: ISI Books, 2008); Pitirim Sorokin, *Social and Cultural Dynamics*, vol. 4 (Boston, MA: Porter Sargent, 1957); and Daniel Heimbach, "The Future Based on Science," in Daniel Heimbach, *True Sexual Morality* (Wheaton, IL: Crossway, 2004), pp. 345-348.

Christopher Oleson, "Phony Matrimony: Or What King Kamehameha II Teaches Us About the Last Marriage Taboo," *Touchstone Magazine*, (January/February 2009), accessible at http://www.touchstonemag/com/archives/article.php?id=22-01-032-f.

Nelson Lund, "The Case Against Boies-Olson: Wrong on the Law, and on Civilization," *National Review Online* (September 24, 2009), accessible at http://article.nationalreview.com/?q=MmI0NWU2ZTU4ZGJ1NDUwYWZjNzI4MzFmZjYwMDA1MGY=.

40

You May Hear Proponents Argue ...

Same-sex marriage should be allowed because it will not lead to including other sexual preferences. Allowing same-sex marriage is not a slippery slope to allowing marriage involving incest, pedophilia, polygamy, polyandry, bestiality (sex between humans and animals) or polyamory (any combination of sex). Such thinking is silly and nothing more than fear-mongering. No one is poised to exploit the legalizing of same-sex marriage in ways that will plunge the nation into a nebulous state of sexual abandon. Homosexuality is different from other sexual attractions. While there is much demand for same-sex marriage, there is no demand for changing marriage in other ways.

You Can *Graciously Refute* This By Saying ...

Proponents of this argument rely on sheer emotion and not on what is objectively true and verifiable for everyone. The truth is that giving public recognition and approval to same-sex marriage will open the door—both logically and legally—to using marriage as a way of affirming endless varieties of bizarre sexual behaviors. Regardless of how strongly anyone denies it, organizations such as the Alternatives to Marriage Project (AtMP) and the North American Man-Boy Love Association (NAMBLA) *are* poised to exploit changes made by legalizing same-sex marriage.

If marriage law becomes a matter of affirming sexual desires, it will not only justify gay marriage but will also introduce into law a basis on which other groups can demand treating their sexual desires the same way. The procreational structure of marriage cannot be removed without generating a basis for allowing practitioners of pedophilia, bestiality, and perhaps even necrophilia to marry as well. According to commentator Stanley Kurtz, "Gradual transition from gay marriage to state-sanctioned polyamory [any sexual combination of any number] and the eventual abolition of marriage itself as a legal category, is now the most influential paradigm within academic family law."

Legalizing the free-for-all model of marriage that proponents of this argument desire is indeed a slippery slope that will destroy marriage altogether. Redefining marriage to affirm homosexual desires will lead to various groups using marriage to affirm whatever desires they happen to have. It will redefine marriage in a way that erases the difference between marriage and non-marriage—destroying marriage as a viable social institution in the process.

The Truth Is ...

Same-sex marriage is wrong because it turns marriage into a way of affirming whatever attractions people happen to have.

References and Further Reading

For an example of an advocate making this argument, see Courtney Megan Cahill, "Same-Sex Marriage: Slippery Slope Rhetoric, and the Politics of Disgust: A Critical Perspective on Contemporary Family Discourse and the Incest Taboo," *Northwestern University Law Review*, 99/4 (2005), pp. 1543-1611.

Stanley Kurtz, "Beyond Gay Marriage: The Road to Polyamory," *Weekly Standard* (August 4/August 11, 2003), pp. 26-33.

Stanley Kurtz, "Here Comes the Brides: Plural Marriage Is Waiting in the Wings," *Weekly Standard* (December 26, 2005), pp. 19-27.

Peter Singer, "Heavy Petting," accessible at http://www.nerve.com. Posted March 12, 2001).

Midas Dekkers, *Dearest Pet: On Bestiality* (London and New York: Verso, 1994).

Barbara Sumner Burstyn, "The Love That Dare Not Bark Its Name," *Men's News Daily* (April 29, 2002), accessible at http://www.mensnewsdaily.com/archive/a-b/burstyn/burstyn042902.htm.

Arthur Weinreb, "And They Call It Puppy Love," *Canada Free Press* (July 22, 2002), accessible at http://www.canadafreepress.com/2002/weinreb72202.htm.

Dorian Solot and Marshall Miller, "The Alternatives to Marriage Project Welcomes Same-Sex Marriage in Massachusetts—and Looks Ahead," *Press Release*, Alternatives to Marriage Project (Albany, New York: May 16, 2004), accessible at http://www.unmarried.org/massachusetts-same-sex-marriage.html.

For exploitation by NAMBLA, see David Thorstad, "Man/Boy Love and the American Gay Movement," *Journal of Homosexuality*, 20 (1990), p. 255. See also Edward Brongersma, et al., *Male Intergenerational Intimacy: Historical, Socio-Psychological, and Legal Perspectives* (Binghamton, NY: Hayworth Press, 1993).

Christopher Oleson, "Phony Matrimony: Or What King Kamehameha II Teaches Us About the Last Marriage Taboo," *Touchstone Magazine*, (January/February 2009), accessible at http://www.touchstonemag/com/archives/article.php?id=22-01-032-f.

Nelson Lund, "The Case Against Boies-Olson: Wrong on the Law, and on Civilization," *National Review Online* (September 24, 2009), accessible at http://article.nationalreview.com/?q=MmI0NWU2ZTU4ZGJ1NDUwYWZjNzI4MzFmZjYwMDA1MGY=.

41

You May Hear Proponents Argue …

Same-sex marriage should be allowed because any social costs involved will be worth it. Even if allowing same-sex marriage leads to some individuals trying homosexual sex for the wrong reasons, or even if it results in producing fewer children, whatever society loses from allowing it will not be worth as much as the value of winning greater freedom and acceptance for homosexuals. The difference same-sex marriage may have on producing children will affect so few that it will never harm the interest society has in reproducing itself. Whatever confusion results from individuals feeling freer to experiment will be worth reducing the pressure on homosexuals to conform with rigid expectations.

You Can *Graciously Refute* This By Saying …

Proponents of this argument are wrong in assuming that society has nothing to gain and everything to lose by approving same-sex marriage. In fact, society has *nothing* to gain and *everything* to lose by allowing it, because each of the *benefits* alleged to come from same-sex marriage (such as greater freedom, flexibility, and satisfaction) involve personal matters affecting private life, while most of the bad results involve general matters affecting public life. Furthermore, no society can afford to deny public interest in preserving the procreational structure of institutional marriage. Even homosexual activist Andrew Sullivan admits there is an "inherent difference between homosexual and heterosexual adults," because "the latter group is committed to the procreation of a new generation [and] the former simply isn't."

The problem with legalizing same-sex marriage is that it redefines marriage in a way that denies the institution has any fixed structure. In so doing, it destroys marriage as a social institution by reducing it to nothing more than a way of affirming whatever desires people have. It *deinstitutionalizes* the institution, and when that happens, society loses cohesion and falls apart. Carle C. Zimmerman, the eminent professor of sociology at Harvard University, studied how family life affects social survival. He discovered that when individual freedom and self-satisfaction become overriding values affecting marriage and family commitments, they limit the expansive power of civilization and cause civilized social order to weaken and eventually die.

The Truth Is ...

Same-sex marriage is wrong because it provides no social benefits while inflicting substantial and irrevocable social costs.

References and Further Reading

For an example of an advocate using this argument, see Andrew Sullivan, *Virtually Normal* (New York: Vintage, 1995), p. 196.

For examples of gay social revolutionaries admitting they are using same-sex marriage as a way to completely abolish the institution of marriage, see Thomas B. Stoddard, "Why Gay People Should Seek the Right to Marry," chapter 35 in *Families in the US: Kinship and Domestic Politics*, ed. Karen V. Hansen (Philadelphia, PA: Temple University Press, 1998); Richard D. Mohr, *A More Perfect Union: Why Straight America Must Stand Up for Gay Rights* (Boston, MA: Beacon, 1994); Gretchen A. Stiers, *From This Day Forward: Commitment, Marriage, and Family in Lesbian and Gay Relationships* (New York: St. Martin's Press, 1999); Michelangelo Signorile, "Bridal Wave," *Out* (December/January 1994); "Sociologist Says Gay Marriage Does Threaten Established Order and That's Good," *Ascribe Law News Service* (November 16, 2003); and Margaret Gullette, "The New Case for Marriage," *American Prospect* (March 1, 2004).

For how abandoning the procreational structure of marriage threatens civilization, see Joseph Daniel Unwin, *Sex and Culture* (London: Oxford University Press, 1937); Joseph Daniel Unwin, *Sexual Regulations and Cultural Behavior: An Address Delivered Before the Medical Section of the British Psychological Society* (London: Oxford University Press, 1935); Carle Zimmerman, *Family and Civilization* (Wilmington, DE: ISI Books, 2008); Pitirim Sorokin, *The Crisis of Our Age* (Richmond, VA: Dutton, 1941); Pitirim Sorokin, *Social and Cultural Dynamics*, vol. 4 (Boston, MA: Porter Sargent, 1957); and Daniel Heimbach, "The Future Based on Science," in Daniel Heimbach, *True Sexual Morality* (Wheaton, IL: Crossway, 2004), pp. 345-348.

William C. Duncan, "The State Interest in Marriage," *Ave Maria Law Review,* 2/1 (Spring 2004), pp. 153-182.

Maggie Gallagher, "The Case Against Same-Sex Marriage," chapter 3 in *Debating Same-Sex Marriage* (New York: Oxford University Press, 2012), pp. 91-178.

Carle Zimmerman develops this thesis in *Family and Civilization* (Wilmington, DE: ISI Books, 2008).

Christopher Oleson, "Phony Matrimony: Or What King Kamehameha II Teaches Us About the Last Marriage Taboo," *Touchstone Magazine*, (January/February 2009), accessible at http://www.touchstonemag/com/archives/article.php?id=22-01-032-f.

Nelson Lund, "The Case Against Boies-Olson: Wrong on the Law, and on Civilization," *National Review Online* (September 24, 2009), accessible at http://article.nationalreview.com/?q=Mml 0NWU2ZTU4ZGJ1NDUwYWZjNzI4MzFmZjYwMDA1MGY=.

42

You May Hear Proponents Argue ...

Same-sex marriage should be allowed because the survival of society does not matter as compared to the value of affirming homosexuals. Societies that depend on limiting marriage to heterosexuals do not deserve to survive and should be allowed to collapse. They must be forced to change—or die. A good social order should be preserved and maintained, but a bad one should not. Gays cannot be full participants of any social system that does not allow them to marry partners of the same sex, and solving this problem is worth more than continuing whatever order happens to exist. Social collapse is better than continuing a bad system.

You Can *Graciously Refute* This By Saying ...

Proponents of this argument admit that radically redefining marriage to affirm homosexuals could destroy American society, but that this outcome would be better than continuing what we currently have. As homosexual activist Michelangelo Signorile demands, "The right to marry [is not] a way of adhering to society's moral codes but rather to debunk America and radically alter an archaic institution." However, these proponents are wrong for two reasons: (1) because there is nothing wrong to fix, and (2) because whatever gays hope to gain is minor compared to what will be lost.

Just as the institution of President of the United States is greater than any person occupying the office, so the institution of marriage is greater than any person who gets married. In both cases, the public reason for justifying what structures the institution is completely different from what motivates people to participate or from what satisfies those who do. There is nothing wrong to fix in marriage because the public interest in justifying legal marriage is getting biological mothers and fathers to have and raise their own children, which has nothing to do with satisfying adult appetites.

Worst of all, proponents of this argument grossly underestimate the value of what everyone will lose as compared to what homosexuals hope to gain. Legalizing same-sex marriage will only help a few individuals feel better about themselves, but it will do so at the cost of threatening the most essential of human institutions. Officially denying as a matter of law and public policy that marriage has any fixed structure will not only destroy marriage but also erode the cohesion on which social order depends.

The Truth Is …

Same-sex marriage is wrong because affirming the way a few like to have sex is not worth collapsing the entire social order.

References and Further Reading

For an example of an advocate using this argument, see Michelangelo Signorile, "Bridal Wave," *Out* (December/January 1994), p. 161.
For how abandoning the procreational structure of marriage threatens civilization, see Joseph Daniel Unwin, *Sex and Culture* (London: Oxford University Press, 1937); Joseph Daniel Unwin, *Sexual Regulations and Cultural Behavior: An Address Delivered Before the Medical Section of the British Psychological Society* (London: Oxford University Press, 1935); Carle Zimmerman, *Family and Civilization* (Wilmington, DE: ISI Books, 2008); Pitirim Sorokin, *The Crisis of Our Age* (Richmond, VA: Dutton, 1941); Pitirim Sorokin, *Social and Cultural Dynamics*, vol. 4 (Boston, MA: Porter Sargent, 1957); and Daniel Heimbach, "The Future Based on Science," in Daniel Heimbach, *True Sexual Morality* (Wheaton, IL: Crossway, 2004), pp. 345-348.
For examples of gay social revolutionaries admitting they are using same-sex marriage as a way to completely abolish the

institution of marriage, see Thomas B. Stoddard, "Why Gay People Should Seek the Right to Marry," chapter 35 in *Families in the US: Kinship and Domestic Politics*, ed. Karen V. Hansen (Philadelphia, PA: Temple University Press, 1998); Richard D. Mohr, *A More Perfect Union: Why Straight America Must Stand Up for Gay Rights* (Boston, MA: Beacon, 1994); Gretchen A. Stiers, *From This Day Forward: Commitment, Marriage, and Family in Lesbian and Gay Relationships* (New York: St. Martin's Press, 1999); Michelangelo Signorile, "Bridal Wave," *Out* (December/ January 1994); "Sociologist Says Gay Marriage Does Threaten Established Order and That's Good," *Ascribe Law News Service* (November 16, 2003); and Margaret Gullette, "The New Case for Marriage," *American Prospect* (March 1, 2004).

William C. Duncan, "The State Interest in Marriage," *Ave Maria Law Review,* 2/1 (Spring 2004), pp. 153-182.

Sherif Gergis, Robert P. George, and Ryan T. Anderson, "What Is Marriage?" *Harvard Journal of Law and Public Policy*, 34/1 (Winter 2011), pp. 245-287.

Christopher Oleson, "Phony Matrimony: Or What King Kamehameha II Teaches Us About the Last Marriage Taboo," *Touchstone Magazine*, (January/February 2009), accessible at http://www.touchstonemag/com/archives/article.php?id=22-01-032-f.

Nelson Lund, "The Case Against Boies-Olson: Wrong on the Law, and on Civilization," *National Review Online* (September 24, 2009), accessible at http://article.nationalreview.com/?q=MmI0NWU2ZTU4ZGJlNDUwYWZjNzI4MzFmZjYwMDA1MGY=.

Daniel R. Heimbach, "Deconstructing the Family," *Religion and Society Report,* 22/7 (October/November 2005), pp. 1-12.

43

You May Hear Proponents Argue ...

Same-sex marriage should be allowed because it makes society stronger by increasing the number of people getting married. Expanding marriage to include same-sex relationships will increase the frequency of marriage, which is a good thing for everyone in society. Homosexual relationships will also add strengths to the practice of marriage that will nourish the broader society. These added strengths include having a more powerful degree of relational commitment, doing a better job of incorporating friendship into marriage, maintaining greater openness to the value of extramarital outlets, and having fewer dependents to harm if a marriage fails.

You Can *Graciously Refute* This By Saying ...

Proponents of this argument assume that legalizing same-sex marriage will merely allow a few more couples to marry without changing anything else. But this is not the case, because legalizing same-sex marriage does not simply enlarge marriage but also redefines it in a radical way. It is not a question of keeping the same thing while including more but of deconstructing a social institution by denying marriage has any fixed structure at all.

Same-sex marriage reduces marriage to non-marriage by redefining it in terms that apply to any sort of personal relation regardless of form, function, motivation, or purpose. This argument does not make sense even in attitudinal terms. There is no evidence for the idea that same-sex couples are more committed to each other or establish stronger friendship bonds. Sexual infidelity is the number one reason for divorce, so it strains credulity to imagine that less fidelity would be a good way to strengthen marriage in the broader society.

Given that the public reason for having marriage laws is to get fathers and mothers to raise their own children, it would be a terribly bad thing for the order and survival of a society to decouple marriage and release men and women from that responsibility. Legalizing same-sex marriage deconstructs marriage, and once marriage law changes to accommodate homosexuals, it will become impossible to stress the social value of procreational over non-procreational relationships. Deconstructing marriage threatens social survival by destroying what makes marriage a social institution. It changes civil marriage into nothing more than a way of affirming whatever private feelings people possess.

The Truth Is …

Same-sex marriage is wrong because it will harm the social order by destroying marriage as a social institution.

References and Further Reading

For examples of advocates using this argument, see Andrew Sullivan, *Virtually Normal* (New York: Vintage, 1995), pp. 202-203; and Theodore B. Olson, "The Conservative Case for Gay Marriage: Why Same-Sex Marriage Is an American Value," *Newsweek* (January 18, 2010), pp. 48-54.

For the weakening effect of same-sex marriage on the institution of marriage, see chapter 6, "Deinstitutionalizing Marriage?" in David Blankenhorn, *The Future of Marriage* (New York: Encounter Books, 2007), pp. 127-169. Also see Stanley Kurtz, "The End of Marriage in Scandinavia: The 'Conservative Case' for Same-Sex Marriage Collapses," *Weekly Standard* (February 2, 2004), pp. 26-33.

For how abandoning the procreational structure of marriage threatens civilization, see Joseph Daniel Unwin, *Sex and Culture* (London: Oxford University Press, 1937); Joseph Daniel Unwin,

Sexual Regulations and Cultural Behavior: An Address Delivered Before the Medical Section of the British Psychological Society (London: Oxford University Press, 1935); Carle Zimmerman, *Family and Civilization* (Wilmington, DE: ISI Books, 2008); Pitirim Sorokin, *The Crisis of Our Age* (Richmond, VA: Dutton, 1941); Pitirim Sorokin, *Social and Cultural Dynamics*, vol. 4 (Boston, MA: Porter Sargent, 1957); and Daniel Heimbach, "The Future Based on Science," in Daniel Heimbach, *True Sexual Morality* (Wheaton, IL: Crossway, 2004), pp. 345-348.

For examples of gay social revolutionaries admitting they are using same-sex marriage as a way to completely abolish the institution of marriage, see Thomas B. Stoddard, "Why Gay People Should Seek the Right to Marry," chapter 35 in *Families in the US: Kinship and Domestic Politics*, ed. Karen V. Hansen (Philadelphia, PA: Temple University Press, 1998); Richard D. Mohr, *A More Perfect Union: Why Straight America Must Stand Up for Gay Rights* (Boston, MA: Beacon, 1994); Gretchen A. Stiers, *From This Day Forward: Commitment, Marriage, and Family in Lesbian and Gay Relationships* (New York: St. Martin's Press, 1999); Michelangelo Signorile, "Bridal Wave," *Out* (December/January 1994); "Sociologist Says Gay Marriage Does Threaten Established Order and That's Good," *Ascribe Law News Service* (November 16, 2003); and Margaret Gullette, "The New Case for Marriage," *American Prospect* (March 1, 2004).

Christopher Oleson, "Phony Matrimony: Or What King Kamehameha II Teaches Us About the Last Marriage Taboo," *Touchstone Magazine*, (January/February 2009), accessible at http://www.touchstonemag/com/archives/article.php?id=22-01-032-f.

Nelson Lund, "The Case Against Boies-Olson: Wrong on the Law, and on Civilization," *National Review Online* (September 24, 2009), accessible at http://article.nationalreview.com/?q=Mml0NWU2ZTU4ZGJlNDUwYWZjNzI4MzFmZjYwMDA1MGY=.

44

You May Hear Proponents Argue ...

Same-sex marriage should be allowed because it strengthens society by domesticating unruly homosexual behavior. Allowing gays and lesbians to marry same-sex partners will encourage them to be less promiscuous. It will enable them to form and maintain stronger, more committed, more stable, and longer-lasting relationships. As it is, homosexuals must choose either to marry someone of the opposite sex or to not marry at all, which gives them no viable options to pursue. Institutionalizing gay marriage will domesticate unruly homosexual behavior by fostering responsibility and commitment, and that, in turn, will make society better and stronger for everyone.

You Can *Graciously Refute* This By Saying ...

The drive to legalize same-sex marriage really is a Trojan horse meant not to protect a threatened minority but to force acceptance of sexual identity as being merely a social construction. In this way, proponents of this argument are not basing their claims on anything objective but only on subjective choices of self-interpretation. Gay activists use this argument to win support from people who fail to realize they really have no interest in conforming to the way straight couples behave.

As the example of Scandinavia proves, once gay marriage was legalized in that region, it did not cause gays to be less promiscuous. Instead, it only weakened support for procreative marriages by placing a weapon in the hands of those who denied marriage had any necessary form at all. As Danish homosexual social theorist Henning Bech observed, the it-will-domesticate-homosexual-behavior argument is nothing but a ploy that gay activists have adopted for tactical purposes to win the political debate—not because they think it will change behavior.

Most members of the homosexual subculture think the idea of domesticating gay behavior is offensive. Few homosexuals care to restrict how they behave, and most actually see same-sex marriage as a way of subverting the ethos of sexual fidelity and complementarity that others expect of marriage. Gay activist Michael Bronski says he knows of hardly any homosexual who wants to be in a monogamous relationship, and for that reason, he dismisses this argument as "idiotic." Andrew Sullivan, who originated this particular claim, has since praised "the beauty and mystery" of anonymous sex and claimed to have no interest in limiting himself to any sexually exclusive relationship.

The Truth Is …

Same-sex marriage is wrong because homosexuals have no real interest in behaving more like heterosexuals.

References and Further Reading

For examples of advocates using this argument, see Michael Bronski, "Over the Rainbow," *The Boston Phoenix*, August 7, 2003, accessible at http://www.bostonphoenix.com/boston/news_features/other_stories/multiple-page/documents/03056855.asp; Andrew Sullivan, "Andrew Sullivan Defends His Politics," letter to the editor, *Salon* (December 15, 1999), accessible at http://www.salon.com/letters/1999/12/15/sullivan; and Theodore B. Olson, "The Conservative Case for Gay Marriage: Why Same-Sex Marriage Is an American Value," *Newsweek* (January 18, 2010), pp. 48-54.

For examples of gay social revolutionaries admitting they are using same-sex marriage as a way to completely abolish the institution of marriage, see Thomas B. Stoddard, "Why Gay People Should Seek the Right to Marry," chapter 35 in *Families in the US: Kinship and Domestic Politics*, ed. Karen V.

Hansen (Philadelphia, PA: Temple University Press, 1998); Richard D. Mohr, *A More Perfect Union: Why Straight America Must Stand Up for Gay Rights* (Boston, MA: Beacon, 1994); Gretchen A. Stiers, *From This Day Forward: Commitment, Marriage, and Family in Lesbian and Gay Relationships* (New York: St. Martin's Press, 1999); Michelangelo Signorile, "Bridal Wave," *Out* (December/January 1994); "Sociologist Says Gay Marriage Does Threaten Established Order and That's Good," *Ascribe Law News Service* (November 16, 2003); and Margaret Gullette, "The New Case for Marriage," *American Prospect* (March 1, 2004).

Mollie Ziegler Hemingway, "Same-Sex, Different Marriage: Many of Those Who Want Marriage Equality Do Not Want Fidelity," *Christianity Today* (May 18, 2010), accessible at http://www.christianitytoday.com/ct/2010/may/11.52.html.

Stanley Kurtz, "The End of Marriage in Scandinavia: The 'Conservative Case' for Same-Sex Marriage Collapses," *Weekly Standard* (February 2, 2004), pp. 26-33.

Nelson Lund, "The Case Against Boies-Olson: Wrong on the Law, and on Civilization," *National Review Online* (September 24, 2009), accessible at http://article.nationalreview.com/?q=MmI0NWU2ZTU4ZGJ1NDUwYWZjNzI4MzFmZjYwMDA1MGY=.

Jeffrey Lord, "A Rebuttal to Theodore Olson," *American Spectator* (January 19, 2010), accessible at http://spectator.org/archives/2010/01/19/a-rebuttal-to-theodore-olson.

Timothy Dailey, "Comparing the Lifestyles of Homosexual Couples to Married Couples," *Family Research Council* (April 29, 2004), accessible at http://www.frc.org/get.cfm?i=IS04C02.

Christopher Oleson, "Phony Matrimony: Or What King Kamehameha II Teaches Us About the Last Marriage Taboo," *Touchstone Magazine*, (January/February 2009), accessible at http://www.touchstonemag.com/archives/article.php?id=22-01-032-f.

45

You May Hear Proponents Argue …

Same-sex marriage should be allowed because it changes how others in society think and behave toward homosexuals. Everyone needs to understand and accept that homosexual relationships are normal and good. For many people, marriage law is the only thing stopping them from accepting this. Same-sex marriage will have a much-needed attitude-altering effect on people. Civil law has a powerful mind-shaping force that affects the way people think. Under current conditions, marriage law affects attitudes toward homosexuals in a bad way. Allowing same-sex marriage and making it legal will change attitudes in a good way.

You Can *Graciously Refute* This By Saying …

Proponents of this argument show that they have little interest in the institution of marriage itself and a great deal of interest in forcing others to affirm and approve their behaviors. Stanley Kurtz observes, "The movement for gay marriage has little to do with an expanded regard for marriage and everything to do with an attempt to gain social approval for homosexuality." In other words, as he says, "Marriage is being *used* to send a message that has little to do with the institution itself."

It is true that civil law does have attitude-shaping power and can affect how people think. But why should the effect of marriage law be reversed when only a small minority believes gender difference is irrelevant to marriage, or that marriage law causes bad attitudes, or that civil law should attack the deepest convictions most people have about marriage, family life, and the common good?

In truth, proponents of this argument base their claims on two false premises: (1) that there are no good reasons for thinking homosexuality is abnormal, and (2) that marriage is no more than a social convention shaped by whatever desires people have. The first premise runs contrary to civilized history, human physiology, and the most reliable scientific evidence. The second premise assumes that the social meaning of marriage has already changed in the way advocates claim it will be changed through same-sex marriage.

In fact, normal marriage does not simply reflect whatever desires people have. Rather, it channels human desires toward the one sort of sexual union that is best for men and women having and raising children in order to assure social survival. In other words, the present law aligns with a social reality that is ignored only at grave peril.

The Truth Is ...

Same-sex marriage is wrong because a social institution should not be changed for reasons unrelated to reasons that institution exists.

References and Further Reading

For an example of an advocate using this argument, see Eugene Volokh, "Same-Sex Marriage and Slippery Slopes," *Hofstra Law Review*, 33/3 (Spring 2005), pp. 1155-1201.

Stanley Kurtz, "Love and Marriage: A Combination Necessarily Exclusive to a Man and a Woman," *National Review Online* (July 30, 2001).

For how legalizing same-sex marriage will align marriage to homosexual categories and not align homosexuals to what marriage is now, see Lawrence Auster, "The Extreme Radicalism of Homosexual 'Marriage,'" *View from the Right* (June 2, 2008), accessible at http://www.amnation.com/vfr/archives/010723. html.

For how the science has been misrepresented and politicized, see Jeffrey Satinover, "The Trojan Couch: How the Mental Health Associations Misrepresent Science," *Conference*

Reports 2005, National Association for Research and Therapy of Homosexuals, accessible at http://www.narth.com/docs/thetrojancouchsatinover.

On disputing the normal view of marriage, see Maggie Gallagher, "Normal Marriage: Two Views," in *Marriage and Same-Sex Unions: A Debate*, ed. Lynn Wardle, Mark Strasser, W. Duncan, and D. Coolidge (Westport, CT: Praeger, 2003), pp. 13-24.

Timothy Dailey, "Comparing the Lifestyles of Homosexual Couples to Married Couples," *Family Research Council* (April 29, 2004), accessible at http://www.frc.org/get.cfm?i=IS04C02.

Christopher Oleson, "Phony Matrimony: Or What King Kamehameha II Teaches Us About the Last Marriage Taboo," *Touchstone Magazine*, (January/February 2009), accessible at http://www.touchstonemag/com/archives/article.php?id=22-01-032-f.

Nelson Lund, "The Case Against Boies-Olson: Wrong on the Law, and on Civilization," *National Review Online* (September 24, 2009), accessible at http://article.nationalrev iew.com/?q=Mm I0NWU2ZTU4ZGJ1NDUwYWZjNzI4MzFmZjYwMDA1MGY=.

For how abandoning the procreational structure of marriage threatens civilization, see Joseph Daniel Unwin, *Sex and Culture* (London: Oxford University Press, 1937); Joseph Daniel Unwin, *Sexual Regulations and Cultural Behavior: An Address Delivered Before the Medical Section of the British Psychological Society* (London: Oxford University Press, 1935); Carle Zimmerman, *Family and Civilization* (Wilmington, DE: ISI Books, 2008); Pitirim Sorokin, *The Crisis of Our Age* (Richmond, VA: Dutton, 1941); Pitirim Sorokin, *Social and Cultural Dynamics*, vol. 4 (Boston, MA: Porter Sargent, 1957); and Daniel Heimbach, "The Future Based on Science," in Daniel Heimbach, *True Sexual Morality* (Wheaton, IL: Crossway, 2004), pp. 345-348.

46

You May Hear Proponents Argue …

Same-sex marriage should be allowed because it strengthens marriage for everyone. Legalizing gay marriage will strengthen the influence of marriage as an anchor in the midst of the chaos of sexual irresponsibility and relational insecurity that characterizes life these days. It will give homosexuals a mechanism for establishing more enduring, more committed, and more stable relationships, while also continuing this effect for heterosexual relationships. This will make the institution of marriage stronger—not weaker—than it is today. It will do this by increasing institutional vitality through a combination of greater participation and greater respect.

You Can *Graciously Refute* This By Saying …

Proponents of this argument make what some call the "conservative" claim for same-sex marriage. However, they can only make their argument work by ignoring that it relies on something totally impossible that most leaders of the homosexual movement consider perfect nonsense. Since gay marriage was legalized in Scandinavia, marriage rates have dropped and family dissolution has exploded. Marriage as a social institution has lost the critical mass needed to be a normative force, and children have been hurt the most. Gay marriage has made things worse by shifting the focus of marriage from procreation, complementarity, and sexual fidelity toward merely affirming sexual appetites regardless of relational structure.

This argument would make sense if and only if the logic of gay marriage and strengthening procreationally structured marriage were compatible. But that is not the case at all. The logic of same-sex marriage is a matter of what scholars call deinstitutionalization, which is a dramatic removal of a fixed social structure sustaining an institution. These logics are not compatible because affirmation and support for the standards and expectations of normal heterosexual marriage will not follow if marriage is redefined in a way that has no fixed social structure.

In the end, same-sex marriage destroys the normative power of institutional marriage by elevating satisfaction of individual appetites over sexual fidelity and procreational responsibility. While normal heterosexual marriage strengthens the institutional value of marriage by reinforcing support for its procreational structure, same-sex marriage threatens marriage by destroying its institutional structure.

The Truth Is …

Same-sex marriage is wrong because it threatens marriage by destroying what gives marriage institutional structure in the first place.

References and Further Reading

Theodore Olson and David Boies used this argument to try to persuade a federal court to invalidate California's Proposition 8, which banned same-sex marriage in the state. See Theodore B. Olson, "The Conservative Case for Gay Marriage: Why Same-Sex Marriage Is an American Value," *Newsweek* (January 18, 2010), pp. 48-54.

David Blankenhorn, "Defining Marriage Down Is No Way to Save It," *Weekly Standard,* 12/28 (April 2, 2007).

Stanley Kurtz, "The End of Marriage in Scandinavia: The 'Conservative Case' for Same-Sex Marriage Collapses," *Weekly Standard* (February 2, 2004), pp. 26-33.

Maggie Gallagher, "Normal Marriage: Two Views," in *Marriage and Same-Sex Unions: A Debate,* ed. Lynn Wardle, Mark Strasser, William Duncan, and David Coolidge (Westport, CT: Praeger, 2003), pp. 13-24.

Stanley Kurtz, "Point of No Return: Marriage Needs a Man and a Woman, and an Amendment," *National Review Online* (August 3, 2001).

Stanley Kurtz, "Love and Marriage: A Combination Necessarily Exclusive to a Man and a Woman," *National Review Online* (July 30, 2001).

For examples of gay social revolutionaries admitting they are using same-sex marriage as a way to completely abolish the institution of marriage, see Thomas B. Stoddard, "Why Gay People Should Seek the Right to Marry," chapter 35 in *Families in the US: Kinship and Domestic Politics*, ed. Karen V. Hansen (Philadelphia, PA: Temple University Press, 1998); Richard D. Mohr, *A More Perfect Union: Why Straight America Must Stand Up for Gay Rights* (Boston, MA: Beacon, 1994); Gretchen A. Stiers, *From This Day Forward: Commitment, Marriage, and Family in Lesbian and Gay Relationships* (New York: St. Martin's Press, 1999); Michelangelo Signorile, "Bridal Wave," *Out* (December/January 1994); "Sociologist Says Gay Marriage Does Threaten Established Order and That's Good," *Ascribe Law News Service* (November 16, 2003); and Margaret Gullette, "The New Case for Marriage," *American Prospect* (March 1, 2004).

Christopher Oleson, "Phony Matrimony: Or What King Kamehameha II Teaches Us About the Last Marriage Taboo," *Touchstone Magazine*, (January/February 2009), accessible at http://www.touchstonemag/com/archives/article.php?id=22-01-032-f.

Nelson Lund, "The Case Against Boies-Olson: Wrong on the Law, and on Civilization," *National Review Online* (September 24, 2009), accessible at http://article.nationalreview.com/?q=MmI0NWU2ZTU4ZGJ1NDUwYWZjNzI4MzFmZjYwMDA1MGY=.

47

You May Hear Proponents Argue …

Same-sex marriage should be allowed because gays provide a model for how to improve society and marriage for everyone. Same-sex marriage will make society and marriage better by affirming *pure relationships*. It will not lead homosexuals to adopt the stifling model of heterosexual normality, and it will loosen up straight society by shedding marriage law of entanglements with gender and procreation. This will make marriage more honest, free, and in line with the open-textured model of homosexual relationships that are characteristically free of restrictions linked to expectations of exclusivity, permanence, children, or limiting sex to just one person.

You Can *Graciously Refute* This By Saying …

Proponents of this argument openly affirm that same-sex marriage will change marriage by making it less committed, stable, or permanent and that it will disconnect marriage from sexual exclusivity and procreation. Rather than hiding or denying these aspects, they embrace them as alleged improvements not only for individuals but also for society as a whole. As gay advocate Mary Bernstein proudly affirms, legalizing same-sex marriage poses what she calls "the ultimate threat to conservatively defined *family values* that view two parents of the opposite sex as necessary for a child's proper gender and sexual development."

While Bernstein's comments are refreshingly honest, she denies reality by embracing something from which nearly everyone on earth (except those making this argument) rightly recoil. It simply makes no sense to pretend that less stability and exclusivity will make marriages stronger, or that disconnecting marriage from permanence and procreation will be good for children and the survival of society.

Heterosexual marriage improves society's regard for the procreational structure of the social institution of marriage. It reinforces society's commitment to protect the relational value of bridging the male-female divide and of getting fathers to join mothers in raising children. Redefining marriage in a way that makes gender combination and procreational ability irrelevant, and in a way that conforms marriage to the open-textured model of homosexual relationships, poses a grave threat to future generations and the survival of society as a whole. As Maggie Gallagher observes, "It is a truism, frequently forgotten by large complex societies, that only societies that reproduce survive."

The Truth Is …

Same-sex marriage is wrong because it disconnects marriage from what links marriage to permanence, children, and exclusivity.

References and Further Reading

For examples of advocates using this argument, see Andrew Sullivan, "What Are Homosexuals For?" in *Virtually Normal* (New York: Random House, 1995), pp. 188-205; Eugene Volokh, "Same-Sex Marriage and Slippery Slopes," *Hofstra Law Review*, 33/3 (Spring 2005), pp. 1155-1201; R. D. Mohr, *A More Perfect Union* (Boston, MA: Beacon, 1994), pp. 41,49-50; and M. Gullette, "The New Case for Marriage," *American Prospect* (March 1, 2004).

For examples of gay social revolutionaries admitting they are using same-sex marriage as a way to completely abolish the institution of marriage, see Thomas B. Stoddard, "Why Gay People Should Seek the Right to Marry," chapter 35 in *Families in the US: Kinship and Domestic Politics*, ed. Karen V. Hansen (Philadelphia, PA: Temple University Press, 1998); Richard D. Mohr, *A More Perfect Union: Why Straight America Must Stand Up for Gay Rights* (Boston, MA: Beacon, 1994); Gretchen A. Stiers, *From This Day Forward: Commitment, Marriage, and Family in Lesbian and Gay Relationships* (New York: St. Martin's Press, 1999); Michelangelo Signorile, "Bridal Wave," *Out* (December/ January 1994); "Sociologist Says Gay Marriage Does Threaten Established Order and That's Good," *Ascribe Law News Service* (November 16, 2003); Margaret Gullette, "The New Case for Marriage," *American Prospect* (March 1, 2004); and Mary Bernstein, "Gender, Queer Family Policies, and the Limits of the Law," in *Queer Families, Queer Politics: Challenging Culture and the State.*, ed. Mary Bernstein and Renate Reimann (New York: Columbia University Press, 2001), p. 433.

For how abandoning the procreational structure of marriage threatens civilization, see Joseph Daniel Unwin, *Sex and Culture* (London: Oxford University Press, 1937); Joseph Daniel Unwin, *Sexual Regulations and Cultural Behavior: An Address Delivered Before the Medical Section of the British Psychological Society* (London: Oxford University Press, 1935); Carle Zimmerman, *Family and Civilization* (Wilmington, DE: ISI Books, 2008); Pitirim Sorokin, *The Crisis of Our Age* (Richmond, VA: Dutton, 1941); Pitirim Sorokin, *Social and Cultural Dynamics*, vol. 4 (Boston, MA: Porter Sargent, 1957); and Daniel Heimbach, "The Future Based on Science," in Daniel Heimbach, *True Sexual Morality* (Wheaton, IL: Crossway, 2004), pp. 345-348.

David Island and Patrick Letellier, *Men Who Beat the Men Who Love Them: Battered Gay Men and Domestic Violence* (New York: Haworth Press, 1991).

Christopher Oleson, "Phony Matrimony: Or What King Kamehameha II Teaches Us About the Last Marriage Taboo," *Touchstone Magazine*, (January/February 2009), accessible at http://www.touchstonemag/com/archives/article. php?id=22-01-032-f.

Nelson Lund, "The Case Against Boies-Olson: Wrong on the Law, and on Civilization," *National Review Online* (September 24, 2009), accessible at http://article.nationalreview.com/?q=MmI 0NWU2ZTU4ZGJ1NDUwYWZjNzI4MzFmZjYwMDA1MGY=.

48

You May Hear Proponents Argue ...

Same-sex marriage should be allowed because an inability to have children does not threaten the way marriage supports social order. If the marriage of infertile heterosexual couples does not pose a hazard to social order, then neither will the marriage of infertile same-sex married couples. The heterosexuality of marriage is civilly intrinsic only if it is understood to be inherently procreative, but that definition was abandoned long ago. Thus, same-sex marriage should be allowed because the inability of same-sex couples to procreate is not relevant to the way marriage sustains social order.

You Can *Graciously Refute* This By Saying ...

It is true that individuals can marry in spite of having problems with fertility. But this does not change the fact that marriage as a social institution is structured for procreation in the same way that cars are structured for transportation. While it is possible for people to sit in cars without going anywhere, that does not mean cars should be classified as something other than vehicles of transportation.

Claiming there is no longer any public interest in supporting marriage except as a way of bestowing social approval on private feelings changes marriage into something it has never been. As a matter of fact, the only legitimate public interest in favoring and supporting marriage has nothing to do with affirming private feelings. Rather, it has to do with trying to make sure that children have fathers and mothers and that society continues from one generation to another. By denying the procreational structure of institutional marriage, same-sex marriage turns the institution into non-marriage, which is bad not only for children but also for social survival.

Gay activists see same-sex marriage as a way of forcing everyone to affirm gay behavior without asking gays to alter anything they are doing. But as Maggie Gallagher says, this ignores the "truism … that only societies that reproduce survive." Marriage is the one social institution that is most essential not just for having and raising children but also for social survival. *Deinstitutionalizing* that same institution by gutting its structure to further adult interests in extending sexual liberty is nothing short of morally reckless, intellectually insane, and socially catastrophic.

The Truth Is …

Same-sex marriage is wrong because affirming gay behavior is not worth hazarding social collapse by deconstructing marriage.

References and Further Reading

Patrick Lee, Robert P. George, and Gerard V. Bradley, "Marriage and Procreation: The Intrinsic Connection," *Public Discourse: Ethics, Law and the Common Good* (March 28, 2011), accessible at http://www.thepublicdiscourse.com.

Maggie Gallagher, "Normal Marriage: Two Views," in *Marriage and Same-Sex Unions: A Debate*, ed. Lynn Wardle, Mark Strasser, William Duncan, and David Coolidge (Westport, CT: Praeger, 2003), pp. 13-24.

Maggie Gallagher, "What Marriage Is For: Children Need Mothers and Fathers," *Weekly Standard* (August 4/August 11, 2003), pp. 22-25.

For how abandoning the procreational structure of marriage threatens civilization, see Joseph Daniel Unwin, *Sex and Culture* (London: Oxford University Press, 1937); Joseph Daniel Unwin, *Sexual Regulations and Cultural Behavior: An Address Delivered Before the Medical Section of the British Psychological Society* (London: Oxford University Press, 1935); Carle Zimmerman,

Family and Civilization (Wilmington, DE: ISI Books, 2008); Pitirim Sorokin, *The Crisis of Our Age* (Richmond, VA: Dutton, 1941); Pitirim Sorokin, *Social and Cultural Dynamics*, vol. 4 (Boston, MA: Porter Sargent, 1957); and Daniel Heimbach, "The Future Based on Science," in Daniel Heimbach, *True Sexual Morality* (Wheaton, IL: Crossway, 2004), pp. 345-348. For examples of gay social revolutionaries admitting they are using same-sex marriage as a way to completely abolish the institution of marriage, see Thomas B. Stoddard, "Why Gay People Should Seek the Right to Marry," chapter 35 in *Families in the US: Kinship and Domestic Politics*, ed. Karen V. Hansen (Philadelphia, PA: Temple University Press, 1998); Richard D. Mohr, *A More Perfect Union: Why Straight America Must Stand Up for Gay Rights* (Boston, MA: Beacon, 1994); Gretchen A. Stiers, *From This Day Forward: Commitment, Marriage, and Family in Lesbian and Gay Relationships* (New York: St. Martin's Press, 1999); Michelangelo Signorile, "Bridal Wave," *Out* (December/ January 1994); and Margaret Gullette, "The New Case for Marriage," *American Prospect* (March 1, 2004).

William C. Duncan, "The State Interest in Marriage," *Ave Maria Law Review*, 2/1 (Spring 2004), pp. 153-182.

Christopher Oleson, "Phony Matrimony: Or What King Kamehameha II Teaches Us About the Last Marriage Taboo," *Touchstone Magazine*, (January/February 2009), accessible at http://www.touchstonemag/com/archives/article. php?id=22-01-032-f.

Nelson Lund, "The Case Against Boies-Olson: Wrong on the Law, and on Civilization," *National Review Online* (September 24, 2009), accessible at http://article.nationalreview.com/?q=MmI 0NWU2ZTU4ZGJ1NDUwYWZjNzI4MzFmZjYwMDA1MGY=.

Arguments 49 – 54

Gracious Answers to Arguments Regarding History and Tradition

*The long
tradition of marriage in
every society has always connected
procreational sex with biological mothers
and fathers raising children. At no time anywhere
has the institution been confused with
nothing more than friendship, recreation,
or economic partnering. There simply
is no tradition to which gay
marriage advocates
can appeal.*

REGARDING HISTORY AND TRADITION

(Arguments 49–54)

49

You May Hear Proponents Argue …

*S*AME-SEX MARRIAGE SHOULD *be allowed because tradition is no reason for treating people unfairly.* Tradition does not justify itself. Anything old enough to become traditional has, for that reason alone, become obsolete and outmoded. Slavery was traditional but also immoral, and continuing that tradition would have been terrible. Traditional marriage, which limits social approval to heterosexual couples while excluding homosexual couples, perpetuates economic and sexual prejudices that need to be rejected in the same way that slavery was rejected. Same-sex marriage will get rid of a bad tradition that should not have been allowed in the first place.

You Can *Graciously Refute* This By Saying …

Of course, no tradition deserves mindless allegiance, but neither should traditions be discarded simply because they have lasted a long time. It is especially foolish to trash a long-serving institution as important as marriage by misconstruing its essential function. As Lucius Cary is alleged to have said, "If it is not necessary to change, then it is necessary not to change."

Proponents of this argument overlook what has justified *public* promotion of marriage as a social institution so they can instead focus on *private* feelings. They wrongly presume that marriage never was—or is no longer—essentially procreative. In truth, what justifies *public* interest in favoring marriage is to support its value for getting men and women together to reproduce and take responsibility for raising their own children. There never has been any *public* reason for favoring marriage except to support this procreational structure. For this reason, the *public* interest in favoring marriage has not had—nor does it now have—anything to do with favoring or affirming *private* feelings.

Marriage as a man-woman union has been (until the recent rise of the homosexual movement) the only way any society ever has structured marriage. Marriage is a tradition that does not come from any one society but from the entire human race, and this kind of human tradition must not be rejected just to affirm how a few individuals like to have sex. In addition, because gay marriage attacks the structure of marriage itself, it is nothing like interracial marriage. Race has no bearing on marital structure, but how people have sex does. While interracial marriage affirms the structure of marriage, gay marriage destroys it completely.

The Truth Is ...

Same-sex marriage is wrong because universal tradition should not be deconstructed to affirm the private feelings of just a few people.

References and Further Reading

For examples of advocates making this argument, see Franklin E. Kameny, "Deconstructing the Traditional Family," *The World and I* (October 1993), pp. 388-389; and Kevin Bourassa, "Love and the Lexicon of Marriage," *Feminism and Psychology* 14, no. 1 (2004), pp. 58,61.

Oliver O'Donovan, *Church in Crisis: The Gay Controversy and the Anglican Communion* (Eugene, OR: Cascade Books, 2008), p. 108.

Carson Holloway, "Same-Sex Marriage and the Death of Tradition," *First Things* (June 10, 2009), accessible at http://www.firstthings.com/onthesquare/2009/06/same-sex-marriage-and-the-deat.

Lucius Cary, a seventeenth-century viscount of Falkland, is credited with saying the quote in this piece in a speech delivered before the British House of Commons on November 22, 1641. Edmund Burke, Benjamin Disraeli, and John F. Kennedy are also credited for having repeated what Lucius Cary said on that occasion.

Anthropologist Claude Lévi-Strauss shows that procreationally structured marriage is not necessarily or uniquely religious, but rather should be categorized as a universally practiced "social institution with a biological foundation." See Claude Lévi-Strauss, "Introduction," in *A History of the Family*, by André Burguière (Cambridge, MA: Harvard University Press, 1996), p. 5. Lévi-Strauss also observes that marriage everywhere is structured as "a union, more or less durable, but socially approved, of two individuals of opposite sexes who establish a household and bear and raise children," and he notes that this marital form is found "to be a practically universal phenomenon, present in every type of society." See Claude Lévi-Strauss, *The View from Afar* (New York: Basic Books, 1985), pp. 40-41.

For how abandoning the procreational structure of marriage threatens civilization, see Joseph Daniel Unwin, *Sex and Culture* (London: Oxford University Press, 1937); Joseph Daniel Unwin,

Sexual Regulations and Cultural Behavior: An Address Delivered Before the Medical Section of the British Psychological Society (London: Oxford University Press, 1935); Carle Zimmerman, *Family and Civilization* (Wilmington, DE: ISI Books, 2008); Pitirim Sorokin, *The Crisis of Our Age* (Richmond, VA: Dutton, 1941); Pitirim Sorokin, *Social and Cultural Dynamics*, vol. 4 (Boston, MA: Porter Sargent, 1957); and Daniel Heimbach, "The Future Based on Science," in Daniel Heimbach, *True Sexual Morality* (Wheaton, IL: Crossway, 2004), pp. 345-348.

William C. Duncan, "The State Interest in Marriage," *Ave Maria Law Review*, 2/1 (Spring 2004), pp. 153-182.

Daniel R. Heimbach, "Deconstructing the Family," *Religion and Society Report*, 22/7 (October/November 2005), pp. 1-12.

50

You May Hear Proponents Argue ...

Same-sex marriage should be allowed because it has been commonly practiced throughout history. Marriages uniting homosexual couples are nothing new, so allowing it now is no leap in the dark. Same-sex marriage continues something well-tested and traditionally accepted throughout history. Gay marriages have long been used to integrate homosexuals into the larger culture. The only surprise now is how common same-sex marriages have been in other times and in other cultures. Allowing them is not radical, threatening, or even unusual. Same-sex marriage has been accepted by most societies through history, and ours should be no exception.

You Can *Graciously Refute* This By Saying ...

Proponents of this argument fail because they rely on data that assumes so-called *marriage* has never had anything to do with sex or children. Using this assumption, of course it is easy to find all sorts of practices, customs, and rituals involving members of the same sex. But these unions are all irrelevant to marriage itself, and they say nothing about any society treating partners of the same sex the same as men and women who unite to become fathers and mothers and have children of their own.

The long tradition of marriage has always connected sex with parents having children and has never, at any time, confused marriage with non-sexual friendship or economic partnering. For this reason, there is no tradition—rich or otherwise—on which gay marriage advocates can justify this appeal. There simply is nothing there.

In fact, William Eskridge Jr., the biggest proponent of this argument, wrecks his case by admitting his evidence comes from changing marriage to mean any of several functions—such as emotional support, economic security, division of labor, or helping with children—none of which are sexual. In other words, he uses data from various nonsexual ways of relating as *evidence* to prove that the most important sex-based tradition in history has never had anything to do with sex. This is like saying that because cars carry groceries, grocery bags are cars; or that it proves cars do not need engines, and that engineless cars are common. The fact is that marriage has always been about more than friendship or economic partnering. Pretending otherwise is both unprecedented and a dangerous leap in the dark indeed.

The Truth Is …

Same-sex marriage is wrong because until now no society has ever pretended marriage has nothing to do with sex or children.

References and Further Reading

For examples of advocates using this argument, see "For the First Time Ever? Same-Sex Marriage in History," chapter 1 in *Same-Sex Marriage: Pro and Con: A Reader*, ed. Andrew Sullivan (New York: Random House, 1997), pp. 3-45; William N. Eskridge Jr., "A History of Same-Sex Marriage," chapter 2 in *The Case for Same-Sex Marriage: From Sexual Liberty to Civilized Commitment* (New York: Simon and Schuster, 1996), pp. 15-50; William N. Eskridge Jr., "A History of Same-Sex Marriage," 79/7, *Virginia Law Review* (1993), pp. 1419-1513; Jonathan Rauch, "The Debt to Tradition," chapter 9 in *Gay Marriage: Why It Is Good for Gays, Good for Straights, and Good for America* (New York: Time Books, 2004), pp. 159-171; and John Boswell, *Same-Sex Unions in Pre-Modern Europe*, (New York: Villard Books, 1994).

For how abandoning the procreational structure of marriage threatens civilization, see Joseph Daniel Unwin, *Sex and Culture*

(London: Oxford University Press, 1937); Joseph Daniel Unwin, *Sexual Regulations and Cultural Behavior: An Address Delivered Before the Medical Section of the British Psychological Society* (London: Oxford University Press, 1935); Carle Zimmerman, *Family and Civilization* (Wilmington, DE: ISI Books, 2008); Pitirim Sorokin, *The Crisis of Our Age* (Richmond, VA: Dutton, 1941); Pitirim Sorokin, *Social and Cultural Dynamics*, vol. 4 (Boston, MA: Porter Sargent, 1957); and Daniel Heimbach, "The Future Based on Science," in Daniel Heimbach, *True Sexual Morality* (Wheaton, IL: Crossway, 2004), pp. 345-348.

Carson Holloway, "Same-Sex Marriage and the Death of Tradition," *First Things* (June 10, 2009), accessible at http://www.firstthings.com/onthesquare/2009/06/same-sex-marriage-and-the-deat.

John Witte Jr., "The Tradition of Traditional Marriage," in *Marriage and Same-Sex Unions: A Debate*, ed. Lynn Wardle, Mark Strasser, William Duncan, and David Coolidge (Westport, CT: Praeger, 2003), pp. 47-59.

Peter Lubin and Dwight Duncan, "Follow the Footnote or the Advocate as Historian of Same-Sex Marriage," *Catholic University Law Review*, 47 (Summer 1998), pp. 1271-1324.

Nelson Lund, "The Case Against Boies-Olson: Wrong on the Law, and on Civilization," *National Review Online* (September 24, 2009), accessible at http://article.nationalreview.com/?q=MmI0NWU2ZTU4ZGJ1NDUwYWZjNzI4MzFmZjYwMDA1MGY=.

Joseph Farah, "Same-Sex Marriage Through History," *Human Events* (June 18, 2008), accessible at http://www.humanevents.com/article.php?id=27076.

Josephine Ross, "Sex, Marriage and History: Analyzing the Continued Resistance to Same-Sex Marriage," *Southern Methodist University Law Review*, 55 (2002), pp. 1657-1681.

51

You May Hear Proponents Argue ...

Same-sex marriage should be allowed because it represents one more small step in the ever-changing evolution of marriage. Changing marriage for the better is not new. Marriage is not something static or fixed but has always been evolving toward greater freedom and equality. Over the years, we have made divorce easier, prohibited polygamy, eliminated parental control over mate selection, stopped requiring dowries, criminalized marital rape, and legalized interracial marriage. After all this, it makes no sense to stop now by saying marriage could be improved for the sake of everyone except homosexuals, who alone must accept what tradition dictates.

You Can *Graciously Refute* This By Saying ...

Although marriage has changed in many ways, it cannot be changed in any way at all. Not all marriage systems have looked like that found in the United States, but until the present homosexual movement, they have all been about bridging the male-female divide, encouraging procreation, and compelling people to take responsibility for the future. No society until now has ever redefined marriage so completely as to make it just a way for approving private appetites unrelated to having and raising children.

All social traditions are formed to safeguard realities, and while tradition must defer to morality, no tradition should be abandoned without considering the reality it was formed to safeguard. The reality proponents of this argument overlook is that successful cultures affirm marriage because societies need babies and cannot survive otherwise. The only valid *public* reason for supporting marriage is the stake all societies have in sustaining the one institution universally structured to get men and women to have and raise their own children. It does not now, and never has had, anything to do with affirming *private* feelings.

Because same-sex marriage attacks the structure of marriage itself, it does not represent just the next step in the *evolution* of marriage. All other variations of marriage have affirmed the value of maintaining the procreational structure of the institution, but proponents of same-sex marriage seek to dismantle it completely. It is terribly wrong and irresponsible to take the one institution all societies have affirmed as being essential for giving children mothers and fathers and for ensuring social survival and to dismantle its structure in order to affirm how some adults like to have sex.

The Truth Is …

Same-sex marriage is wrong because alterations in marriage have never before now sought to dismantle its procreational structure.

References and Further Reading

For examples of advocates using this argument, see Jonathan Rauch, *Gay Marriage: Why It Is Good for Gays, Good for Straights, and Good for America* (New York: Times Books, 2004), pp. 167-168; John Borneman and Laurie Hart, "An Elastic Institution," *Washington Post* (April 14, 2004), accessible at http://www. aaanet.org/ress/min_borneman_4-15-04.htm; and Theodore B. Olson, "The Conservative Case for Gay Marriage: Why Same-Sex Marriage Is an American Value," *Newsweek* (January 18, 2010), pp. 48-54.

For how abandoning the procreational structure of marriage threatens civilization, see Joseph Daniel Unwin, *Sex and Culture* (London: Oxford University Press, 1937); Joseph Daniel Unwin,

Sexual Regulations and Cultural Behavior: An Address Delivered Before the Medical Section of the British Psychological Society (London: Oxford University Press, 1935); Carle Zimmerman, *Family and Civilization* (Wilmington, DE: ISI Books, 2008); Pitirim Sorokin, *The Crisis of Our Age* (Richmond, VA: Dutton, 1941); Pitirim Sorokin, *Social and Cultural Dynamics*, vol. 4 (Boston, MA: Porter Sargent, 1957); and Daniel Heimbach, "The Future Based on Science," in Daniel Heimbach, *True Sexual Morality* (Wheaton, IL: Crossway, 2004), pp. 345-348.

John Witte Jr., "The Tradition of Traditional Marriage," in *Marriage and Same-Sex Unions: A Debate*, ed. Lynn Wardle, Mark Strasser, William Duncan, and David Coolidge (Westport, CT: Praeger, 2003), pp. 47-59.

Maggie Gallagher, "What Marriage Is For: Children Need Mothers and Fathers," *Weekly Standard* (August 4/August 11, 2003), pp. 22-25.

Maggie Gallagher, "Normal Marriage: Two Views," in *Marriage and Same-Sex Unions: A Debate*, ed. Lynn Wardle, Mark Strasser, William Duncan, and David Coolidge (Westport, CT: Praeger, 2003), pp. 13-24.

Anthropologist Claude Lévi-Strauss shows that procreationally structured marriage is not necessarily or uniquely religious, but rather should be categorized as a universally practiced "social institution with a biological foundation." See Claude Lévi-Strauss, "Introduction," in *A History of the Family*, by André Burguière (Cambridge, MA: Harvard University Press, 1996), p. 5. Lévi-Strauss also observes that marriage everywhere is structured as "a union, more or less durable, but socially approved, of two individuals of opposite sexes who establish a household and bear and raise children," and he notes that this marital form is found "to be a practically universal phenomenon, present in every type of society." See Claude Lévi-Strauss, *The View from Afar* (New York: Basic Books, 1985), pp. 40-41.

Nelson Lund, "The Case Against Boies-Olson: Wrong on the Law, and on Civilization," *National Review Online* (September 24, 2009), accessible at http://article.nationalreview.com/?q=MmI 0NWU2ZTU4ZGJ1NDUwYWZjNzI4MzFmZjYwMDA1MGY=.

52

You May Hear Proponents Argue ...

Same-sex marriage should be allowed because it moves society in a direction that is profoundly traditional and conservative. Legalizing same-sex marriage is a traditional and conservative step in the best sense of the word. It is not a leap in the dark at great social risk; in fact, homosexual marriages already exist in contemporary American society and only lack public recognition and support. A law institutionalizing same-sex marriage will initiate nothing new but will only add public recognition, support, and accountability to a healthy trend. Same-sex marriage is not a radical step but a profoundly humanizing and traditional one.

You Can *Graciously Refute* This By Saying ...

Proponents of this argument are making a claim similar to stating that poison would be safe to drink if people called it tea. Their logic only *appears* to make sense after they redefine marriage in a radically nontraditional way. The world has never seen a phenomenon like the contemporary same-sex marriage movement. While there have been various pockets of homosexual practice in various cultures, none of these has had the constellation of features and persistent self-assertion that this movement presents.

Proponents of the gay agenda have invented a whole new relational form and called it *marriage*, and they pretend people's standards and expectations of traditionally defined heterosexual marriage will come along for the ride. But simply using the same term will never make that happen. Contrary to what those who promote this argument claim, same-sex marriage *is* a radical attack on the fundamental structure of marriage. It will sever marriage from the unique dynamics of heterosexuality, deconstruct traditional marriage by discarding its procreational structure, and replace what society supports as marriage with a series of infinitely flexible contracts shaped only by personal appetites.

Marriage involves social approval of committed relationships, but not just *any* form of relationship. The idea that marriage law functions to bestow approval on undefined private appetites changes marriage into something radically different and contrary to universal marriage tradition. Throughout history, marriage has always united a man with a woman, and we should not easily set aside the longstanding structure of such a critically important social institution.

The Truth Is ...

Same-sex marriage is wrong because it radically attacks the longstanding structure of the well-proven social institution of marriage.

References and Further Reading

Theodore Olson and David Boies used this argument to try to persuade a federal court to invalidate California's Proposition 8, which banned same-sex marriage in the state. See Theodore B. Olson, "The Conservative Case for Gay Marriage: Why Same-Sex Marriage Is an American Value," *Newsweek* (January 18, 2010), pp. 48-54.

Carson Holloway, "Same-Sex Marriage and the Death of Tradition," *First Things* (June 10, 2009), accessible at http://www.firstthings.com/onthesquare/2009/06/same-sex-marriage-and-the-deat.

For how abandoning the procreational structure of marriage threatens civilization, see Joseph Daniel Unwin, *Sex and Culture* (London: Oxford University Press, 1937); Joseph Daniel Unwin, *Sexual Regulations and Cultural Behavior: An Address Delivered Before the Medical Section of the British Psychological Society* (London: Oxford University Press, 1935); Carle Zimmerman,

Family and Civilization (Wilmington, DE: ISI Books, 2008); Pitirim Sorokin, *The Crisis of Our Age* (Richmond, VA: Dutton, 1941); and Daniel Heimbach, "The Future Based on Science," in Daniel Heimbach, *True Sexual Morality* (Wheaton, IL: Crossway, 2004), pp. 345-348.

Stanley Kurtz, "The End of Marriage in Scandinavia: The 'Conservative Case' for Same-Sex Marriage Collapses," *Weekly Standard* (February 2, 2004), pp. 26-33.

Stanley Kurtz, "Point of No Return: Marriage Needs a Man and a Woman, and an Amendment," *National Review Online* (August 3, 2001).

Maggie Gallagher, "Normal Marriage: Two Views," in *Marriage and Same-Sex Unions: A Debate*, ed. Lynn Wardle, Mark Strasser, William Duncan, and David Coolidge (Westport, CT: Praeger, 2003), pp. 13-24.

Maggie Gallagher, "The Case Against Same-Sex Marriage," chapter 3 in *Debating Same-Sex Marriage* (New York: Oxford University Press, 2012), pp. 91-178.

Sherif Girgis, Ryan T. Anderson, and Robert P. George, "Marriage: Merely a Social Construct?" *Public Discourse: Ethics, Law and the Common Good* (December 29, 2010), accessible at http://www.thepublicdiscourse.com.

Nelson Lund, "The Case Against Boies-Olson: Wrong on the Law, and on Civilization," *National Review Online* (September 24, 2009), accessible at http://article.nationalreview.com/?q=MmI0NWU2ZTU4ZGJ1NDUwYWZjNzI4MzFmZjYwMDA1MGY=.

Jeffrey Lord, "A Rebuttal to Theodore Olson," *American Spectator* (January 19, 2010), accessible at http://spectator.org/archives/2010/01/19/a-rebuttal-to-theodore-olson.

53

You May Hear Proponents Argue ...

Same-sex marriage should be allowed because it follows the same social model as traditional marriage. There is nothing inconsistent with celebrating same-sex marriage along with traditional marriage. Both should be affirmed because same-sex marriage is, in fact, modeled after traditional marriage. Same-sex marriage merely emulates traditional marriage, so traditionalists should rejoice and not fear allowing homosexuals to marry. Imitation is the highest form of praise, and marriage traditionalists should be honored by the fact that homosexuals now want to follow their good example.

You Can *Graciously Refute* This By Saying ...

Proponents of this argument fail to realize that there are two different views of marriage at stake in the same-sex marriage debate. One side is fighting to preserve the *traditional* procreational structure of marriage as an enduring social institution, while the other side is fighting to *deconstruct* marriage by denying it has any fixed structure at all. Same-sex marriage proponents are not trying to *imitate* traditional marriage but change it into something radically new and different.

In making this argument, these individuals try to get people to think that gays will somehow act like heterosexuals, even if marriage is left with no structure. But because one view destroys the other, that cannot happen. With traditional marriage, societies reward couples for embracing procreatively structured relationships because they know this will ensure stability and intergenerational survival. However, by legalizing same-sex marriage, a society *deconstructs* marriage by changing it into a merely private and emotional relationship formed by couples for their own reasons. This leaves marriage with no particular structure and no connection to the way in which people have sex to bear and raise children.

Proponents of this deconstructionist view change marriage into something it never has been at the cost of abandoning public interest in supporting marriage as a procreationally structured institution that is essential for assuring social stability and intergenerational survival. In truth, public interest in favoring marriage as a social institution never has had anything to do with affirming personal feelings. Same-sex marriage will not *imitate* procreationally structured *traditional* marriage at all, and allowing it will only *deconstruct* the public meaning of marriage for everyone.

The Truth Is ...

Same-sex marriage is wrong because it will destroy traditional marriage by deconstructing its public meaning for everyone.

References and Further Reading

Andrew Sullivan uses this argument to claim that "it is perfectly possible to combine a celebration of the traditional family with the celebration of a stable homosexual relationship," because gay marriage is, after all, "modeled on the other." For those who accept that idea, Sullivan goes one step farther to suggest that same-sex marriage "might even serve to buttress the ethic of heterosexual marriage by showing how even those excluded from it can wish to model themselves on its shape and structure." See Andrew Sullivan, *Virtually Normal* (New York: Random House, 1995), p. 112.

For how abandoning the procreational structure of marriage threatens civilization, see Joseph Daniel Unwin, *Sex and Culture* (London: Oxford University Press, 1937); Joseph Daniel Unwin, *Sexual Regulations and Cultural Behavior: An Address Delivered Before the Medical Section of the British Psychological Society*

(London: Oxford University Press, 1935); Carle Zimmerman, *Family and Civilization* (Wilmington, DE: ISI Books, 2008); Pitirim Sorokin, *The Crisis of Our Age* (Richmond, VA: Dutton, 1941); Pitirim Sorokin, *Social and Cultural Dynamics*, vol. 4 (Boston, MA: Porter Sargent, 1957); and Daniel Heimbach, "The Future Based on Science," in Daniel Heimbach, *True Sexual Morality* (Wheaton, IL: Crossway, 2004), pp. 345-348.

Maggie Gallagher, "Normal Marriage: Two Views," in *Marriage and Same-Sex Unions: A Debate*, ed. Lynn Wardle, Mark Strasser, William Duncan, and David Coolidge (Westport, CT: Praeger, 2003), pp. 13-24.

William C. Duncan, "The State Interest in Marriage," *Ave Maria Law Review*, 2/1 (Spring 2004), pp. 153-182.

Stanley Kurtz, "Point of No Return: Marriage Needs a Man and a Woman, and an Amendment," *National Review Online* (August 3, 2001).

Daniel R. Heimbach, "Deconstructing the Family," *Religion and Society Report*, 22/7 (October/November 2005), pp. 1-12.

Nelson Lund, "The Case Against Boies-Olson: Wrong on the Law, and on Civilization," *National Review Online* (September 24, 2009), accessible at http://article.nationalreview.com/?q=MmI 0NWU2ZTU4ZGJ1NDUwYWZjNzI4MzFmZjYwMDA1MGY=.

Louis P. Sheldon, "The Destruction of Marriage Precedes the Death of a Culture," *Traditional Values Coalition Special Report* (Anaheim, CA: Traditional Values Coalition Education and Legal Institute), accessible at http://www.traditionalvalues.org/ pdf_files/deathofmarriage.pdf.

54

You May Hear Proponents Argue ...

Same-sex marriage should be allowed because it will abolish traditional marriage and radically change civilization as we know it. Human culture has been institutionally homophobic for millennia. It is time people changed this by removing the traditional gender-based structure of marriage. Traditional marriage is a bad and oppressive institution that must be replaced with something new. Gay marriage will do this by removing the gender-based structure of socially recognized marriage, which will transform marriage into a *pure relationship* with no structural limits. Once this is in place, marriage can include and affirm whatever sort of relationship satisfies those involved.

You Can *Graciously Refute* This By Saying ...

Proponents of this argument seek to radically change the centerpiece of civilized order and cease all public favor and support for the only institution ever structured to bridge the male-female divide and assure that children have mothers and fathers. They do all this merely to pretend there is no significant reason to treat procreationally structured relationships any differently than other sorts of associations. Nowhere do they put this effort put more starkly than in this argument. As such, they should be commended for their clarity and full disclosure.

Like a poker player laying his hand on the table, those who make this argument are being brutally honest about the implications same-sex marriage will cause to the bottom line. Thomas Stoddard, a significant early leader of the same-sex marriage movement in the United States, employed this argument openly. He saw marriage as "the centerpiece of our entire social structure," and he realized that same-sex marriage would transform traditional marriage into something new by removing "the traditional gender requirements of marriage" for everyone.

Only when the public meaning of marriage has been redefined to have no gender base will society treat heterosexuals and homosexuals as exactly the same. That is true enough. The trouble is that redefining marriage in this way comes at the terrible cost of deconstructing, and thus losing, what Stoddard called "the centerpiece of our entire social structure." It annihilates the very entity without which no society can survive.

The Truth Is ...

Same-sex marriage is wrong because it removes structure from the institution that is at the very center of social order.

References and Further Reading

For Stoddard's argument, see Thomas B. Stoddard, "Why Gay People Should Seek the Right to Marry," chapter 35 in *Families in the US: Kinship and Domestic Politics*, ed. Karen V. Hansen (Philadelphia, PA: Temple University Press, 1998).

Others making this argument include Richard Mohr, *A More Perfect Union* (Boston, MA: Beacon, 1994); Gretchen Stiers, *From This Day Forward: Commitment, Marriage, and Family in Lesbian and Gay Relationships* (New York: St. Martin's Press, 1999); Michelangelo Signorile, "Bridal Wave," *Out* (December/January 1994); "Sociologist Says Gay Marriage Does Threaten Established Order and That's Good," *Ascribe Law News Service* (November 16, 2003); and Margaret Gullette, "The New Case for Marriage," *American Prospect* (March 1, 2004).

For how abandoning the procreational structure of marriage threatens civilization, see Joseph Daniel Unwin, *Sex and Culture* (London: Oxford University Press, 1937); Joseph Daniel Unwin,

Sexual Regulations and Cultural Behavior: An Address Delivered Before the Medical Section of the British Psychological Society (London: Oxford University Press, 1935); Carle Zimmerman, *Family and Civilization* (Wilmington, DE: ISI Books, 2008); Pitirim Sorokin, *The Crisis of Our Age* (Richmond, VA: Dutton, 1941); Pitirim Sorokin, *Social and Cultural Dynamics*, vol. 4 (Boston, MA: Porter Sargent, 1957); and Daniel Heimbach, "The Future Based on Science," in Daniel Heimbach, *True Sexual Morality* (Wheaton, IL: Crossway, 2004), pp. 345-348. For related discussion, see Franklin E. Kameny, "Deconstructing the Traditional Family," *The World and I* (October 1993), pp. 383-395; Daniel R. Heimbach, "Deconstructing the Family," *Religion and Society Report*, 22/7 (October/November 2005), pp. 1-12; and Stanley Kurtz, "Point of No Return: Marriage Needs a Man and a Woman, and an Amendment," *National Review Online* (August 3, 2001).

Michael Gaynor notes that while history shows some of the legal incidentals of marriage have changed, the fundamental nature and procreational structure of the institution has remained essentially unchanged throughout human history. See Michael Gaynor, "Lambda Legal: Please Say Marriage for 'Same-Sex Partners,' NOT 'Same-Sex Marriage,'" *RenewAmerica* (March 9, 2011), accessible at http://www.renewamerican.com/columns/gaynor/110309. Gaynor says, "History shows some of the legal incidents of marriage have changed, [but] not the fundamental nature of marriage."

William C. Duncan, "The State Interest in Marriage," *Ave Maria Law Review*, 2/1 (Spring 2004), pp. 153-182.

Daniel R. Heimbach, "Deconstructing the Family," *Religion and Society Report*, 22/7 (October/November 2005), pp. 1-12.

Arguments 55 – 65

Gracious Answers to Arguments Regarding Constitutional Law

*The freedom to
marry in our Constitution
comes from the even more basic
freedom to procreate without government
interference. This means that
the constitutional right to
marry only applies to
uniting a man with a
woman.*

REGARDING CONSTITUTIONAL LAW

(Arguments 55–65)

55

You May Hear Proponents Argue ...

SAME-SEX MARRIAGE SHOULD be allowed because the U.S. Constitution guarantees people the right to privacy. The U.S. Supreme Court has found same-sex marriage to be within the fundamental right to privacy as guaranteed by the Fourteenth Amendment of the Constitution. Given this, any law that refuses to allow or recognize same-sex marriage violates the Constitution by denying the right that same-sex couples have to privacy. The Constitution prohibits government interference in private matters, and this right extends to same-sex couples who desire to marry.

You Can *Graciously Refute* This By Saying ...

Proponents of this argument confuse private decisions to marry with public purposes that justify having laws to protect marriage. They also confuse private reasons that motivate people to get married with what makes marriage a public institution. The U.S. Supreme Court has found that marriage is part of the fundamental right to privacy guaranteed by the Fourteenth Amendment, but the Court has never even hinted that this could affect the legal status of same-sex unions.

In *Skinner v. Oklahoma* (1942), the Court held that an individual's right to marry is guaranteed by the right to privacy. However, the Court found that this right evolved out of the more basic right people have to procreate without government interference, which makes marriage something that can only apply to procreationally structured unions that join a man with a woman. In addition, in *Zablocki v. Redhail* (1978), the Court declared once more that the right to marry as protected by the Constitution depends entirely on the prior right to procreate. Therefore, the Court's finding again only related to uniting men with women.

The claim same-sex couples now raise through this argument is that the same constitutional right to marry applies to them. However, this is not the case, as the constitutional right to marry the Court afforded comes from the more basic right to procreate. Furthermore, because there is no such thing as a constitutional right to redefine what marriage means, the gay movement has no legitimate basis for finding a right for same-sex marriage in the Constitution, and there is nothing unconstitutional about leaving marriage laws as they are. Should a constitutional right to same-sex marriage be declared, it will not protect something already in the Constitution but will corrupt constitutional law by redefining what it protects.

The Truth Is ...

Same-sex marriage is wrong because there is no right to redefine marriage within the constitutional right to privacy.

References and Further Reading

For examples of advocates using this argument, see Theodore B. Olson, "The Conservative Case for Gay Marriage: Why Same-Sex Marriage Is an American Value," *Newsweek* (January 18, 2010), pp. 48-54; and Eugene Volokh, "Same-Sex Marriage and Slippery Slopes," *Hofstra Law Review*, 33/3 (Spring 2005), pp. 1155-1201.

Skinner v. Oklahoma, 316 U.S. 535 (1942).

Zablocki v. Redhail, 434 U.S. 374 (1978).

The Hawaiian Supreme Court made a good refutation of this claim in *Baehr v. Lewin*, 74 Hawaii 645, 852 P.2d 44 (1993).

William C. Duncan, "The State Interest in Marriage," *Ave Maria Law Review*, 2/1 (Spring 2004), pp. 153-182.

Nelson Lund, "The Case Against Boies-Olson: Wrong on the Law, and on Civilization," *National Review Online* (September 24, 2009), accessible at http://article.nationalreview.com/?q=MmI 0NWU2ZTU4ZGJ1NDUwYWZjNzI4MzFmZjYwMDA1MGY=.

Jeffrey Lord, "A Rebuttal to Theodore Olson," *American Spectator* (January 19, 2010), accessible at http://spectator.org/ archives/2010/01/19/a-rebuttal-to-theodore-olson.

Maggie Gallagher, "(How) Will Gay Marriage Weaken Marriage as a Social Institution," *University of Saint Thomas Law Journal*, 2/1 (Fall 2004), pp. 33-70.

Robert P. George, Sherif Girgis, and Ryan T. Anderson, "Brief of *Amici Curiae* in Support of Reversal and the Intervening Defendants-Appellants," *Appeal from the United States District Court for the Northern District of California* (September 24, 2010), regarding *Perry v. Schwarzenegger*, Civil Case No. 09-CV-2292 VRW.

Patrick Lee, Robert P. George, and Gerard V. Bradley, "Marriage and Procreation: The Intrinsic Connection," *Public Discourse:*

Ethics, Law and the Common Good (March 28, 2011), accessible at http://www.thepublicdiscourse.com.

Patrick Lee, Robert P. George, and Gerard V. Bradley, "Marriage and Procreation: The Intrinsic Connection," *Public Discourse: Ethics, Law and the Common Good* (March 28, 2011), accessible at http://www.thepublicdiscourse.com.

Glenn T. Stanton, "How Good Is Goodridge? An Analysis of *Goodridge v. Department of Public Health*," in *Same-Sex Marriage: The Moral and Legal Debate*, ed. Robert M. Baird and Stuart E. Rosenbaum (New York: Prometheus Books, 2004), pp. 69-79.

56

You May Hear Proponents Argue …

Same-sex marriage should be allowed because family formation is a right protected by the Constitution. The right to form families is a matter of sexual freedom that the Supreme Court has already recognized as falling under the constitutional right to privacy. The way in which people form families has changed, and now it makes sense to give the protection of marriage to couples who are forming families—regardless of gender combination. Because American law no longer polices family structure, there is no reason for civil law to interfere with the gender combination of couples who seek marriage licenses to strengthen formation of new family units.

You Can *Graciously Refute* This By Saying …

Proponents of this argument (1) confuse individual family behaviors (which are private) with how the institution of marriage is structured in relation to family formation (which is public), (2) reverse the relationship between marriage and family formation by wrongly assuming family formation justifies marriage, and (3) confuse the right to marry with an alleged right to redefine marriage.

The constitutional right to marry within the right of privacy arises out of a more basic right to procreate. In fact, the constitutional right people have to form a family follows *from*—but does not *precede*—the right to marry. Thus, there is nothing in the rights people have to marry or form a family that provides proponents of this argument with any basis for claiming a constitutional right to change the structure of marriage to something it never has been. Rather, the Constitution recognizes a legitimate state interest in preserving the procreational structure of marriage, which is to ensure the survival of society by getting parents to cooperate in raising their biological children.

Because (1) the constitutional right to marry comes from the constitutional right to procreate, (2) the constitutional right to form a family arises out of the constitutional right to marry, and (3) the public interest in justifying marriage law is based on supporting the procreational structure of family formation, there is nothing in the constitutional right to privacy that justifies recognizing new rights to reconceive and redefine the meaning of marriage or family in ways that render the procreational structure of these institutions irrelevant to what connects them together.

The Truth Is ...

Same-sex marriage is wrong because there is no constitutional basis for claiming a constitutional right to pursue new family forms.

References and Further Reading

For examples of advocates using this argument, see Donald J. Cantor, "The Evolution of State Law Toward Sexual Privacy" in *Same-Sex Marriage: The Legal and Psychological Evolution in America*, by Donald J. Cantor, Elizabeth Cantor, James C. Black, and Campbell D. Barrett (Middleton, CT: Wesleyan University Press, 2006), pp. 11-21; and Eugene Volokh, "Same-Sex Marriage and Slippery Slopes," *Hofstra Law Review*, 33/3 (Spring 2005), pp. 1155-1201.

Theodore Olson and David Boies also used this argument to try to persuade a federal court to invalidate California's Proposition 8, which banned same-sex marriage in the state. See Theodore B. Olson, "The Conservative Case for Gay Marriage: Why Same-Sex Marriage Is an American Value," *Newsweek* (January 18, 2010), pp. 48-54.

Martha B. Sosman, Justice of the Massachusetts Supreme Judicial Court, Dissent to *Goodridge v. Massachusetts*, 798 N.E. 2d 941 (Massachusetts 2003).

Sandra Day O'Connor, concurring with *Lawrence v. Texas* (02-102) 539 U.S. 558 (2003), p. 7.

William C. Duncan, "The State Interest in Marriage," *Ave Maria Law Review,* 2/1 (Spring 2004), pp. 153-182.

Nelson Lund, "The Case Against Boies-Olson: Wrong on the Law, and on Civilization," *National Review Online* (September 24, 2009), accessible at http://article.nationalreview.com/?q=MmI0NWU2ZTU4ZGJ1NDUwYWZjNzI4MzFmZjYwMDA1MGY=.

Jeffrey Lord, "A Rebuttal to Theodore Olson," *American Spectator* (January 19, 2010), accessible at http://spectator.org/archives/2010/01/19/a-rebuttal-to-theodore-olson.

Maggie Gallagher, "(How) Will Gay Marriage Weaken Marriage as a Social Institution: A Reply to Andrew Koppelman," *University of Saint Thomas Law Journal,* 2/1 (Fall 2004), pp. 33-70.

Daniel R. Heimbach, "Deconstructing the Family," *Religion and Society Report,* 22/7 (October/November 2005), pp. 1-12.

Sherif Girgis, Robert P. George, and Ryan T. Anderson, "What Is Marriage?" *Harvard Journal of Law and Public Policy*, 34/1 (Winter 2011), pp. 245-287.

Robert P. George, Ryan T. Anderson, and Sherif Girgis, "The Argument Against Gay Marriage: And Why It Doesn't Fail," *Public Discourse: Ethics, Law and the Common Good* (December 17, 2010), accessible at http://www.thepublicdiscourse.com.

57

You May Hear Proponents Argue ...

Same-sex marriage should be allowed because the morality of marriage is a private matter that should have no bearing on civil law. The United States consists of many moral communities, some of which believe homosexual relations are morally wrong and some of which do not. However, civil law should be morally neutral. Marriage laws govern the sphere of life about which people hold their strongest moral opinions, and for the last four decades the American legal system has moved toward leaving sex between consenting adults as free of interference as possible. It is time to apply this to marriage by allowing all couples to marry regardless of conflicting moral views.

You Can *Graciously Refute* This By Saying ...

Proponents of this argument confuse subjectivity with objectivity in relation to morality and law. They claim that something subjective (homosexual feelings) must be treated objectively (recognized by marriage law). They do so by falsely alleging that something objective (marriage as a legal institution) is merely subjective (just private moral feelings). There are only two ways they can be consistent on this subject: (1) leave marriage law as it is, because it is already well justified in ways that have nothing to do with private feelings; or (2) get rid of marriage law for all, because it only expresses private feelings. There is no neutral ground between these positions, which means their argument really makes sense for no one.

Good law is not subjective, and it is wrong to say morality is simply a matter of private feelings, personal opinion, or individual satisfaction. Contending that morality has no bearing on the law is absurd. It is the fundamental duty of lawmakers to decide what laws are needed to correct wrong or promote good. The legitimate interest the public has in justifying laws that protect the procreational structure of marriage has nothing to do with expressing private feelings or opinions but with the objectively defined and commonly relevant public good of ensuring social stability and survival. It is foolish to pretend marriage law should be morally neutral or blind. Justice is a matter of morality, for it defines public good served by law. Pretending marriage law should be non-moral or morally irrelevant will produce laws that are foolish and unjust as far as they concern the public interest and common good.

The Truth Is ...

Same-sex marriage is wrong because public law on marriage cannot be morally neutral without being publicly foolish and unjust.

References and Further Reading

For examples of advocates using this argument, see Martha Ertman, "Marriage as a Trade: Bridging the Private/Private Distinction," 36, *Harvard Civil Rights and Civil Liberties Law Review* (2001), pp. 79, 85-98; Chai R. Feldblum, "Moral Conflict and Liberty; Gay Rights and Religion," *Brooklyn Law Review*, 72/1 (2006), pp. 61-123; and Eugene Volokh, "Same-Sex Marriage and Slippery Slopes," *Hofstra Law Review*, 33 (Spring 2005), pp. 1155-1201.

Theodore Olson and David Boies also used this argument to try to persuade a federal court to invalidate California's Proposition 8, which banned same-sex marriage in the state. See Theodore B. Olson, "The Conservative Case for Gay Marriage: Why Same-Sex Marriage Is an American Value," *Newsweek* (January 18, 2010), pp. 48-54.

Homosexual activist Michelangelo Signorile has stated that the goal of legalizing same-sex marriage is to abolish marriage as a social institution. He explains that what homosexuals must do is "fight for same-sex marriage and its benefits and then, once granted, redefine the institution of marriage completely." He states that the homosexuals' strategy is "to demand the right to marry not as a way of adhering to society's moral codes but rather to debunk America and radically alter an archaic institution." See Michelangelo Signorile, "Bridal Wave," *Out* (December/January 1994), p. 161.

In *Maynard v. Hill*, 125 U.S. 190 (1888), the U.S. Supreme Court recognized that the public legal understanding of marriage springs from the fundamental morality of a people, which is to say that constitutionally protected marriage law is not moral neutrality. In that case, the court described marriage as "creating the most important relation in life" and as "having more to do with the morals and civilization of a people than any other institution."

William C. Duncan, "The State Interest in Marriage," *Ave Maria Law Review,* 2/1 (Spring 2004), pp. 153-182.

Nelson Lund, "The Case Against Boies-Olson: Wrong on the Law, and on Civilization," *National Review Online* (September 24, 2009), accessible at http://article.nationalreview.com/?q=MmI 0NWU2ZTU4ZGJ1NDUwYWZjNzI4MzFmZjYwMDA1MGY=.

Jeffrey Lord, "A Rebuttal to Theodore Olson," *American Spectator* (January 19, 2010), accessible at http://spectator.org/ archives/2010/01/19/a-rebuttal-to-theodore-olson.

Maggie Gallagher, "(How) Will Gay Marriage Weaken Marriage as a Social Institution: A Reply to Andrew Koppelman," *University of Saint Thomas Law Journal,* 2/1 (Fall 2004), pp. 33-70.

Daniel R. Heimbach, "Deconstructing the Family," *Religion and Society Report,* 22/7 (October/November 2005), pp. 1-12.

58

You May Hear Proponents Argue …

Same-sex marriage should be allowed because there is no public basis for using the power of civil law to limit marriage to heterosexuals. Same-sex and opposite-sex relationships are identical with respect to the purpose of civil marriage. The public interest in marriage only concerns an emotional and financial bond that unites people—not one that is intrinsically procreative. The right to privacy as protected by the Constitution prohibits state intervention in the realm of individuals selecting a marriage partner. Thus, there is no compelling state purpose, independent of invidious discrimination, to justify continuing to deny civil marriage to same-sex couples.

You Can *Graciously Refute* This By Saying …

Laws prohibiting same-sex couples to marry do prevent those couples from marrying only because they are members of the same sex. However, that is irrelevant to the constitutional right of privacy in relation to civil marriage. In truth, proponents of this argument are wrong for at least three reasons.

First, the issue being contested is not a matter of *privacy* but one that concerns the structure of marriage as a *public* institution. It has nothing at all to do with private feelings, desires, or choices.

Second, same-sex couples are not in the same relational category as opposite-sex couples when it comes to the pubic interest in favoring and supporting marriage as a social institution. What justifies the public interest in marriage is the need all societies have to encourage men and women to have and raise children, which in turn is driven by the social interest in assuring intergenerational survival.

Third, as far as the Constitution is concerned, the state is warranted in protecting the procreational structure of civil marriage in order to serve the greatest public interest possible—to assure the survival of society. Thus, regardless of how it affects individual freedom, there is no greater possible justification than in keeping the laws regarding marriage the way we have them now.

Gays have the same freedom as all Americans to pursue personal goals in line with the common good. What gays do not have—and what no one else does either—is the right to change the institutional structure of marriage in ways that threaten the common good of maintaining social stability and assuring intergenerational survival.

The Truth Is …

Same-sex marriage is wrong because there is no greater public interest than preserving the procreational structure of marriage.

References and Further Reading

For examples of advocates using this argument, see justice Kennedy writing for the majority in *United States v. Windsor*, 570 U.S. ___ (2013); justices Marshall and Greaney writing for the majority in *Goodridge v. Massachusetts*, 798 N.E. 2d 941 (Massachusetts 2003); and Chai R. Feldblum, "Moral Conflict and Liberty; Gay Rights and Religion," *Brooklyn Law Review*, 72/1 (2006), pp. 61-123.

Theodore Olson and David Boies also used this argument to try to persuade a federal court to invalidate California's Proposition 8, which banned same-sex marriage in the state. See Theodore B. Olson, "The Conservative Case for Gay Marriage: Why Same-Sex Marriage Is an American Value," *Newsweek* (January 18, 2010), pp. 48-54.

Justice Francis Spina refuted this argument in his dissent to *Goodridge v. Massachusetts*, 798 N.E. 2d 941 (Massachusetts 2003).

William C. Duncan, "The State Interest in Marriage," *Ave Maria Law Review*, 2/1 (Spring 2004), pp. 153-182.

Nelson Lund, "The Case Against Boies-Olson: Wrong on the Law, and on Civilization," *National Review Online* (September 24, 2009), accessible at http://article.nationalreview.com/?q=MmI 0NWU2ZTU4ZGJ1NDUwYWZjNzI4MzFmZjYwMDA1MGY=.

Jeffrey Lord, "A Rebuttal to Theodore Olson," *American Spectator* (January 19, 2010), accessible at http://spectator.org/ archives/2010/01/19/a-rebuttal-to-theodore-olson.

Maggie Gallagher, "(How) Will Gay Marriage Weaken Marriage as a Social Institution: A Reply to Andrew Koppelman," *University of Saint Thomas Law Journal*, 2/1 (Fall 2004), pp. 33-70.

Daniel R. Heimbach, "Deconstructing the Family," *Religion and Society Report*, 22/7 (October/November 2005), pp. 1-12; and Daniel Heimbach, "The Future Based on Science," in Daniel Heimbach, *True Sexual Morality* (Wheaton, IL: Crossway, 2004), pp. 345-348.

For how abandoning the procreational structure of marriage threatens civilization, see Joseph Daniel Unwin, *Sex and Culture* (London: Oxford University Press, 1937); Joseph Daniel Unwin, *Sexual Regulations and Cultural Behavior: An Address Delivered Before the Medical Section of the British Psychological Society* (London: Oxford University Press, 1935); Carle Zimmerman, *Family and Civilization* (Wilmington, DE: ISI Books, 2008); Pitirim Sorokin, *The Crisis of Our Age* (Richmond, VA: Dutton, 1941); Pitirim Sorokin, *Social and Cultural Dynamics*, vol. 4 (Boston, MA: Porter Sargent, 1957); Daniel R. Heimbach, "Deconstructing the Family," *Religion and Society Report* 22/7 (October/November 2005), pp. 1-12; and Daniel Heimbach, "The Future Based on Science," in Daniel Heimbach, *True Sexual Morality* (Wheaton, IL: Crossway, 2004), pp. 345-348.

In *Baehr v. Lewin*, 74 Hawaii 645, 852 P.2d 44 (1993), the Hawaiian Supreme Court explained refutation of a constitutional right to same-sex marriage was implicit in the constitutional right to privacy.

59

You May Hear Proponents Argue ...

Same-sex marriage should be allowed because the only legitimate reason for the Constitution to protect marriage is to support social relationships. The public contract of marriage is a legally recognized bond between people who desire to make a life-long commitment to one another, and same-sex couples are identical to opposite-sex couples in this respect. The Constitution entitles gay partners to marry under the inalienable right to pursue happiness and the duty of government to provide for the general welfare. Limiting marriage to only opposite-sex couples violates this entitlement by not serving the one constitutional purpose for supporting civil marriage.

You Can *Graciously Refute* This By Saying ...

The public's interest in supporting laws regarding civil marriage does not come from the way people relate to pursuing happiness through relationships but from pursuing the common good of guarding the procreational structure of marriage. Proponents of this argument pose a nonsensical rationale for marriage that is unrelated to what structures the legal institution. While the law recognizes a fundamental right of people to marry, it does not allow them to marry their sister, their mother, their twelve-year-old child, their dog, or anyone already married to someone else.

Individuals who fall in these relational categories may not marry because these unions would not serve the public interest of assuring the common good of intergenerational survival. Same-sex couples may not marry for the same reason that children, blood relatives, and animal-human partners may not marry—because those relationships would not be in the same category as male-female couples in terms of what justifies the public's interest in marriage.

Fair laws should not be made unfair merely to stir demand for changing them.

Homosexuals already have the same legally protected opportunity that everyone else has to marry, because the institution is structured to serve the common good. What homosexuals want, however, is not the same right others have but an alleged right to change marriage into something different and impossible. Homosexuals want to change the structure of marriage into something with no structure and change an institution into something that is no longer institutional. They want to create a type of "marriage" affirmed by law that no longer serves the public interest in assuring social survival.

The Truth Is ...

Same-sex marriage is wrong because the only legitimate purpose for marriage is protecting the procreational structure of the institution.

References and Further Reading

For examples of advocates using this argument, see Andrew Sullivan, *Virtually Normal* (New York: Random House, 1995), especially pages 178-180; Franklin E. Kameny, "Deconstructing the Traditional Family," *The World and I* (October 1993), pp. 383-395; Jonathan Rauch, *Gay Marriage: Why It Is Good for Gays, Good for Straights, and Good for American* (New York: Time Books, 2004), especially chapter 1; and Theodore B. Olson, "The Conservative Case for Gay Marriage: Why Same-Sex Marriage Is an American Value," *Newsweek* (January 18, 2010), pp. 48-54.

For the public value of procreationally structured marriage, see Maggie Gallagher, "What Marriage Is For: Children Need Mothers and Fathers," *Weekly Standard* (August 4/August 11, 2003), pp. 22-25; Robert P. George and Jean Bethke Elshtain, eds., *The Meaning of Marriage: Family, State, Market, and Morals*

(Dallas, TX: Spence Publishing, 2006); and William C. Duncan, "The State Interest in Marriage," *Ave Maria Law Review,* 2/1 (Spring 2004), pp. 153-182.

For how abandoning the procreational structure of marriage threatens civilized order and social survival, see Joseph Daniel Unwin, *Sex and Culture* (London: Oxford University Press, 1937); Joseph Daniel Unwin, *Sexual Regulations and Cultural Behavior: An Address Delivered Before the Medical Section of the British Psychological Society* (London: Oxford University Press, 1935); Carle Zimmerman, *Family and Civilization* (Wilmington, DE: ISI Books, 2008); Pitirim Sorokin, *The Crisis of Our Age* (Richmond, VA: Dutton, 1941); Pitirim Sorokin, *Social and Cultural Dynamics,* vol. 4 (Boston, MA: Porter Sargent, 1957); Daniel R. Heimbach, "Deconstructing the Family," *Religion and Society Report* 22/7 (October/November 2005), pp. 1-12; and Daniel Heimbach, "The Future Based on Science," in Daniel Heimbach, *True Sexual Morality* (Wheaton, IL: Crossway, 2004), pp. 345-348.

Nelson Lund, "The Case Against Boies-Olson: Wrong on the Law, and on Civilization," *National Review Online* (September 24, 2009), accessible at http://article.nationalreview.com/?q=MmI 0NWU2ZTU4ZGJ1NDUwYWZjNzI4MzFmZjYwMDA1MGY=.

Jeffrey Lord, "A Rebuttal to Theodore Olson," *American Spectator* (January 19, 2010), accessible at http://spectator.org/ archives/2010/01/19/a-rebuttal-to-theodore-olson.

Maggie Gallagher, "(How) Will Gay Marriage Weaken Marriage as a Social Institution: A Reply to Andrew Koppelman," *University of Saint Thomas Law Journal,* 2/1 (Fall 2004), pp. 33-70.

For a well-stated legal refutation of this argument, see Sherif Girgis, Robert P. George, and Ryan T. Anderson, "What Is Marriage?" *Harvard Journal of Law and Public Policy,* 34/1 (Winter 2011), pp. 245-287.

60

You May Hear Proponents Argue ...

Same-sex marriage should be allowed because the Constitution guarantees equal protection for homosexuals under the law. The Equal Protection Clause in the Fourteenth Amendment of the Constitution says that no law can make social distinctions unless it is shown to be necessary for serving a public purpose greater than any harm that comes to members of a disadvantaged class. There is no public purpose independent of invidious discrimination that can justify limiting civil marriage to opposite-sex couples. All that gay and lesbian people demand is the same equal treatment under the law, which all Americans are entitled to receive under the Constitution.

You Can *Graciously Refute* This By Saying ...

Proponents of this argument make two errors. First, same-sex relationships are *not* in the same category as opposite-sex relationships when it comes to justifying the public's interest in regulating marriage, so there is no basis for alleging the right of marriage applies to same-sex couples. Alleging that same-sex relationships *are the same* as opposite-sex relationships in regard to marriage is like alleging that people who cannot see are *the same* as those who can when it comes to binoculars. Binoculars are not structured for the blind, and marriage is not structured for non-procreating unions.

As binoculars cannot be redefined in a way that makes seeing irrelevant without turning them into something totally different, so marriage cannot be redefined in a way that makes gender difference irrelevant without turning it into something completely different. In fact, legalizing same-sex marriage without first redefining marriage will not treat gay couples *the same* as heterosexuals but will treat them different from everyone else—which will violate the Equal Protection Clause.

Second, even if gay relationships were to be classified in the same legal category (which would be wrong), it would still be constitutionally warranted by the most compelling of state interests to deny same-sex couples an equal right to marry. The Constitution allows denying equal treatment to individuals when it is justified by an overriding state interest. There is truly no greater overriding state interest in favoring legal marriage than in assuring the survival of society.

The Truth Is ...

Same-sex marriage is wrong because same-sex couples are not in the same relational category as opposite-sex couples when it comes to legal marriage.

References and Further Reading

This argument was made by justices writing for the majority in *Baehr v. Lewin*, 74 Hawaii 645, 852 P.2d 44 (1993); and in *Goodridge v. Massachusetts*, 798 N.E. 2d 941 (Massachusetts 2003).

Theodore Olson and David Boies also used this argument to try to persuade a federal court to invalidate California's Proposition 8, which banned same-sex marriage in the state. See Theodore B. Olson, "The Conservative Case for Gay Marriage: Why Same-Sex Marriage Is an American Value," *Newsweek* (January 18, 2010), pp. 48-54.

William C. Duncan, "The State Interest in Marriage," *Ave Maria Law Review*, 2/1 (Spring 2004), pp. 153-182.

Nelson Lund, "The Case Against Boies-Olson: Wrong on the Law, and on Civilization," *National Review Online* (September 24,

2009), accessible at http://article.nationalreview.com/?q=MmI
0NWU2ZTU4ZGJ1NDUwYWZjNzI4MzFmZjYwMDA1MGY=.

Jeffrey Lord, "A Rebuttal to Theodore Olson," *American Spectator*
(January 19, 2010), accessible at http://spectator.org/
archives/2010/01/19/a-rebuttal-to-theodore-olson.

Maggie Gallagher, "(How) Will Gay Marriage Weaken Marriage as
a Social Institution: A Reply to Andrew Koppelman," *University
of Saint Thomas Law Journal*, 2/1 (Fall 2004), pp. 33-70.

Sherif Girgis, Robert P. George, and Ryan T. Anderson, "What
Is Marriage?" *Harvard Journal of Law and Public Policy*, 34/1
(Winter 2011), pp. 245-287.

Robert P. George, Ryan T. Anderson, and Sherif Girgis, "The
Argument Against Gay Marriage: And Why It Doesn't Fail,"
Public Discourse: Ethics, Law and the Common Good (December
17, 2010), accessible at http://www.thepublicdiscourse.com.

Sherif Girgis, Ryan T. Anderson, and Robert P. George, "Does
Marriage, or Anything, Have Essential Properties?" *Public
Discourse: Ethics, Law and the Common Good* (January 12, 2011),
accessible at http://www.thepublicdiscourse.com.

Patrick Lee, Robert P. George, and Gerard V. Bradley, "Marriage
and Procreation: The Intrinsic Connection," *Public Discourse:
Ethics, Law and the Common Good* (March 28, 2011), accessible
at http://www.thepublicdiscourse.com.

61

You May Hear Proponents Argue …

Same-sex marriage should be allowed because under the Constitution no one can be denied fundamental freedoms without due process. Defining marriage as a union between people who have always been able to marry does not justify continuing to exclude people who have never been able to do so. In 1967, the U.S. Supreme Court declared that freedom to marry is a vital right that cannot be abridged without showing a supportable basis for denying that right. Not allowing same-sex couples to marry violates this right of due process because the freedom to marry includes allowing people to choose whom they will marry. For this reason, there is no supportable reason for restricting same-sex marriage.

You Can *Graciously Refute* This By Saying …

Proponents of this argument make three fatal errors in their reasoning. First, the category of individuals whom they claim have "due process protection" have no such protection when it comes to the right to marry. The due process clause protects the *existing* rights of people against unwarranted government intrusion and cannot be used to *redefine* something well established to *generate* something new and different. This would be like saying basketball players must have a protected right to be called tennis players. Nothing is being denied unless people first *redefine* "tennis" to mean playing any sort of game with a ball. If tennis is redefined in that manner, excluding basketball players would be unfair—but then tennis would no longer be tennis.

Second, the due process clause only protects freedoms considered "fundamental." In 1997, the Supreme Court held that for a right to be fundamental, it had to be one "deeply rooted in this nation's history and traditions." Although homosexuality is ancient, gay marriage is new and thus does not qualify.

Third, even if same-sex couples were the same as others in relation to marriage (which is not true), keeping the laws we have about marriage would be warranted to preserve the greatest public good possible—to maintain social stability and assure intergenerational survival. Gays have the same freedoms as everyone else to pursue personal goals in line with maintaining and preserving the common good. What gays do not have—and no one else has—is due process protection of a novel right to *redefine*, and in essence *remove*, the structure of an institution like marriage so essential to the common good.

The Truth Is ...

Same-sex marriage is wrong because marriage law should not be changed to make legally irrelevant differences legally relevant.

References and Further Reading

According to the U.S. Supreme Court's decision in *Loving v. Virginia*, 388 U.S. 1 (1967), freedom to marry is "essential to the orderly pursuit of happiness by free men" (see http://supreme. justia.com/us/388/1/case.html). However, according to the U.S. Supreme Court's decision in *Washington v. Glucksberg*, 521 U.S. 702 (1997), the standard for a fundamental right protected by constitutional due process is that it must be "deeply rooted in this nation's history and traditions." (See http://www.law. cornell.edu/supct/html/96-110.ZS.html.)

Theodore Olson and David Boies used this argument to try to persuade a federal court to invalidate California's Proposition 8, which banned same-sex marriage in the state. See Theodore B. Olson, "The Conservative Case for Gay Marriage: Why Same-Sex Marriage Is an American Value," *Newsweek* (January

18, 2010), pp. 48-54. See also Neil S. Seigel, "Beware the Anti-Freedom Amendment," *News and Observer* (June 9, 2006), Raleigh, North Carolina, p. 15A.

William C. Duncan, "The State Interest in Marriage," *Ave Maria Law Review*, 2/1 (Spring 2004), pp. 153-182.

Nelson Lund, "The Case Against Boies-Olson: Wrong on the Law, and on Civilization," *National Review Online* (September 24, 2009), accessible at http://article.nationalrev iew.com/?q=Mm I0NWU2ZTU4ZGJ1NDUwYWZjNzI4MzFmZjYwMDA1MGY=.

Jeffrey Lord, "A Rebuttal to Theodore Olson," *American Spectator* (January 19, 2010), accessible at http://spectator.org/archives/2010/01/19/a-rebuttal-to-theodore-olson.

Maggie Gallagher, "(How) Will Gay Marriage Weaken Marriage as a Social Institution," *University of Saint Thomas Law Journal*, 2/1 (Fall 2004), pp. 33-70.

Dan Cere, *The Future of Family Law: Law and the Marriage Crisis in North America* (New York: Institute for American Values, 2005), accessible at http://www.marriagedebate.com/pdf/future_of_family_law.pdf.

Robert P. George, Sherif Girgis, and Ryan T. Anderson, "Brief of *Amici Curiae* in Support of Reversal and the Intervening Defendants-Appellants," *Appeal from the United States District Court for the Northern District of California* (September 24, 2010), regarding *Perry v. Schwarzenegger*, Civil Case No. 09-CV-2292 VRW.

Sherif Girgis, Robert P. George, and Ryan T. Anderson, "What Is Marriage?" *Harvard Journal of Law and Public Policy*, 34/1 (Winter 2011), pp. 245-287.

Robert P. George, Ryan T. Anderson, and Sherif Girgis, "The Argument Against Gay Marriage: And Why It Doesn't Fail," *Public Discourse: Ethics, Law and the Common Good* (December 17, 2010), accessible at http://www.thepublicdiscourse.com.

62

You May Hear Proponents Argue …

Same-sex marriage should be allowed because under the Constitution same-sex couples have the same right to marry as interracial couples. What the Constitution guarantees to interracial couples it guarantees to same-sex couples. The constitutionally guaranteed rights of equal treatment, privacy, and due process apply no differently to same-sex couples than to interracial couples. Because the Constitution prohibits states from denying the freedom right to marry based on race, it also prohibits states from denying marriage based on sexual orientation. There is no legally defensible reason for treating sexual orientation differently from race when it comes to the right to marry.

You Can *Graciously Refute* This By Saying …

It is true that in *Loving v. Virginia* (1967), the U.S. Supreme Court said, "Freedom to marry has long been recognized as one of the vital personal rights essential to the orderly pursuit of happiness by free men" and that "under our Constitution, the freedom to marry, or not marry, a person of another race … cannot be infringed by the States." It is also true that in *Planned Parenthood v. Casey* (1992), the Court said the Constitution protects "personal decisions relating to marriage." However, racial difference is not the same as gender difference when it comes to the right to marry.

Everyone in the United States has a right to marry a partner of the opposite sex, but no one has freedom to marry any partner he or she desires. The legally protected structure of institutional marriage is not shaped by desire but by procreation. It is not shaped by personal appetite but by what is best for encouraging the survival of future generations. Under these conditions, race is not relevant to this structure, but gender is.

The Constitution prohibits the government from treating unrelated differences as if they are related and from treating related differences as if they are not. Both are forms of "invidious discrimination." However, what the Constitution does *not* prohibit (and actually *requires*) is treating related differences as related. In other words, it requires "benign discrimination," because without doing so laws would be unjust and social institutions would collapse. Limiting the freedom to marry by racial difference is unconstitutional, but limiting it by gender difference is not. In fact, giving same-sex couples a right to marry would not be constitutional unless marriage was first redefined and turned into something else.

The Truth Is ...

Same-sex marriage is wrong because it would redefine constitutional marriage laws into something that was unconstitutional.

References and Further Reading

See *Loving v. Virginia*, 388 U.S. 1 (1967); and *Planned Parenthood v. Casey*, 505 U.S. 833 (1992).

Theodore Olson and David Boies used this argument to try to persuade a federal court to invalidate California's Proposition 8, which banned same-sex marriage in the state. See Theodore B. Olson, "The Conservative Case for Gay Marriage: Why Same-Sex Marriage Is an American Value," *Newsweek* (January 18, 2010), pp. 48-54.

Nelson Lund, "The Case Against Boies-Olson: Wrong on the Law, and on Civilization," *National Review Online* (September 24, 2009), accessible at http://article.nationalrev iew.com/?q=Mm I0NWU2ZTU4ZGJ1NDUwYWZjNzI4MzFmZjYwMDA1MGY=.

Jeffrey Lord, "A Rebuttal to Theodore Olson," *American Spectator* (January 19, 2010), accessible at http://spectator.org/archives/2010/01/19/a-rebuttal-to-theodore-olson.

Maggie Gallagher, "(How) Will Gay Marriage Weaken Marriage as a Social Institution: A Reply to Andrew Koppelman," *University of Saint Thomas Law Journal*, 2/1 (Fall 2004), pp. 33-70.

William C. Duncan, "The State Interest in Marriage," *Ave Maria Law Review*, 2/1 (Spring 2004), pp. 153-182.

Glenn T. Stanton and Bill Maier, "Isn't Banning Gay Marriage Just Like Banning Interracial Marriage?" in *Why Marriage Matters: Reasons to Believe in Marriage in Postmodern Society* (Colorado Springs, CO: Pinion Press, 1997), pp. 36-39.

In challenging this particular argument, Sherif Girgis, Robert George, and Ryan Anderson note that "antimiscegenation [opposing interracial marriage] was about whom to allow to marry, not what marriage was essentially about; and sex, unlike race, is rationally relevant to the latter question ... [in direct contrast], there is nothing unjustly discriminatory in marriage law's reliance on genuinely relevant distinctions." See Sherif Girgis, Robert P. George, and Ryan T. Anderson, "What Is Marriage?" *Harvard Journal of Law and Public Policy*, 34/1 (Winter 2011), pp. 245-287.

Robert P. George, Ryan T. Anderson, and Sherif Girgis, "The Argument Against Gay Marriage: And Why It Doesn't Fail," *Public Discourse: Ethics, Law and the Common Good* (December 17, 2010), accessible at http://www.thepublicdiscourse.com.

Sherif Girgis, Ryan T. Anderson, and Robert P. George, "Marriage: Merely a Social Construct?" *Public Discourse: Ethics, Law and the Common Good* (December 29, 2010), accessible at http://www.thepublicdiscourse.com.

63

You May Hear Proponents Argue ...

Same-sex marriage should be allowed because marriage laws must conform to the Texas v. Lawrence decision. Under the *Texas v. Lawrence* decision, the U.S. Supreme Court dismantled the basis by which states can limit marriage to only opposite-sex unions. This decision gave individuals equal liberty to choose what defines their personal identity as a spouse, lover, or sex partner, which means that states can no longer distinguish homosexuals from heterosexuals. Because this decision linked the right to marry with prohibiting states from intruding into consensual adult sexual intimacy and choice of sexual partner, it is no longer constitutional to deny same-sex marriage.

You Can *Graciously Refute* This By Saying ...

The *Texas v. Lawrence* (2003) decision did not convert the traditional, long-established, and constitutionally protected right of a man and woman to marry into something it never was. In this case, the Supreme Court only prohibited criminalizing privately expressed sexual behavior, which means the decision has no bearing on marriage law. There are at least three reasons why this is true.

The first is because marriage law does not fall into the category of criminal law, so traditional laws that only recognize unions between a man and a woman criminalize nothing, including same-sex relationships. The second reason is because in *Texas v. Lawrence,* the Court explicitly disavowed the ruling had any bearing on marriage. In fact, the Court warned against using the decision to alter definitions of marriage. The third reason is because *Texas v. Lawrence* prohibited using criminal law to demean private sexual activity, but just being in a union not classified as marriage implies no such breach of this ruling.

Keeping marriage as it is has nothing to do with approving or disapproving what homosexuals do in private. Civilization has long maintained legal boundaries on marriage that—along with excluding unions between members of the same sex—also exclude unions between near relatives, adults with children, and humans with animals. These boundaries do not demean those who engage in such activities any more than trucks are demeaned by laws not allowing them to use lanes reserved for cars. There is no wrong done by laws that maintain boundaries to guard what an institution was designed to be. There is nothing wrong with keeping marriage law as it is, and *Texas v. Lawrence* has does nothing to change that fact.

The Truth Is …

Same-sex marriage is wrong because decriminalizing sodomy implies no right to change marriage into something it never was.

References and Further Reading

See *Lawrence v. Texas*, accessible at http://supreme.justia.com/us/539/558/case.html. Note especially Justice Scalia's dissent, in which he disputed the U.S. Supreme Court's discovery of a constitutional power to regulate actions based on a self-defined "concept of existence."

Theodore Olson and David Boies used this argument to try to persuade a federal court to invalidate California's Proposition 8, which banned same-sex marriage in the state. See Theodore B. Olson, "The Conservative Case for Gay Marriage: Why Same-Sex Marriage Is an American Value," *Newsweek* (January 18, 2010), pp. 48-54.

For a thorough legal refutation of this argument, see Robert P. George, Sherif Girgis, and Ryan T. Anderson, "Brief of *Amici Curiae* in Support of Reversal and the Intervening Defendants-Appellants," *Appeal from the United States District Court for the*

Northern District of California (September 24, 2010), regarding *Perry v. Schwarzenegger*, Civil Case No. 09-CV-2292 VRW.

Sandra Day O'Connor, concurring with *Lawrence v. Texas* (02-102) 539 U.S. 558 (2003), p. 7.

Nelson Lund, "The Case Against Boies-Olson: Wrong on the Law, and on Civilization," *National Review Online* (September 24, 2009), accessible at http://article.nationalrev iew.com/?q=Mm I0NWU2ZTU4ZGJ1NDUwYWZjNzI4MzFmZjYwMDA1MGY=.

Jeffrey Lord, "A Rebuttal to Theodore Olson," *American Spectator* (January 19, 2010), accessible at http://spectator.org/ archives/2010/01/19/a-rebuttal-to-theodore-olson.

Martha B. Sosman, Justice of the Massachusetts Supreme Judicial Court, Dissent to *Goodridge v. Massachusetts*, 798 N.E. 2d 941 (Massachusetts 2003).

Sherif Girgis, Robert P. George, and Ryan T. Anderson, "What Is Marriage?" *Harvard Journal of Law and Public Policy*, 34/1 (Winter 2011), pp. 245-287.

Patrick Lee and Robert P. George, *Body-Self Dualism in Contemporary Ethics and Politics* (New York: Cambridge University Press, 2008).

William C. Duncan, "The State Interest in Marriage," *Ave Maria Law Review*, 2/1 (Spring 2004), pp. 153-182.

For how legalizing same-sex marriage will align marriage to homosexual categories and not align homosexuals to what marriage is now, see Lawrence Auster, "The Extreme Radicalism of Homosexual 'Marriage,'" *View from the Right* (June 2, 2008), accessible at http://www.amnation.com/vfr/archives/010723. html.

64

You May Hear Proponents Argue …

Same-sex marriage should be allowed because civil marriage laws are now inconsistent and need fixing. Some states allow same-sex marriages, while others refuse to recognize them. Some states treat civil unions differently from marriage, while others (like Massachusetts) not only recognize same-sex marriages but also prohibit distinguishing civil unions from civil marriage. Marriage laws should be clear and consistent from state to state. As it now stands, they are in a terrible mess. This can only be fixed by the U.S. Supreme Court declaring that the Constitution requires all states to recognize same-sex marriages, no matter where a couple gets married.

You Can *Graciously Refute* This By Saying …

It is true that some states recognize same-sex marriages while others do not; that some states distinguish civil unions from marriage while others do not; and that some states prohibit their courts from requiring legal recognition of same-sex marriages that were done in other states. It is also true the U.S. Supreme Court, in striking down the *Defense of Marriage Act*, recognized that the Constitution reserves marriage law to the states and allows state laws regulating marriage to vary from state to state—even though Article 4 of the Constitution says that all states shall give "full faith and credit" to acts, records, and proceedings performed by other states. Furthermore, it is true that state marriage laws will never reach a state of consistency unless the Court intervenes to require it.

However, while this all may be true, none of these factors means the Supreme Court should fix this problem or assume it has proper authority to address it. What passes for law should above all be honest, and legalizing same-sex marriage perpetrates a legal lie. Even though it would be good to have consistency in marriage law from state to state, honesty in law would be better still, and spreading a legal lie would make law worse, not better.

The Constitution does not require states to regulate marriage in a consistent manner, and no state (or even the Supreme Court) has any legitimate authority to redefine non-marriage as marriage. In fact, the Eleventh Amendment of the Constitution actually prohibits the Supreme Court from forcing states to redefine something in state law merely to conform with how other states are redefining their laws.

The Truth Is ...

Same-sex marriage is wrong because attempting to fix the mess in state marriage laws would only make the situation worse than it is already.

References and Further Reading

Justice Kennedy, writing for the majority in *United States v. Windsor*, 570 U.S. ___ (2013), recognized that "the regulation of civil marriages is central to state domestic law applicable to its residents and citizens" and held that the Constitution allows marriage law to vary from state to state. In fact, the U.S. Supreme Court struck down the *Defense of Marriage Act* precisely because federal law interfered with allowing "the incidents, benefits, and obligations of marriage" to vary "from one State to the next."

Amendment 11 of the U.S. Constitution reads, "The judicial power of the United States shall not be construed to extend to any suit in law or equity, commenced or prosecuted against one of the United States by citizens of another state, or citizens or subjects of any foreign state."

Nelson Lund, "The Case Against Boies-Olson: Wrong on the Law, and on Civilization," *National Review Online* (September 24,

2009), accessible at http://article.nationalrev iew.com/?q=Mm I0NWU2ZTU4ZGJ1NDUwYWZjNzI4MzFmZjYwMDA1MGY=.

Jeffrey Lord, "A Rebuttal to Theodore Olson," *American Spectator* (January 19, 2010), accessible at http://spectator.org/archives/2010/01/19/a-rebuttal-to-theodore-olson.

Maggie Gallagher, "(How) Will Gay Marriage Weaken Marriage as a Social Institution: A Reply to Andrew Koppelman," *University of Saint Thomas Law Journal*, 2/1 (Fall 2004), pp. 33-70.

William C. Duncan, "The State Interest in Marriage," *Ave Maria Law Review*, 2/1 (Spring 2004), pp. 153-182.

Dan Cere, *The Future of Family Law: Law and the Marriage Crisis in North America* (New York: Institute for American Values, 2005), accessible at http://www.marriagedebate.com/pdf/future_of_family_law.pdf.

Sherif Girgis, Ryan T. Anderson, and Robert P. George, "Does Marriage, or Anything, Have Essential Properties?" *Public Discourse: Ethics, Law and the Common Good* (January 12, 2011), accessible at http://www.thepublicdiscourse.com.

Patrick Lee, Robert P. George, and Gerard V. Bradley, "Marriage and Procreation: The Intrinsic Connection," *Public Discourse: Ethics, Law and the Common Good* (March 28, 2011), accessible at http://www.thepublicdiscourse.com.

Patrick Lee, Robert P. George, and Gerard V. Bradley, "Marriage and Procreation: The Intrinsic Connection," *Public Discourse: Ethics, Law and the Common Good* (March 28, 2011), accessible at http://www.thepublicdiscourse.com.

65

You May Hear Proponents Argue ...

Same-sex marriage should be allowed because civil marriage laws already accept no-fault divorce, which is a lot worse than same-sex marriage. What could be worse for the old view of marriage than legalizing no-fault divorce? No-fault divorce already redefines marriage into something vastly different than it was intended to be. Americans today live in a world of no-strings heterosexual hookups, 50-percent divorce rates, and no-fault divorce laws, so there is no reason to keep on excluding homosexuals from marriage. Same-sex marriage is required to keep things legally fair and up to date.

You Can *Graciously Refute* This By Saying ...

Proponents of this argument make four errors: (1) they assume two things are one thing, (2) they assume courts have power they don't have, (3) they treat divorce as if it doesn't matter, and (4) they treat marriage as not worth saving. For the first point, these proponents assume that no-fault divorce is just as bad for society as same-sex marriage. However, no-fault divorce does not change the legal meaning of marriage, while same-sex marriage does. The two are not the same. Just using the same word does not make gay unions the same thing as real marriage any more than calling Justin Beiber a "star" makes him the same thing as the sun.

Second, no court has the authority simply to change what marriage means according to the law. Citizens of a state can do that through elected representatives, but there is no constitutional basis to allow courts to usurp the democratic process other than through the democratic process required by the Constitution itself.

Third, everyone knows that homosexual behavior is highly promiscuous. Gays pursuing same-sex marriage have no interest in changing their behavior by limiting sex to one partner. Today, the number one reason for divorce is sexual infidelity, so it strains credulity to imagine that injecting civil marriage with a huge dose of infidelity would be good for civil marriage, children, or broader society.

Fourth, proponents of this argument assume marriage is so far gone that causing it to crumble even further doesn't matter. However, it is terribly inconsistent for gays to say on the one hand that the institution we have is so good they must be included, while on the other hand saying the institution is not worth saving without changing it into something radically new and different.

The Truth Is …

Same-sex marriage is wrong because practicing marriage badly is no reason to deconstruct marriage as well.

References and Further Reading

For examples of advocates using this argument, see Andrew Sullivan, "Unveiled," *New Republic*, August 13, 2001, p. 6, accessible at www.andrewsullivan.com/print.php? artnum=20011083; and Jonathan Rauch, *Gay Marriage: Why It Is Good for Gays, Good for Straights, and Good for America* (New York: Times Books, 2004), pp. 167-168.

Mollie Ziegler Hemingway, "Same-Sex, Different Marriage: Many of Those Who Want Marriage Equality Do Not Want Fidelity," *Christianity Today* (May 18, 2010), accessible at http://www.christianitytoday.com/ct/2010/may/11.52.html.

Stanley Kurtz, "Point of No Return: Marriage Needs a Man and a Woman, and an Amendment," *National Review Online* (August 3, 2001).

Erwin W. Luzer, "Look at the Divorce Rate!" in *The Truth about Same-Sex Marriage* (Chicago: Moody, 2004), pp. 84-86.

Peter Sprigg and Timothy Dailey, eds., Getting *It Straight: What the Research Shows About Homosexuality* (Washington, DC: Family Research Council, 2004).

Timothy Dailey, "Comparing the Lifestyles of Homosexual Couples to Married Couples," *Family Research Council* (April 29, 2004), accessible at http://www.frc. org/get.cfm?i=IS04C02.

Nelson Lund, "The Case Against Boies-Olson: Wrong on the Law, and on Civilization," *National Review Online* (September 24, 2009), accessible at http://article.nationalrev iew.com/?q=Mm I0NWU2ZTU4ZGJ1NDUwYWZjNzI4MzFmZjYwMDA1MGY=.

Jeffrey Lord, "A Rebuttal to Theodore Olson," *American Spectator* (January 19, 2010), accessible at http://spectator.org/ archives/2010/01/19/a-rebuttal-to-theodore-olson.

Maggie Gallagher, "(How) Will Gay Marriage Weaken Marriage as a Social Institution," *University of Saint Thomas Law Journal*, 2/1 (Fall 2004), pp. 33-70.

William C. Duncan, "The State Interest in Marriage," *Ave Maria Law Review*, 2/1 (Spring 2004), pp. 153-182.

Sherif Girgis, Robert P. George, and Ryan T. Anderson, "What Is Marriage?" *Harvard Journal of Law and Public Policy*, 34/1 (Winter 2011), pp. 245-287.

Robert P. George, Ryan T. Anderson, and Sherif Girgis, "The Argument Against Gay Marriage: And Why It Doesn't Fail," *Public Discourse: Ethics, Law and the Common Good* (December 17, 2010), accessible at http://www.thepublicdiscourse.com.

Arguments 66 – 73

Gracious Answers to *Arguments Regarding* Government and Religion

Good
government
will never knowingly
deconstruct the one institution
on which social survival most
depends, because that would
destroy what government
is most responsible
to protect.

REGARDING GOVERNMENT AND RELIGION

(Arguments 66–73)

66

You May Hear Proponents Argue ...

*S*AME-SEX MARRIAGE SHOULD *be allowed because government should not favor one view of marriage over another.* Why should the government be in the business of deciding who can get married and who cannot? Such judgments rightly belong to individuals or private groups like churches. Individuals and private groups should not try to restrict marriage law, and government should not try to limit how individuals or groups practice marriage. It is not the state's job to privilege one kind of marriage over others. Instead of choosing between sorts, the law should get out of the way and allow same-sex marriage for those who favor it, even if others do not.

You Can *Graciously Refute* This By Saying ...

The value, meaning, and significance of marriage to society is not defined by private desires that change over time or from individual to individual. Traditional marriage law that limits marriage to opposite-sex couples does not deny anyone anything. Homosexuals already have the same rights as everyone else to marry in accordance to the way marriage is now and has always been structured—along lines justified by the common public interest to reward and protect procreation, maintain social stability, and assure intergenerational survival. What homosexuals do not have—and no else has either—is a right to redefine civil marriage so completely that it deconstructs marriage as a fundamental social institution. Deconstructing marriage in this manner would be bad for everyone, because it would cause long-lasting harm to the common good of social cohesion and endurance.

The real reason behind the current drive for same-sex marriage is not access to benefits. Homosexuals living together can already avail themselves of most legal benefits connected with marriage without changing marriage itself to get them. They can access domestic partner health benefits; own property together; set up wills passing on property to each other; agree to leave joint property to whatever person, charity, or trust they desire; set up hospital visiting rights for each other; and be beneficiaries of each other's life insurance. What they have no right to—and no government should ever recognize—is ruin marriage for everyone by deconstructing the one institution every good government is most responsible to protect.

The Truth Is …

Same-sex marriage is wrong because a government taking a hands-off approach would only harm what a good government should most protect.

References and Further Reading

For the real reason behind the homosexual push for same-sex marriage, see Jonathan D. Katz's (former executive coordinator of the Larry Kramer Initiative for Lesbian and Gay Studies at Yale University) comments to a National Public Radio interviewer in "Gay Marriage Debate within the Gay Community," *Talk of the Nation*, National Public Radio, February 16, 2004.

For examples of advocates making this argument, see Theodore B. Olson, "The Conservative Case for Gay Marriage: Why Same-Sex Marriage Is an American Value," *Newsweek* (January 18, 2010), pp. 48-54; and Chai R. Feldblum, "Moral Conflict and Liberty; Gay Rights and Religion," *Brooklyn Law Review*, 72/1 (2006), pp. 61-123 (see especially page 121).

Nelson Lund, "The Case Against Boies-Olson: Wrong on the Law, and on Civilization," *National Review Online* (September 24, 2009), accessible at http://article.nationalrev iew.com/?q=Mm I0NWU2ZTU4ZGJ1NDUwYWZjNzI4MzFmZjYwMDA1MGY=.

Jeffrey Lord, "A Rebuttal to Theodore Olson," *American Spectator* (January 19, 2010), accessible at http://spectator.org/archives/2010/01/19/a-rebuttal-to-theodore-olson.

For how legalizing same-sex marriage weakens marriage as a social institution, see Cynthia Harper and Sara McLanahan, "Father Absence and Youth Incarceration," *Journal of Research on Adolescence*, 14 (September 2004), pp. 369-397; Robert L. Flewelling and Karl Bauman, "Family Structure as a Predictor of Initial Substance Abuse and Sexual Intercourse in Early Adolescence," *Journal of Marriage and Family*, 52/1 (February 1990), pp. 171-181; David Blankenhorn, "Defining Marriage Down Is No Way to Save It," *Weekly Standard*, 12/28 (April 2, 2007); Stanley Kurtz, "The End of Marriage in Scandinavia," *Weekly Standard* (February 2, 2004), pp. 26-33; Stanley Kurtz, "Point of No Return: Marriage Needs a Man and a Woman, and an Amendment," *National Review Online* (August 3, 2001); Daniel R. Heimbach, "Deconstructing the Family," *Religion and Society Report*, 22/7 (October/November 2005), pp. 1-12; Maggie Gallagher, "(How) Will Gay Marriage Weaken Marriage as a Social Institution," *University of Saint Thomas Law Journal*, 2/1 (Fall 2004), pp. 33-70.

William C. Duncan, "The State Interest in Marriage," *Ave Maria Law Review*, 2/1 (Spring 2004), pp. 153-182.

Sherif Girgis, Robert P. George, and Ryan T. Anderson, "What Is Marriage?" *Harvard Journal of Law and Public Policy*, 34/1 (Winter 2011), pp. 245-287.

Sherif Girgis, Ryan T. Anderson, and Robert P. George, "Does Marriage, or Anything, Have Essential Properties?" *Public Discourse: Ethics, Law and the Common Good* (January 12, 2011), accessible at http://www.thepublicdiscourse.com.

67

You May Hear Proponents Argue …

Same-sex marriage should be allowed because the federal govern-ment should not preempt the freedom of states to experiment. The various states must be left free of federal interference to try different approaches toward improving marriage. Variety is a good thing, and experimenting is how things get better. Accepting differences between states and allowing states to experiment will make marriage better, not worse. Marriage laws govern a sphere of life in which people often hold their most strongly opposed views. This means that marriage laws are best left to the level of government closest to home and that they work best when a government interferes least.

You Can *Graciously Refute* This By Saying …

If there is anything on which government cannot afford to experiment, it is marriage. What proponents of this argument suggest is similar to saying that the federal government should allow states to "experiment" and work things out by instituting slavery or lying to policemen. Marriage is an essential social institution that has worked perfectly fine for millennia, and it is foolish at this point to act as if marriage is something experimental and untested. Marriage is not a fashion on which to experiment how it meets personal whims, but something essential to social survival.

Marriage is an entity without which society will collapse and children will suffer. In many ways, experimenting with marriage makes as little sense as experimenting with installing screen doors on submarines while underwater or removing airplane wings while in midair. Changing marriage in a way that no longer favors getting mothers and fathers to raise their children threatens the public good of raising well-adjusted children. Research shows that children are best raised by their own biological parents and, when that is not possible, are best parented by a man-woman couple whose interaction duplicates biological parents.

By contrast, children raised by same-sex couples are more likely to experiment sexually at younger ages. This higher rate of promiscuity is linked to a much higher risk of sexually transmitted diseases, educational failure, unhappiness, teen pregnancy, anti-social behavior, unemployment, and poverty. We already face a huge crisis in this country caused by states experimenting with the structure of marriage. Rather than allow things to get worse, we should pass a single national definition of marriage that overrules all state and local laws allowing same-sex marriage.

The Truth Is ...

Same-sex marriage is wrong because it threatens something essential by acting as if it is experimental and untested.

References and Further Reading

For an example of an advocate making this argument, see Jonathan Rauch, *Gay Marriage: Why It Is Good for Gays, Good for Straights, and Good for America* (New York: Times Books, 2004), p. 176.

Paul Cameron and Kirk Cameron, "Homosexual Parents," *Adolescence*, 31 (1996), pp. 757-776.

Robert L. Flewelling and Karl Bauman, "Family Structure as a Predictor of Initial Substance Abuse and Sexual Intercourse in Early Adolescence," *Journal of Marriage and Family*, 52/1 (February 1990), pp. 171-181.

Cynthia Harper and Sara McLanahan, "Father Absence and Youth Incarceration," *Journal of Research on Adolescence*, 14 (September 2004), pp. 369-397.

According to Rebecca O'Neal, for the past 30 years America has been conducting a vast "experiment" with the family. The results of the experiment show that the decline of the heterosexual, two-parent, married-couple family has resulted in poverty, ill-health, educational failure, unhappiness, anti-social behavior, isolation and social exclusion for thousands of men, women and children. See Rebecca O'Neal, "Experiments in Living: The Fatherless Family," *CIVITAS* (September 2002), pp. 2-20.

Maggie Gallagher, "(How) Will Gay Marriage Weaken Marriage as a Social Institution: A Reply to Andrew Koppelman," *University of Saint Thomas Law Journal*, 2/1 (Fall 2004), pp. 33-70.

William C. Duncan, "The State Interest in Marriage," *Ave Maria Law Review*, 2/1 (Spring 2004), pp. 153-182.

Dan Cere, *The Future of Family Law: Law and the Marriage Crisis in North America* (New York: Institute for American Values, 2005), accessible at http://www.marriagedebate.com/pdf/future_of_family_law.pdf.

Maggie Gallagher, "Should Gay Marriage Be Legal? No," *ProCon.org* (May 22, 2009), accessible at http://gaymarriage.procon.org/view.answers.php?questionID=001607.

Sherif Girgis, Robert P. George, and Ryan T. Anderson, "What Is Marriage?" *Harvard Journal of Law and Public Policy*, 34/1 (Winter 2011), pp. 245-287.

Robert P. George, Ryan T. Anderson, and Sherif Girgis, "The Argument Against Gay Marriage: And Why It Doesn't Fail," *Public Discourse: Ethics, Law and the Common Good* (December 17, 2010), accessible at http://www.thepublicdiscourse.com.

68

You May Hear Proponents Argue ...

Same-sex marriage should be allowed because government is responsible for overturning laws limiting the freedom of same-sex couples to marry. There are truly people for whom opposite-sex love is not an option, and society owes them the approval and support they need as much as anyone else. These individuals should not be made to wait a minute longer for what society owes them and should never have denied in the first place. States that resist must be forced to accept same-sex marriages just as they were forced to accept interracial marriages. Democratic freedom must not be used to excuse denying what every society owes every human being.

You Can *Graciously Refute* This By Saying ...

Proponents of this argument employ draconian, tyrannical, circular, and false reasoning to make their claim. They call for oppressive force, are anti-democratic, and proceed unfairly by presuming the very thing for which they argue. They begin by assuming that same-sex marriage has already been proven to be absolutely necessary, and then they focus on getting rid of their opposition. Not only is this is terribly unfair, but it also proposes a course of action that is contrary to our system of government—an action that would override the democratic process, states' rights, and federalism.

Furthermore, it is not true that gays are people "for whom opposite-sex love is not an option." There is no credible basis for making such a statement. In fact, strong evidence exists that shows homosexual desires can be resisted, can change, and can be treated—and that they rarely ever last into old age. With this being the case, there is no good reason at all for claiming the state owes gays access to marriage, much less a right that will deconstruct marriage and ruin it for everyone.

Opposition to same-sex marriage is not based on bigotry but on fidelity to what makes a marriage real. Government does not discriminate when it favors real procreationally structured marriage over fake same-sex marriage any more than it favors people driving cars on freeways instead of roller-skating on them. People who like roller-skating are perfectly free to apply for licenses that allow them to drive real cars on freeways anywhere they like, but they have no right to roller-skate on freeways simply by pretending that roller-skates are the same as cars.

The Truth Is ...

Same-sex marriage is wrong because the federal government should not overturn state laws that are perfectly justified as they are.

References and Further Reading

Glenn T. Stanton and Bill Maier, "Isn't Banning Gay Marriage Just Like Banning Interracial Marriage?" in *Why Marriage Matters: Reasons to Believe in Marriage in Postmodern Society* (Colorado Springs, CO: Pinion Press, 1997), pp. 36-39.

Carson Holloway, "Same-Sex Marriage and the Death of Tradition," *First Things* (June 10, 2009), accessible at http://www.firstthings.com/onthesquare/2009/06/same-sex-marriage-and-the-deat.

For how the science has been misrepresented and politicized, see Jeffrey Satinover, "The Trojan Couch: How the Mental Health Associations Misrepresent Science," *Conference Reports 2005*, National Association for Research and Therapy of Homosexuals, accessible at http://www.narth.com/docs/thetrojancouch-satinover; Robert Lerner and Althea Nagia, *No Basis: What the Studies Don't Tell Us About Same-Sex Parenting*, Marriage Law Project (Washington, DC, January 2001); A. Dean Byrd, "When

Activism Masquerades as Science," National Association for Research and Therapy of Homosexuals, accessible at http://www.narth.com/docs/masquerades (posted 2004, updated September 3, 2008); and Michael L. Brown, "Is Gay the New Black? Analyzing the Argument That 'I Was Born That Way,'" in *A Queer Thing Happened to America* (Concord, NC: Equal Time Books, 2011), pp. 197-225.

Maggie Gallagher, "(How) Will Gay Marriage Weaken Marriage as a Social Institution," *University of Saint Thomas Law Journal*, 2/1 (Fall 2004), pp. 33-70.

William C. Duncan, "The State Interest in Marriage," *Ave Maria Law Review*, 2/1 (Spring 2004), pp. 153-182.

Sherif Girgis, Ryan T. Anderson, and Robert P. George, "Marriage: Merely a Social Construct?" *Public Discourse: Ethics, Law and the Common Good* (December 29, 2010), accessible at http://www.thepublicdiscourse.com.

Sherif Girgis, Ryan T. Anderson, and Robert P. George, "Marriage: Real Bodily Union," *Public Discourse: Ethics, Law and the Common Good* (December 30, 2010), accessible at http://www.thepublicdiscourse.com.

Sherif Girgis, Ryan T. Anderson, and Robert P. George, "Marriage: No Avoiding the Central Question," *Public Discourse: Ethics, Law and the Common Good* (January 3, 2011), accessible at http://www.thepublicdiscourse.com.

Sherif Girgis, Ryan T. Anderson, and Robert P. George, "Does Marriage, or Anything, Have Essential Properties?" *Public Discourse: Ethics, Law and the Common Good* (January 12, 2011), accessible at http://www.thepublicdiscourse.com.

69

You May Hear Proponents Argue …

Same-sex marriage should be allowed because it is not the role of government to link marriage with procreation. The gendered meaning of marriage is archaic and no longer relevant to the public meaning of modern marriage. Marriage is no longer intrinsically connected to bringing males and females together to procreate and share a common life, and to be fair, the government should not be encouraging this to happen. Legalizing same-sex marriage will get rid of the idea that government has any proper role in sustaining the gendered and procreative elements of marriage.

You Can *Graciously Refute* This By Saying …

Proponents of this argument base their claims on three ideas: (1) the public meaning of marriage has changed, (2) any change made has been good, and (3) we must get rid of something that no longer exists. While the first and second ideas are false, the third is just plain nonsense.

First, proponents of this argument assume that something has changed that cannot change. The procreational structure of marriage cannot change, because it precedes culture and is something on which social order depends—not the other way around. Public interest in supporting marriage comes from how marriage moves gendered people toward bridging the male-female divide and connecting sex with having and raising children.

Second, proponents of this argument reverse what is truly good and what is truly bad for society. If the public reason for supporting marriage shifts from favoring its procreational structure toward affirming private feelings, marriage will lose structure and cease to be a social institution. This will be very bad, not good. Purging public marriage of all connections with gender and procreation and replacing those connections with an open-textured model that normalizes homosexual relationships will pose a grave threat to the welfare of future generations and to the survival of society as a whole.

Third, proponents of this argument basically say we must change something that does not need changing, or that we should get rid of something that is no longer real. However, the only sensible options would be to argue either that what we have is something bad and should change, or that what we have is something good and should stay. Because what we currently have is good and essential, their argument must be rejected as pernicious nonsense.

The Truth Is ...

Same-sex marriage is wrong because it is circular nonsense to argue that government must change marriage because marriage has changed.

References and Further Reading

Gretchen Stiers says that "by claiming the legal right to have a commitment or wedding ceremony, lesbians and gay men challenge the gender component of marriage as well as its underlying procreative function." See Gretchen A. Stiers, *From This Day Forward: Commitment, Marriage, and Family in Lesbian and Gay Relationships* (New York: St. Martin's Press, 1999), p. 109.

Mary Bernstein confirms that same-sex marriage will change so much in law and public policy regarding the meaning of marriage that it poses "the ultimate threat to conservatively defined *family values* that view two parents of the opposite sex as necessary for a child's proper gender and sexual development." Mary Bernstein, "Gender, Queer Family Policies, and the Limits of Law," in *Queer Families, Queer Politics: Challenging Culture and the State*, ed. Mary Bernstein and Renate Reimann

(New York: Columbia University Press, 2001), p. 433. See also Jeffrey Weeks, Brian Heaphy, and Catherine Donovan, *Same Sex Intimacies: Families of Choice and Other Life Experiments* (London: Routledge, 2001), p. 47.

William C. Duncan, "The State Interest in Marriage," *Ave Maria Law Review*, 2/1 (Spring 2004), pp. 153-182.

For more on the public meaning of marriage see Maggie Gallagher, "What Marriage Is For: Children Need Mothers and Fathers," *Weekly Standard* (August 4/August 11, 2003), pp. 22-25; and Robert P. George and Jean Bethke Elshtain, eds., *The Meaning of Marriage: Family, State, Market, and Morals* (Dallas, TX: Spence Publishing, 2006).

Maggie Gallagher, "(How) Will Gay Marriage Weaken Marriage as a Social Institution," *University of Saint Thomas Law Journal*, 2/1 (Fall 2004), pp. 33-70.

Daniel R. Heimbach, "Deconstructing the Family," *Religion and Society Report*, 22/7 (October/November 2005), pp. 1-12.

Sherif Girgis, Robert P. George, and Ryan T. Anderson, "What Is Marriage?" *Harvard Journal of Law and Public Policy*, 34/1 (Winter 2011), pp. 245-287.

Patrick Lee, Robert P. George, and Gerard V. Bradley, "Marriage and Procreation: The Intrinsic Connection," *Public Discourse: Ethics, Law and the Common Good* (March 28, 2011), accessible at http://www.thepublicdiscourse.com.

Patrick Lee, Robert P. George, and Gerard V. Bradley, "Marriage and Procreation: The Intrinsic Connection," *Public Discourse: Ethics, Law and the Common Good* (March 28, 2011), accessible at http://www.thepublicdiscourse.com.

70

You May Hear Proponents Argue …

Same-sex marriage should be allowed to bring our nation into line with other nations that have already legalized same-sex marriage. If Americans do not go along with the international trend to approve same-sex marriage, we will lose the respect of nations that are more progressive than ourselves. Instead of being respected for visionary leadership, the United States will be criticized for thinking that lags behind international advances in social justice. Our nation is not so big and successful that we have nothing to learn from others. In this case, we must set aside our national pride and adopt policies that reflect the changing world opinion.

You Can *Graciously Refute* This By Saying …

Proponents of this argument wrongly assume that the procreational structure of marriage is so trivial that it can be discarded to reflect whims of popular opinion. They also unwisely assume that we should adopt whatever other nations do without criticism. Both assumptions are irresponsible.

Just as the spread of fascism in Europe preceding World War II did not justify the United States adopting fascism, and just as the spread of communist ideology in Europe and elsewhere during the Cold War did not justify America adopting communism, so too would it be foolish for us to adopt same-sex marriage just because it is spreading among those same nations that previously fell victim to these dangerous ideologies. Proponents of this argument naively assume that anything popular anywhere in the world is beyond criticism or that other nations somehow have better judgment than we do about an institution as essential as marriage. Neither assumption provides a wise basis for deciding anything important, much less something on which our nation's survival literally depends.

Whether it concerns personal relations or international relations, some things are truly dangerous and must be avoided for the common good. There is no honor in being the first nation to give up something essential to securing the common good of self-preservation, nor is there any honor in mindlessly following other nations toward certain disaster. That is what lemmings do, and we in the United States are not lemmings. It is foolish to put our nation on a path toward social self-annihilation, regardless of how many other nations are already on that path.

The Truth Is ...

Same-sex marriage is wrong because change to be like other nations is not good when it sets society on a path to disaster.

References and Further Reading

For examples of advocates using this argument, see James D. Wilets, "The Inexorable Momentum Toward National and International Recognition of Same-Sex Relationships," in *Marriage and Same-Sex Unions*, ed. Lunn Wardle, Mark Strasser, William Duncan, and David Coolidge (Westport, CT: Praeger, 2003), pp. 349-360; and Campbell Barrett, "The Present Status of the Law of Marriage in the United States and Abroad," in *Same-Sex Marriage: The Legal and Psychological Evolution in America*, ed. Donald Cantor, Elizabeth Cantor, James Black, and Campbell Barrett (Middletown, CT: Wesleyan University Press, 2006), pp. 115-133.

Donald Cantor states, "[If] developments outside the United States evidence ... a continuing and growing acceptance of same-sex marriage ... then why is there opposition to same-sex marriage (in the United States)?" See Donald Cantor, "Conclusion: The Case for Same-Sex Marriage," in *Same-Sex Marriage: The Legal and Psychological Evolution in America*, ed. Donald

Cantor, Elizabeth Cantor, James Black and Campbell Barrett (Middletown, CT: Wesleyan University Press, 2006), pp. 149-150.

For how abandoning the procreational structure of marriage threatens civilization, see Joseph Daniel Unwin, *Sex and Culture* (London: Oxford University Press, 1937); Joseph Daniel Unwin, *Sexual Regulations and Cultural Behavior: An Address Delivered Before the Medical Section of the British Psychological Society* (London: Oxford University Press, 1935); Carle Zimmerman, *Family and Civilization* (Wilmington, DE: ISI Books, 2008); Pitirim Sorokin, *The Crisis of Our Age* (Richmond, VA: Dutton, 1941); Pitirim Sorokin, *Social and Cultural Dynamics*, vol. 4 (Boston, MA: Porter Sargent, 1957); Daniel R. Heimbach, "Deconstructing the Family," *Religion and Society Report* 22/7 (October/November 2005), pp. 1-12; and Daniel Heimbach, "The Future Based on Science," in Daniel Heimbach, *True Sexual Morality* (Wheaton, IL: Crossway, 2004), pp. 345-348.

Stanley Kurtz, "The End of Marriage in Scandinavia: The 'Conservative Case' for Same-Sex Marriage Collapses," *Weekly Standard* (February 2, 2004), pp. 26-33.

David Coolidge, "Let's Not Go Dutch," *Weekly Standard* (May 7, 2001), pp. 17-19.

Stanley Kurtz, "Going Dutch? Lessons of the Same-Sex Marriage Debate in the Netherlands," *Weekly Standard* (May 31, 2004), pp. 26-29.

Maggie Gallagher, "(How) Will Gay Marriage Weaken Marriage as a Social Institution," *University of Saint Thomas Law Journal*, 2/1 (Fall 2004), pp. 33-70.

William C. Duncan, "The State Interest in Marriage," *Ave Maria Law Review*, 2/1 (Spring 2004), pp. 153-182.

71

You May Hear Proponents Argue …

Same-sex marriage should be allowed because there is no secular reason for government to prefer heterosexual over homosexual coupling. Civil marriage is not the same as religious marriage. Religious people see traditional marriage as a sacrament ordained by God, but civil marriage is a purely secular matter. Government regulates marriage for the common good, but religion favors one group against another. Religious people made up the male-female view of marriage and then used laws to impose it on others for theological reasons rather than the common good. Allowing same-sex marriage will separate civil marriage from dangerous religious ideology.

You Can *Graciously Refute* This By Saying …

Proponents of this argument make a false charge so they can offer a false solution to a false problem. It is true that Christianity, Judaism, and Islam all believe that God instituted marriage with a male-female procreational structure. However, that is not what justifies the public's interest in maintaining that same structure. The public's interest in favoring procreational marriage is to assure the survival and stability of society, which has nothing to do with privately held religious convictions. The public's value in marriage comes from the way it brings men and women together to have and raise children. It has nothing to do with what people feel or believe.

The main reason homosexual radicals are demanding same-sex marriage is not to participate in something others have but to radically change the public meaning of marriage for everyone. In truth, those who are honest openly admit they are using the issue of same-sex marriage to affect change for all people—whether heterosexual, homosexual, religious, or secular. Sociologist Gretchen Stiers states that legalizing gay marriages "has a radical potential to alter religious, social, and legal definitions of what a marriage is supposed to be." In other words, she understands perfectly well that it will transform the public relevance of marriage for all.

Proponents of this argument pretend that male-female marriage is just a matter of personal taste and that civil marriage should be distanced from anything remotely religious. However, we should remain focused on serving the established and legitimate secular interest government has in assuring the survival of society by favoring procreationally structured unions that get fathers and mothers to have and raise their own children.

The Truth Is ...

Same-sex marriage is wrong because government has good secular reasons for preserving the procreational structure of civil marriage.

References and Further Reading

For examples of advocates making this argument, see Daniel A. Crane, "Pick Your Shibboleths Wisely," *Christianity Today* (October 2004), pp. 60-64; Alan M. Dershowitz, "To Fix Gay Marriage, Government Should Quit the Marriage Business," *Los Angeles Times*, December 3, 2003; Alisa Solomon, "State to Church: I Want a Divorce," *Village Voice*, February 24, 2004; Jo Ann Citron, "Will It Be Marriage or Civil Union?" *Gay and Lesbian Review*, 11, no. 2 (2004), pp. 10-12; and Steve Swayne, "Church, State, and Marriage," *Rutland Herald*, May 4, 2004.

Christian writer C.S. Lewis favored an earlier version of this argument in relation to legal divorce. He contended, "There ought to be to be two distinct kinds of marriage: one governed by the State with rules enforced on all citizens, the other governed by the Church with rules enforced by her on her own members. The distinction ought to be quite sharp, so that a man knows which couples are married in a Christian sense and which are not." See C. S. Lewis, *Mere Christianity* (New York: Simon and Schuster, 1980), p. 102.

Anthropologist Claude Lévi-Strauss shows that procreationally structured marriage is not necessarily or uniquely religious, but rather should be categorized as a universally practiced "social institution with a biological foundation." See Claude Lévi-Strauss, "Introduction," in *A History of the Family*, by André Burguière (Cambridge, MA: Harvard University Press, 1996), p. 5. Lévi-Strauss also observes that marriage everywhere is structured as "a union, more or less durable, but socially approved, of two individuals of opposite sexes who establish a household and bear and raise children," and he notes that this marital form is found "to be a practically universal phenomenon, present in every type of society." See Claude Lévi-Strauss, *The View from Afar* (New York: Basic Books, 1985), pp. 40-41.

For the public meaning of marriage, see Maggie Gallagher, "What Marriage Is For: Children Need Mothers and Fathers," *The Weekly Standard* (August 4/August 11, 2003), pp. 22-25; Robert P. George and Jean Bethke Elshtain, eds., *The Meaning of Marriage: Family, State, Market, and Morals* (Dallas, TX: Spence Publishing, 2006); Claude Lévi-Strauss, *The Elementary Structures of Kinship* (Boston, MA: Beacon Press, 1969); and Carle Zimmerman, *Family and Civilization* (Wilmington, DE: ISI Books, 2008).

Douglas Laycock, Anthony Picarello and Robin Wilson, eds., *Same-Sex Marriage and Religious Liberty: Emerging Conflicts* (New York: Rowman and Littlefield, 2008).

Maggie Gallagher, "Banned in Boston: The Coming Conflict Between Same-Sex Marriage and Religious Liberty," *The Weekly Standard* (May 15, 2006), pp. 20-26.

Marc D. Stern, "Liberty v. Equality; Equality v. Liberty," *Northwestern Journal of Law and Social Policy*, 5/2 (Fall 2010), pp. 307-317, accessible at http://acadia.law.northwestern.edu/journals/njlsp/v5/n2/5/5Stern.pdf.

72

You May Hear Proponents Argue ...

Same-sex marriage should be allowed because government needs to affirm and support all marriages that are recognized and performed by communities of faith. Denying civil recognition to any marriage blessed by a faith community dishonors that community. Government in a secular society should not affirm the convictions of one faith group while restricting others, and it has no reason to allow fewer marriage options than what different faith communities affirm and practice. While secular government may allow more options than particular faith communities accept, it should never have fewer options than practiced by the various faith groups within its jurisdiction.

You Can *Graciously Refute* This By Saying ...

Proponents of this argument—in the name of equal treatment of faith communities—wrongly assume that government should recognize and support *any* activity endorsed by *any* religion simply because that particular religion endorses the activity. This violates the Non-establishment Clause of the U.S. Constitution by wrongly suggesting that secular government should establish practices endorsed by religion for no reason other than religious endorsement. It also is irresponsible, because it employs a principle that could require government to allow and support activities such as human sacrifice.

The interest that secular government has in prohibiting dangerous activities (such as human sacrifice) comes from the social value and common good of protecting innocent human life. The prohibition has nothing to do with favoring any one religion over another—even though one religion might allow human sacrifice while others do not. In the same way, the interest secular government has in protecting the procreational structure of marriage comes from the important social value and common good of assuring social survival and stability by uniting men with women to have and raise children. Again, it has nothing to do with dishonoring one faith community in favor of another—even though some faith groups bless and affirm same-sex unions while others do not.

Rather than aligning legal marriage with whatever any one religious group does, secular government should stay focused on supporting and protecting the institution of marriage. After all, it is the one institution that unites men and women long enough to have and raise children and keep children connected with their biological parents.

The Truth Is …

Same-sex marriage is wrong because government should not automatically endorse just any behavior a religious community happens to promote.

References and Further Reading

Chai R. Feldblum makes a similar argument in "Moral Conflict and Liberty; Gay Rights and Religion," *Brooklyn Law Review*, 72/1 (2006), pp. 61-123. Feldblum claims that "protecting one group's identity liberty may, at times, require that we burden others' belief liberty. This is an inherent and irreconcilable reality of our complex society" (p. 123).

Maggie Gallagher, "Banned in Boston: The Coming Conflict Between Same-Sex Marriage and Religious Liberty," *The Weekly Standard* (May 15, 2006), pp. 20-26.

Douglas Laycock, Anthony Picarello, and Robin Wilson, eds., *Same-Sex Marriage and Religious Liberty: Emerging Conflicts* (New York: Rowman and Littlefield, 2008).

Marc D. Stern, "Liberty v. Equality; Equality v. Liberty," *Northwestern Journal of Law and Social Policy*, 5/2 (Fall 2010), pp. 307-317, accessible at http://acadia.law.northwest ern.edu/journals/njlsp/v5/n2/5/5Stern.pdf.

Robin F. Wilson, "Same-Sex Marriage and Religious Liberty: Life after Prop 8," 14 NEXUS 101 (2009), accessible at http://heinonline. org/HOL/LandingPage?collection =journalsandhandle=hein. journals/nex14anddiv=14andid=andpage=.

Katie Zezima, "Obey Same-Sex Marriage Law, Officials Told," *New York Times* (April 26, 2004), p. A15.

John Jalsevac, "U.S. Christian Camp Loses Tax-Exempt Status over Same-Sex Civil-Union Ceremony," *LifeSiteNews* (September 19, 2007), accessible at http://www.lifesite.net/ldn/2007/sep/07091902.html. Jalsevac reported that the New Jersey Department of Environmental Protection revoked the tax-exemption of a Methodist ministry after it refused to allow a same-sex couple to use its boardwalk pavilion for their civil commitment ceremony.

Mary Ann Glendon, "For Better or for Worse?" *Wall Street Journal* (February. 25, 2004), p. A14, accessible at http://www.catholic-fidelity.com/for-better- or-for-worse-by-mary-ann-glendon/.

Tom Strode, "Scholars: 'Gay Marriage' Will Cause Church-State Clashes," *Baptist Press* (June 2006), accessible at http://www.bpnews.net/printerfriendly.asp?ID=23383.

Emily Donohue, "Same-Sex Marriage Would Have Disastrous Effects on Churches," *Rhode Island Catholic* (March 13, 2008), accessible at http://www.thericatholic.com/news/detail.html?sub_id=968.

M. V. Lee Badgett, *When Gay People Get Married: What Happens When Societies Legalize Same-Sex Marriage* (New York: New York University Press, 2009).

73

You May Hear Proponents Argue …

Same-sex marriage should be allowed because government must honor and protect religious freedom. Freedom of religion includes freedom from religious intrusions that limit what a government does as well as freedom from government intrusions that limit what religions do. Some religions believe their holy writings say that homosexual activity is wrong, while others do not. However, we live under a secular form of government, and faith convictions about what a holy writing says have no bearing on matters of law and public policy. Opposing same-sex marriage comes from religious convictions that everyone does not share, so resisting it is not consistent with religious liberty.

You Can *Graciously Refute* This By Saying …

Proponents of this argument wrongly suppose that there is a problem with existing law as it relates to religious freedom that legalizing same-sex marriage will fix. However, that is totally false and reverses the true situation. There is no problem with the present law, but legalizing same-sex marriage *will* create a significant problem as it relates to religious liberty that must be avoided.

What justifies the male-female procreational structure of marriage does not come from religion but from the public's interest in assuring social survival and stabilizing the social order. However, legalizing gay marriage will deny that marriage has any necessary structure, which will make it impossible to reconcile with any religious doctrine or tradition that treats marriage as having any structure at all. If gay marriage is legalized, all separate treatment of gay unions will become illegal, and religious exceptions will not be allowed because they will be classified in the same legal category as racial discrimination.

Under such law, people and groups who oppose gay marriage will be treated like bigots who oppose racial integration. Just as no religious exception is allowed for racial bigotry, no religious exemption will be allowed for people who refuse to accept gay marriage or refuse to treat same-sex marriages any different from other marriages. It is precisely because marriage is a legally protected public act that religious individuals and groups who refuse to honor or accept gay marriages will be made to suffer a host of negative consequences. These consequences include loss of tax-exempt status, punitive fines, and perhaps even incarceration.

The Truth Is ...

Same-sex marriage is wrong because it introduces conflicts of religious liberty into law that do not now exist and are totally unnecessary.

References and Further Reading

For example, Harvard professor Alan Dershowitz argues that because those who reject gay marriage view the institution of marriage as a religious sacrament, "the entire concept of marriage has no place in our civil society, which recognizes the separation between the sacred and the secular, between church and state." (See "To Fix Gay Marriage, Government Should Quit the Marriage Business," *Los Angeles Times*, December 3, 2003.) Alisa Solomon, a professor at City University of New York believes that the problem on which the same-sex marriage debate should focus is how "marriage itself violates the establishment clause by defining matrimony according to particular religious beliefs." (See "State to Church: I Want a Divorce," *Village Voice*, February 24, 2004.)

Maggie Gallagher, "Banned in Boston: The Coming Conflict Between Same-Sex Marriage and Religious Liberty," *The Weekly Standard* (May 15, 2006), pp. 20-26.

Chai Feldblum, EEOC commissioner for the Obama Administration and former Georgetown law professor, has claimed that if our government passes a law prohibiting discrimination on the basis of sexual orientation, it will at the same time require burdening "those who have an alternative moral assessment of gay men and lesbians." In other words, legalizing gay marriage will require burdening religiously based moral judgment, which will affect every level of human interaction. See Gallagher, "Banned in Boston," p. 22.

Marc Stern, general counsel for the American Jewish Congress, says that legalizing same-sex marriage will "work a sea change in American law ... [that] will reverberate across the legal and religious landscape." He believes this change will affect religious educational institutions, religious camps, religious retreats, religious social services, religious homeless shelters, religiously affiliated family services, religious marital counselors, religious adoption agencies, and religious community programs. See Gallagher, "Banned in Boston," p. 23.

Robin Wilson, professor of law at Washington and Lee University, says that if same-sex marriage is legalized, "Churches that oppose same-sex marriage today may perceive a credible, palpable threat to their tax-exemption status." Wilson believes this will occur because under Section 501(c) (3) of the Internal Revenue Code, for an organization to be recognized as tax-exempt, it must have purposes and activities that do not violate fundamental "public policy." See Gallagher, "Banned in Boston," p. 25.

Douglas Laycock, Anthony Picarello and Robin Wilson, eds., *Same-Sex Marriage and Religious Liberty: Emerging Conflicts* (New York: Rowman and Littlefield, 2008).

Emily Donohue, "Same-Sex Marriage Would Have Disastrous Effects on Churches," *Rhode Island Catholic* (March 13, 2008), accessible at http://www.thericatholic.com/news/detail.html?sub_id=968.

Gracious Answers to *Arguments Regarding* Science and Research

*There is
no more scientific basis for
institutionalizing same-sex marriage
anymore than there is for institutionalizing
a taste for tobacco. Institutions are not structured
by tastes that vary from person to person,
fluctuate over time, and cannot be
reliably measured. The fact is that
trustworthy science shows that
same-sex attractions vary from
person to person, fluctuate
over time, and cannot be
reliably measured.*

REGARDING SCIENCE AND RESEARCH

(Arguments 74–81)

74

You May Hear Proponents Argue …

*S*AME-SEX MARRIAGE SHOULD *be allowed because science has determined that homosexual attraction cannot change*. Science has proven that some people are biologically predisposed to same-sex attraction. This predisposition is genetically fixed and is impossible for people to change. Homosexuals do not choose to be gay. Just as they cannot be held responsible for changing something as genetically permanent as their eye color, skin color, or race, so they cannot be held responsible for changing their sexual orientation. Scientific evidence shows that we cannot treat homosexuality as if it is something a person can change, redirect, or deny. Legalizing same-sex marriage is needed to bring marriage up to date with current science.

You Can *Graciously Refute* This By Saying …

Statements by proponents of this argument—such as the American Psychological Association (APA), which denies the orientation of homosexuals can change—tend to be driven more by politics than by science. Most of these arguments are amazingly dogmatic given the large body of evidence certifying that not only can same-sex attraction be reduced but also changed to complete heterosexuality. The claim that homosexuality cannot be altered has no similar body of supporting evidence.

In fact, research compiled over more than a century convincingly shows that men and women *can* change their orientation from homosexuality to heterosexuality. This same research also shows that treating homosexuals is not harmful; that homosexuals do have more medical, psychological, and relational problems than heterosexuals; and that reorientation therapies are fairly successful. Opposing claims about the "science" of homosexuality come from a number of politicized studies conducted by activists—many of whom have admitted they were just trying to justify their own behavior—that were touted by the media as having proven same-sex attraction is beyond changing.

None of these studies has been replicated, all have failed to follow standard scientific procedure, and some have been exposed as blatantly fallacious. Even Dr. Robert Spitzer, who believed for years that changing sexual orientation was impossible and who worked to declassify homosexuality as a mental disorder, has since revised his stance. In a study he conducted he found that everyone "gave evidence of achieving degrees of long-term change in their sexual orientation up to and including complete heterosexuality without suffering any negative consequences from therapy."

The Truth Is ...

Same-sex marriage is wrong because homosexual orientation can change, and marriage cannot rely on something that can change.

References and Further Reading

For the American Psychological Association opposing change therapy, see "Insufficient Evidence that Sexual Orientation Change Efforts Work, Says APA: Practitioners Should Avoid Telling Clients They Can Change from Gay to Straight," (August 5, 2009), accessible at http://www.apa.org/news/press/releases/2009/08/therapeutic.aspx.

For Robert Spitzer's revised stance, see Robert L. Spitzer, "Can Some Gay Men and Lesbians Change Their Sexual Orientation?" 32/5, *Archives of Sexual Behavior* (October 2003), pp. 403-417.

For evidence that sexual orientation is subject to treatment and change, see Brian S. Mustanski, et al., "A Critical Review of Recent Biological Research on Human Sexual Orientation," *Annual Review of Sex Research*, 13 (2002), pp. 89-140; William Byne and Bruce Parsons, "Human Sexual Orientation: The Biologic Theories Reappraised," 50/3, *Archives of General Psychiatry* (March 1993), pp. 228-239; William Byne, "The Biological Evidence Challenged," *Scientific American* (May 1994), pp. 50-55; William Byne, "Why We Cannot Conclude that Sexual Orientation is Primarily a Biological Phenomenon," 34/1, *Journal of Homosexuality* (1997), pp. 73-80; John Horgan, "Gay Genes, Revisited: Doubts Arise Over Research on the Biology of Homosexuality," 273/5, *Scientific American* (November 1995), p. 26; and Eliot Marshall, "NIH's 'Gay Gene' Study Questioned," 268/5219, *Science* (June 30, 1995), p. 1841.

The National Association for Research and Therapy of Homosexuality (NARTH), "What Research Shows: NARTH's Response to the American Psychological Association's (APA) Claims on Homosexuality," *Journal of Human Sexuality* (2009), pp. 1-128, accessible at http://www.narth.com/docs/journalsummary.html.

"Reparative Therapy—Understanding and Diminishing Unwanted Attractions," National Association for Research and Therapy of

Homosexuality (video posted February 19, 2011), accessible at
http://www.narth.com/2011/02/therapy-from-gay-to-straight/.
For how the science has been misrepresented and politicized, see
Jeffrey Satinover, "The Trojan Couch: How the Mental Health
Associations Misrepresent Science," *Conference Reports 2005*,
National Association for Research and Therapy of Homosexuals,
accessible at http://www.narth.com/docs/thetrojancouch-
satinover; Robert Lerner and Althea Nagia, *No Basis: What the
Studies Don't Tell Us About Same-Sex Parenting*, Marriage Law
Project (Washington, DC, January 2001); A. Dean Byrd, "When
Activism Masquerades as Science," National Association for
Research and Therapy of Homosexuals, accessible at http://
www.narth.com/docs/masquerades (posted 2004, updated
September 3, 2008); and Michael L. Brown, "Is Gay the New
Black? Analyzing the Argument That 'I Was Born That Way,'"
in *A Queer Thing Happened to America* (Concord, NC: Equal
Time Books, 2011), pp. 197-225.

75

You May Hear Proponents Argue …

Same-sex marriage should be allowed because science has determined that same-sex attraction is as normal for homosexuals as opposite-sex attraction is for heterosexuals. The APA states, "The reality is that homosexuality is not an illness." There is nothing mentally unnatural, abnormal, deviant, or unhealthy about same-sex attraction for homosexuals as compared to opposite-sex attraction for heterosexuals. Thus, because there is no psychological basis for treating same-sex attraction as unnatural or abnormal for homosexuals, there is nothing abnormal or deviant about allowing same-sex marriage for homosexuals.

You Can *Graciously Refute* This By Saying …

The APA changed its position on homosexuality more as a result of political pressure than for valid scientific reasons. It is not true that homosexual behavior can be classified as biologically "natural" in the same way as heterosexual behavior. It is an obvious and irrefutable scientific fact that homosexual behavior is *very unnatural*. There are at least three reasons for this.

First, homosexuality is unnatural because there is no scientifically verifiable basis for believing the desire to stimulate sexual passion between members of the same sex is caused by naturally occurring biological factors. Researchers have speculated there is, but they have never proven any scientifically valid cause. In fact, there is a great body of valid evidence that links homosexual attraction to abuse or acquired taste.

Second, homosexual sex is physiologically unnatural for everyone. That is, the human body is not shaped to have sex in a way that is conducive to homosexuality. Homosexual behavior is

biologically destructive to human health—and, by functional definition—biologically destructive behavior is biologically *unnatural*.

Third, homosexuality is unnatural because reliable science does
not support the idea that sexual orientation is immutable. In fact,
the research verifies that all therapeutic approaches taken to reorient
people's feelings of homosexual attraction toward heterosexual
attraction have achieved significant results. In addition, nearly all
people who self-identify themselves as *homosexual* or *lesbian* end
up reorienting as heterosexuals by the time they reach old age.

The Truth Is …

*Same-sex marriage is wrong because it approves something that is
biologically unnatural and destructive.*

References and Further Reading

For the American Psychological Association (APA) position, see
"Sexual Orientation and Homosexuality," APA Help Center,
American Psychological Association, accessible at http://www.
apahelpcenter.org/articles/article.php?id+31.

For how the science relating to homosexuality has been misrepre-
sented and politicized, see Jeffrey Satinover, "The Trojan Couch:
How the Mental Health Associations Misrepresent Science,"
Conference Reports 2005, National Association for Research
and Therapy of Homosexuals, accessible at http://www.narth.
com/docs/thetrojancouchsatinover; Robert Lerner and Althea
Nagia, *No Basis: What the Studies Don't Tell Us About Same-Sex
Parenting*, Marriage Law Project (Washington, DC, January
2001); A. Dean Byrd, "When Activism Masquerades as Science,"
National Association for Research and Therapy of Homosexuals,
accessible at http://www.narth.com/docs/masquerades (posted
2004, updated September 3, 2008); Charles W. Socarides,
"How America Went Gay," *The Journal of Human Sexuality*

(1996), pp. 29-32; Ronald Bayer, *Homosexuality and American Psychiatry: The Politics of Diagnosis* (New York: Basic Books, 1981); and Michael L. Brown, "Is Gay the New Black? Analyzing the Argument That 'I Was Born That Way,'" in *A Queer Thing Happened to America* (Concord, NC: Equal Time Books, 2011), pp. 197-225.

Jeffrey B. Satinover, *Homosexuality and the Politics of Truth* (Grand Rapids, MI: Baker, 1996).

"Empowering Parents of Gender Discordant and Same-Sex Attracted Children," American College of Pediatricians (April 2008), accessible at http://www.acpeds.org/index/cgi?BISKIT+6792andCONTEXT=artandcat=1005andarthttp://www.acpeds.org/index/index.cgi?cat.

Warren Throckmorton, "Attempts to Modify Sexual Orientation: A Review of Outcome Literature and Ethical Issues," *Journal of Mental Health,* 20 (October 1998), pp. 283-304, accessible at http://www.narth.com/docs/atemptstohttp://www.narth.com/docs/attemptstomodify.html.

Charles W. Socarides, "Sexual Politics and Scientific Logic: The Issue of Homosexuality," *Journal of Psychohistory,* 10/3 (Winter 1992), pp. 307-329.

Charles W. Socarides, *Homosexuality: Psychoanalytic Therapy* (Northvale, NJ: Jason Aronson, 1989).

Charles W. Socarides, *Homosexuality: A Freedom too Far* (Phoenix, AZ: Margrave Books, 1995).

Joseph Nicolosi, *Reparative Therapy of Male Homosexuality: A New Clinical Approach* (New York: Jason Aronson, 1991).

76

You May Hear Proponents Argue …

Same-sex marriage should be allowed because psychologists say that homosexuals must actualize their human personhood with same-sex partners. Leading psychologists such as Sigmund Freud, Carl Jung, Erich Fromm, Abraham Maslow, and Carl Rogers all agreed that persons self-actualize themselves through sex and that this only occurs when they satisfy sexual desires in the form in which they arise. This means that homosexuals can only actualize themselves through homosexual sex. Discouraging gays from doing this is like withholding food from someone who is starving. Same-sex marriage will support efforts made by gays to achieve what psychologists say they must achieve.

You Can *Graciously Refute* This By Saying …

Proponents of this argument are saying that homosexuals have a psychologically necessary duty to pursue and fulfill whatever sexual desires they happen to possess. This concept comes from a false belief system, not from hard evidence that scientists can prove to be literally true or false. It represents the dangerous idea that society must redefine and restructure all institutions—especially marriage—to affirm whatever sexual desires people have.

Proponents wish to make this change in the name of actualizing an immeasurable, amorphic (formless), nebulous (hazy or unclear), ambiguous (open to interpretation), subjective, idiosyncratic (peculiar to the one claiming it), fluctuating, and relative notion of *personhood*. They base their claim on scientifically unverifiable psycho-philosophical theories that have been soundly discredited for normalizing and excusing pathological behaviors that are detrimental to human life and health.

Numerous studies over the years have documented that issues such as life-threatening behaviors, substance abuse, domestic violence, and suicidality are all several times higher among homosexual than heterosexual populations. These differences persist even when the stress of social disapproval is not present, and they result from behaviors most gays would not change even if they were allowed to marry same-sex partners. One sobering study led by David Fergusson in 2005 found that homosexuals were five times more likely to suffer major depression, four times more likely to be drug addicts, and 17.5 times more likely to attempt suicide as compared to a general heterosexual population.

The Truth Is …

Same-sex marriage is wrong because it radically redefines marriage based on a false ideology that harms homosexuals themselves.

References and Further Reading

For examples of famous figures in the field of psychology who have developed psycho-philosophical theories based on this argument, see Sigmund Freud, "Civilized Sexual Morality and Modern Nervousness," in *Sigmund Freud: Collected Papers*, trans. Joan Riviere, vol. 2 (New York: Basic Books, 1959); Carl G. Jung, *The Undiscovered Self* (Boston, MA: Little, Brown, 1958); Carl G. Jung, *Aspects of the Masculine* (Princeton, MA: Princeton University Press, 1989); Erich Fromm, *The Art of Loving* (New York: Harper and Brothers, 1956); Abraham Maslow, *Toward a Psychology of Being* (New York: Van Nostrand, 1968); and Carl R. Rogers, *Becoming Partners: Marriage and Its Alternatives* (New York: Delacorte, 1972).

While a poor mental state can be aggravated by discrimination, the main source of these negative results is intrinsic and arises from the pathology of homosexuality itself. For studies linking homosexual activity with a higher risk of poor mental and physical health and suicidality, see Theo Sandfort, Ron de Graaf, Rob Bojl, and Paul Schnabel, "Same-Sex Sexual Behavior and Psychiatric Disorders," *Archives of General Psychiatry*, 58 (January 2001), pp. 85-91; Susan Cochran and Vickie Mays, "Lifetime Prevalence of Suicide Symptoms and Affective Disorders Among Men Reporting Same-Sex Partners," *American Journal of Public Health*, 90/4 (April 2000), pp. 573-578; Stephen Gilman, Susan Cochran, Vickie Mays, M. Hughes, D. Ostrow, and R.C. Kessler, "Risk of Psychiatric Disorders Among Individuals Reporting Same-Sex Sexual Partners in the National Comorbidity Survey," *American Journal of Public Health*, 91/6 (June 2001), pp. 933-939; and David Fergusson, John Horwood, Elizabeth Ridder, and Annette Beautrais, "Sexual Orientation and Mental Health in a Birth Cohort of Young Adults," *Psychological Medicine*, 35/7 (2005), pp. 971-981.

For evidence of sexual orientation being subject to treatment and change, see Brian S. Mustanski, et al., "A Critical Review of Recent Biological Research on Human Sexual Orientation," *Annual Review of Sex Research*, 13 (2002), pp. 89-140; William Byne and Bruce Parsons, "Human Sexual Orientation: The Biologic Theories Reappraised," 50/3, *Archives of General Psychiatry* (March 1993), pp. 228-239; William Byne, "The Biological Evidence Challenged," *Scientific American* (May 1994), pp. 50-55; William Byne, "Why We Cannot Conclude That Sexual Orientation is Primarily a Biological Phenomenon," 34/1, *Journal of Homosexuality* (1997), pp. 73-80; John Horgan, "Gay Genes, Revisited: Doubts Arise Over Research on the Biology of Homosexuality," 273/5, *Scientific American* (November 1995), p. 26; and Eliot Marshall, "NIH's 'Gay Gene' Study Questioned," 268/5219, *Science* (June 30, 1995), p. 1841.

The National Association for Research and Therapy of Homosexuality (NARTH), "What Research Shows: NARTH's Response to the American Psychological Association's (APA) Claims on Homosexuality," *Journal of Human Sexuality* (2009), pp. 1-128, accessible at http://www.narth.com/docs/journalsummary.html.

77

You May Hear Proponents Argue …

Same-sex marriage should be allowed because there is no scientific basis for drawing a clear line between heterosexual and homosexual orientation. People's sexual orientation tends to fall in a continuum, with total heterosexuality being one extreme and total homosexuality being the other. People are rarely ever completely one way or the other, but tend to fall somewhere between the two extremes, so that they possess sexual orientations that are mixed. Thus, because there is no clear division separating one from the other, marriage should be made to accommodate this diversity by removing a barrier that imposes a distinction not supported by scientific fact.

You Can *Graciously Refute* This By Saying …

It is true that sexual feelings vary not only from person to person but also over time in the same person. However, this variation has nothing to do with sexual physiology (with how members of a species mate), much less with what structures marriage as a social institution. This creates two main problems with this argument.

First, proponents reverse how science fits what is subjective to what is objective. Science uncovers objective facts to which people's subjective feelings must adapt, not the other way around. Instead of shaping feelings (which is subjective) to marriage (which is objective), proponents of this argument shape marriage (which is objective) to feelings of sexual attraction (which is subjective). This is like saying auto safety should be made to fit how people feel about cars, instead of requiring people's feelings about cars to be made to fit what auto safety requires.

Second, proponents confuse ideology with science. In many ways, they make a claim similar to saying they believe the moon is made of Swiss cheese (an ideology); and because they hold this belief, it must necessarily be so (a scientific fact). Of course, ideologies do not necessarily lead to scientific fact.

Third, the biggest problem proponents have in making this argument is that science absolutely proves that humans are completely dimorphic creatures. In every human cell, women have two X chromosomes and men have one X and one Y chromosome. There is no sliding continuum—every person is either completely male or completely female. Because of this, there is no scientific basis to justify that what draws one person to mate with another can be rightly distinguished from how sexual physiology fits male to female bodies. Nothing else fits, nothing else is complete, and nothing else works.

The Truth Is ...

Same-sex marriage is wrong because marriage should not be made to conflict with human physiology and cellular science.

References and Further Research

Physiology is the branch of biology dealing with the functions and activities of living organisms and their parts.

For an example of an advocate making a claim on which this argument is based, see Sivahn Barsade, "The Many Colors of the Sexuality Spectrum," *The Merionite*, Lower Merion High School, accessible at http://www.themerionite.org/?p=1901.

For evidence of sexual orientation being subject to treatment and change, see Brian S. Mustanski, et al., "A Critical Review of Recent Biological Research on Human Sexual Orientation," *Annual Review of Sex Research*, 13 (2002), pp. 89-140; William Byne and Bruce Parsons, "Human Sexual Orientation: The Biologic Theories Reappraised," 50/3, *Archives of General Psychiatry* (March 1993), pp. 228-239; William Byne, "The Biological Evidence Challenged," *Scientific American* (May 1994), pp. 50-55; William Byne, "Why We Cannot Conclude

that Sexual Orientation is Primarily a Biological Phenomenon,"
34/1, *Journal of Homosexuality* (1997), pp. 73-80; and John
Horgan, "Gay Genes, Revisited: Doubts Arise Over Research
on the Biology of Homosexuality," 273/5, *Scientific American*
(November 1995), p. 26.

Oliver O'Donovan states that because "human beings come into
existence with a dimorphically differentiated sexuality ...
ordered at the biological level towards heterosexual union
as the human mode of procreation [it cannot be argued that]
the biological endowment from which the psychological and
behavioral possibilities arise [is a graduated continuum] with a
masculine and feminine pole and a wide range of intermediate
variations." Rather, science clearly proves "the starting point for
dimorphic differentiation is already present at the conception
of a child in the presence or absence of a 'Y' chromosome, the
effect of which is to differentiate the development of a male
from the female gonadal structure [in every single cell of the
body]." On this basis, O'Donovan declares "the either-or of
biological maleness and femaleness to which the human race is
bound is not a meaningless or oppressive condition of nature."
See Oliver O'Donovan, *Transsexualism and Christian Marriage*
(Bramcote, UK: Grove Books, 1982), pp. 6-7.

For how legalizing same-sex marriage will align marriage to
homosexual categories and not align homosexuals to what
marriage is now, see Lawrence Auster, "The Extreme Radicalism
of Homosexual 'Marriage,'" *View from the Right* (June 2, 2008),
accessible at http://www.amnation.com/vfr/archives/010723.html.

Timothy J. Dailey and Peter Sprigg, *Getting It Straight: What
Research Says About Homosexuality* (Washington, DC: Family
Research Council, 2004).

Ronald Bayer, *Homosexuality and American Psychiatry: The Politics
of Diagnosis* (New York: Basic Books, 1981).

78

You May Hear Proponents Argue …

Same-sex marriage should be allowed because science shows that homosexuals have different brains and cannot marry opposite-sex partners. Biological research into areas of the brain shows there is nothing scientifically abnormal or wrong with same-sex orientation. In fact, new findings add to an increasingly convincing body of evidence proving that sexual orientation comes from developmental brain differences occurring in the womb. Sexual differentiation of the human brain occurs during fetal and neo-natal development, and this is what programs sexual orientation. Denying same-sex marriage clashes with the findings of neurological science.

You Can *Graciously Refute* This By Saying …

The brain studies to which proponents of this argument refer are highly dubious, but even if accepted, the alleged findings are totally irrelevant to the significance of marriage. The public value of marriage has nothing to do with feelings or desires that vary from person to person but only with preserving intergenerational continuity and getting mothers and fathers to stay with and raise their own biological children. The claim that scientists are amassing evidence that proves the existence of a neurological basis for homosexual behavior is totally false.

These studies have all failed to distinguish cause from effect, and so they prove nothing about homosexual desires having a biological origin. The idea that there is a brain status for *sexual orientation* apart from physiological gender is pure fiction. Scientists cannot even agree on what *sexual orientation* means, much less how to measure such a nebulous concept. The most recent and reliable neurological research confirms that sexual activity produces powerful changes in the human brain, rather than the other way around.

In the end, the physiological gender identity of a person comes down to three unchanging and easy-to-identify scientific criteria: (1) the presence or absence of a Y chromosome in every cell, (2) the possession of male or female gonads, and (3) the possession of either male or female genitalia. When all three point in the same direction, they determine a person's sexual status for the public purpose of civil marriage. These characteristics cannot be replaced by psychological, emotional, or even purely neurological criteria.

The Truth Is …

Same-sex marriage is wrong because brain studies do not justify adopting a deconstructionist redefinition of marriage.

References and Further Reading

For the studies on which this argument is based, see Ivanka Savic, Hans Berglund, and Per Lindström, "Brain Responses to Putative Pheronomes in Homosexual Men," *Proceedings of the National Academy of Sciences of the United States*, 102/20 (May 17, 2005), pp. 7356-7361; Ivanka Savic and Per Lindström, "PET and MRI Show Differences in Cerebral Asymmetry and Functional Connectivity between Homo- and Hetero-sexual Subjects," *Proceedings of the National Academy of Sciences of the United States*, 105/27 (July 8, 2008), pp. 9403-9408; Nicholas Wade, "For Gay Men, An Attraction to a Different Kind of Scent," *The New York Times* (May 11, 2005); and J. R. Atwood, "The Gay Brain? Neuroscientists Find Evidence that Homosexuality Is Hard-Wired," *Playthink* (June 17, 2008), accessible at http://playthink.wordpress.com/2008/06/17/the-gay-brain/.

For criticism of these studies, see Rob Stein, "Brain Study Shows Differences Between Gays, Straights," *The Washington Post* (June 23, 2008); and NARTH, "Latest Gay Brain Study Scrutinized,"

(May 11, 2005), accessible at http://narth.com/2010/09/latest-gay-brain-study-scrutinized/.

For evidence of sexual orientation being subject to treatment and change, see Brian S. Mustanski, et al., "A Critical Review of Recent Biological Research on Human Sexual Orientation," *Annual Review of Sex Research*, 13 (2002), pp. 89-140; William Byne and Bruce Parsons, "Human Sexual Orientation: The Biologic Theories Reappraised," *Archives of General Psychiatry*, 50/3 (March 1993), pp. 228-239; William Byne, "The Biological Evidence Challenged," *Scientific American* (May 1994), pp. 50-55; William Byne, "Why We Cannot Conclude That Sexual Orientation Is Primarily a Biological Phenomenon," *Journal of Homosexuality*, 34/1 (1997), pp. 73-80; and John Horgan, "Gay Genes, Revisited: Doubts Arise Over Research on the Biology of Homosexuality," *Scientific American*, 273/5 (November 1995), p. 26.

Jeffrey Elman, Elizabeth A. Bates, Mark H. Johnson, et al, *Rethinking Innateness: A Connectionist Perspective on Development* (Cambridge, MA: MIT Press, 1996).

Charles A. Nelson, "Neural Plasticity and Human Development: The Role of Early Experience in Sculpting Memory Systems," *Current Directions in Psychological Science*, 8/2 (2000), pp. 42-45.

Helen Fisher, *Why We Love: The Nature and Chemistry of Romantic Love* (New York: Henry Holt, 2004).

Andreas Bartels and Semir Zeki, "The Neural Basis of Romantic Love," *NeuroReport*, 11/17 (November 27, 2000), pp. 3829-3834.

79

You May Hear Proponents Argue …

Same-sex marriage should be allowed because the "ick" response some feel toward it has no scientific justification. Revulsion toward homosexual marriage comes from social conditioning and has no basis in human biology or psychology. People are tricked into wrongly thinking that anything other than heterosexual behavior is abnormal and are trained to react with disgust. Such reaction is unnaturally imposed by nothing more than blind prejudice, and it only shows that people are stuck in old-fashioned ways of thinking that have no scientific basis. Same-sex marriage must be legalized to cleanse marriage law from unreflective social prejudice.

You Can *Graciously Refute* This By Saying …

It is true that what shocked people yesterday is often accepted today and that some repugnancies express blind prejudice. But this does not mean that all do, or that all such change is good, or that feelings of revulsion are never scientifically grounded. Some visceral reactions clash with scientific reality, but others come from instincts rooted in human anatomy and physiology.

The "ick" response that some people feel toward same-sex marriage belongs in the second category, not the first. People instinctively recoil from the idea of severing marriage from the anatomy of human procreation. We should not renounce this response but respect it, because it comes from deep emotions connecting basic humanity with the science of reproduction. There is a difference between biologically rooted natural instincts and biologically irrelevant social conditioning. Neither starts with reason, but that does not mean that both are therefore beyond justification. Instinctive revulsion is grounded in biological reality and therefore justified, while conditioning contrary to natural instinct is groundless and unjustifiable.

The "ick" response some feel toward same-sex marriage thus does not come from baseless prejudice but from scientifically warranted natural instincts. What has no scientific basis—and only expresses blind prejudice—is claiming instinctive revulsion toward same-sex marriage has no objective relation to biology. Real science will never justify overriding the natural alignment of human instinct with human physiology. After all, it is possible for people to override their intuitive revulsion and get used to things such as cannibalism, father-daughter incest, or same-sex marriage, but they only do so to the detriment of humanity.

The Truth Is …

Same-sex marriage is wrong because it overrides scientifically justified alignment of human instinct with human physiology.

References and Further Reading

For examples of advocates using this argument, see "Dog Poop, Religion, Homosexuality and the 'Ick' Factor," *Trip to the Outhouse* blog (posted August 13, 2008), accessible at http://triptotheouthouse.wordpress.com/2008/08/13/dog-poop-religion-and-the-ick-factor/; Damon Linker, "The Great Gay Marriage Debate: Round Three," *The New Republic* (posted April 2, 2009), accessible at http://www.tnr.com/print/blog/damon-linker/the-great-gay-marriage-debate-round-three; Tony Jones, "Getting Beyond the 'Ick Factor' in the Gay Marriage Debate," *The New Christians* blog, *BeliefNet* (posted April 20, 2009), accessible at http://blog.beliefnet.com/tonyjones/2009/04/getting-beyond-the-ick-factor.html; and Nick Wing, "Mike Huckabee 'Ick Factor' Comments Slammed by Gay Rights Groups," *The Huffington Post* (posted June 22, 2010).

Matt Kennedy, "The 'Ick Factor'," *StandFirm* blog (June 17, 2008), accessible at http://www.standfirminfaith.com/index.php/site/article/13451/.

Leon R. Kass, "The Wisdom of Repugnance," *The New Republic*, 22 (1997), pp. 12-26, accessible at http://www.catholiceducation.org/articles/medical_ethics/me0006.html.

Robert M. L. Winston, *Human Instinct* (New York: Bantam Press, 2002).

A.D. Paltiel and A.A. Stinnett, "Making Health Policy Decisions: Is Human Instinct Rational? Is Rational Choice Human?" *Chance*, 9/2 (1996), pp. 34-39.

Nigel Nicholson, "How Hardwired Is Human Behavior?" *Harvard Business Review* (July-August, 1998), pp. 135-147.

In *Crime and Punishment*, Dostoevsky has the character Raskolnikov say, "Man grows used to everything, the brute!" In making that comment, Dostoevsky was observing that men acclimatize to some things only at loss to their humanity. See Fyodor Dostoevsky, *Crime and Punishment* (New York: Modern Library, 1994), chapter 2.

For how the science has been misrepresented and politicized, see Jeffrey B. Satinover, "The Trojan Couch: How the Mental Health Associations Misrepresent Science," *Conference Reports 2005*, National Association for Research and Therapy of Homosexuals, accessible at http://www.narth.com/docs/thetrojancouchsatinover; Jeffrey B. Satinover, *Homosexuality and the Politics of Truth* (Grand Rapids, MI: Baker, 1996); Jeffrey B. Satinover, "The Gay Gene?" *The Journal of Human Sexuality*, (1996), pp. 3-10; Robert Lerner and Althea Nagia, *No Basis: What the Studies Don't Tell Us About Same-Sex Parenting*, Marriage Law Project (Washington, DC, January 2001); and A. Dean Byrd, "When Activism Masquerades as Science," National Association for Research and Therapy of Homosexuals, accessible at http://www.narth.com/docs/masquerades (posted 2004, updated September 3, 2008).

80

You May Hear Proponents Argue ...

Same-sex marriage should be allowed in order to end the damage being done to the mental health of homosexual partners. Homosexuals have the same need we all have for human connection through sex, and they differ only in their sexual orientation. Studies have shown that denying same-sex marriage to homosexuals harms their psychological health. This is why the American Medical Association (AMA) has declared that "exclusion from civil marriage contributes to health care disparities affecting same-sex households." Same-sex marriage is required to stop the psychological damage homosexuals suffer when they are made to feel ostracized and abnormal.

You Can *Graciously Refute* This By Saying ...

Dr. Jeffrey Satinover, a distinguished expert in psychoanalysis and psychiatry, has documented through his experience and extensive scientific analysis how the professional medical associations in the United States—including the AMA and the APA—have been radically corrupted to accommodate homosexual activists and have seriously misinterpreted and misrepresented the scientific record. Based on Satinover's observations, proponents of this argument are wrong on at least five accounts.

First, they misrepresent science by claiming their evidence supports something that cannot be reliably measured, much less validated. Because the sexual orientation of homosexuals fluctuates over time and from person to person, attempting to measure *harm* to such a person is like trying to measure harm to the shape of Jell-O.

Second, these proponents wrongly assume that homosexuals do not now have what heterosexuals have when they get married. This is not the case at all—or at least it cannot be the same, unless *marriage* is redefined into what homosexuals want to make it by legalizing same-sex marriage.

Third, these proponents rely on the idea that homosexuals are not having sex, or cannot experience psychologically satisfying sex, until or unless they are allowed to marry partners of the same sex. This is also not the case.

Fourth, they wrongly reduce sex to nothing but psychology, and then they mistake an effect that sex produces with what marriage is intended to produce. Finally, they confuse sexual intimacy with friendship intimacy, which, of course, are different categories that have no automatic connection.

The Truth Is …

Same-sex marriage is wrong because it relies on bad psychology to justify confusing an effect of sex with the purpose of marriage.

References and Further Reading

For examples of advocates using this argument, see Christopher Munsey, "Psychology's Case for Same-Sex Marriage," *Monitor,* 41/9 (October 2010), p. 46; and Sharon Scales Rostosky, Ellen D.B. Riggle, Sharon G. Horne, and Angela D. Miller, "Marriage Amendments and Psychological Distress in Lesbian, Gay, and Bisexual (LGB) Adults," *Journal of Counseling Psychology,* 56/1 (January 2009), pp. 56-66.

For how the mental health sciences have been misrepresented and politicized, see Jeffrey B. Satinover, "The Trojan Couch: How the Mental Health Associations Misrepresent Science," *Conference Reports 2005,* National Association for Research and Therapy of Homosexuals, accessible at http://www.narth.com/docs/ thetrojancouchsatinover; Jeffrey B. Satinover, *Homosexuality and the Politics of Truth* (Grand Rapids, MI: Baker, 1996);

Jeffrey B. Satinover, "The Gay Gene?" *The Journal of Human Sexuality* (1996), pp. 3-10; Robert Lerner and Althea Nagia, *No Basis: What the Studies Don't Tell Us About Same-Sex Parenting*, Marriage Law Project (Washington, DC, January 2001); Dean Byrd, "When Activism Masquerades as Science," National Association for Research and Therapy of Homosexuals, accessible at http://www.narth.com/docs/masquerades (posted 2004, updated September 3, 2008); Michael L. Brown, "Is Gay the New Black? Analyzing the Argument That 'I Was Born That Way,'" in *A Queer Thing Happened to America* (Concord, NC: Equal Time Books, 2011), pp. 197-225; Ronald Bayer, *Homosexuality and American Psychiatry: The Politics of Diagnosis* (New York: Basic Books, 1981); Warren Throckmorton, "Initial Empirical and Clinical Findings Concerning the Change Process for Ex-Gays," *Professional Psychology: Research and Practice*, 33/3 (June 2002), pp. 242-248; and Paul Billings and Jonathan Beckwith, "Born Gay?" *Technology Review*, 96/5 (July 1993), pp. 60-22.

Contrary to what proponents of this argument assume, there is a well-documented connection linking homosexual activity with poor mental health and greater risk of suicide. While a poor mental state can be aggravated by discrimination, the main source of these negative results intrinsically arises from the pathology of homosexuality itself. For documentation and details, see Theo Sandfort, Ron de Graaf, Rob Bojl, and Paul Schnabel, "Same-Sex Sexual Behavior and Psychiatric Disorders," *Archives of General Psychiatry*, 58 (January 2001), pp. 85-91; Susan Cochran and Vickie Mays, "Lifetime Prevalence of Suicide Symptoms and Affective Disorders Among Men Reporting Same-Sex Partners," *American Journal of Public Health*, 90/4 (April 2000), pp. 573-578; Stephen Gilman, Susan Cochran, Vickie Mays, et al., "Risk of Psychiatric Disorders Among Individuals Reporting Same-Sex Sexual Partners in the National

Comorbidity Survey," *American Journal of Public Health*, 91/6 (June 2001), pp. 933-939; and David Fergusson, John Horwood, Elizabeth Ridder, and Annette Beautrais, "Sexual Orientation and Mental Health in a Birth Cohort of Young Adults," *Psychological Medicine*, 35/7 (2005), pp. 971-981.

81

You May Hear Proponents Argue ...

Same-sex marriage should be allowed to enhance the mental health of homosexual couples. In the same way that denying same-sex marriage harms homosexuals' mental health, so allowing same-sex couples to marry will strengthen it. Psychological wholeness is a matter of integrating life with sexual desires that are aligned to the way they arise. Denying this natural alignment is unhealthy, while pursuing relationships that accept and affirm this alignment is healthy. Legalizing same-sex marriage is needed not only to cease damaging the mental health of homosexual couples but also to ensure they can become as psychologically strong and healthy as married heterosexual couples.

You Can *Graciously Refute* This By Saying ...

Proponents of this argument make three errors. First, they incorrectly assume that marriage is already what they want it to be and that they are only being made to feel bad for being left out. However, that is not the case, because homosexuals want to radically change marriage before they get married and do *not* want what others currently have. Same-sex couples are not allowed to marry for the same reason people are not allowed to marry an animal, a dead body, a plant, or their own son, daughter, sister, mother, or father. The structure of civil marriage has nothing to do with affirming psychology but only with the state's legitimate interest in assuring social survival.

Second, these proponents wrongly assume that marriage produces psychological health. People should be psychologically healthy *before* they get married and should not think that marriage will solve their mental problems. Even traditional marriage does not ensure a person will get psychologically better, and sometimes it can even aggravate a person's mental problems. In the same way, marriage restructured to affirm a homosexual's feelings will only make his or her mental state worse by intensifying tension between the psychological and biological. Scientifically speaking, if there is psychological and biological conflict within a person, it is the psychological that must change to fit the biological, not the other way around.

Third, proponents of this argument anticipate scientifically invalid results, because all evidence indicates that same-sex couples continue to generate the same psychological problems whether they are allowed to marry or not. Countries where same-sex marriage is allowed have continued to report much higher rates of depression, suicide, and anxiety among homosexuals as compared to the general population.

The Truth Is …

Same-sex marriage is wrong because it will increase the tension that same-sex couples experience between the psychological and biological.

References and Further Reading

For examples of advocates justifying same-sex marriage based on psychology, see Christopher Munsey, "Psychology's Case for Same-Sex Marriage," *Monitor*, 41/9 (October 2010), p. 46; Sharon S. Rostosky, Ellen D. B. Riggle, Sharon G. Horne, and Angela D. Miller, "Marriage Amendments and Psychological Distress in Lesbian, Gay, and Bisexual (LGB) Adults," *Journal of Counseling Psychology*, 56/1 (January 2009), pp. 56-66; Sharon S. Rotosky, Ellen D. B. Riggle, Sharon G. Horne, et al., "Lesbian, Gay, and Bisexual Individuals' Psychological Reactions to Amendments Denying Access to Civil Marriage," *American Journal of Orthopsychiatry*, 80/3 (July 2010), pp. 302-310; Brian

Musanski, "Why Not Allow Gay Marriage?" posted November 28, 2008, on *The Sexual Continuum* blog for *Psychology Today*; Saul Levin and Gal Mayer, "Statement of the American Medical Association to the Institute of Medicine Re: Lesbian, Gay, Bisexual and Transgender (LGBT) Health Issues and Research Gaps and Opportunities," issued and presented February 1, 2010; and Ilan H. Meyer, "Prejudice, Social Stress, and Mental Health in Lesbian, Gay, and Bisexual Populations: Conceptual Issues and Research Evidence," *Psychological Bulletin,* 129/5 (September 2003), pp. 674-697.

For evidence of sexual orientation being subject to treatment and change, see Brian S. Mustanski, et al., "A Critical Review of Recent Biological Research on Human Sexual Orientation," *Annual Review of Sex Research*, 13 (2002), pp. 89-140; William Byne and Bruce Parsons, "Human Sexual Orientation: The Biologic Theories Reappraised," 50/3, *Archives of General Psychiatry* (March 1993), pp. 228-239; William Byne, "The Biological Evidence Challenged," *Scientific American* (May 1994), pp. 50-55; William Byne, "Why We Cannot Conclude That Sexual Orientation is Primarily a Biological Phenomenon," 34/1, *Journal of Homosexuality* (1997), pp. 73-80; John Horgan, "Gay Genes, Revisited: Doubts Arise Over Research on the Biology of Homosexuality," 273/5, *Scientific American* (November 1995), p. 26; and Eliot Marshall, "NIH's 'Gay Gene' Study Questioned," 268/5219, *Science* (June 30, 1995), p. 1841.

The National Association for Research and Therapy of Homosexuality (NARTH), "What Research Shows: NARTH's Response to the American Psychological Association's Claims on Homosexuality," *Journal of Human Sexuality* (2009), pp. 1-128, accessible at http://www.narth.com/docs/journalsummary.html.

On how the science has been misrepresented and politicized see, Jeffrey B. Satinover, "The Trojan Couch: How the Mental Health Associations Misrepresent Science," *Conference Reports 2005,*

National Association for Research and Therapy of Homosexuals, accessible at http://www.narth.com/docs/thetrojancouchsatinover; A. D. Byrd, "When Activism Masquerades as Science," National Association for Research and Therapy of Homosexuals, accessible at http://www.narth.com/docs/masquerades, updated September 3, 2008; and Ronald Bayer, *Homosexuality and American Psychiatry: The Politics of Diagnosis* (New York: Basic Books, 1981).

Arguments 82 – 91

Gracious Answers to Arguments Regarding Morality and Ethics

*It cannot
be moral to ruin
an essential institution
by changing it in a way that
denies what is best for children,
affirms behavior harmful to
those who embrace it, and
ultimately threatens
social collapse.*

REGARDING MORALITY
AND ETHICS

(Arguments 82–91)

82

You May Hear Proponents Argue ...

*S*AME-SEX MARRIAGE SHOULD *be allowed because it greatly improves the morality of homosexual relationships.* Conservatives who deplore the sexual promiscuity of homosexuals should be the first to support same-sex marriage. The only possible effect gay marriage can have is to encourage homosexuals to behave in more responsible ways. So why not use same-sex marriage to coax homosexuals into embracing traditional family values rather than railing incoherently against them? Same-sex marriage will help homosexual relationships become more faithful, responsible, and enduring. In the end, this will improve the morality of homosexual relationships in general.

You Can *Graciously Refute* This By Saying ...

This is the moral form of what some call the "conservative" argument for same-sex marriage. However, proponents of this claim depend on the assumption that homosexuals will accept their behavior is morally wrong and needs to change, which is something to which no homosexual will agree. Ultimately, this argument does not represent something that homosexuals respect but is just a ploy designed to weaken the resistance of gullible conservatives.

In reality, gay and lesbian couples have no interest in ever conforming to conservative sexual values or in taking moral cues from the way straight couples behave. Most homosexuals look on same-sex marriage as a way to weaken and marginalize the ethic of sexual fidelity and complementarity traditional marriage law has reinforced. Contrary to what proponents of this argument say, same-sex marriage will not change the ethic of homosexuals but will only change the kind of ethic that marriage law affirms and supports. It will shift what marriage law endorses away from reinforcing an ethos of procreation, complementarity, and sexual fidelity toward condoning and supporting an ethos indulging personal appetite.

Sociologist Gretchen Stiers has done a study showing that "many radical gays and lesbians actually yearn to see marriage abolished" and favor same-sex marriage only "as part of a self-conscious attempt to subvert the institution of marriage from within." In addition, Andrew Sullivan, the progenitor and original proponent of this argument, now admits that what he calls the *richness* of homosexual experience actually *dissolves* the morality by which everything is structured and defined in society, law, and the church—including marriage.

The Truth Is …

Same-sex marriage is wrong because it will not improve the morality of homosexuals but will dissolve the morality of regular marriage.

References and Further Reading

For examples of advocates using this argument, see Andrew Sullivan, "Here Comes the Groom," *New Republic* (August 28, 1989), accessible at www.andrewsullivan.com/print. php?artnum=19890828; Andrew Sullivan, *Virtually Normal: An Argument About Homosexuality* (New York: Random House, 1995), p. 107; and William N. Eskridge, Jr., "Civilizing Gays, Civilizing Straights, " in *The Case for Same-Sex Marriage: From Sexual Liberty to Civilized Commitment* (New York: Simon and Schuster, 1996), pp. 1-13.

For examples of gays having no interest in restricting sex to marriage, see Michelangelo Signorile, "Bridal Wave," *Out* (December/January 1994), p. 161; Gretchen A. Stiers, *From This Day Forward: Commitment, Marriage, and Family in Lesbian and Gay Relationships* (New York: St. Martin's Press, 1999); William Aaron, *Straight* (New York: Bantam Books, 1972), p. 208; and Mollie Hemingway, "Same-Sex, Different Marriage: Many Who Want Marriage Equality Do Not Want Fidelity," *Christianity Today* (May 18, 2010), accessible at http://www. christianitytoday.com/ct/2010/may/11.52.html.

For examples of gay social revolutionaries admitting they are using same-sex marriage as a way to completely abolish the institution of marriage, see Thomas B. Stoddard, "Why Gay People Should Seek the Right to Marry," chapter 35 in *Families in the US: Kinship and Domestic Politics*, ed. Karen V. Hansen (Philadelphia, PA: Temple University Press, 1998); Richard D. Mohr, *A More Perfect Union: Why Straight America Must Stand Up for Gay Rights* (Boston, MA: Beacon, 1994); Gretchen A. Stiers, *From This Day Forward: Commitment, Marriage, and Family in Lesbian and Gay Relationships* (New York: St. Martin's Press, 1999); Michelangelo Signorile, "Bridal Wave," *Out* (December/ January 1994); "Sociologist Says Gay Marriage Does Threaten

Established Order and That's Good," *Ascribe Law News Service* (November 16, 2003); and Margaret Gullette, "The New Case for Marriage," *American Prospect* (March 1, 2004).

Stanley Kurtz, "The End of Marriage in Scandinavia: The 'Conservative Case' for Same-Sex Marriage Collapses," *Weekly Standard* (February 2, 2004), pp. 26-33.

John M. Finnis, "The Good of Marriage and the Morality of Sexual Relations: Some Philosophical and Historical Observations," *The American Journal of Jurisprudence*, 42 (1997), pp. 97-134.

For how legalizing same-sex marriage will align marriage to homosexual categories and not align homosexuals to what marriage is now, see Lawrence Auster, "The Extreme Radicalism of Homosexual 'Marriage,'" *View from the Right* (June 2, 2008), accessible at http://www.amnation.com/vfr/archives/010723.html.

Sherif Girgis, Robert P. George, and Ryan T. Anderson, "What Is Marriage?" *Harvard Journal of Law and Public Policy*, 34/1 (Winter 2011), pp. 245-287.

83

You May Hear Proponents Argue …

Same-sex marriage should be allowed because morality requires rejecting what is mean-spirited and hateful. It is hurtful and wrong to deny marriage to homosexuals and insist they must instead choose to marry someone they do not find sexually attractive. Everyone should have a chance to marry a mate he or she finds attractive, and denying this to homosexuals is bigoted, selfish, and cruel. The state's case for opposing same-sex marriage rests on nothing more than homophobia, which is not a productive policy because it engenders irrational hatred. Civilizing America means taking homophobia off the national agenda.

You Can *Graciously Refute* This By Saying …

Proponents of this argument unfairly disparage those who defend the traditional structure of marriage as heartless zealots bent on harming homosexuals. Political disagreement is not hate speech, and opposition to same-sex marriage is not based on bigotry but on good moral reason. The state's interest in keeping marriage as it is does not come from irrational views about gay people but from legitimate public concern in assuring intergenerational social survival.

Seen in this light, existing marriage laws are not any more mean or hateful than saying a dog is not a cat or that only American citizens can vote in American elections. All people—both heterosexuals and homosexuals—have an equal right to find and marry a willing partner within the categories structuring the institution. No one—neither heterosexuals nor homosexuals—can get a marriage license for categories outside that structure. So, for example, no one can marry a child, or a near relative, or a person married to someone else, or a corpse, or an animal.

No one in his or her right mind would think of calling these limits bigoted, mean-spirited, or hateful. These restrictions just follow from recognizing something for what it is and then treating everyone the same in relation to that thing. Thus, opposition to same-sex marriage is not hateful in the same way that not going along with calling a clock a chair is not hateful—even if some people like to sit on clocks. What is truly bigoted, mean-spirited, and hateful is smearing the character of those who try to keep marriage from being radically deconstructed and then charging them with having improper motives for their actions.

The Truth Is ...

Same-sex marriage is wrong because marriage law is not hateful and should not be made to change by maligning the character of others.

References and Further Reading

For examples of advocates using this argument, see "Civil Rights Commission Calls Gay Marriage Amendment 'Hateful'," accessible at http://www.gaypasg.org/gaypasg/PressClippings/2004/October/civil_rights_commissioni_calls_g.htm; "Rick Perry Signs NOM's Hateful Anti-Gay Marriage Pledge," *Gay-Geek Number One* (posted August 26, 2011), accessible at http://southern4life.blogspot.com/2011/08/rick-perry-signs-noms-hateful-anti-gay.html; Fred Karger, "Open Letter to Maggie Gallagher," *Californians Against Hate*, posted March 9, 2010, accessible at http://www.californiansagainsthate.com/category/national-organization-for-marriage/page/2/; "Gay Rights, Gay Marriage, Homophobia: Ethical, Political Issues," http://atheism.about.com/od/gaymarriage/Gay_Rights_Gay_Marriage_Homophobia_Ethical_Political_Issues.htm; Matthew Urdan, "Gay Marriage: Our Choice Between Hate and Civil Society," *Inside Government* blog, posted March 10, 2011, accessible at http://www.insidegov.org/?p=583andprint=1; and "Bishop Cordileone's Masses Threatened," *California Catholic Daily* blog, posted December 1, 2009, accessible at http://calcatholic.com/news/newsArticle.aspx?id= 2273e73a-daals-47d7-81ef-39b61fb4a49e.

On the rationality of normal marriage, see Maggie Gallagher, "Normal Marriage: Two Views," in *Marriage and Same-Sex Unions: A Debate*, ed. Lynn Wardle, Mark Strasser, William Duncan, and David Coolidge (Westport, CT: Praeger, 2003), pp. 13-24.

Sherif Girgis, Ryan T. Anderson, and Robert P. George, "Marriage: Merely a Social Construct?" *Public Discourse: Ethics, Law and the Common Good* (December 29, 2010), accessible at http:// www.thepublicdiscourse.com.

Sherif Girgis, Ryan T. Anderson, and Robert P. George, "Does Marriage, or Anything, Have Essential Properties?" *Public Discourse: Ethics, Law and the Common Good* (January 12, 2011), accessible at http://www.thepublicdiscourse.com.

William C. Duncan, "The State Interest in Marriage," *Ave Maria Law Review*, 2/1 (Spring 2004), pp. 153-182.

Justin Quinn, "Why Some Conservatives Oppose Gay Marriage," *U.S. Conservative Politics* blog, © 2011, accessible at http://usconservatives.about.com/od/conservativemyths/a/ MYTH_GayMarriage.htm.

Matthew Shaffer, "Stop the Hate," *National Review Online* blog, posted May 31, 2011, accessible at http://www.nationalreview. com/articles/print/268419.

Matthew J. Franck, "On Gay Marriage, Stop Playing the Hate Card," *The Washington Post*, December 19, 2010, p. B01, accessible at http://www.washingtonpost.com/wp-dyn/content/ article/2010/12/17/AR2010121707043_pf.html.

84

You May Hear Proponents Argue ...

Same-sex marriage should be allowed because morality requires people to love their neighbors as they love themselves. If marriage is something people want for themselves, they should also want it for all their neighbors—whether gay or straight. Allowing homosexuals to marry is what neighborly love requires. It is not loving to deny gay couples what others have and enjoy, and heterosexuals who love their gay neighbors as themselves will want them to enjoy the same benefits of marriage as they do. Neighborly love requires affirming loving relationships of all kinds. While affirming same-sex marriage is consistent with loving one's neighbor, opposing it is not.

You Can *Graciously Refute* This By Saying ...

Proponents of this argument misconstrue love by confusing it with sentimentality. Real love does not simply affirm whatever one's neighbors want but seeks what truly is best for them. After all, it is never loving to affirm destructive behavior. Thus, in the same way that friends should not let their friends drive drunk even when they demand to do so, friends should not affirm same-sex marriage even if their homosexual friends demand for them to do so.

Affirming homosexual behavior by legalizing same-sex marriage is not loving toward homosexuals, children, or everyone else in society. It is not loving toward homosexuals because it affirms behavior for which the human body is not biologically suited, which sets a person's psychology at war with his or her physiology. Reliable studies have found that homosexual populations have much higher levels of life-threatening behaviors, substance abuse, domestic violence, and suicidality when compared to heterosexual populations. These differences persist even where social disapproval is not present.

Same-sex marriage is not loving toward children because it places young people raised by homosexuals at greater risk of gender confusion, suicide, long-term depression, mood disorders, bipolar disorders, sexual promiscuity, out-of-wedlock pregnancies, and sexually transmitted diseases. It is also not loving toward everyone else in society because same-sex marriage deconstructs, deinstitutionalizes, and destroys the one institution on which social survival most depends. For these reasons, neighborly love requires *opposing* same-sex marriage. While such love includes loving non-gay neighbors and children, it especially includes loving gay neighbors themselves.

The Truth Is …

Same-sex marriage is wrong because neighborly love requires seeking what is best for others and not simply affirming what they want.

References and Further Reading

For examples of advocates using this argument, see Emilia Barrosse, "Love Your Neighbor . . . Unless He Voted for Gay Marriage," *NY comPRESSED* blog, posted July 2006, accessible at http://www.nypress.com/print-blog-9342-print.html#; Santi Tafarella, "Love Your Gay Neighbor? *Prometheus Unbound* blog, posted August 10, 2010, accessible at http://santitafarella.wordpress.com/2010/08/10/love-your-gay-neighbor/; and Elizabeth Esther, "Apologizing to My Gay Neighbors," *Elizabeth Esther: I Use My Own Words* blog, posted September 14, 2011, accessible at http://www.elizabethesther.com/2011/09/apologizing-gay-neighbors.html.

Doug Eaton, "Gay Marriage: Rights, Scripture and That Whole 'Love Your Neighbor Thing,'" *Godward Thoughts* blog, posted October 28, 2008, accessible at http://godwardthoughts.blogspot.com/2008/10/gay-marriage-rights-scripture-and-that.html.

Christine Sneeringer, "Loving Your Gay Neighbor as Yourself," *Topics*, posted February 14, 2011, The Ethics and Religious Liberty Commission, accessible at http://erlc.com/article/loving-your-gay-neighbor-as-yourself/.

Joe Dallas, "Love Thy Homosexual Neighbor," *Enrichment J.* (2011), accessible at http://enrichmentjournal.ag.org/201103/201103_086_Love_Homosexual_Neighbor.cfm.

Daniel R. Heimbach, *True Sexual Morality: Recovering Biblical Standards for a Culture in Crisis* (Wheaton, IL: Crossway, 2004).

Oliver O'Donovan, *Common Objects of Love: Moral Reflection and the Shaping of Community* (Grand Rapids, MI: William B. Eerdmans, 2002).

For studies linking homosexual activity with mental and physical health problems see Theo Sandfort, Ron de Graaf, Rob Bojl, and Paul Schnabel, "Same-Sex Sexual Behavior and Psychiatric Disorders," *Archives of General Psychiatry*, 58 (January 2001), pp. 85-91; S. Cochran and V. Mays, "Lifetime Prevalence of Suicide Symptoms and Affective Disorders Among Men Reporting Same-Sex Partners," *American Journal of Public Health*, 90/4 (April 2000), pp. 573-578; Stephen Gilman, et al., "Risk of Psychiatric Disorders Among Individuals Reporting Same-Sex Sexual Partners in the National Comorbidity Survey," *American Journal of Public Health*, 91/6 (June 2001), pp. 933-939; and David Fergusson, John Horwood, Elizabeth Ridder, and Annette Beautrais, "Sexual Orientation and Mental Health in a Birth Cohort of Young Adults," *Psychological Medicine*, 35/7 (2005), pp. 971-981.

For reasons why same-sex marriage is bad for children, see "Marriage Rights for Homosexuals: Not the Best for Children: Critique of AAP Special Report," *American College of Pediatricians* (posted prior to January 22, 2004), accessible at http://www. acpeds. org/Marriage-Rights-for-Homosexual-Couples-Not-the-Best-for-Children.html.

85

You May Hear Proponents Argue ...

Same-sex marriage should be allowed because morality requires people to behave toward homosexuals in ways that are unselfish and humble. It is selfishly arrogant to think anyone has the last word on marriage and to limit others to the approach a group of people prefers. Moral humility requires societies to keep an open door to finding new ways of thinking and behaving that can improve what has been done in the past. It is prideful and rigid to insist in advance—with no proof of harm—that society can never enlarge marriage to include same-sex partners. On the other hand, it is magnanimous to revise the public's opinions of traditional marriage, allow more people to marry, and reconsider social views on marriage.

You Can *Graciously Refute* This By Saying ...

Proponents of this argument are actually arrogant themselves in insisting that marriage be deconstructed, contrary to the public good, to affirm nothing more than what amounts to satisfying the private appetite of a few individuals. In making this argument, they show that they are willfully oblivious both to the damage this change will cause and the utter foolishness of deinstitutionalizing an essential social institution.

As for charging opponents with selfish close-mindedness, it cannot be either close-minded or selfish to resist destroying by radical redefinition the one institution on which the intergenerational survival of society most depends. Homosexuals already have—and will continue to have—the same moral and legal right that everyone has to marry. But what they do not have—and no else has—is the moral or legal right to deconstruct marriage as a structured relational form or deinstitutionalize marriage as a social institution.

Aside from being blind, narrow-minded and arrogant themselves, the main problem proponents have with this argument is how it assumes marriage has no necessary structure and can be redefined in any way at all—even to the point of leaving it with no structure at all. Redefining institutional marriage based on nothing more than feelings leaves the institution with no structure, which changes marriage into non-marriage. What these proponents seek is not in the same relational or institutional category as marrying a partner of the opposite sex. Treating these different things as if they are the same is neither honest nor wise, and appealing to people's humility to justify something foolish and irresponsible is not moral at all.

The Truth Is …

Same-sex marriage is wrong because it places moral value on failing to defend what is true rather than defending it.

References and Further Reading

For examples of advocates using this argument, see Lori W. Hollander, "Gay Marriage Opponents Need to Get the Facts about Homosexuality," *Light for All*, blog for *The Baltimore Sun*, accessible at http://articles.baltimoresun.com/2011-08-25/news/bs-ed-homosexuality-20110825_1_sexual-orientation-homosexuality-gay-marriage (posted August 25, 2011); and Steve Lenius, "Gay Pride: A Celebration of True Humility," *The Wild Reed* blog, posted June 4, 2011, accessible at http://thewildreed.blogspot.com/2011/06/gay-pride-celebration-of-true-humility.html.

State interest in supporting the institution of marriage does not come from close-minded proud individuals looking down on gay people but from humble individuals who understand the legitimate public stake that society has in supporting the procreational structure of marriage as a necessary social institution. This has nothing to do with satisfying people's private feelings but with getting biological fathers and mothers to share in raising their own children and, through this process, to ensure the intergenerational survival of society as a whole. See David M. Wagner, "Over to You California," *Weekly Standard* (October 8, 2007), pp. 21-22.

David Benikof, "It's Time for Gay Humility to Go Along with Gay Pride," *Houston Chronicle* (June 26, 2009), accessible at http://www.chron.com/opinion/outlook/article/It-s-time-for-gay-humility-to-go-along-with-gay-1741204.php.

Rod Dreher, "We Are All Ideologues to Some Degree," *Beliefnet* blog, posted July 21, 2010, accessible at http://blog.beliefnet.com/roddreher/2010/07/we-are-all-ideologues-to-some-degree.html.

John C. Cress, "Compassion: An Alternative Lifestyle," *Ministry* (November, 1996), accessible at http://www.gladventist.org/lead/h-crress.html.

Robert P. George, Ryan T. Anderson, and Sherif Girgis, "The Argument Against Gay Marriage: And Why It Doesn't Fail," *Public Discourse: Ethics, Law and the Common Good* (December 17, 2010), accessible at http://www.thepublicdiscourse.com.

"The Validity of Moral Arguments" in *The Slippery Slope of Same-Sex Marriage* (Washington, DC: Family Research Council, 2004), pp. 12-13.

Daniel Maguire, "The Morality of Homosexual Marriage," in Robert Baird and Stuart Rosenbaum, eds., *Same-Sex Marriage: The Moral and Legal Debate* (Amherst, NY: Prometheus Books, 2004), pp. 147-161.

John M. Finnis, "The Good of Marriage and the Morality of Sexual Relations: Some Philosophical and Historical Observations," *The American Journal of Jurisprudence*, 42 (1997), pp. 97-134.

86

You May Hear Proponents Argue ...

Same-sex marriage should be allowed because morality requires treating others in the same way that people want to be treated. If straight people want gays to treat their relationships as normal and good, then they must treat gay relationships in the same way. Love expressed by those who are straight, gay, or bisexual is all morally good, while denying gender equality is morally bad. Forcing homosexuals to choose between marrying someone to whom they are not attracted or never marrying at all is unjust and immoral. Marriage law should follow the Golden Rule, and limiting marriage to opposite-sex couples is rooted in ignorance contrary to this ideal.

You Can *Graciously Refute* This By Saying ...

The Golden Rule can never justify behavior that is inherently hurtful, harmful, and unnatural, and the harmful effects resulting from gay sex have been well documented. Proponents of this argument are not really interested in fair treatment for gays, because marriage law already treats homosexuals fairly in accordance to the way marriage has always been defined. Those who push for same-sex marriage are thus employing a strategy to pry people loose from traditional views on marriage.

The whole point of the same-sex marriage movement is actually to use marriage law as the means to force people—against their better judgment—to approve same-sex relationships. Same-sex marriage is driven by the desire to force others to affirm gay sex in a public way that is policed by law. As gay writer Andrew Sullivan remarks, "Including homosexuals within marriage would be a means of conveying the highest form of social approval imaginable."

However, this is precisely what Americans should *not* be forced into doing. This is not because people should ignore the

Golden Rule, but because there are relevant social, scientific, and moral distinctions involved that *really do* matter. By abolishing the freedom to respect differences that distinguish same-sex relationships from opposite-sex matrimony, mandating same-sex marriage will turn those who respect such differences into *enemies of state policy*. Those who do will be treated the same as racial bigots in the eyes of the law. They will no longer be allowed to respect relevant differences when applying the Golden Rule, but will be shamed, shunned, targeted for lawsuits, and driven out of public life. Others will then misuse the Golden Rule to justify forcing people to ignore the differences that still truly matter.

The Truth Is …

Same-sex marriage is wrong because it misuses the Golden Rule to justify affirming behavior that actually harms those who pursue it.

References and Further Reading

Chai Feldblum used this argument to launch what she called The Moral Values Project. Feldblum alleged that "heterosexuality, homosexuality and bisexuality are all morally neutral. But the love that is expressed by those who are straight, gay or bisexual is morally good—and all equally morally good. All forms of gender are morally neutral. But lack of gender equity is morally bad." See Chai Feldblum, "A Conversation with Chai Feldblum," *The Moral Values Project* (November 27, 2006), accessible at http://www.law.georgetown.edu/moralvaluesproject/.

For studies linking homosexual activity with mental and physical health problems, see Theo Sandfort, Ron de Graaf, Rob Bojl, and Paul Schnabel, "Same-Sex Sexual Behavior and Psychiatric Disorders," *Archives of General Psychiatry*, 58 (January 2001), pp. 85-91; S. Cochran and V. Mays, "Lifetime Prevalence of Suicide Symptoms and Affective Disorders Among Men Reporting

Same-Sex Partners," *American Journal of Public Health*, 90/4 (April 2000), pp. 573-578; Stephen Gilman, et al., "Risk of Psychiatric Disorders Among Individuals Reporting Same-Sex Sexual Partners in the National Comorbidity Survey," *American Journal of Public Health*, 91/6 (June 2001), pp. 933-939; and David Fergusson, John Horwood, Elizabeth Ridder, and Annette Beautrais, "Sexual Orientation and Mental Health in a Birth Cohort of Young Adults," *Psychological Medicine*, 35/7 (2005), pp. 971-981.

For examples of gay revolutionaries admitting they are using same-sex marriage to abolish marriage as a social institution, see Thomas Stoddard, "Why Gay People Should Seek the Right to Marry," chapter 35 in *Families in the US: Kinship and Domestic Politics*, ed. Karen Hansen (Philadelphia, PA: Temple University Press, 1998); Richard Mohr, *A More Perfect Union: Why Straight America Must Stand Up for Gay Rights* (Boston, MA: Beacon, 1994); Gretchen A. Stiers, *From This Day Forward: Commitment, Marriage, and Family in Lesbian and Gay Relationships* (New York: St. Martin's Press, 1999); Michelangelo Signorile, "Bridal Wave," *Out* (December/January 1994); "Sociologist Says Gay Marriage Does Threaten Established Order and That's Good," *Ascribe Law News Service* (November 16, 2003); and Margaret Gullette, "The New Case for Marriage," *American Prospect* (March 1, 2004).

Alan F.H. Wisdom, "This Isn't Tolerance: Same-Sex Marriage in Washington, DC Will Trample on Religious Liberty," *The Weekly Standard*, posted November 30, 2009), accessible at http://67.43.13.183/Content/Public/Articles/000/000/017/281eyfhv.asp.

Patrick Lee, Robert P. George, and Gerard V. Bradley, "Marriage and Procreation: The Intrinsic Connection," *Public Discourse: Ethics, Law and the Common Good* (March 28, 2011), accessible at http://www.thepublicdiscourse.com.

Daniel R. Heimbach, "Deconstructing the Family," *Religion and Society Report*, 22/7 (October/November 2005), pp. 1-12.

87

You May Hear Proponents Argue ...

Same-sex marriage should be allowed because universal human conscience demands it. If we are honest with ourselves, there is a common moral conscience within all of us. We may ignore it or suppress it, but that does not give us a pass or get us off the hook. We still know what that moral conscience requires. We know what our hearts say we must do. And when we rid our minds of all unworthy motives and distractions, we see that allowing same-sex marriage for homosexuals is the right thing to do. All of us who hear and follow the still small voice of universal human conscience agree that we must support legalizing same-sex marriage.

You Can *Graciously Refute* This By Saying ...

Most of the world overwhelmingly opposes accepting gay sex as moral, which effectively destroys this claim. While proponents of this argument certainly want to change how others think about the morality of homosexual behavior, what their argument amounts to is nonsensically alleging that others must change their morality for what these proponents affirm. The fact that most people in the world currently (and have always) considered homosexual behavior to be grossly immoral is good evidence that universal moral conscience more likely rejects than demands treating same-sex marriage as morally necessary.

Every person in the world—regardless of culture or religion—who understands the deadly personal and social consequences of deconstructing marriage is obligated by shared human conscience to reject same-sex marriage as fundamentally immoral. If those who know and sense this moral obligation are weak or compromising, then the personal and social harm that results will prove their moral hesitation comes more from self-interest and fear than from a sense of universal moral conscience. There is indeed a moral conscience shared by all humanity, but a truly honest assessment of commonly held moral sentiment transcending place, time, and culture must conclude that it aligns *against* and not in favor of what proponents of this argument say.

Universal conscience has always aligned to affirm and guard procreationally structured marriage as being essential to the stability and intergenerational survival of society. That makes same-sex marriage completely contrary to what the universal moral conscience requires.

The Truth Is …

Same-sex marriage is wrong because it ignores and rejects what the universal moral conscience of humanity requires.

Reference and Further Reading

While some gay marriage advocates use this argument, others criticize it. For an example of a gay advocate criticizing this argument see Reg Domingo, "Push for Policy Change on Gay Marriage to Continue Despite Conscience Vote," *Gay News Network*, November 6, 2011, accessible at http://www.gaynewsnetwork.com.au/news/national/2672-push-for-change-on-gay-marriage-to-continue-despite-conscience-vote.html.

James Q. Wilson, "Against Homosexual Marriage," *Commentary*, 101 (March 1996), pp. 34-39. Wilson argues it is wrong for a few homosexuals to impose social/legal change that overrides the moral conscience of most other persons in a shared social/legal system.

Thomas V. Smith, *Beyond Conscience: A Critical Examination of Various Doctrines of Conscience* (New York: McGraw-Hill, 1934).

C. D. Broad, "Some Reflections on Moral-Sense Theories in Ethics," *Proceedings of the Aristotelian Society*, vol. 45 (1944-1945), pp. 131-166.

John Hass, *Crisis of Conscience* (New York: Crossroad, 1996).

Mary Hasson, "Same-Sex Marriage: Lessons in Conscience," *Catholic News Agency*, July 22, 2011, accessible at http://www.catholicnewsagency.com/cw/post.php?id=568.

Clyde Haberman, "When Conscience and the New Marriage Law Collide," *The New York Times*, November 10, 2011, accessible at http://cityroom.blogs.nytimes.com/2011/07/18/when-conscience-and-the-new-marriage-law-collide/.

In *Maynard v. Hill*, 125 U.S. 190 (1888), the U.S. Supreme Court recognized that the public legal understanding of marriage springs from the fundamental morality of a people, which is to say that constitutionally protected marriage law is not moral neutrality. In that case, the court described marriage as "creating the most important relation in life" and as "having more to do with the morals and civilization of a people than any other institution."

For studies linking homosexual activity with mental and physical health problems, see Theo Sandfort, Ron de Graaf, Rob Bojl, and Paul Schnabel, "Same-Sex Sexual Behavior and Psychiatric Disorders," *Archives of General Psychiatry*, 58 (January 2001), pp. 85-91; S. Cochran and V. Mays, "Lifetime Prevalence of Suicide Symptoms and Affective Disorders Among Men Reporting Same-Sex Partners," *American Journal of Public Health*, 90/4 (April 2000), pp. 573-578; Stephen Gilman, et al., "Risk of Psychiatric Disorders Among Individuals Reporting Same-Sex Sexual Partners in the National Comorbidity Survey," *American Journal of Public Health*, 91/6 (June 2001), pp. 933-939; and David Fergusson, John Horwood, Elizabeth Ridder, and Annette Beautrais, "Sexual Orientation and Mental Health in a Birth Cohort of Young Adults," *Psychological Medicine*, 35/7 (2005), pp. 971-981.

88

You May Hear Proponents Argue …

Same-sex marriage should be allowed because moral views about sex and marriage have no place in laws regulating marriage. It is true that Americans hold different views on the morality of gay marriage. However, morality is a matter of personal conviction, and marriage laws must remain neutral on these convictions. If we have learned anything from history, it is that we should avoid regulating moral differences by force of law. Law and morality are not the same thing, and they should not be confused. Law regulates what is, while morality declares what should be. Gay relationships need to be protected in spite of people's morality, which means not privileging one morality over others.

You Can *Graciously Refute* This By Saying …

The contention that morality has no place in formulating marriage law is patently absurd. It is the fundamental legal and moral duty of legislators to make laws that correct wrong and promote good on matters relating to the public welfare. Those who deny the relevance of morality for laws on marriage have no trouble relying on morality when dealing with issues such as racism, torture, capital punishment, or wars. In other words, they are using this argument only to discredit moral realities they do not like.

Pretending that the way people have sex is not relevant to marriage destroys the value and power of the institution for linking sex with procreation and procreation with raising children. Changing marriage in this manner will cause children to suffer, because fewer fathers and mothers will raise their own biological children. Society will also suffer because families will be less enduring if the adults care more for satisfying their own personal appetites than for providing what their children most need. This will also lead to affirming behaviors that harm human health and shortens the lives of those who pursue it. That can never be morally right and should never be affirmed by law, regardless of how strongly certain people desire it.

Proponents of same-sex marriage do not desire to protect a threatened minority. Rather, they desire to use law to impose a social construct that comes not from anything objectively real but from something that is subjective and self-interpreted. Civil law must affirm what truly is right. The sort of morality on which the social order depends is not something that comes from private preference but from something real—and laws must conform to this reality or ignore it to society's peril.

The Truth Is …

Same-sex marriage is wrong because it denies the relevance of moral realities on which general respect for marriage law depends.

References and Further Reading

For examples of advocates using this argument, see Sarah Braasch, "Morality Has No Place in the Law," *Daylight Atheism* blog, posted January 14, 2011, accessible at http://www.daylightathe ism.org/2011/01/morality-has-no-place-in-the-law.html; "Gay Marriage Is Issue of Rights, Not Morals," *The Flor-Ala*, posted September 15, 2011, accessible at http://www.florala.net/opinion/article_c4152d92-deeb-11e0-acc7-0019bb30f31a.html.

Alan Charles, "How Legalizing Gay Marriage Undermines Society's Morals," *The Christian Science Monitor*, December 9, 2003, accessible at http://www.csmonitor.com/2003/1209/p11s02-coop.html.

In *Maynard v. Hill*, 125 U.S. 190 (1888), the U.S. Supreme Court recognized that the public legal understanding of marriage springs from the fundamental morality of a people, which is to say that constitutionally protected marriage law is not moral neutrality. In that case, the court described marriage as "creating the most important relation in life" and as "having more to do with the morals and civilization of a people than any other institution."

For studies linking homosexual activity with a higher risk of poor mental and physical health and suicidality, see Theo Sandfort, Ron de Graaf, Rob Bojl, and Paul Schnabel, "Same-Sex Sexual Behavior and Psychiatric Disorders," *Archives of General Psychiatry,* 58 (January 2001), pp. 85-91; Susan Cochran and Vickie Mays, "Lifetime Prevalence of Suicide Symptoms and Affective Disorders Among Men Reporting Same-Sex Partners," *American Journal of Public Health,* 90/4 (April 2000), pp. 573-578; Stephen Gilman, Susan Cochran, Vickie Mays, M. Hughes, D. Ostrow, and R.C. Kessler, "Risk of Psychiatric Disorders Among Individuals Reporting Same-Sex Sexual Partners in the National Comorbidity Survey," *American Journal of Public Health,* 91/6 (June 2001), pp. 933-939; and David Fergusson, John Horwood, Elizabeth Ridder, and Annette Beautrais, "Sexual Orientation and Mental Health in a Birth Cohort of Young Adults," *Psychological Medicine,* 35/7 (2005), pp. 971-981.

For how same-sex marriage is harming children, see Marriage Rights for Homosexuals: Not the Best for Children: Critique of AAP Special Report," *American College of Pediatricians* (posted prior to January 22, 2004), accessible at http://www.acpeds.org/Marriage-Rights-for-Homosexual-Couples-Not-the-Best-for-Children.html; Maggie Gallagher and Joshua K. Baker, "Do Moms and Dads Matter? Evidence from the Social Sciences on

Family Structure and the Best Interests of the Child," 4/161, *Margins* (2004), pp. 161-180; and Robert Lerner and Althea Nagia, *No Basis: What the Studies Don't Tell Us About Same-Sex Parenting*, Marriage Law Project (Washington, DC, January 2001).

"Yet Another Study Confirms Gay Life Expectancy 20 Years Shorter," *LifeSiteNews* blog, posted June 6, 2005, accessible at http://www.lifesitenews.com/news/archive/ldn/1950/60/5060606.

89

You May Hear Proponents Argue ...

Same-sex marriage should be allowed because morality requires lifting oppression from the shoulders of innocent people. Oppressing any class of people for no good reason is terribly wrong, as is causing any group to systematically suffer at the hands of an unwelcoming community. Homosexual behavior is normal and good for homosexuals, so denying same-sex marriage serves no purpose other than to lessen the human dignity of gays and lesbians by classifying their relationships as inferior. People who still believe homosexual behavior is immoral must realize that such thinking interferes with the duties of responsible government.

You Can *Graciously Refute* This By Saying ...

Of course, using the power of government to oppress people is terribly wrong, but traditional marriage law does not do this. However, changing marriage to affirm gay relationships will cause—rather than prevent—what proponents of this argument allege to oppose. They want to replace a true reality with a false one to produce a false view of morality that leads to a false view of oppression.

Morality of the sort by which good government operates does not come from feelings but from facts. The true good of marriage as a social institution comes not from the false morality of pursuing personal fulfillment but from the true morality of limiting appetites to assure the common good. This requires the true morality of assuring generational replacement by getting fathers and mothers to have and raise their own children, not from pretending all feelings are the same.

What is at stake is the underlying nature of marriage because no oppression will exist unless legal marriage has already been changed into what gays want it to become. Much like refusing to give drivers' licenses to people who cannot drive, no one is oppressed by not having licenses for a function he or she cannot perform. It is both immoral and dangerous to pretend people are oppressed when they are not.

Legalizing same-sex marriage will change marriage into nothing more than a way to affirm feelings, which will make gay relationships the legal norm for everyone. Marriage law will shift from assuring the public good of social survival to just a way of affirming private feelings. It will be forced to treat something private as if it were public and to treat something public as if it were private. In the end, those who deny this false reality will be oppressed.

The Truth Is …

Same-sex marriage is wrong because it replaces moral reality with a lie that produces—rather than prevents—oppression.

References and Further Reading

For an example of advocates using this argument, see Gregory Turner, "Gay Marriage: Fear and Oppression Also Won at the Ballot Box," *The Seattle Times* (Seattle), November 7, 2008, accessible at http://seattletimes.nwsource.com/html/opinion/2008364665opin09turner.htm.

For how legalizing same-sex marriage will align marriage to homosexual categories and not align homosexuals to what marriage is now, see Lawrence Auster, "The Extreme Radicalism of Homosexual 'Marriage,'" *View from the Right* (June 2, 2008), accessible at http://www.amnation.com/vfr/archives/010723.html.

For how abandoning the procreational structure of marriage threatens civilization, see Joseph Daniel Unwin, *Sex and Culture* (London: Oxford University Press, 1937), Carle Zimmerman,

Family and Civilization (Wilmington, DE: ISI Books, 2008); and Pitirim Sorokin, *The Crisis of Our Age* (Richmond, VA: Dutton, 1941).

Maggie Gallagher, "Normal Marriage: Two Views," in *Marriage and Same-Sex Unions: A Debate*, ed. Lynn Wardle, Mark Strasser, William Duncan, and David Coolidge (Westport, CT: Praeger, 2003), pp. 13-24.

Patrick Lee, Robert P. George, and Gerard V. Bradley, "Marriage and Procreation: The Intrinsic Connection," *Public Discourse: Ethics, Law and the Common Good* (March 28, 2011), accessible at http://www.thepublicdiscourse.com.

Robert P. George and Jean Bethke Elshtain, eds., *The Meaning of Marriage: Family, State, Market, and Morals* (Dallas, TX: Spence Publishing, 2006).

John M. Finnis, "Law, Morality, and 'Sexual Orientation,'" *Notre Dame Law Review*, 69/5 (1994), pp. 1049-1076.

Sherif Girgis, Robert P. George, and Ryan T. Anderson, "What Is Marriage?" *Harvard Journal of Law and Public Policy*, 34/1 (Winter 2011), pp. 245-287.

Sherif Girgis, Ryan T. Anderson, and Robert P. George, "Does Marriage, or Anything, Have Essential Properties?" *Public Discourse: Ethics, Law and the Common Good* (January 12, 2011), accessible at http://www.thepublicdiscourse.com.

Daniel Maguire, "The Morality of Homosexual Marriage," in Robert Baird and Stuart Rosenbaum, eds., *Same-Sex Marriage: The Moral and Legal Debate* (Amherst, NY: Prometheus Books, 2004), pp. 147-161.

William C. Duncan, "The State Interest in Marriage," *Ave Maria Law Review*, 2/1 (Spring 2004), pp. 153-182.

90

You May Hear Proponents Argue ...

Same-sex marriage should be allowed because morality prohibits ruining the lives of other people. Homosexuals must not be forced to assume roles they are not equipped to play and perform disastrously when they try. Homosexuals pressured into entering heterosexual marriages inevitably reach a point at which they find the dishonesty too great to bear. This produces a trail of betrayed spouses, abandoned children, and broken families. It also leaves homosexuals deeply wounded by a history of failing to find love and acceptance. Moral duty demands allowing same-sex marriage in order to stop this progression of lives ruined by relational failure.

You Can *Graciously Refute* This By Saying ...

Of course, true morality rejects laws that systematically ruin the lives of innocent people and favors laws that encourage relational fidelity. However, traditional marriage laws do not do that. Furthermore, radically changing what marriage means only to affirm what homosexuals want it to mean will more likely *increase* the number of lives ruined by relational failure.

Proponents of this argument note that gay relationships tend to leave a trail of ruined lives in their wake. This is sad but true, but it shifts the blame away from the real cause by blaming the wrong thing. What causes the string of relational failures is not that traditional marriage laws force innocent people to behave badly but rather that gays insist on imagining a false reality that allows them to break promises regardless of how their actions hurt other people. The fact is that homosexuals want something impossible and are blaming everyone (except themselves) for not being able to find what they seek. People do not ruin their lives by conforming to false reality, but they do ruin their lives by demanding the impossible without regard for how it affects others.

If gays could find deep relational satisfaction with partners of the same-sex, those leaving heterosexual marriages would settle into long-lasting and stable relationships with one life partner. But that hardly ever happens. The fact is that gays live unstable relational lives and continue to behave in unreliable ways even when they are surrounded by an atmosphere of acceptance. The deep sense of relational dissatisfaction that homosexuals experience is psychological and internal, not legal and external. Gays with same-sex partners do not stop ruining lives, including their own.

The Truth Is ...

Same-sex marriage is wrong because gays who leave heterosexual partners for same-sex partners do not stop ruining the lives of others.

References and Further Reading

For examples of proponents using this argument, see Andrew Sullivan, *Virtually Normal* (New York: Random House, 1995), pp. 203-204; and Heidi, "Living a Lie," *Peoples Insight blog*, accessible at http://www.peoplesinsight.com/articles/8-secrets/84-living-a-lie.

David Island and Patrick Letellier, *Men Who Beat the Men Who Love Them: Battered Gay Men and Domestic Violence* (New York: Haworth Press, 1991).

Timothy Dailey, "Comparing the Lifestyles of Homosexual Couples to Married Couples," *Family Research Council* (April 29, 2004), accessible at http://www.frc.org/get.cfm?i=IS04C02.

Gwat Yong Lie and Sabrina Gentlewarrier, "Intimate Violence in Lesbian Relationships: Discussion of Survey Findings and Practice Implications," *Journal of Social Service Research*, 15/1-2 (1991), pp. 41-59.

For gays having no interest in limiting sex to marriage, see Michelangelo Signorile, "Bridal Wave," *Out* (December/January 1994), p. 161; William Aaron, *Straight* (New York: Bantam Books, 1972), p. 208; Gretchen A. Stiers, *From This Day Forward: Commitment, Marriage, and Family in Lesbian and Gay Relationships* (New York: St. Martin's Press, 1999); and Mollie Ziegler Hemingway, "Same-Sex, Different Marriage: Many of Those Who Want Marriage Equality Do Not Want Fidelity," *Christianity Today* (May 18, 2010), accessible at http://www.christianitytoday.com/ct/2010/may/11.52.html.

Gretchen Stiers reveals (1) that few dedicated gay and lesbian couples actually expect that same-sex marriage will limit their own promiscuity, (2) that nearly half of these same couples openly despise straight marriage, and (3) that most homosexuals look on same-sex marriage as a strategy for subverting the institution from within. See Gretchen A. Stiers, *From This Day Forward: Commitment, Marriage, and Family in Lesbian and Gay Relationships* (New York: St. Martin's Press, 1999).

For studies linking homosexual activity with a higher risk of poor mental and physical health and suicidality, see Theo Sandfort, Ron de Graaf, Rob Bojl, and Paul Schnabel, "Same-Sex Sexual Behavior and Psychiatric Disorders," *Archives of General Psychiatry,* 58 (January 2001), pp. 85-91; Susan Cochran and Vickie Mays, "Lifetime Prevalence of Suicide Symptoms and Affective Disorders Among Men Reporting Same-Sex Partners," *American Journal of Public Health,* 90/4 (April 2000), pp. 573-578; Stephen Gilman, Susan Cochran, Vickie Mays, et al., "Risk of Psychiatric Disorders Among Individuals Reporting Same-Sex Sexual Partners in the National Comorbidity Survey," *American Journal of Public Health,* 91/6 (June 2001), pp. 933-939; and David Fergusson, John Horwood, Elizabeth Ridder, and Annette Beautrais, "Sexual Orientation and Mental Health in a Birth Cohort of Young Adults," *Psychological Medicine,* 35/7 (2005), pp. 971-981.

91

You May Hear Proponents Argue …

Same-sex marriage should be allowed because morality requires enabling gays to pursue and achieve their own happiness. There is no reason to discourage people from embracing gay identities other than to spare them the unhappiness caused by social rejection. However, when social attitudes change and gays are allowed to marry partners of the same-sex, this will no longer be the case. Gay identity will be affirmed, and the happiness of gay couples will be enhanced by social acceptance. Same-sex marriage is necessary in order to make sure that gays are able to pursue and achieve their own happiness. It is morally wrong to have laws that stop them from doing so.

You Can *Graciously Refute* This By Saying …

Proponents of this argument are basically saying that people should be allowed to try slavery, or lie on their tax returns, if it makes them feel happy. Marriage is a social institution on which social stability and survival both depend, so redefining marriage in a way that it no longer has anything to do with having children is like pretending submarines need not operate underwater or that airplanes can fly without wings. Same-sex marriage is a radical attack on real marriage and threatens the public good.

The public interest in marriage has nothing to do with making people happy but with the common good of ensuring intergenerational survival. Proponents of this argument wrongly confuse subjective happiness with objective happiness. No government can make everyone feel subjectively happy, and pretending that it can is a horrible lie. The happiness a person seeks is not identical with the happiness he or she wants, because the first is objective and the second is not. Objective happiness represents a person's true wellbeing, which means the person can be objectively happy when feeling unhappy about not getting what he or she wants. People can also feel subjectively happy in situations that are bad for their true wellbeing.

With objective happiness, a person's psychology cannot be separated from that same person's physiology. A person's objective happiness depends on *conforming* psychology (wants) to physiology (bodily form)—never the other way around. This means the objective happiness of homosexuals, like everyone else, depends on conforming what they want to their own bodily form, not pretending their bodies can be used in harmful ways just because that is what they want.

The Truth Is …

Same-sex marriage is wrong because feeding sensual desires does not generate the relational strength needed to produce real happiness.

References and Further Reading

For examples of proponents using this argument, see Andrew Sullivan, *Virtually Normal* (New York: Random House, 1995), pp. 115-117; and Megan Carpentier, "Gay Marriage In California Make Some People Happy, Others Blithering Idiots," *Jezebel* blog, accessible at http://www.peoplesinsight.com/articles/http://jezebel.com/5017207/gay-marriage-in-california-makes-some-people-happy-others-blathering-idiots.

Richard B. Brandt, "Happiness," in *Encyclopedia of Philosophy*, ed. Paul Edwards, vol. 3, (New York: Macmillan, 1972), pp. 413-414.

Karl Duncker, "On Pleasure, Emotion, and Striving," *Philosophy and Phenomenological Research*, vol. 1, no. 4 (June 1941), pp. 391-430.

Aristotle, *Eudemian Ethics*, bks. I-III; *Nicomachaean Ethics*, bks. I,X.

William C. Duncan, "The State Interest in Marriage," *Ave Maria Law Review*, 2/1 (Spring 2004), pp. 153-182.

For studies linking homosexual activity with a higher risk of poor mental and physical health and suicidality, see Theo Sandfort, Ron de Graaf, Rob Bojl, and Paul Schnabel, "Same-Sex Sexual Behavior and Psychiatric Disorders," *Archives of General Psychiatry,* 58 (January 2001), pp. 85-91; Susan Cochran and Vickie Mays, "Lifetime Prevalence of Suicide Symptoms and Affective Disorders Among Men Reporting Same-Sex Partners," *American Journal of Public Health,* 90/4 (April 2000), pp. 573-578; Stephen Gilman, Susan Cochran, Vickie Mays, M. Hughes, D. Ostrow, and R.C. Kessler, "Risk of Psychiatric Disorders Among Individuals Reporting Same-Sex Sexual Partners in the National Comorbidity Survey," *American Journal of Public Health,* 91/6 (June 2001), pp. 933-939; and David Fergusson, John Horwood, Elizabeth Ridder, and Annette Beautrais, "Sexual Orientation and Mental Health in a Birth Cohort of Young Adults," *Psychological Medicine,* 35/7 (2005), pp. 971-981.

For how abandoning the procreational structure of marriage threatens civilized order and social survival, see Joseph Daniel Unwin, *Sex and Culture* (London: Oxford University Press, 1937); Joseph Daniel Unwin, *Sexual Regulations and Cultural Behavior: An Address Delivered Before the Medical Section of the British Psychological Society* (London: Oxford University Press, 1935); Carle Zimmerman, *Family and Civilization* (Wilmington, DE: ISI Books, 2008); Pitirim Sorokin, *The Crisis of Our Age* (Richmond, VA: Dutton, 1941); Pitirim Sorokin, *Social and Cultural Dynamics,* vol. 4 (Boston, MA: Porter Sargent, 1957); Daniel R. Heimbach, "Deconstructing the Family," *Religion and Society Report,* 22/7 (October/November 2005), pp. 1-12; and Daniel Heimbach, "The Future Based on Science," in Daniel Heimbach, *True Sexual Morality* (Wheaton, IL: Crossway, 2004), pp. 345-348.

Arguments 92 – 101

Gracious Answers to Arguments Regarding God and Theology

*It is
absurd to think
that gays require same-
sex marriage to fulfill God's
call to be holy. Holiness
cannot be expressed by
actions that God
declares sinful.*

REGARDING GOD AND THEOLOGY

(Arguments 92–101)

92

You May Hear Proponents Argue ...

SAME-SEX MARRIAGE SHOULD *be allowed because it affirms what God is doing in the lives of gay couples.* God is leading gay couples to marry, so hindering them from doing so resists the will of God. The Holy Spirit is ingrafting openly gay couples into the lives of our communities in the same way He once ingrafted Gentiles into the life of the Christian community. Refusing to allow same-sex couples to marry opposes the work of God. Whether that happens in the church or in civil life, opposing God is spiritually dangerous, and those who do can lose their salvation. All who love and respect God must affirm what God is now doing by accepting same-sex marriage.

You Can *Graciously Refute* This By Saying ...

Eugene Rogers made this argument in his book *Sexuality and the Christian Body*, basing it on a text in which Paul warns

Christians to be afraid of losing connection with God (see Rom. 11:20-21). But Rogers reverses what Paul meant. Paul was addressing people who arrogantly thought they could redefine life with God by reducing Him to their desires rather than shaping their desires to God. Even more amazing, Rogers claims that what homosexuals desire comes from a new moving of God's Spirit—a moving that contradicts the moral character of God, even though the Bible says God's moral character never changes (see Ps. 102:27; Mal. 3:6; Heb. 13:8; Jas. 1:17).

Treating same-sex intercourse as normal and good is nothing less than a frontal attack on the work of God in creation. Paul says this clearly in Romans 1:18-27 and also states that doing so prevents people from inheriting the kingdom of God (see 1 Cor. 6:9-10). Jesus never loosened God's moral law (see Matt. 5:17-18) but affirmed God's absolute prohibition of same-sex intercourse (see Lev. 18:22; 20:13). When addressing marriage, Jesus took a back-to-creation approach to sexuality that presupposed the male-female duality God established for marriage at creation (see Mark 10:6-9).

Scripture can never be interpreted fairly to legitimize same-sex marriage. Redefining marriage is not the same as treating people fairly, and it has nothing to do with following God's example of welcoming repentant sinners into the kingdom of God. Claiming the Bible requires Christians to take a non-gendered view of marriage that makes male-female duality irrelevant is a false portrait that must be deconstructed.

The Truth Is …

Same-sex marriage is wrong because it blames God for sinful behavior by supposing He considers male-female duality to be irrelevant.

References and Further Reading

For examples of advocates using this argument, see Eugene F. Rogers Jr., *Sexuality and the Christian Body* (Oxford, UK: Blackwell Publishers, 1999), pp. 51-52; Eugene F. Rogers, "An Argument for Gay Marriage," *The Christian Century* (June 15, 2004), pp. 26-29; and Eugene F. Rogers Jr., "An Argument for Gay Marriage," *Return to Religion-Online* blog, posted June 15, 2004, accessible at http://www.peoplesinsight.com/articles/ http://www.religion-online.org/showarticle.asp?title=3069.

Robert A.J. Gagnon, "Why 'Gay Marriage' Is Wrong" (July 2004), accessible at http://www.robgagnon.net/homopresbytodayarticle. htm.

Robert A.J. Gagnon, "The Bible and Homosexual Practice: Theology, Analogies, and Genes," *Theology Matters* (November/ December 2001), pp. 1-16, accessible at http://wordalone. com/t/gagnon-summary.doc and at http://theologymatters. com/NovDec01.pdf.

Robert A.J. Gagnon, *The Bible and Homosexual Practice: Texts and Hermeneutics* (Nashville, TN: Abingdon Press, 2001).

Robert A.J. Gagnon, "The Bible and Homosexual Practice: Key Issues," in *Homosexual and the Bible: Two Views*, by Dan O. Via and Robert A. J. Gagnon (Minneapolis, MN: Augsburg Fortress, 2003).

Robert A.J. Gagnon, "More than 'Mutual Joy': Lisa Miller of *Newsweek* Against Scripture and Jesus," accessible at http:// www.robgagnon.net/NewsweekMillerHomosexResp.htm.

James B. DeYoung, *Homosexuality: Contemporary Claims Examined in Light of the Bible and Other Ancient Literature and Law* (Grand Rapids, MI: Kregel, 2000).

Alan Sears and Craig Osten, *The Homosexual Agenda: Exposing the Principle Threat to Religious Freedom Today* (Nashville, TN: Broadman and Holman, 2003).

Joe Dallas, *The Gay Gospel? How Pro-Gay Advocates Misread the Bible* (Eugene, OR: Harvest House, 2007).

Thomas E. Schmidt, *Straight and Narrow? Compassion and Clarity in the Homosexual Debate* (Downers Grove, IL: InterVarsity Press, 1995).

Albert Mohler, "Newsweek Argues the Religious Case for Gay Marriage," *Crosswalk* blog, posted December 10, 2008, accessible at http://www.crosswalk.com/news/newsweek-argues-the-religious-case-for-gay-marriage-11596776.html.

93

You May Hear Proponents Argue …

Same-sex marriage should be allowed because the chief purpose of marriage is not to make children of human beings but to make children of God. Sex and marriage are related to religion. However, what connects them has more to do with sanctification than with procreation; has more to do with giving one's self to another for the sake of holiness than with avoiding lust; and has more to do with forming the family of God than with forming biological families. Sexual intimacy with same-sex partners is the way gay and lesbian people fulfill their calling to pursue sanctification. Denying same-sex marriage thus prevents homosexuals from achieving their spiritual destiny.

You Can *Graciously Refute* This By Saying …

The Bible does teach that human marriage serves a higher purpose than just producing children. Even so, we should not suppose that the biblical view of marriage serves this higher purpose in a way that makes gender difference irrelevant or relational fruitfulness unnecessary. God made human beings for marriage, not marriage for human beings. However, while the chief and ultimate purpose of marriage goes beyond biology, this does not mean that gender duality in God's design for marriage is merely one of several options.

Gender duality in marriage is so critically important that the Bible says it expresses the same moral union (see Eph. 5:32) by which human beings are "conformed to the likeness" of Christ (Rom. 8:29, NIV). It is not a union of identical partners but of partners formed to unite for relational productivity. This argument takes a pagan—rather than a Christian or biblical—approach to sex and marriage. It changes the meaning of sex and marriage, and even of God, in order to justify whatever desires human beings have. In truth, God says that to fulfill our calling to sanctification, we need to become "imitators of God … [by avoiding] even a hint of sexual immorality" (Eph. 5:1,3 NIV).

Claiming that same-sex marriage is a path to biblical sanctification is thus absurd for two reasons. First, because biblical sanctification is not something anyone can achieve by his or her own efforts; and second, because it is nonsense to think that the holiness God requires comes from activity God declares to be sin worthy of death (see Lev. 18:22; 20:13).

The Truth Is …

Same-sex marriage is wrong because God does not accept anyone who redefines sanctification, holiness, or spirituality to excuse sin.

References and Further Reading

For examples of advocates using this argument, see Eugene F. Rogers Jr., *Sexuality and the Christian Body* (Oxford, UK: Blackwell Publishers, 1999), p. 206; and Eugene F. Rogers Jr., "An Argument for Gay Marriage," *Return to Religion-Online* blog, posted June 15, 2004, accessible at http://www.peoples-insight.com/articles/http://www.religion-online.org/showarticle.asp?title=3069.

Sherif Girgis, Robert P. George, and Ryan T. Anderson, "What Is Marriage?" *Harvard Journal of Law and Public Policy*, 34/1 (Winter 2011), pp. 245-287.

Patrick Lee, Robert P. George, and Gerard V. Bradley, "Marriage and Procreation: The Intrinsic Connection," *Public Discourse: Ethics, Law and the Common Good* (March 28, 2011), accessible at http://www.thepublicdiscourse.com.

Robert A.J. Gagnon, "Why 'Gay Marriage' Is Wrong" (July 2004), accessible at http://www.robgagnon.net/homopresbytodayarticle.htm.

Robert A.J. Gagnon, *The Bible and Homosexual Practice: Texts and Hermeneutics* (Nashville, TN: Abingdon Press, 2001).

James B. DeYoung, *Homosexuality: Contemporary Claims Examined in Light of the Bible and Other Ancient Literature and Law* (Grand Rapids, MI: Kregel, 2000).

Joe Dallas, *The Gay Gospel? How Pro-Gay Advocates Misread the Bible* (Eugene, OR: Harvest House, 2007).

Thomas E. Schmidt, *Straight and Narrow? Compassion and Clarity in the Homosexual Debate* (Downers Grove, IL: InterVarsity Press, 1995).

Oliver O'Donovan, *Common Objects of Love: Moral Reflection and the Shaping of Community* (Grand Rapids, MI: William B. Eerdmans, 2002).

John-Henry Westen, "The Real Reason Christians Oppose Same-Sex Marriage," *LifeSiteNews.com*, posted April 14, 2005, accessible at http://www.lifesitenews.com/news/archive/ldn/1950/41/5041403.

Daniel R. Heimbach, *True Sexual Morality: Recovering Biblical Standards for a Culture in Crisis* (Wheaton, IL: Crossway, 2004).

Edward Collins Vacek, *Love, Human and Divine: The Heart of Christian Ethics* (Washington, DC: Georgetown University Press, 1994).

94

You May Hear Proponents Argue …

Same-sex marriage should be allowed because the Bible defies convention to include social outcasts, and gay couples are social outcasts. The Bible calls for lifting up and embracing marginalized and downtrodden people. Therefore, it favors rather than prohibits allowing same-sex marriage. Religious conservatives are wrong about what the Bible requires. The Bible never defines marriage as only uniting men with women. Instead, it treats same-sex intimacy as a gift of God, envisions relational perfection in ways that make gender differences irrelevant, and affirms and encourages marriages that defy social conventions in order to achieve a better life for all.

You Can *Graciously Refute* This By Saying …

Lisa Miller made this argument in *Newsweek* (December 15, 2008). She claimed that because the Bible defies social conventions by welcoming social outcasts into God's family, it requires people who believe and respect the Bible to support same-sex marriage. The problem with Miller's argument is that she mistakes the Bible's merciful forgiveness and inclusion of repentant sinners into the family of God with an outright denial of the reality and relevance of sin. She insists that God's people should accept sinners who persist in rebelling and refuse to repent as if rejecting God's terms makes no difference at all.

Despite claims to the contrary, the Bible clearly condemns homosexual behavior for everyone without exception as both materially unnatural (see Rom. 1:26-27) and seriously immoral (see Lev. 18:22; 20:13). The Bible also calls all who accept God's authority to expose and not normalize (see Eph. 5:11-12) all forms of sexual immorality, including sex with persons of the same sex (see 1 Cor. 6:9-10). There is no way that Scripture can be interpreted honestly and legitimately to require supporting same-sex marriage.

Redefining sin and marriage cannot be equated either with the Bible's insistence on treating social outcasts fairly or with welcoming repentant sinners who are seeking forgiveness. Proponents of this argument rely on respecting biblical authority in order to reject biblical authority. They use what the Bible says in order to dismiss what the Bible says. Doing so is totally incoherent and self-contradictory, which, of course, destroys any credibility they hope to achieve by appealing to the Bible in the first place.

The Truth Is ...

Same-sex marriage is wrong because the Bible cannot be used to demand, require, or promote what the Bible clearly condemns.

References and Further Reading

For examples of advocates using this argument, see Eugene F. Rogers, Jr., *Sexuality and the Christian Body* (Oxford, UK: Blackwell Publishers, 1999), pp. 155-156,232; and Chris Glaser, *Coming Out As Sacrament* (Louisville: Westminster/John Knox, 1998), pp. 7-9,82, http://www.newsweek.com/id/172653/output/printhttp://religion.blogs.cnn.com/2011/02/09/.

For research on sexual orientation being subject to treatment and change, see Brian S. Mustanski, et al., "A Critical Review of Recent Biological Research on Human Sexual Orientation," *Annual Review of Sex Research*, 13 (2002), pp. 89-140; William Byne and Bruce Parsons, "Human Sexual Orientation: The Biologic Theories Reappraised," 50/3, *Archives of General Psychiatry* (March 1993), pp. 228-239; William Byne, "The Biological Evidence Challenged," *Scientific American* (May 1994), pp. 50-55; William Byne, "Why We Cannot Conclude That Sexual Orientation is Primarily a Biological Phenomenon,"

34/1, *Journal of Homosexuality* (1997), pp. 73-80; John Horgan, "Gay Genes, Revisited: Doubts Arise Over Research on the Biology of Homosexuality," 273/5, *Scientific American* (November 1995), p. 26; and Eliot Marshall, "NIH's 'Gay Gene' Study Questioned," 268/5219, *Science* (June 30, 1995), p. 1841. For how the science has been misrepresented and politicized, see Jeffrey Satinover, "The Trojan Couch: How the Mental Health Associations Misrepresent Science," *Conference Reports 2005*, National Association for Research and Therapy of Homosexuals, accessible at http://www.narth.com/docs/thetrojancouch-satinover; Robert Lerner and Althea Nagia, *No Basis: What the Studies Don't Tell Us About Same-Sex Parenting*, Marriage Law Project (Washington, DC, January 2001); A. Dean Byrd, "When Activism Masquerades as Science," National Association for Research and Therapy of Homosexuals, accessible at http://www.narth.com/docs/masquerades (posted 2004, updated September 3, 2008); and Michael L. Brown, "Is Gay the New Black? Analyzing the Argument That 'I Was Born That Way,'" in *A Queer Thing Happened to America* (Concord, NC: Equal Time Books, 2011), pp. 197-225.

Robert A.J. Gagnon, "The Bible and Homosexual Practice: Theology, Analogies, and Genes," *Theology Matters* (November/December 2001), pp. 1-16, accessible at http://wordalone.com/t/gagnon-summary.doc and at http://theologymatters.com/NovDec01.pdf.

Robert A.J. Gagnon, *The Bible and Homosexual Practice: Texts and Hermeneutics* (Nashville, TN: Abingdon Press, 2001).

Thomas E. Schmidt, *Straight and Narrow? Compassion and Clarity in the Homosexual Debate* (Downers Grove, IL: InterVarsity Press, 1995).

Stanton L. Jones and Mark A. Yarhouse, *Homosexuality: The Use of Scientific Research in the Church's Moral Debate* (Downers Grove, IL: InterVarsity, 2000).

95

You May Hear Proponents Argue ...

Same-sex marriage should be allowed because without it homosexuals cannot enter into the divine love for which they were created. Homosexuals were made gay by the creative act of God Himself. Gayness is a gift from God, and rejecting the gift offends the Giftgiver. Just as heterosexuals come into God's love heterosexually and can only love God that way, so homosexuals come into God's love homosexually and can only love God that way. Homosexuals have no other way into God, and denying same-sex marriage separates homosexuals from God. Without same-sex marriage, homosexuals cannot enter the love of God for which they were made.

You Can *Graciously Refute* This By Saying ...

By making sex the means through which humans connect with God, proponents of this argument exchange biblical sexual morality for pagan sexual morality. In doing so, they demonstrate what the Bible calls exchanging "the truth of God for a lie" (Rom. 1:25, NIV). In the Bible, God clearly prohibits gay sex for everyone without exception (see Lev. 18:22), and this prohibition comes directly from the mouth of God. It comes by audible dictation directly from God to Moses and not from any human source. It did not start with Moses, or with a group of elders, or with social customs evolving into tradition, but from the Creator of all things Himself.

This makes the Bible's no-exceptions prohibition of gay sex a word of God from God, not a word of man from men. Another direct word of God in the Bible states that no one who has sex with a same-sex partner can ever shift blame to God for how he or she was made (see Lev. 20:13). This means that justifying or normalizing gay sex is an egregious attack on the veracity and goodness of God's created order—and on God Himself.

A third word of God in the Bible states that gay desires are not fixed or irrepressible. They can be strengthened or weakened, are subject to discipline and control, and may even be completely eliminated (see 1 Cor. 6:9-11). Homosexuality is a combination of desires and behaviors for which individuals are personally responsible. Gay sex alienates same-sex partners from God's love, and same-sex marriage will only offend the Creator and Giver of human sexuality.

The Truth Is …

Same-sex marriage is wrong because God does not make persons in a manner that requires behavior He condemns.

References and Further Reading

For examples of advocates using this argument, see Eugene F. Rogers Jr., *Sexuality and the Christian Body* (Oxford, UK: Blackwell Publishers, 1999), pp. 155-156, 232; and Chris Glaser, *Coming Out As Sacrament* (Louisville, KY: Westminster/John Knox, 1998), pp. 7-9, 82, http://www.newsweek.com/id/172653/output/printhttp://religion.blogs.cnn.com/2011/02/09/

For research on sexual orientation being subject to treatment and change, see Brian S. Mustanski, et al., "A Critical Review of Recent Biological Research on Human Sexual Orientation," *Annual Review of Sex Research*, 13 (2002), pp. 89-140; William Byne and Bruce Parsons, "Human Sexual Orientation: The Biologic Theories Reappraised," 50/3, *Archives of General Psychiatry* (March 1993), pp. 228-239; William Byne, "The Biological Evidence Challenged," *Scientific American* (May 1994), pp. 50-55; William Byne, "Why We Cannot Conclude That Sexual Orientation is Primarily a Biological Phenomenon," 34/1, *Journal of Homosexuality* (1997), pp. 73-80; John Horgan, "Gay Genes, Revisited: Doubts Arise Over Research on the Biology of Homosexuality," 273/5, *Scientific American* (November 1995), p. 26; and Eliot Marshall, "NIH's 'Gay Gene' Study Questioned," 268/5219, *Science* (June 30, 1995), p. 1841. For how the science has been misrepresented and politicized, see Jeffrey Satinover, "The Trojan Couch: How the Mental Health Associations Misrepresent Science," *Conference Reports 2005*, National Association for Research and Therapy of Homosexuals, accessible at http://www.narth.com/docs/thetrojancouch-satinover; Robert Lerner and Althea Nagia, *No Basis: What the Studies Don't Tell Us About Same-Sex Parenting*, Marriage Law Project (Washington, DC, January 2001); A. Dean Byrd, "When Activism Masquerades as Science," National Association for Research and Therapy of Homosexuals, accessible at http://www.narth.com/docs/masquerades (posted 2004, updated September 3, 2008); and Michael L. Brown, "Is Gay the New Black? Analyzing the Argument That 'I Was Born That Way,'" in *A Queer Thing Happened to America* (Concord, NC: Equal Time Books, 2011), pp. 197-225.

Robert A.J. Gagnon, "The Bible and Homosexual Practice: Theology, Analogies, and Genes," *Theology Matters* (November/December 2001), pp. 1-16, accessible at http://wordalone.com/t/gagnon-summary.doc and at http://theologymatters.com/NovDec01.pdf.

Robert A.J. Gagnon, *The Bible and Homosexual Practice: Texts and Hermeneutics* (Nashville, TN: Abingdon Press, 2001).

Thomas E. Schmidt, *Straight and Narrow? Compassion and Clarity in the Homosexual Debate* (Downers Grove, IL: InterVarsity Press, 1995).

Stanton L. Jones and Mark A. Yarhouse, *Homosexuality: The Use of Scientific Research in the Church's Moral Debate* (Downers Grove, IL: InterVarsity, 2000).

96

You May Hear Proponents Argue ...

Same-sex marriage should be allowed because the Bible does not unfairly limit God's blessing of marriage—and neither should we. God never restricts marriage to some people while denying it to others. God is perfectly fair, and we must not limit marriage in ways that God never intended. Refusing to recognize and support the marriage of same-sex partners reduces marriage to something less than God desires and treats marriage in a way God never intended. Allowing same-sex marriage will restore marriage to the blessing God intended and will enable all to rejoice when homosexuals receive and celebrate God's perfect plan for their lives.

You Can *Graciously Refute* This By Saying ...

Proponents of this argument are wrong because God would never change marriage by making the way He established it at creation to be unfair (see Gen. 2:18-25), or by making the way He treats marriage in the rest of the Bible to be unfair (see Eph. 5:25-31), or by making how Jesus treated marriage to be unfair (see Matt. 19:4-6). He would never make His command to "be fruitful and increase in number" (Gen. 1:28, NIV) irrelevant to how marriage is structured. He would never unfairly deconstruct marriage as an enduring social institution for everyone or unfairly threaten the intergenerational continuity and survival for everyone in society.

God is fair and loving (see 1 Pet. 1:17; 1 John 4:16), but He stresses justice and equality (see Amos 5:24; 2 Cor. 13) only where differences are really not relevant. However, allowing same-sex couples to marry turns marriage into something radically different and totally inconsistent with the institution God made marriage to be at creation. It does this by unfairly treating relevant differences in human behavior as if they were irrelevant to God's design for marriage. Proponents of this argument are thus themselves being unfair, because they start by assuming what they conclude. They unfairly use their assumptions to conclude that homosexuals are being treated unjustly.

Proponents of this argument conclude that God would not be unfair when applying a definition of marriage to which He did not agree in the first place. However, if marriage is not redefined, there is no unfairness to resolve. Homosexuals are not demanding a fair chance to share a blessing from which they are excluded but an unfair chance to deconstruct a blessing they already share with everyone else. Doing so not only is unfair but also foolish and downright dangerous.

The Truth Is …

Same-sex marriage is wrong because it unfairly transforms God's blessing of marriage into something He never intended.

References and Further Reading

For examples of advocates using this argument, see Bernard H. Cochran, "No Biblical Basis for Ban," *News and Observer* (Raleigh), March 14, 2012, p. 11A; Rusty and Carol Parks, "Against Exclusion," Letter to the Editor, *News and Observer* (Raleigh), January 10, 2012; Chris Glaser, "Marriage as We See It," *Newsweek* (September 16, 1998), p. 19; and Dan O. Via, "The Bible, the Church, and Homosexuality," in *Homosexual and the Bible: Two Views*, by Dan O. Via and Robert A. J. Gagnon (Minneapolis, MN: Augsburg Fortress, 2003), pp. 37-39.

For examples of gay social revolutionaries admitting they are using same-sex marriage as a way to completely abolish the institution of marriage, see Thomas B. Stoddard, "Why Gay People Should Seek the Right to Marry," chapter 35 in *Families in the US: Kinship and Domestic Politics*, ed. Karen V. Hansen

(Philadelphia, PA: Temple University Press, 1998); Richard D. Mohr, *A More Perfect Union: Why Straight America Must Stand Up for Gay Rights* (Boston, MA: Beacon, 1994); Gretchen A. Stiers, *From This Day Forward: Commitment, Marriage, and Family in Lesbian and Gay Relationships* (New York: St. Martin's Press, 1999); Michelangelo Signorile, "Bridal Wave," *Out* (December/January 1994); "Sociologist Says Gay Marriage Does Threaten Established Order and That's Good," *Ascribe Law News Service* (November 16, 2003); Margaret Gullette, "The New Case for Marriage," *American Prospect* (March 1, 2004); and Mary Bernstein, "Gender, Queer Family Policies, and the Limits of Law," in *Queer Families, Queer Politics: Challenging Culture and the State*, ed. Mary Bernstein and Renate Reimann (New York: Columbia University Press, 2001). Especially note what she says on page 433.

Daniel R. Heimbach, "Deconstructing the Family," *Religion and Society Report*, 22/7 (October/November 2005), pp. 1-12.

Gary Thomas, *Sacred Marriage: What If God Designed Marriage to Make Us Holy More Than to Make Us Happy* (Grand Rapids, MI: Zondervan, 2000).

Christopher Ash, *Marriage: Sex in the Service of God* (Vancouver, Canada: Regent College Publishing, 2003).

Andreas Köstenberger and David W. Jones, with Mark Liederbach, *God, Marriage, and Family: Rebuilding the Biblical Foundation*, 2nd edition (Wheaton, IL: Crossway, 2010).

Barrett Duke and Bill Wylie-Kellerman, "The Good Book and Gay Marriage: A Faith-Based Debate over What Scripture Teaches About Same-Sex Marriage," *The Daily Beast* blog, from *Newsweek* (December 15, 2008, accessible at http://www.thedaily beast.com/newsweek/2008/12/15/the-good-book-and-gay-marriage.html.

97

You May Hear Proponents Argue ...

Same-sex marriage should be allowed because limiting marriage to heterosexuals places boundaries on God's limitless love. God's love has no conditions; it is boundless and free. He loves everyone—even His enemies—and no human authority should place boundaries and restrictions on something God made to be boundless and free. For this reason, we should allow all to marry in whatever way God's love happens to lead.

You Can *Graciously Refute* This By Saying ...

Proponents of this argument state something that makes no sense. Of course God's love has limits, much in the same way that the law of logical non-contradiction has limits. God's love is limited by those who reject His love in the same way that honesty rejects dishonesty and light rejects darkness. God's love is transcendent and extends to all who accept His authority, live by His standards, submit to His judgment, and repent for their desires and behaviors that conflict with His holiness (see 1 Pet. 1:14-16). God in His love forgives all who come to Him in repentance, but He does not ignore rebellion, is not blind to the difference separating right from wrong, and does not affirm desires and behaviors that He says are wrong and sinful (see Gal. 6:7).

Proponents of this argument falsely imagine that God's love is not consistent with His righteousness and that sinners can escape His wrath without repenting. This not only accuses God of being inconsistent with Himself but also turns Him into something that is hateful and not loving at all. After all, telling someone who is on a path to destruction that he or she should stay on that path is not loving but hateful. God's perfect love for gay and lesbian couples is expressed by urging them to cease gay sexual behavior, not by pretending that what they desire and do is good and normal.

God's perfect love does include everyone in a same-sex sexual relationship, but it does not include affirming or encouraging those individuals' desires and behaviors. God's love does not embrace sexual behavior that He says is abnormal and sinful for everyone without exception (see Rom. 1:26; Lev. 18:22). In addition, while God's love embraces everyone who comes to Him in repentance, it does not include those who do not repent on His terms (see Rev. 22:16).

The Truth Is ...

Same-sex marriage is wrong because God's love does not overlook, embrace, or affirm sinful behavior for which people refuse to repent.

References for Further Reading

For examples of advocates using this argument, see Jimmy Creech, *Adam's Gift: A Memoir of a Pastor's Calling to Defy the Church's Persecution of Lesbians and Gays* (Durham, NC: Duke University Press, 2001); John J. McNeill, *Taking a Chance on God: Liberating Theology for Gays, Lesbians, and Their Lovers, Families, and Friends* (Boston, MA: Beacon, 1988); and Carter Heyward, *Touching Our Strength: The Erotic as Power and the Love of God* (San Francisco: Harper and Row, 1989).

For studies linking homosexual activity with a much higher risk of poor mental and physical health and suicidality, see Theo Sandfort, Ron de Graaf, Rob Bojl, and Paul Schnabel, "Same-Sex Sexual Behavior and Psychiatric Disorders," *Archives of General Psychiatry*, 58 (January 2001), pp. 85-91; Susan Cochran and Vickie Mays, "Lifetime Prevalence of Suicide Symptoms and Affective Disorders Among Men Reporting Same-Sex Partners," *American Journal of Public Health*, 90/4

(April 2000), pp. 573-578; Stephen Gilman, Susan Cochran, Vickie Mays, M. Hughes, D. Ostrow, and R.C. Kessler, "Risk of Psychiatric Disorders Among Individuals Reporting Same-Sex Sexual Partners in the National Co-morbidity Survey," *American Journal of Public Health*, 91/6 (June 2001), pp. 933-939; John R. Diggs Jr., "The Health Risks of Gay Sex," Catholic Education Resource Center, copyright 2002, accessible at http://www. catholiceducation.org/articles/homosexuality/ho0075.html; and David Fergusson, John Horwood, Elizabeth Ridder, and Annette Beautrais, "Sexual Orientation and Mental Health in a Birth Cohort of Young Adults," *Psychological Medicine*, 35/7 (2005), pp. 971-981.

Robert A. J. Gagnon, "Does the Bible Regard Same-Sex Intercourse as Intrinsically Sinful?" in *Christian Sexuality: Normative and Pastoral Principles*, ed. Russell E. Saltzman (Delhi, NY: Kirk House, 2003).

James B. DeYoung, *Homosexuality: Contemporary Claims Examined in Light of the Bible and Other Ancient Literature and Law* (Grand Rapids, MI: Kregel, 2000).

Joe Dallas, *The Gay Gospel? How Pro-Gay Advocates Misread the Bible* (Eugene, OR: Harvest House, 2007).

Oliver O'Donovan, *Common Objects of Love: Moral Reflection and the Shaping of Community* (Grand Rapids, MI: William B. Eerdmans, 2002).

Edward Collins Vacek, *Love, Human and Divine: The Heart of Christian Ethics* (Washington, DC: Georgetown University Press, 1994).

Sherif Girgis, Robert P. George, and Ryan T. Anderson, "What Is Marriage?" *Harvard Journal of Law and Public Policy*, 34/1 (Winter 2011), pp. 245-287.

98

You May Hear Proponents Argue ...

Same-sex marriage should be allowed because God only cares about how people love, not whom they love. God is pleased by every loving relationship that is strong and true, regardless of sexual identity. Social differences based on race, economic status, and gender make no difference to God's love for His children. God loves everyone equally without regard to such differences. All that matters is that we love one another in the manner God loves us. Because He loves us without regard to gender differences, God wants us to also ignore gender differences in the way we love each other. Rejecting same-sex marriage is thus not consistent with loving each other the way God loves us.

You Can *Graciously Refute* This By Saying ...

Proponents of this argument rightly argue that God wants people to love one another, but they twist the proper understanding of God's love. God's love is part of an ordered reality aligned to His holiness, which means there are boundaries that distinguish what God loves from what He hates. The love God made marriage to express is not mere sentimentality. Rather, it is love that serves three eternal purposes: (1) that gender dualism in marriage serves to manifest God's image (see Gen. 1:27), (2) that it perpetuates the human race through biological reproduction (see Gen. 1:28), and (3) that it expresses the union of corresponding difference by which the church is united with Christ (see Eph. 5:32).

Same-sex marriage flatly denies and structurally erases all three eternal purposes God's love designed marriage to serve. God, in His love, cannot possibly condone behavior He declares to be sinful and wrong for everyone without exception (see Lev. 18:22). Nor can He affirm people He says are heading for eternal death (see Rom. 1:32; John 3:36).

What proponents of this argument call *love* is nothing of the sort. They confuse real love with grandmotherly indulgence that simply feeds appetites and has no regard for ultimate welfare. Feeding sexual desires is not real love, nor is merely affirming feelings of affection. Real love pursues what is ultimately best, which is something God defines. What gay couples feel for each other is not real love because it affirms what God abhors (see Lev. 18:22). It substitutes sensual gratification for what God declares is truly in their own best interests.

The Truth Is …

Same-sex marriage is wrong because God's love conforms to God's holiness, and leaving sinners under God's wrath is not loving at all.

References and Further Reading

For examples of advocates using this argument, see Lisa Miller, "Our Mutual Joy: Opponents of Gay Marriage Often Cite Scripture. But What the Bible Teaches About Love Argues for the Other Side," *Newsweek*, December 15, 2008, accessible at http://www.newsweek.com/id/172653/output/print; David G. Meyers and Letha Dawson Scanzoni, *What God Has Joined Together? A Christian Case for Gay Marriage* (San Francisco: HarperSanFrancisco, 2005), pp. 105-113; and Dan O. Via, "The Bible, the Church, and Homosexuality," in *Homosexual and the Bible: Two Views*, by Dan O. Via and Robert A. J. Gagnon (Minneapolis, MN: Augsburg Fortress, 2003).

Oliver O'Donovan, *Common Objects of Love: Moral Reflection and the Shaping of Community* (Grand Rapids, MI: William B. Eerdmans, 2002).

Edward Collins Vacek, *Love, Human and Divine: The Heart of Christian Ethics* (Washington, DC: Georgetown University Press, 1994).

Carl F. H. Henry, "Love, the Divine Imperative," chapter 9 in *Christian Personal Ethics* (Grand Rapids, MI: William B. Eerdmans, 1957), pp. 219-235.

John R. Diggs Jr., "The Health Risks of Gay Sex," *Catholic Education Resource Center*, copyright 2002, accessible at http://www.catholiceducation.org/articles/homosexuality/ho0075.html.

David Island and Patrick Letellier, *Men Who Beat the Men Who Love Them: Battered Gay Men and Domestic Violence* (New York: Haworth Press, 1991).

Timothy Dailey, "Comparing the Lifestyles of Homosexual Couples to Married Couples," *Family Research Council* (April 29, 2004), accessible at http://www.frc.org/get.cfm?i=IS04C02.

Gwat Yong Lie and Sabrina Gentlewarrier, "Intimate Violence in Lesbian Relationships: Discussion of Survey Findings and Practice Implications," *Journal of Social Service Research*, 15/1-2 (1991), pp. 41-59.

Robert A. J. Gagnon, "Does the Bible Regard Same-Sex Intercourse as Intrinsically Sinful?" In *Christian Sexuality: Normative and Pastoral Principles*, ed. R.E. Saltzman (Delhi, NY: Kirk House, 2003).

Daniel R. Heimbach, "Deconstructing the Family," *Religion and Society Report*, 22/7 (October/November 2005), pp. 1-12.

99

You May Hear Proponents Argue …

Same-sex marriage should be allowed because Jesus stood for social justice, and same-sex marriage is a matter of social justice. Denying marriage to homosexuals goes against the example Jesus set on social justice and conflicts with what He taught about how we should treat the oppressed and downtrodden. Jesus said we should lift up those who were despised by people in power, defend the disadvantaged, and favor the weak over the strong. If Jesus were here today, He would overturn laws that protect heterosexual power and treat homosexuals like outcasts on the margins of society.

You Can *Graciously Refute* This By Saying …

Proponents of this argument fail because they assume the thing for which they aim and then misrepresent the ministry of Jesus. They begin by assuming that gay sex is normal and that denying same-sex marriage must therefore be terribly unjust. But Jesus would not have accepted their starting premise, and so He would not have thought denying same-sex marriage to be unjust at all.

While Jesus had compassion for the downtrodden, He never pursued social justice for its own sake. In addition, while He truly cared for the poor, the sick, and the suffering, He did not lead a movement to change social structures simply to satisfy human wants and desires. Instead, Jesus' ministry and teaching focused on doing what God the Father sent Him to do, which was freeing sinners from their bondage to sin and making a way for them to escape the eternal death sentence required by God's wrath (see John 3:16-17).

Jesus did not come to earth to solve social problems but to save sinners who were oppressed by sin. He would not have championed same-sex marriage because He supported every standard in God's moral law (see Matt. 5:17), including God's strict prohibition of gay sex (see Lev. 18:22). He insisted that gender duality was required to achieve the sort of relational union for which God designed marriage (see Mark 10:5-6). He also would have viewed treating the gender duality in God's design for marriage (see Gen. 2:18-24) as if it made no difference to the practice of marriage to be unjust—not only in a morally theoretical or theological sense, but also in the practical sense of violating social justice.

The Truth Is ...

Same-sex marriage is wrong because Jesus would have never viewed changing marriage to accommodate gays as being socially unjust.

References and Further Reading

For examples of advocates using this argument, see Fredrick Herzog, *Justice Church: The New Function of the Church in North American Christianity* (Maryknoll, NY: Orbis, 1980); and Carter Heyward, *Our Passion for Justice: Images of Power, Sexuality, and Liberation* (New York: Pilgrim, 1984).

Robert A. J. Gagnon, "Does the Bible Regard Same-Sex Intercourse as Intrinsically Sinful?" In *Christian Sexuality: Normative and Pastoral Principles*, ed. R.E. Saltzman (Delhi, NY: Kirk House, 2003).

Robert A. J. Gagnon, "The Bible and Homosexual Practice: Key Issues," in *Homosexual and the Bible: Two Views*, by Dan O. Via and Robert A. J. Gagnon (Minneapolis, MN: Augsburg Fortress, 2003).

Robert A. J. Gagnon, "The Bible and Homosexual Practice: Theology, Analogies, and Genes," *Theology Matters* (November/ December 2001), pp. 1-16, accessible at http://wordalone. com/t/gagnon-summary.doc and at http://theologymatters.com/ NovDec01.pdf.

Robert A. J. Gagnon, *The Bible and Homosexual Practice: Texts and Hermeneutics* (Nashville, TN: Abingdon Press, 2001).

Joe Dallas, *The Gay Gospel? How Pro-Gay Advocates Misread the Bible* (Eugene, OR: Harvest House, 2007).

Thomas E. Schmidt, *Straight and Narrow? Compassion and Clarity in the Homosexual Debate* (Downers Grove, IL: InterVarsity Press, 1995).

Albert Mohler, "*Newsweek* Argues the Religious Case for Gay Marriage," *Crosswalk* blog, posted December 10, 2008, accessible at http://www.crosswalk.com/news/news week-argues-the-religious-case-for-gay-marriage-11596776.html.

Barrett Duke and Bill Wylie-Kellerman, "The Good Book and Gay Marriage: A Faith-Based Debate over What Scripture Teaches About Same-Sex Marriage," *The Daily Beast* blog, from *Newsweek* (December 15, 2008, accessible at http://www.thedaily beast.com/newsweek/2008/12/15/the-good-book-and-gay-marriage.html.

John-Henry Westen, "The Real Reason Christians Oppose Same-Sex Marriage," *LifeSiteNews.com*, posted April 14, 2005, accessible at http://www.lifesitenews.com/news/archive/ldn/1950/41/5041403.

100

You May Hear Proponents Argue ...

Same-sex marriage should be allowed because Jesus only taught that marriage requires fidelity and did not limit marriage by sexual orientation. Jesus never claimed that marriage is only for heterosexuals or can only unite a man with a woman. Jesus focused on fidelity as the central theme in marriage, not on gender. He defined marriage and family relationships in spiritual terms, not biological ones. In His teaching on marriage Jesus opposed divorce, but restricting marriage to opposite-gendered couples goes beyond what He taught. Thus, because Jesus never limited marriage to some while denying it to others, neither should we.

You Can *Graciously Refute* This By Saying ...

Proponents of this argument fail because Jesus not only stressed marital fidelity but also the dual-gender structure of marriage. They depend on a false claim that is contrary to the biblical-historical record. They suggest that Jesus never restricted marriage to opposite-gendered couples, when He obviously did. While Jesus did stress the importance of marital fidelity, He also affirmed the dual-gendered structure of marriage just as strongly—if not more so.

In Mark 10:6-10, before Jesus stressed marital fidelity, He first emphasized the dual-gender structure of marriage by appealing to Genesis 1:27, where "God 'made them male and female,'" and to Genesis 2:24, where God declared "a man will leave his father and mother and be united to his wife" (vv. 6-7, NIV). In doing so, Jesus taught that marriage is defined in a way that makes same-sex relationships irrelevant. He also showed that fidelity in marriage only concerns unions where a man leaves his father and mother and is united with his wife (see Gen. 2:24).

Same-sex marriage rejects the dual-gender structure that God designed marriage to have and replaces it with a sentimental definition that denies marriage has any fixed structure at all. In fact, nothing could be further from what Jesus actually taught, and it is totally contrary to what He would affirm today. Lisa Miller, who makes this argument, also says "we cannot look to the Bible as a marriage manual." However, in making this statement she destroys what she claims in the first place. One cannot appeal to the Bible for authority in one breath and then dismiss it in the next.

The Truth Is …

Same-sex marriage is wrong because Jesus taught that from the beginning marriage was made only to unite a man with a woman.

Reference and Further Reading

For examples of advocates using this argument, see Chris Glaser, "Marriage as We See It: When My Partner and I Took Vows and Received the Church's Blessing, I Was Transformed," *Newsweek* (September 16, 1998), p. 19; Peter J. Gomes, *The Good Book: Reading the Bible with Mind and Heart* (New York: William Morrow, 1996); David G. Meyers and Letha Dawson Scanzoni, *What God Has Joined Together? A Christian Case for Gay Marriage* (San Francisco: HarperSanFrancisco, 2005), pp. 92,103; and Lisa Miller, "Our Mutual Joy: Opponents of Gay Marriage Often Cite Scripture. But What the Bible Teaches about Love Argues for the Other Side," *Newsweek*, December 15, 2008, accessible at http://www.newsweek.com/id/172653/output/print.

Robert A. J. Gagnon, "The Bible and Homosexual Practice: Key Issues," in *Homosexual and the Bible: Two Views*, by Dan O. Via and Robert A. J. Gagnon (Minneapolis, MN: Augsburg Fortress, 2003).

Robert A. J. Gagnon, "The Bible and Homosexual Practice: Theology, Analogies, and Genes," *Theology Matters* (November/December 2001), pp. 1-16, accessible at http://wordalone.com/t/gagnon-summary.doc and at http://theologymatters.com/NovDec01.pdf.

Robert A. J. Gagnon, *The Bible and Homosexual Practice: Texts and Hermeneutics* (Nashville, TN: Abingdon Press, 2001).

Robert A. J. Gagnon, "More than 'Mutual Joy': Lisa Miller ... Against Scripture and Jesus," accessible at http://www.robgagnon.net/NewsweekMillerHomosexResp.htm.

Albert Mohler, "*Newsweek* Argues the Religious Case for Gay Marriage," *Crosswalk* blog, posted December 10, 2008, accessible at http://www.crosswalk.com/news/newsweek-argues-the-religious-case-for-gay-marriage-11596776.html.

Sue Bohlin, "*Newsweek*'s Gay Marriage Propaganda Piece," *Tapestry*, the Bible.org Women's blog, accessible at http://www.probe.org/site/c.fdKEIMNsEoG/b.4839319/k.E937/Newsweeks_Gay-Marriage_Propaganda_Piece.html.

Barrett Duke and Bill Wylie-Kellerman, "The Good Book and Gay Marriage: A Faith-Based Debate over What Scripture Teaches About Same-Sex Marriage," *The Daily Beast* blog, from *Newsweek* (December 15, 2008, accessible at http://www.thedaily beast.com/newsweek/2008/12/15/the-good-book-and-gay-marriage.html.

Daniel R. Heimbach, *True Sexual Morality: Recovering Biblical Standards for a Culture in Crisis* (Wheaton, IL: Crossway, 2004).

101

You May Hear Proponents Argue …

Same-sex marriage should be allowed because civil laws have no effect on how God views marriage. Nothing in civil law changes God's view of marriage, so there is no need for Christians to defend God's view of marriage by opposing legalization of same-sex marriage. However, when Christians oppose legalization of same-sex marriage, they promote the false idea that religious marriage requires state approval to be legitimate. The solution is to detach religious marriage from civil marriage altogether. This will be good for those practicing religious marriage and good for gays seeking legal recognition for their deepest commitments.

You Can *Graciously Refute* This By Saying …

Proponents of this argument overlook the public's interest that underlies marriage law and then misidentify what leads Christian citizens to oppose legalizing same-sex marriage. Of course, changing marriage law has no effect on God's view of marriage. However, it will change how people view and practice marriage in ways that are bad for themselves, for their children, and for society.

Traditional marriage law guards the dual-gender structure of marriage as a social institution, and it does so for justified secular reasons—not religious ones. If the state legally redefines marriage as nothing more than a way to affirm personal feelings, it will open the door to allowing people to legally marry anything they desire. If the objectively defined procreational structure of civil marriage is replaced by entitlement to have subjective feelings affirmed, then whatever feelings people possess will have the same claim. By universal tradition and practice, marriage is a procreationally structured institution. However, legalizing same-sex marriage will deinstitutionalize the institution by deconstructing its structure, which will destroy the social institution on which the survival of society most depends.

The problem with same-sex marriage is not the way in which it affects God's view of marriage but in how it harms the common good of people and society at large. Christians oppose legalizing same-sex marriage not because it harms God's view of marriage but because neighborly love and good citizenship require them to oppose a legal revision that threatens to collapse the institution on which the common good of their social order most depends.

The Truth Is …

Same-sex marriage is wrong because it is socially necessary to keep marriage a dual-gender union.

References and Further Reading

For examples of advocates using this argument, see Daniel A. Crane, "Pick Your Shibboleths Wisely," *Christianity Today* (October 2004), pp. 60-64; Alan Dershowitz, "Government Should Quit the Marriage Business," *Los Angeles Times*, December 3, 2003; Alisa Solomon, "State to Church: I Want a Divorce," *Village Voice*, February 24, 2004; and Steve Swayne, "Church, State, and Marriage," *Rutland Herald*, May 4, 2004.

C. S. Lewis, the widely respected Christian writer, proposed something similar to this argument when addressing laws on divorce (not same-sex marriage). He wrote, "There ought to be two distinct kinds of marriage: one governed by the State with rules enforced on all citizens, the other governed by the Church with rules enforced by her on her own members." Since Lewis approached divorce law in this manner, he may have taken a similar approach to legalizing same-sex marriage. C. S. Lewis, *Mere Christianity* (New York: Simon and Schuster, 1980), p. 102.

Douglas Laycock, Anthony Picarello and Robin Wilson, eds., *Same-Sex Marriage and Religious Liberty: Emerging Conflicts* (New York: Rowman and Littlefield, 2008).

Maggie Gallagher, "Banned in Boston: The Coming Conflict Between Same-Sex Marriage and Religious Liberty," *The Weekly Standard* (May 15, 2006), pp. 20-26.

Marc D. Stern, "Liberty v. Equality; Equality v. Liberty," *Northwestern Journal of Law and Social Policy*, 5/2 (Fall 2010), pp. 307-317, accessible at http://acadia.law.northwest ern.edu/journals/njlsp/v5/n2/5/5Stern.pdf.

Daniel R. Heimbach, "Deconstructing the Family," *Religion and Society Report*, 22/7 (October/November 2005), pp. 1-12.

Sherif Girgis, Robert P. George, and Ryan T. Anderson, "What Is Marriage?" *Harvard Journal of Law and Public Policy*, 34/1 (Winter 2011), pp. 245-287.

William C. Duncan, "The State Interest in Marriage," *Ave Maria Law Review* 2/1 (Spring 2004), pp. 153-182.

Homosexual activist Michelangelo Signorile has stated that the goal of legalizing same-sex marriage is to abolish marriage as a social institution. He states that it is the goal of the gay rights movement to "fight for same-sex marriage … and then, once granted, redefine the institution of marriage completely … not as a way of adhering to society's moral codes but rather to debunk America and radically alter an archaic institution." Michelangelo Signorile, "Bridal Wave," *Out* (December/January 1994), p. 161.

PART II

For Further Consideration

*The main
reason homosexual
activists are demanding same-sex
marriage is not to participate in something
others have but rather to radically
change the public meaning of
marriage for everyone.*

I THOUGHT CHANGE
WAS IMPOSSIBLE

by Eric Garner

I WAS BORN into a family of five. My father died when I was four years old, and my mother did what she could to raise me as a single parent. She spent the early years of my childhood in survival mode. Mom worked hard at low-paying jobs with less-than-desirable hours, which meant I had little adult supervision and got into mischief much of the time. She took me to church, and at age 10 I went forward in a service to become a Christian. But I merely went through the motions. Nothing changed, and the experience made no difference in my life.

I deeply grieved losing my Dad. Mom says I would pour over his pictures for hours. My brother didn't do that, and neither did my sister. But I did. My father's death affected me deeply and in ways I still do not completely understand.

When Mom finally remarried, it was to an alcoholic. At first I was delighted to have a father. But he handled pressure by getting inebriated, and he had little time for me. In fact, he was verbally abusive and emotionally distant toward everyone in the family, including me, which had a detrimental effect on how I viewed men. I missed my real father, despised my stepfather, and had no other male role model in my life. Everything was up for grabs, including my sexual identity.

With no male role model, I became fascinated with male nudity. I remember being drawn to ads for men's underwear. I was looking for masculine affirmation, which led me to viewing pictures of men in the nude and then to experimenting with guys once or twice while in high school. However, at that point I had not yet settled who I was sexually, so I began a sexual relationship with a girl as well. I asked God to take away my attraction for men and got engaged to my high school sweetheart.

On graduating from high school my feelings were in turmoil, so I held off getting married and enlisted in the Navy. I thought the Navy would be a good place to discover myself. I believed that if I surrounded myself with men, I might get more interested in women. But rather than solidify my desire for women, my Navy experience only increased my desire for men. That was 1985, and I was surprised even then by how many gay men there were in the Navy.

I had agreed to a standard four-year tour, but after two years I wanted out. Of course, the Navy expected me to fulfill my enlistment, but I knew that if the officers found out that I was gay, I could leave in a hurry. So that's what I did. I was out of the Navy in 60 days.

When I came out to my officers, I thought I might receive counseling, or at least an evaluation. But that never happened. Instead, I was accused of playing games and lying. I was put under pressure and made to feel nervous. I held my ground, and eventually the Navy had to accept what I said. After that everyone treated me differently. Some understood, but most shunned me. That was hard to endure.

I did not act on gay desires while I was in the Navy, and I remained engaged to my high school sweetheart until I was discharged. But after leaving the Navy, I called her, broke off our engagement, and went to a gay bar—all in one evening. I immersed myself in everything gay. It became my life, my culture, and my entire world.

My first serious relationship lasted about a year and ended in a way that left me devastated. How it ended took me by surprise. My partner announced one day that he thought I was looking for a "daddy," and he did not want the job. He said he needed a relationship with a peer and did not want to raise a child. That hurt so badly and felt like more than I could bear. I was so upset that I tried to take my own life.

However, even though I felt terrible at that point, I was still happy most of the time. Or so I told myself. Looking back, I realize that even then I knew something was missing, but I was in denial. I was intoxicated with feeling I could "do whatever I pleased." In my honest moments, I knew I didn't feel truly complete, didn't have lasting security, and wasn't totally satisfied. I feared that what I had would not last and would never be profound. Was I happy? The truth was that almost every time I engaged in homosexual sex, I was inebriated—either under the influence of drugs or alcohol.

After attempting suicide, I went to a vacant church and asked God to give me someone to fill the emptiness in my life. I did not like being alone, so I asked God to send a man who would know everything about me and love me as I was. Right after that a new man came along, and for a while I thought God had answered my prayer. This man—let's call him "Joe"—and I were in a committed relationship for two-and-a-half years. While this relationship did not last either, it led me down a different path than I have been on ever since.

Joe grew up in the church, but he had stopped going before we met. After we linked up, he went back to attending the church where his family went. Joe took me along, and I soon got acquainted with his family. I found that they were people who believed the Bible and accepted God on biblical terms. This impressed me, and in the end it was members of Joe's family who made the most difference in my life.

When Joe and I started going to church, he wanted us to act as if no one knew we were a gay couple. I was sure his family knew, and I thought others in the church did as well. But to please him, I went along with keeping things under wraps at church. Joe and I went regularly, and I started listening to a preacher who understood God better than anyone I had ever known. He also seemed to know me better than I knew myself.

Then, on January 7, 1990, I got saved. I have never been the same since! The experience was so different than when I was age 10. The only way I can explain it is that I had an encounter with the Holy Spirit. At the invitation I began to shake and knew I needed to get right with God. I was scared to walk out of that church without submitting to the Holy Spirit. I asked God to save me, and I got up knowing that things were different.

When I got home, I started reading the Bible. It was not long before the Holy Spirit led me to Leviticus 20:13, where it says, "If a man lies with a male as he lies with a woman, both of them have committed an abomination. They shall surely be put to death. Their blood shall be upon them" (NKJV). Well, that scared me to death, because I had been living as a homosexual for 10 years and had been in a homosexual relationship with Joe for two-and-a-half years.

Then I read 1 Corinthians 6:9-10, where Paul says, "Do you not know that the unrighteous will not inherit the kingdom of God? Do not be deceived. Neither fornicators, nor idolaters, nor adulterers, nor homosexuals, nor sodomites … will inherit the kingdom of God." That was bad. But when I saw the next verse, I got excited, because Paul says, "And such were some of you. But you were washed, but you were sanctified, but you were justified in the name of the Lord Jesus and by the Spirit of our God" (1 Cor. 6:11, NKJV). This was great! Here was a way out! For the first time in my life, the pieces started coming together.

But I thought I might perhaps be acting hasty. I knew that Joe, my gay partner, had been raised in church and knew the Bible better than I did, so I went to see what he thought. I don't remember what I expected, but I do remember that Joe responded in a way that astounded me when I showed him what I was reading. He said, "Eric, if you're looking for something in the Bible that will justify homosexuality, you will never find it." When I asked why not, he said, "Because the Bible condemns homosexuality!"

I was floored. "Then what are we doing?" I asked. "How can we call ourselves Christians and go to church every week if the Bible condemns what we're doing?" Joe got angry and said I would need to deal with that on my own. So I studied the Bible more intensely. Soon I told Joe, "I can't go on living this way and have peace with God. I'm losing sleep and becoming a nervous wreck. Something has to give, and I need to talk with someone." He said, "Fine! Talk with anyone you want." I didn't have a car, so I asked Joe if I could borrow his, and he agreed. At first I wasn't sure where to go, but then I got a strong feeling that God wanted me to go over to Joe's older brother's house.

I felt nervous about that, because I didn't know Joe's older brother very well, and because he was a deacon at our church. I was afraid he might turn against me. But the conviction I had grew stronger, so I headed over there. I arrived late at night and knocked on the door. Both Joe's brother and his wife both opened the door.

I said, "I hope I haven't bothered you, but I really need to talk." When they invited me in, I asked, "Do you have any idea how I'm living with your brother?" They said, "We do, and we've been praying for you." I was so relieved I started weeping. I told them I didn't know what to do, but I was afraid of what I had read in the Bible. I knew I could not go on living as I had been doing.

We went into their den, and this couple confirmed that I was reading the Bible correctly. They told me that feeling alarmed over what I read meant I was under conviction. They said it meant God was telling me to head in a new direction, and they would help in any way they could. I appreciated this, but I couldn't believe they actually understood my situation. Sometimes in a crisis you feel as if you are dealing with something totally unique—like you are the only one who has ever gone through it. In such cases, when others say they "understand," it seems trite, regardless of how they might have intended it. That's how I felt. So when Joe's brother and sister-in-law told me they "understood," I didn't believe them.

When I started to put them off, Joe's wife stood up and said with big tears in her eyes, "Eric, there's something I need to tell you. Before meeting my husband, I lived with a woman for five years in the same way you're living with my brother-in-law. I do know what you are going through, because I have been there myself."

Well, I had never been more speechless in my life! I had sat across the dinner table from this woman at least once each month for the last two-and-a-half years. She had known what I was doing all along, and she had never uttered a word in judgment. Instead, she and her husband had loved me and had been praying for me. I was stunned. I still get chills just thinking about it.

She went on to say, "Eric, look at me now! I have a wonderful husband, this wonderful home, and I'm six months pregnant with child. I am the happiest I've been in my whole life! And it's all because I got right with God and decided to live on His terms rather than my own."

When I asked her what I should do, she told me to stop sleeping in the same bed with Joe and to move into his spare bedroom. Then she suggested that I simply ask God every day what He wanted me to do and do whatever He told me. At that, she put her hands on my shoulders and said, "This will be the hardest thing you ever do in your life. But I promise if you do this, God will bless you!"

So that is what I did. I went home and had a long discussion with Joe. He said that if moving into his spare bedroom was what I needed to get over what I was experiencing in this situation, it was fine with him. So we started sleeping in different rooms while living in the same house. But it didn't work out well. Joe realized he was no longer the center of my life, and knowing that caused tension between us. Now it seemed we were at each other's throats all the time.

I called Joe's brother and sister-in-law again to say that living in separate rooms in the same house wasn't working, and I needed somewhere else to stay. They said they had an extra room over their garage that I could move into right away. I still had no transportation, and again I had to borrow Joe's car—this time to move out completely. Joe asked if I could be happy living with his older brother and his wife, because up until that point we had considered them snobs. I said I didn't know—I only knew that God was telling me to move out because I could not stay in the relationship we had. Joe said he couldn't believe God was telling me to rip his heart out like that. I had nothing more to say and just finished packing.

I moved out of Joe's house and into the little room that Joe's brother and sister-in-law gave me over their garage. When I arrived there and found myself alone, I was overwhelmed and feared that I had just thrown away everything that I had built my life on for years. I told God, "I can't do this!" In fact, to be blunt, I wanted to deal with my pain the way I always had, which was to get a beer and smoke a joint. But that was part of the life I was leaving, so I resisted.

I got on my knees and told God, "You are asking me do something I do not know how to do! I've been going one way for 10 years, and now all of a sudden You are sending me in a whole new direction. Even if I knew what to do, I don't have the strength for it. This does not match my feelings. It's not making me happy. It's not like anything else I have ever done."

I had no straight friends, and everyone knew I was gay. So I got totally honest with God and said, "I don't know how *not* to be gay!

I need help, and I need it now!" At that point, I made a promise that made all the difference. I told God, "I don't know how not to be gay, but I know what Your Word says. I can listen to Your voice, and I can do what You tell me. I will no longer focus on thinking about my sin problem but on thinking about my Savior. I will start listening to You and obeying You *regardless of how I feel*. I'm leaving the results to you."

Strangely enough, one of the people who encouraged me the most at that time was a woman named Kelly, who is now my wife. I met Kelly shortly after meeting Joe. Joe and Kelly knew each other in high school and had played in the marching band together. Joe considered Kelly to be one of his best friends, and because of that I had attended Kelly's first wedding. She invited Joe to be one of the ushers in her wedding, and of course he brought me along. But Kelly's first marriage ended tragically. Her first husband was emotionally unstable, and two years later he committed suicide in a way that Kelly saw but could not prevent. As a result, Kelly and I ended up in the same singles group at church—she as a recent widow, and I because I was on my own again.

After moving out of Joe's place, Joe's older brother asked if I had any interest in dating or getting married someday. I wasn't sure that could happen. But when he saw me hesitate, he said, "Don't worry if the feelings aren't there right now. If God has a woman for you, He will give you the feelings you need." After that, based on *faith* more than feeling, I started asking God for a wife. Even though my feelings were confused, I was sure I did not have the gift of celibacy. If going back to my old life was not an option, finding a wife was the only alternative.

I was in cosmetology school at the time, and I started going over to where Kelly lived with her mother and father to practice pedicures on them. One night, I was working on Kelly's feet when I started experiencing feelings for her that I had never had before. It was as if God was saying, "Do you see this beautiful woman I have set before you?" This man who had been so totally gay was falling in love with a woman! What I felt was not what I had known for my gay partners. This was something new, pure, good, and overwhelming, all at the same time.

As I drove home that night, God told me, "Eric, that's the woman I have prepared to be your wife!" I didn't hear an audible voice, but I sensed God's presence so strongly that I knew it was not wishful thinking. Well, I got excited, but I still found it hard to believe. I was overjoyed and scared to death at the same time. All of this made me a nervous wreck.

I started acting awkwardly around Kelly, and it wasn't long before she realized something was up. She asked me what was wrong, which only made me feel worse. I put her off, but she persisted. She said that she knew something was upsetting me, but that if I didn't want to discuss it that was fine. No pressure. But then she said that if I did ever want to talk, I needed to tell her the truth and not lie about it.

Well, that did it! I opened up and said I had feelings for her that went way beyond friendship. In all my confusion and self-doubt, I was in love with Kelly—not as an object of self-gratification but as a person! She smiled and said, "That's okay, because I feel the same about you!" God brought us together in an amazing way. I had no idea what I was doing. All I can say is that what I least expected took place at the time I least expected and in the way I least expected. We had a beautiful wedding. I cried through the whole thing, and now Kelly laughs every time she watches the video.

Kelly and I have been married for two decades, and in my mind she grows more beautiful every day. I finished cosmetology school just before we got married, and I have supported myself and my family in that trade ever since. My job puts me around homosexuals all the time, and I have many gay friends. But while interacting with gay men and women remains a large part of my life, my motives have changed.

I no longer self-identify as gay, but I have a very real non-sexual affection for people who are in the same place I was. Because I have been there, I know their feelings and experiences from the inside out. So now, in addition to working on hair and nails, I also have a ministry that offers a listening ear and advice to anyone who struggles with sexual identity issues, especially if he or she is interested in trying to overcome same-sex attractions. Anyone interested can reach me at www.EricGarnerSetFree.com.

I am sometimes asked if the passion I feel for my wife is the same I once felt for men. That's a great question, because it gets to the heart of something important. My answer is no. The passion I had for men was powerful and intense, but it was wrong. It came from something good, but it was misdirected. I do not have the kind of passion for my wife as I had for men, because they are entirely different things. What I had for men was lust, which is sin, while what I have now for my wife is wholesome love. It is not misshapen but is what sexual attraction was designed to be in the first place. I love and enjoy my wife for the wonderful person she is, and I do not depersonalize her by reducing her to a means for feeding my appetites.

Yes, I find her attractive. But my attraction to her is selfless, not selfish. I want to please her more than myself, and together we want to please God more than pleasing each other. It is something radically different than what I had with men—and a whole lot better. Having tasted what I have now, I would never trade it for what I had before. But I am saying this in retrospect, and I admit that I did not feel like that right away. It wasn't easy, and I encountered difficulties along the way. I am only saying that the journey is worth taking, no matter how hard it feels at the beginning.

I use the word "overcome" in relation to same-sex attractions because I believe homosexual identity is self-generated and feelings of same-sex attraction can be lessened and stopped. I do not accept the idea that same-sex attraction is a biologically predetermined orientation that is permanent and irresistible. Based on God's Word, the most reliable science, and my own experience, I believe that same-sex attraction is something subjective that varies with choice, experience, and cultivation, and that it can be changed over time.

When I surrendered to God, I accepted His view of sin, asked for His forgiveness, and submitted to His control over my life—not only over my circumstances and behavior but also over my feelings. I still felt gay. I still had strong feelings of same-sex attraction that felt impossible to overcome. I knew I couldn't change myself. But something beyond me started changing me when I prayed and relied on the power of God.

When I became saved, I had to make a choice. I knew that I could either excuse my same-sex desires by accepting all the contrary claims given to justify treating gay sex as normal and good, in which case I would be denying the authority of God's Word; or I could trust God's Word, in which case I would be denying the reliability of contrary claims so widely accepted in our culture these days. It had to be one way or the other. I chose trusting God over man and trusting God's Word over my feelings. This choice has made all the difference in my life.

In my case, my mind changed first and then my sexual attractions followed. Some people experience radical change all at once, but for most it takes time. For me it took place gradually. At first I felt strongly tempted. But temptations are *feelings*, and *feelings come and go*. I persisted in obeying God's Word, and as I did I found that bouts of temptation grew less intense and came less often. My feelings did not change overnight, but when I set my mind on obeying God's Word my feelings slowly shifted. I did not try to replace one form of sexual lust with another but simply chose to obey. The rest came by the power of God.

When some people hear my story they say, "That's nice, but don't you think some people are born gay and have feelings that can never change?" My answer is no. I am firmly convinced that no one is hopelessly enslaved to homosexual feelings. No one is beyond the hope of change. It is not an inescapable destiny. What I experienced is not unique or even that unusual. I was not dabbling. I was not experimenting. I was deeply committed and convinced that I could never change. But I did. And if I did, then others can as well.

Despite claims to the contrary, I have found that there is not a single shred of reliable scientific evidence backing the idea that homosexual attractions are predetermined and permanent. The evidence just isn't there. However, at the same time there is a lot of solid evidence proving that feelings of same-sex attraction do change and can be stopped.

I am living proof that change is possible—and not just possible, but also very worthwhile!

I Didn't Much Like Being a Girl

by Rebekah Mason

IT HAS BEEN said that children are incredible observers of the world but terrible interpreters of it. That was true of me growing up. My story is one of misinterpretation and rediscovering the world through new lenses.

From my earliest memories, I recall feeling different from others, especially when it came to comparing myself with other girls my age. I was a tomboy who preferred playing with my brothers and their friends than to playing with girls. The truth is that I didn't much like being a girl. Girls seemed to be clean, proper, frilly, and silly, and I was none of those things.

When I observed my parents, it seemed far more appealing to be a man. Mom stayed home all day cooking, cleaning, doing laundry, and caring for babies. But Dad got to leave home and enjoy freedom all day; and when he came home, he got to teach kids how to fish and play ball. As I saw it, being a woman meant housework, silliness, fussing over hair, and wearing uncomfortable clothes, while being a man meant freedom, fun, games, and wearing comfortable clothes.

Unlike other women I know who have experienced same-sex attraction, I did not suffer any physical, verbal, or sexual abuse at the hands of other family members. I was raised in a loving and supportive family. My parents loved each other and loved their children. They were good role models and encouraged me to be successful. I faced some difficulties, but looking back most of those resulted from my own misbehavior or unrealistic expectations. The suffering I experienced was self-inflicted and arose from unnecessary self-loathing and believing I deserved recognition without working for it.

I was a study in contradiction. For me, feeling exceptional and deficient were two sides of the same thing. I considered myself exceptional while believing I was deficient compared to other girls. This caused tension between my mother and me, and I rarely did anything she wanted willingly. I wanted to be like other girls, but I disliked them at the same time. I made fun of them, but I also envied them. I did this all because what came naturally to them was never easy for me.

My first "crush" on a woman came in kindergarten. It was not sexual, but not normal either. I just "loved" my music teacher because she was beautiful, kind, and talented—everything I was not. Not only did I want to be *like* her, but I also wanted to *be* her. This desire to *have for myself* what I saw in others became a destructive pattern that would affect my life for decades. I would hang around girls who had qualities I wanted, hoping that what they had would rub off well enough to fool others into thinking I was better than I was.

One of the hardest things I had to deal with growing up was pressure to meet social expectations. I found middle school to be an especially torturous experience. It was in turns both glorious and excruciating. I learned many new things, but some were not age-appropriate. I experimented sexually with boys and quickly reached two conclusions: (1) guys wanted only one thing from girls, and (2) girls could get guys to do anything by giving them what they wanted. With this realization I started disliking guys almost as much as I disliked myself. My view of middle school boys quickly became my view of men in general. I decided that all male human beings were immature, easy to manipulate, and basically stupid.

But this ran counter to the other strong influence in my life. I was immersed at home and at church in a conservative Christian culture that stressed gender roles under male leadership. So, while the guys I knew at school were all bumbling fools controlled by their hormones, I was being told at home and at church that women needed men for protection, care, and leadership—as if we couldn't do those things for ourselves. What I was being taught did not correspond to what I was experiencing, and I knew I had to choose one over the other. Based on what I saw at school, I chose to run my life in ways that did not rely on men.

I felt my decision was confirmed when I noticed how men not only failed to protect women but were also usually the ones from whom women most needed to be protected. I met women who had been badly hurt by the very men on whom they relied for protection. I decided that not only did I know what women needed, but also that I could meet those needs myself. When it came to understanding what women needed, I thought men had no clue. But I did.

Starting as a child and continuing into my teens, I was attracted to women with qualities I found lacking in myself. However, when I became sexually active, those attractions took on a sexual tone. I went from wanting qualities I saw in other women to wanting those women for myself. Because I hungered for love and acceptance, I started looking for a woman who would love and accept me for who I was. I wanted intimate connection with a woman who would allow me to let down my guard and stop pretending. This produced much internal conflict. One side pulled me toward rejecting religious expectations in pursuit of intimacy with another woman, while the other pulled me toward meeting gender-role expectations as required by the Christian culture in which I was raised.

I lived in a rural area where gay stereotypes were ridiculed. The more I heard these statements, the more I saw they applied to me.

Lesbians were tomboys who played softball, drove trucks, had short hair, and listened to music by Melissa Etheridge and the Indigo Girls. That was me on all counts. Because I fit the stereotype, I *had* to be lesbian. It just made sense. No wonder I wasn't like other girls. I was a lesbian.

But I had a troubled conscience. In church I had heard that same-sex attractions and behaviors were sinful. To be gay meant being someone about whom I heard church members say horrible things. It meant being ostracized by the people I most loved and cared about. I could not bear being ostracized, so I suppressed my feelings, kept quiet, and threw myself into being what I thought would assure me of obtaining the most love and acceptance. I tried to be a "super Christian."

I became a leader in my church youth group, helped lead the Christian Forum club at school, and served on a "character committee" tasked with promoting good behavior among fellow students. I went to Young Life meetings and attended Christian camps and concerts. I dated guys, wore hair bows, drove a car instead of a truck, and stopped playing softball. I ran from all the lesbian stereotypes that were haunting me.

But while I tried to avoid lesbian stereotypes, my relational patterns stayed the same. I still felt drawn in a sexual way toward female friends, and I was terrified they would find out my secret and reject me. I went through a lot of emotionally co-dependent friendships that ended badly, either because I acted in some overly friendly way or because I cut them off to avoid possible rejection.

Throughout high school and into college, I never had a regular group of friends. I stayed on the periphery of group activities and focused on trying to find one special person who would meet all my needs. I was a fraud who lived in terror of being discovered. I played relational games and tried to be whatever I thought would gain me acceptance. I was always the performer, hoping that I was playing the right role for that time.

I did this pretty well for a while. But after one intense friendship led me to make some irrational decisions, I decided I needed a fresh start. I transferred to a Christian college and threw myself once again into redefining who I was. Within one week of arriving on campus, I met a girl who lived in the same dorm down the hall. She was outgoing, confident, fun-loving, and popular. She didn't care what people thought, but everyone loved her anyway. She loved baseball but also loved feminine things. She didn't fit into any social stereotype. That drew me like a magnet.

We were soon inseparable, and her friendship became a source of great comfort to me. It gave me identity, defined my place in the world, and fed my hunger for love and acceptance. For the first time in my life, I felt connected with someone who enjoyed me as much as I enjoyed her. We spent hours talking, laughing, and sharing. I let down my walls, and she did too. I learned that her confident exterior hid a wounded soul like my own, and I vowed to give her everything she needed. We moved in together in January and were a lesbian couple by Valentine's Day.

We each thought we completed the other, and we assured ourselves of this frequently. I thought she met all my needs, and she thought I met all hers. That began a two-year relationship, which, in the end, nearly consumed me. At first it seemed that I had all I ever wanted. Life was good. Who wouldn't want to be the center of someone else's world? Then I began to realize that there were no limits to what self-centered love demands. The more I gave, the more she demanded; and the more she gave, the more I demanded. My entire sense of personal worth hung on meeting her every need, and what she needed grew immensely. There was no balance, no brake, no end in sight, and no outside reference by which to measure what we were doing.

I lost all sense of individuality and had no idea of who I was. There was just this one overpowering, all-devouring relationship. I have since run into people who knew us at that time but who—even years later—still did not know which of us was which. They knew our names, but because they never saw us apart, they did not know which name was mine and which was hers. Our relationship became so intense that it finally imploded, and we blew apart.

But who was I now? For two years this intense relationship had defined my identity. It had defined the "real me" not only to others but also to myself. After it blew apart, I was left with no identity, no self-worth, and no place in the world. In fact, it seemed that less remained than what I had in the beginning. I graduated from college deeply disillusioned and moved back in with my parents, still searching for the love and acceptance I so desperately longed for. I told no one. I was convinced that lesbian attractions defined me, but I suppressed them. It was better, I decided, to keep the approval I got from family and church friends than to lose everything trying to find another relationship of the sort that had ended with such terrible pain.

Determined to find answers, I dug into studies of sexuality and theology. I read scholars who argued that God's destruction of Sodom and Gomorrah had nothing to do with sex and that David and Jonathan were gay lovers. I read other scholars who taught that God sends homosexuals to hell. Everything I read seemed either to take a live-and-let-live permissive approach that made same-sex attractions a gift from God or a fire-and-brimstone impersonal approach that made God seem like an ogre who enjoyed damning sinners to everlasting punishment.

I found the live-and-let-live approach to be the more appealing of the two, so I adopted it for myself. But I was angry that my life had not worked out as I thought it should. I had relied on myself, trusted my own wisdom and intelligence, and pursued what I thought was best. But rather than fulfillment and joy, it had ended in disaster.

Then one day, as I was pouring out my frustrations to a friend, she challenged me by asking, "What does God say about that in the Bible?" This friend suggested I study the Bible for myself and let God speak to me through it. So I took her advice. I put away my theology books and began studying the Bible directly for myself.

I started off believing that if God made lesbians like me, He must have provided instructions for how we should live. I assumed that He must have given guidelines for being a good lesbian. But as I pursued this, I found that my expectations were being challenged. I also found that there was another option for understanding God's approach to sex besides "sentimental permissiveness" and "unloving judgmentalism."

As I looked for advice on how to be a good lesbian, I realized there was nothing on that topic in the Bible. God gave clear moral instructions for all approved areas of life and affirmed the value of sex by treating it extensively and in detail. But despite all this, I found nothing on how to practice same-sex relationships properly. Nothing! Well, that struck me as odd, and even unfair. If God made lesbians, why had He left no instructions for them on how to act?

Reading further, I noticed that in places where God dealt with categories of sexual sin—including prohibiting gay sex—He also stressed His intention for people to have what He truly knew was best for them. I began to realize that if God made me, loved me, knew what was best for me, prohibited gay sex, and gave no instructions for practicing same-sex relationships properly, then perhaps this meant identifying as a lesbian was neither moral nor best for me.

One day as I was reading through a long list of Bible verses that condemned gay sex, I came to 1 Corinthians 6:9-10, where Paul says, "Or do you not know that the unrighteous will not inherit the kingdom of God? Do not be deceived: neither the sexually immoral, nor idolaters, nor adulterers, nor men who practice homosexuality, nor thieves, nor the greedy, nor drunkards, nor revilers, nor swindlers will inherit the kingdom of God" (ESV). But instead of stopping at verse 10, this time I went on to read verse 11, which says, "And such were some of you. But you were washed, you were sanctified, you were justified in the name of the Lord Jesus Christ and by the Spirit of our God."

This was a turning point for me. In this verse God promised freedom and blessing to those who accepted His terms and did things His way. God would not bless me using my body as I pleased, but He promised to accept me and bless me as I relied on Him and followed Him over my own desires.

My study of God's Word became a time of discipleship and growth in which I learned to trust the Bible instead of questioning it. The more I trusted God, the more I found Him to be trustworthy. I threw myself at His feet, gave up my previous expectations, and began focusing on God over myself. I saw how God had provided something much better for me than trying to satisfy myself on my own terms. I realized that if I rested in God's loving acceptance, I could stop desperately searching for another person to fill the emptiness in my soul.

After two years of working through these issues, I came to understand that everything I had thought about sex, life, and myself was severely skewed. I reconsidered what I thought about men, women, sex, and God. I also reevaluated my view of Christians and saw that I had been as quick to judge Christians on the basis of a few as some Christians had been to judge me. Instead of focusing on the negative, I studied what positive sexuality should look like. As a friend once told me, I discovered that "every human is sexually broken in one way or another." I studied the purpose of sexuality and began to see it is about more than just sensual pleasure and personal affirmation.

Instead of viewing God as an impersonal judge, I began to see how He is a loving heavenly Father who blesses those who accept His commands. I saw how no human being—either man or woman—could ever fill the emptiness in my soul, and I began to see the holes in secular and liberal arguments used to justify homosexuality. In the process, I also discovered that my sexual attractions were being realigned and that God was blessing me with friends in whom I could trust and rely.

I came to see how my same-sex attractions had been rooted in misperceiving God, myself, and others. As the way I perceived these things changed, so did my sexual desires. I could now distinguish between friendship and sex. I had thought the only way to gain love and acceptance was through sex, and my hunger for female friends had drawn me into lesbian relationships. I had pursued what I thought best but learned I was wrong. What I thought best led to loneliness and pain, but when I admitted being wrong and trusted God instead, I found the love and acceptance I longed for.

Because I am single and not married to a man, people sometimes ask if I am "cured" of sexual attraction toward women. In other words, they wonder if I am still lesbian and simply being celibate. All I can say is, "Yes! I've changed!" But not only has my sexual desire for women faded, but also what I desire no longer defines my core identity. The real me now is defined by the loving relationship I have with Jesus Christ, and when I am in proper relationship with Him, all other relationships are properly aligned as well.

Would I like to marry a Christ-centered man? Sure I would! But unless God brings one my way, I am content with serving Him as a single woman. I welcome the idea of marrying a man, but I do not need to do that to prove myself. Sexual health is not a matter of substituting one lust for another. All lust is sin, whether heterosexual or homosexual. My goal now is holiness, not pursuing lust of any kind. My identity, self-worth, and sense of personal fulfillment are all rooted in Jesus Christ. How I relate to others depends on that.

Having spent years struggling to combine lesbian desires with Christian faith, I understand the incredible loneliness that comes with hanging one's identity on something God reveals to be sin. Feelings of same-sex sexual attraction are not inevitable, and they need not define who a person is. They are what God calls "sin" in the Bible. I know that seems rigid, but it is no more rigid than what the culture claims in reverse. If it seems harsh, I can only attest to how enormously freeing it is to accept God's terms. Agreeing with God about sin makes repentance possible, and with repentance comes forgiveness, renewal, and blessing. I used to recoil when I heard what I strongly desired being called "sin," and would think people who claimed to be delivered were fooling themselves. But I think differently since experiencing it myself.

The culture has bought into the lie that "homosexual" is a noun, an identifier, instead of an adjective, a descriptor. If we discussed any other sin the way our culture treats homosexuality, we would think it absurd. We wouldn't say, "I know greed is a sin, but I was born greedy, which makes me a *greeder*. I can't help wanting things that are not my own." Nor would we say, "I am proud to be a *glutton*. Sure, the Bible says gluttony is sin, but that's out of date because I was born a *glutton* and can't help it." Nor would we say, "I am a *hitter*. I like hitting people. When I get stressed out, I feel better when I hit someone. So, for me, hitting other people is normal and good." Why has homosexuality become the only sin we can't help?

We can't help how we are tempted, but we can help what we do about it. We can, as Paul says, "Take captive every thought to make it obedient to Christ" (2 Cor. 10:5, NIV). I have found that the more I take my thoughts captive and surround myself with godly role models, the less I am tempted by what feels like "uncontrollable" homosexual desires. Not only can such desires be diminished, but they can also be made to cease completely.

Paul speaks about "putting off" the old man and "putting on" the new (see Eph. 4:22-24). The more I put on the "new man" of thinking in a God-glorifying manner, the more I desire to put off the old sinful nature of homosexuality. As I view people as Christ views them, it is impossible for me to see them as "need-meeters" for my own selfish and sinful desires.

I spent years believing it was my cross to bear to be lonely and unfulfilled as a lesbian Christian called to be celibate. How defeatist!

By contrast, Scripture is full of passages describing homosexuality as a past-tense event in the life of a believer. We do a disservice to those struggling with same-sex attractions if we only urge them to be celibate homosexuals. That implies God made them gay or lesbian and then cruelly insisted they suppress whom He created them to be. Is that a fair and accurate picture of the loving and just God we worship? The truth is that we can surrender our sexual attractions to the redeeming work of Christ.

I am not saying that celibacy is defeatist for everyone, only that it is defeatist for someone who thinks gay or lesbian desires can only be endured. Celibacy can be a divine calling, but only when sexual attractions align with God's moral order. Tolerating any desire to sin is sinful all by itself, which makes *continually tolerating* homosexual desires wrong, even if a person never acts on them. Scripture does not allow us the luxury of dividing desires from actions. If an action is sin, then continuing to desire it is as well. The issue I am raising is not celibacy *per se* but also the reason for choosing to be celibate. For a person who desires sinful sex, stopping with celibacy is sinful, enslaving legalism.

I used to identify myself as a lesbian who desired other women sexually, but I do not do so any longer. I am now a female Christian who strives to relate to others in ways that honor the God who made me and saved me. My sexual attractions are not what they were, but I still enjoy baseball and wearing comfortable clothes. My identity is no longer centered on myself or how I feel, is not set by society, and does not depend on what others say, think, or expect. I am a woman created in the image of my Creator and redeemed by the Lamb of God. Stereotypes, feelings, and social expectations no longer play a part in my identity.

If Americans
are persuaded to gamble on
deconstructing marriage to normalize
homosexual behavior, it will be
a sucker's bet in a game
that cannot be won.

—Dr. Daniel Heimbach

DESTROYING MARRIAGE BY DECONSTRUCTION

by Daniel R. Heimbach, Ph.D.

First published by the title "Deconstructing the Family" in
The Religion & Society Report (October/November, 2005): 1-12.
Revised and republished with permission.

*The notion of the family ... is enmeshed in a web ... of
religious, moral and theological precepts, all of which
serve needlessly, harmfully, and perniciously to bind, limit,
and restrain individuals in the exercise of their freedom to
enter into choices as to their intimate relationships.*
—Franklin Kameny

*Being queer means pushing the parameters of sex,
sexuality, and family, and in the process, transforming
the very fabric of society ... we must keep our eyes on
the goals of providing true alternatives to marriage and
of radically reordering society's view of reality.*
—Paula Ettelbrick

No society can survive unless it comes full
forward in favor of heterosexuality.
—William Bennett

AMERICA IS CURRENTLY torn by a *Kulturkampf*. More precisely, the culture is riveted by a full-scale moral war being waged from television screens to the halls of Congress, from newspaper pages to university classrooms, and from offices on Madison Avenue to pews of our local churches.[1] In this war, the most heated line of battle is perhaps the one having to do with the meaning, structure, and definition of the family as relevant to law, public policy, education, business, entertainment, and popular culture—to say nothing of deeper dimensions of morality and faith relating to God and the church. Special tension focuses on what is known as the *traditional* family. This is the long-standing norm for intergenerational family relationships centered on presuming the family ideal consists of two adults of the opposite sex living together in a sexually exclusive and lifelong union—adults that assume primary responsibility for each other's welfare and for raising children born of their union or added to it by adoption.

This has been a long-held standard proven through centuries of practice, by all civilizations, and affirmed and supported by all world religions. But there has risen in recent years an enormously powerful moral-cultural attack on this standard ideal. This attack has been led by social revolutionaries—both feminist and homosexual—who demand approval of sexual relationships based on the belief that individual lust is all that should determine social acceptance and that people have no obligation to conform with any set forms. Leaders of this attack aim at *deconstructing* the traditional family.[2] By this they mean destroying all expectations of gender roles and the importance of gender or age differences between men, women, and children. In so doing, they open socially acceptable sexual relationships to any possibility that individuals happen to desire. If the concept of *family* is not abandoned altogether, then these social-sexual *deconstructionists* would render its meaning so radically inclusive that no relational combination could ever be excluded.

Shocking Statements

Voices favoring family social-sexual *deconstruction* have often been strident, expressing visceral animosity toward relational structures long judged essential for maintaining social health and civil stability. For example, on the militant feminist side, French feminist pioneer Simone de Beauvoir (1908–1986) believed that "since the oppression of women has its cause in the will to perpetuate the family ... woman escapes complete dependency to the degree in which she escapes from the family."[3] She also said, "No woman should be authorized to stay at home to raise her children. Society should be totally different. Women should not have that choice, precisely because if there is such a choice, too many women will make that one."[4]

Robin Morgan, former editor for *Ms.* magazine, once declared that marriage is "a slavery-like practice" and that "we can't destroy the inequities between men and women until we destroy marriage."[5] Feminist author Shulamith Firestone claimed, "The family is ... directly connected to—is even the cause of—the ills of the larger society."[6] Feminist social critic Kate Millett has said, "The complete destruction of traditional marriage and the nuclear family is the *revolutionary or utopian* goal of feminism."[7] And Judith Stacey, a feminist scholar and professor at the University of Southern California, believes that "perhaps the postmodern *family of women* will take the lead in burying The Family at long last. The Family is a concept derived from faulty theoretical premises and an imperialistic logic, which even at its height never served the best interests of women, their children, or even many men."[8]

Feminist writer Vivian Gornick proclaimed that "being a housewife is an illegitimate profession.... The choice to serve and be protected and plan towards being a family-maker is a choice that shouldn't be ... [because] the heart of radical feminism is to change that."[9] Catholic feminist theologian Mary Hunt has said that "it is time to live beyond the family, especially beyond the Christian family.... I picture friends, not families but friends, basking in the pleasures we deserve because our bodies are holy."[10] And Linda Gordon, a feminist scholar and history professor at New York University, has declared, "The nuclear family must be destroyed, and people must find better ways of living together.... Whatever its ultimate meaning, the break-up of families now is an objectively revolutionary process.... Families will be finally destroyed only when a revolutionary social and economic organization permits people's needs for love and security to be met in ways that do not impose divisions of labor, or any external roles, at all."[11]

Anti-family stridency has also been a characteristic among men crusading to normalize homosexual practice. James Nelson, a retired professor of Christian ethics at United Theological Seminary of the Twin Cities, explains that "one of the basic challenges of the church and synagogue, I believe, is to end the sexual hegemony of the nuclear family and the resulting temptation to police the sexuality of everyone who does not fit that mold."[12] Nelson goes on to encourage support for a movement to eliminate "uncritical sanctification of the nuclear family," because he argues that "we have been complicit in equating a relative and fairly recent historical development (i.e., the two-parent, heterosexual family structure) with God's eternal will."[13]

Michael Swift, who styles himself a "gay revolutionary," zealously declares, "The family unit—spawning ground of lies, betrayals, mediocrity, hypocrisy and violence—will be abolished. The family unit, which only dampens imagination and curbs free will, must be eliminated. Perfect boys will be conceived and grown in the genetic laboratory. They will be bonded together in communal setting, under the control and instruction of homosexual savants."[14] Franklin Kameny, founder of the gay movement in Washington, DC, considers the very idea of *family* to be dangerously pernicious. Says Kameny, "The notion of the family … is enmeshed in a web … of religious, moral and theological precepts, all of which serve needlessly, harmfully, and perniciously to bind, limit, and restrain individuals in the exercise of their freedoms to enter into choices as to their intimate relationships."[15]

As an advocate for the social normalization of homosexual behavior, Kameny explained in a 1993 article on deconstructing the traditional family that he thought Americans should not even be discussing "whether or not *alternative families* can and should be tolerated, legalized, encouraged, and taught." Instead, he argued, we should realize that American society has always been socially permissive. Therefore, trying to maintain a rigid, unchanging notion of *family* is simply contrary to honoring the spirit of individual freedom that has characterized Americans throughout history. In his view, people have not resisted family evolution because deconstructing the family is somehow anti-American, but rather because "the notion of the family—or, more recently, the *traditional* family—has been placed upon such a lofty pedestal of unquestioning and almost mindless, ritualistic worship and endlessly declared but quite unproven importance that rational discussion of it is often well-nigh impossible."[16]

Kameny goes on to allege that "there is no legitimate basis for limiting the freedom of the individual to structure his family in nontraditional ways that he finds satisfying."[17] For Kameny and the movement he represents, "Human ingenuity is infinite, so the possibility of varieties of human relationships are innumerable." Thus, he concludes that Americans have "an affirmative moral and ethical obligation" to provide young people with models for a wide range of nontraditional family structures presented in a way that makes clear they are all every bit as valid, good and valuable as the traditionally accepted monogamous, two-parent, heterosexual family model."[18]

Movement Demands

For those taking part in the 1993 March on Washington for Lesbian, Gay, and Bi Equal Rights, changing the meaning of *family* was a central theme that was hard for anyone there to avoid.[19] A group labeled "gay fathers" marched in the parade. Lesbians pushed young children in strollers and were eager to explain that they were indeed a "family." A group representing the Gay and Lesbian Parents Coalition International chanted, "We're here! We're gay! We're in the P.T.A.!" A banner proclaimed, "Love Makes a Family." And a threesome consisting of one man and two women explained that because families are all about "love," and because feelings of "love" are entirely subjective, that has to mean marriages formed to establish family life should not matter to anyone except their participants. For them, family definition had no public significance. In addition, lest anyone miss their aim to radically revolutionize the family, lesbian activist Robin Tyler screamed from the organizers' podium to the assembled marchers, "WE ARE GOING TO SAVE OUR CHILDREN!!!"[20]

The homosexual plan to radically redefine the family was not only observable on the parade route or from individual speakers but was also the main emphasis expressed in the March Platform. This well-articulated and widely published March Platform made it clear that radically redefining the family was central to the homosexual agenda—not just a matter they considered somewhere on the radical fringe. Out of seven demands that proponents listed in the March Platform, five were specifically aimed at altering the fundamental structure of family relationships:

- Demand #1 called for legalizing any sort of "non-coercive sexual behavior between adults" and replacing age-of-consent laws with more lenient "graduated age-of-consent laws."

- Demand #3 called for removing legal barriers that restricted family diversity and requiring "recognition and legal protection of the whole range of family structures." This included "recognition of domestic partnerships," "legalization of same-sex marriages," and revising child custody, adoption, and foster care laws to remove any preferences favoring the traditional family structure over other possible arrangements.

- Demand #4 focused on education and included a call to promote normalizing social acceptance of homosexual behavior "at all levels," starting with preschool children.

- Demand #5 called for providing "alternative insemination" services to lesbians at the taxpayers' expense.

- Demand #6 called for ending "religious oppression." They understood this to mean the influence of religious teaching that denies the morality of homosexual behavior and opposes the formation of family structures based on assuming the normality and value of homosexual sex.

- Demand #7 called for ending "all programs of the Boy Scouts of America [and, by implication, other private sector social programs] that openly favor monogamous, two-parent, heterosexual families and discourage normalizing homosexual behavior."[21]

Deconstructing Marriage

Throughout the 1970s and 1980s, the stance taken by most militant feminists and homosexuals was firmly anti-marriage, and they had little interest in trying to change the meaning of marriage to include non-heterosexual or non-monogamous categories of behavior. For example, in 1979 Shulamith Firestone said, "The institution of marriage consistently proves itself unsatisfactory, even rotten."[22] Marlene Dixon, a feminist leader in the 1960s and 1970s, proclaimed, "The institution of marriage is the chief vehicle for the perpetuation of the oppression of women; it is through the role of wife that the subjugation of women is maintained. In a very real way the role of wife has been the genesis of women's rebellion throughout history."[23] Helen Sullinger and Nancy Lehman, in their *Declaration on Feminism*, published in 1971, said, "Marriage has existed for the benefit of men and has been a legally sanctioned method of control over women…. Now we know it is the institution that has failed us and we must work to destroy it…. The end of the institution of marriage is the necessary condition for the liberation of women. Therefore it is important for us to encourage women to leave their husbands and not to live individually with men."[24]

As recently as the early 1990s, Paula Ettelbrick, then policy director for the National Gay and Lesbian Task Force, strongly opposed the idea of making same-sex marriage part of the gay rights agenda, much less a priority. Rejecting marriage, she said, was a long-held feature of radical feminism, and encouraging lesbian women and gay men to marry would "assimilate" the movement to American social norms and interfere with their ultimate goal of "transforming the very fabric of society."[25] Instead, she argued, "Being queer means pushing the parameters of sex, sexuality, and family, and in the process, transforming the very fabric of society…. We must keep our eyes on the goals of providing true alternatives to marriage and of radically reordering society's view of reality."[26]

Similarly, in 1996 Nancy Polikoff, faculty member at the American University Law School, strongly attacked lesbian promotion of same-sex marriage because until that time the lesbian feminist movement had always rejected marriage as an oppressive institution.[27] Polikoff feared that promoting same-sex marriage in any form would favor thinking marriage was good for society thus leaving homosexuals at the margins of an essentially monogamous institution. It was better she thought to attack the fundamental legitimacy of marriage itself. At about the same time, Martha Fineman, a professor at Cornell University and leader in gay normalization of family law, published the book *The Neutered Mother, the Sexual Family, and Other Twentieth Century Tragedies*, in which she argued that rather than revising marriage to include persons of the same sex, the social-legal category of marriage needed to be abolished altogether.[28]

However, midway through the 1990s, something changed in America to redirect the policy of militant feminists and homosexuals in regard to marriage and family life. Gay and lesbian leaders began promoting marriage—not because they had changed their goals, but because they began to see that a radical restructuring of marriage and family would achieve the same ultimate purpose. They began to understand that revolutionizing the socially accepted and legally enforced meaning of marriage—to the point of making gender identity irrelevant and severing parenting from the social purpose of marriage—would eventually lead toward the abolition of marriage as a legally relevant social category.[29]

Thus, by the end of the 1990s, most gay and lesbian advocates, including Ettelbrick and Polikoff, had fallen in line to promote same-sex marriage as the new face of the revolutionary movement to normalize homosexual behavior in American culture. This did not mean, however, that leaders of the gay normalizing movement had developed a more hopeful view of marriage. The gay movement had hushed overt statements on abolishing the institution, but this general shift in tone was more a matter of strategy than conversion, and some could not refrain from saying they still desired the demise of marriage altogether. If they could not abolish marriage by rendering it illegal, perhaps they could achieve the same result by rendering it so meaningless that there would be no social incentives for people to get married in the first place.

Gay normalizing family law specialist Martha Ertman revised Martha Fineman's plan for abolishing legal recognition of marriage by suggesting that the meaning of marriage in law should be replaced with a contract system accepting and affirming any combination of gender or number. Her plan called for immediately marginalizing and ultimately collapsing legal recognition for any social convention that treated heterosexual and monogamous marriages as somehow preferable, normal, or superior to any other sexual combination.[30] David Chambers, another gay revisionist in family law, argued in 1996 that supporting legal recognition for same-sex marriage was entirely consistent with the ultimate goal of abolishing the notion of marriage as a publically recognized social institution.

Chambers held that legalizing same-sex marriage would lead society away from treating heterosexual monogamous relationships as socially preferable or in some way superior to other sexual combinations. He wrote, "By ceasing to conceive of marriage as a partnership composed of one person of each sex, the state may become more receptive to units of three or more."[31] He believed once society legitimized same-sex marriage, it would be more likely to legitimize other sexual combinations—eventually including so many relational categories that society would be forced in time to abolish marriage as a legal category. By supporting same-sex marriage, the feminist and gay movements would eventually reach the same anti-marriage goal they had been seeking all along. As Chambers explained, "All desirable changes in family law need not be made at once."[32]

Deconstruction by Deconstruction

In 1989, Andrew Sullivan of *The New Republic* recognized that "much of the gay leadership clings to notions of gay life as essentially outsider, anti-bourgeois, radical. Marriage, for them [for most leaders of the gay normalizing movement], is cooptation into straight society. For the Stonewall generation, it is hard to see how this vision of conflict will ever fundamentally change."[33] But then, only a few years later, nearly every gay and feminist leader was so "pro-marriage" they were insisting gay and lesbian couples had to be included as a matter of social equality. What happened? How could so many social revolutionaries in sexual policy and family law suddenly change their tone from being anti-marriage and anti-family to being pro-marriage and pro-family? The answer can be found in the popularity of French intellectuals Jacques Derrida (1930–2004) and Michel Foucault (1926–1984) and their philosophy of *deconstructionism.*

As a member of the American Academy of Religion (AAR), I remember the overwhelming positive interest engendered by the new approach these men offered toward social analysis and revision. During the 1990s, their philosophy became enormously popular in elite circles. It swept the country and was quickly adopted by militant feminist and gay activists working in sexuality studies and family law.

Jacque Derrida, a leader in the postmodern movement in France and creator of deconstructionism, basically held that all thinking was so filled with hidden confusion and contradiction that nothing could be what it seemed. Language itself was so impossibly confused that there could be no hope of finding anything reliably true in literature, history, or philosophy. To arrive at truth, Derrida argued, a new method of inquiry called *deconstruction* was needed. Under this method, all structures defining truth—especially truth that formed the basis of value systems and organized the moral principles of society—were dismissed and replaced by a form of libertarianism in which nothing was assumed to be right, wrong, normal, or abnormal. As one writer concluded, Derrida "showed us how to take the world apart."[34]

As a political strategy, deconstructionism combined Marxist social analysis with Freudian psychological techniques to justify removing (or "deconstructing") the main supports of Western civilization, such as long-held notions of morality, marriage, the family, male leadership, and responsibility. Deconstructionism has sometimes been called *poststructuralism* in that it has to do with taking apart whatever structures have been accepted in a social context. It rarely, if ever, has anything to do with offering something to replace what has been deconstructed. In other words, it has more to do with erasing the concept of structure itself than with replacing one sort of structure with another. Of course, the implications of such thinking are incompatible with any social order, whether it is economic, political, linguistic, moral, religious, historical, or sexual.

In his book *Glas*, Derrida systematically deconstructed the concept of family by affirming the power of sexuality while, at the same time, denying that sexual differences were truly essential to human existence. Derrida claimed that sexual difference was not an essential trait and did not "belong to the existential structure of *Dasein* [fundamental human existence]."[35] He went on to say, "If *Dasein* as such belongs to neither of the sexes, that does not mean that its being is deprived of sex. On the contrary, here one must think of a pre-differential [non-sexually differentiated], or rather a pre-dual [non-male/female] sexuality ... a matter here of the positive and powerful source of *every possible sexuality*."[36] Thus the reason why Derrida titled his work *Glas*, or "death knell," for denying the essential reality of sexual difference indeed rings a "death knell" for the family.

Michel Foucault, an openly homosexual psycho-philosopher under whom Derrida studied at the elite Ecole Normale Superieure in Paris, also played a major role in developing deconstruction-ism—especially in regard to persuading Western thinkers to revise their views on sex and sexuality. Although Foucault came before Derrida and did not use the term "deconstruction," he was largely responsible for developing the initial radical deconstructionist postmodern approach to social analysis that would later be carried forward by Derrida. Foucault has thus become enormously influential among social radicals in America.

Foucault began by rejecting modernity's faith in reason. He argued instead that true understanding arises not from reason but from observing relations of power and domination. According to Foucault, so called "knowledge" was never more than beliefs constructed to justify existing power relationships, and there was no such thing as objective truth on which to base social structures such as marriage and family. Throughout human history, repression had always been the fundamental link connecting power, knowledge, and sexuality. Therefore, he concluded, the key to all truth was removing sexual repression and pursuing unrestrained sexual desires in whatever form they took. Of course, to achieve this required overturning all laws, limitations, and social structures standing in the way of unhindered sexual expression. And because marriage and family were social structures arising from limitations placed on sexual expression, Foucault believed these structures should either be entirely removed or so redefined as to leave them amorphous—without any objectively necessary meaning, shape, or content.

Rather than conforming sex, marriage, and family to objective standards—either moral or social—Foucault held that "sexuality [and social structures depending on sexuality like marriage and family] is something we ourselves create—it is our own creation, and much more than the discovery of a secret [unchangeable] side of our desire. We have to understand that with our desires, through our desires, go new forms of love, new forms of creation. Sex is not a fatality: it is a [formless] possibility for creative life."[37] Foucault also made clear that he rejected the objectivity of all morality, and so denied the existence of any fixed basis for either evaluating sexual activity or defining sexual relationships.

For Foucault, this meant that conceptions of marriage and family were merely illusionary. He believed that clinging to fixed expectations (standards, structures, norms) regarding marriage and family was an arbitrary and repressive activity that achieved nothing more than protecting positions of power from those whose freedom threatened that power. "Today," he said, "it is sex that serves as a support for the ancient form—so familiar and important in the West—of preaching. A great sexual sermon—which has had its subtle theologians and its popular voices—has swept through our societies over the last decades; it has chastised the older [Judeo-Christian] order, denounced hypocrisy, and praised the rights of the immediate and the real [the sensual embodiment of human life]; it has made people dream of a New City [a brand new approach to social order]."[38] Obviously, when human sexuality is deconstructed in this manner, the institutions of marriage and family are either destroyed or rendered absolutely meaningless.

Why Attack the Family?

Why are proponents of the movement to normalize homosexual behavior so bent on attacking the traditional family structure? What is it about the traditional family that so offends them? Why can they not go about freely living their preferred lifestyle and just leave the structure of marriage and family alone?

From the literature, four convictions seem most likely to attract the ire of gay or lesbian militants. The first conviction is that the value of the traditional family is uniquely worthy and deserves a place of honor over all other types of human relationship. The second conviction is that morality properly limits sexual relationships to marriage between two—and only two—adults of the opposite gender, so that the traditional heterosexual family is the only proper venue for morally acceptable sexual activity. This third conviction is that traditional families are necessary to the welfare and preservation of society. The fourth conviction is that children are best raised in a traditional family structure and are disadvantaged for lack of something essential or at least vital if raised in *alternative* family structures.

An especially good place to study an insider's view on family deconstruction within the gay rights movement is the 1993 article by Franklin E. Kameny called "Deconstructing the Traditional Family," which was quoted at the beginning of this chapter. Kameny was (and continues to be) a key player for normalizing homosexual behavior in American culture. He was revered as a leader especially at the time when other leaders in the movement were transitioning to adopt the strategy of deconstructionism. Kameny, who earned a Ph.D. from Harvard in 1956, was for years considered the most influential homosexual leader in Washington, DC.

Kameny founded the homosexual movement in the capital region in 1961, led the first gay demonstration at the White House in 1965, founded the Gay Activists Alliance (now the Gay and Lesbian Activist Alliance) in 1971, and co-founded the National Gay Task Force and the National Gay Rights Lobby (the first national political lobbying organization for gay and lesbian rights). He served in World War II and is personally responsible for launching a national crusade for lifting the ban on homosexuals in the military. He served on the DC board of the ACLU and was appointed commissioner on the Washington, DC, city commission on human rights. All of this is to say that Kameny's article—written just as leaders in the movement were transitioning from their virulently anti-marriage, anti-family stance to favoring both—shows not only how insiders in the gay movement came to adopt a deconstructionist approach but also how their purposes never really changed.

Kameny claims the traditional family structure does not truly merit the place of honor that it has been accorded historically, and he savages the social preferences, legal protections, and moral standards used to encourage the formation, stability, and permanence of traditional family commitments. However, in presenting his case, Kameny ignores the basic physiology of human reproduction, transcultural moral principles, scientific studies relating the traditional family structure to social strength, and centuries of historical experience. Instead, he supports deconstructing the family by severing the whole discussion from anything objective, and he only appeals to subjective considerations. In particular, Kameny asserts (1) the universal priority of individuality over society, (2) the unworthiness of all tradition (social or otherwise), (3) the ultimate subjectivity and essential irrelevance of all morality for public policy, and (4) the denial that there is any risk to radically deconstructing the meaning of *family* as to include "*any* relationship entered into freely, openly, informedly, and without coercion."[39] We will now consider each step in Kameny's methodical deconstruction of the traditional family structure.

Exalting Individual Desire

The first step in Kameny's deconstruction of the family is in denying that individuals should ever defer their desires to favor the common good. Individuals, Kameny believes, live independent of social norms unless they accept such norms as favoring whatever they view as personally desirable. He believes the very notion of *society* is simply a linguistic construct designed to serve and benefit only individuals.

As such, he believes that society "has no legitimacy in its own right and no rights to which the interests of the individual need properly be subordinated."[40] For Kameny, society is something radically tentative and subject to the fancy of the individuals who happen to be living in proximity. He alleges, "There is no legitimate basis for limiting the freedom of the individual to structure his family in nontraditional ways that he finds satisfying, on the basis of the alleged interests or supposed preservation of a society that has another *raison d'etre* beyond the promotion of his satisfactions."[41]

Kameny elevates individual autonomy to such extremes that a person has to wonder how society exists at all. Is there anything about which a random set of individuals ever fully agrees? Unless society as a whole can constrain individual conduct at some level—unless some sort of limit is set on individual desires—society is simply impossible. And, if society does not exist, then there can be no common effort to achieve goals transcending individual abilities, no economy of effort to magnify individual resources, no legacy to outlast individual lives, and no heritage by which individuals can benefit from those who have gone before.

Although heroic individuals must at times stand against the group when society becomes corrupt, thinking that individual desires should *never* submit to any higher good only creates a Hobbesian state of anarchy in which people are doomed to lives that are solitary, poor, nasty, brutish, and short. The family is the most necessary of all social units because it is the most important social structure for defining how individual desires should be restrained, disciplined, and directed toward the common good.

Trashing Tradition

Kameny's second step in deconstructing the meaning and purpose of family life is to deny there is any good reason for respecting traditions of any kind. He objects to supposing "that those things that are deemed traditional are good and desirable on that count alone, and that the longer a tradition has existed, the less reason there is for changing it, when actually, precisely the opposite is true." Kameny believes it is far preferable to start by supposing traditions are ill-advised or outmoded until proven otherwise. This is because favoring tradition makes "millennia-old, backward, and benighted cultures the model to which we are supposed to aspire." Kameny also believes that "anything that has lasted long enough to have become traditional has, on that ground alone, become potentially obsolete, outmoded, and archaic."[42]

Instead of thinking tradition is a distillation of practical wisdom proven by experience, Kameny argues that tradition of any kind is at best outmoded, and at the least a mixture of superstition and prejudice. He believes tradition proves nothing by itself and should be rejected unless validated on other grounds. He claims that "characterization of anything as traditional should render it suspect and should trigger a heightened, intensified, skeptical scrutiny."[43] Consequently, he believes that simply because the traditional family has been around a long time does not necessarily mean it should be given special honor. What counts is what appears to make sense in the here and now, regardless of what past humanity has experienced.

However, Kameny's case for automatically disfavoring tradition—especially tradition regarding family structure—is strictly an abstract exercise that consists of nothing more than reversing suppositions. It is neither based on factual experience nor on any record of proven success. If there has ever been a social experiment proven through human experience, it is the value and necessity of the traditional structuring of the basic family unit. Tradition distilled from so vast and varied a basis in human experience is neither arbitrary nor irrelevant. The traditional family structure has endured from before the beginning of recorded history. It has been proven by experience across every society, culture, and civilization to be the most viable, stable, and secure arrangement for nurturing children, cultivating intimacy, honing moral character, and disciplining individual desires so they promote and do not disintegrate the strength and stability of social order.

Denying Moral Foundations

The third step in Kameny's deconstruction of society favoring monogamous, two-parent, heterosexual families is to deny the reality of objective moral authority. In so doing, Kameny also denies that society even needs moral foundations on which to base laws and policies governing social institutions, including the structure of marriage and family. For Kameny, all morality is voluntary, idiosyncratic, and therapeutic. That is, he assumes moral claims are never objective and so can never be properly used to evaluate the legitimacy or value of individual behavior. In his view, individuals should be free to select their own moral standards and should do so according to whatever satisfies their individual sense of wellbeing.

Kameny believes people must respect "an inescapable moral relativism" in public policy, so he argues that there is no legitimate reason for restricting the pursuit of individual happiness with laws favoring one family structure over another.[44] He believes that "the only position that can validly be taken, consistent with basic American principles, is that morality and immorality are and must remain matters of personal opinion and individual religious belief … upon which American governments at any level may take no explicit positions at all…. [These] may not properly intervene [by limiting the definition of family] upon a claim of immorality alone."[45]

Again, we should look carefully at where Kameny's case for family deconstruction must lead in the end. All decisions about value or non-value, or judgments about right or wrong, or evaluations about good, better, or best—whether in private or public life—are exercises in moral judgment. Some moral reference is presupposed. In addition, unless some moral reference is employed, the decision, judgment, or evaluation made is entirely arbitrary and capricious.

However, Kameny also believes that the U.S. government has a duty to encourage the formation of families based on homosexual relationships. He cannot have it both ways. His denial that there is any legitimate public basis for making value judgments in matters of public policy does more than disqualify laws supporting the traditional family structure he dislikes. It necessarily eliminates the possibility of laws and policies he would have enacted.

Whistling in the Dark

The final step in Kameny's deconstruction of the family is to deny there is any risk in dismissing fixed notions about the preferred structure of marriage and family as social institutions. Kameny says that removing the *traditional* family from its place of honor and protection in law and social policy—and opening the notion of *family* to include all possible arrangements—will actually enhance the common welfare of society as a whole. "Homosexuality," he says, "is affirmatively good in every sense of the word *good*, morally, culturally, [and] societally."[46] That is because "variety and diversity in family arrangements add zest to our communities and make them exciting and stimulating, to the benefit of all, to the detriment of none, to the enhancement of our individual and collective happiness."[47] The reason Kameny believes there is no risk is because he thinks removing all structural expectations what *the family* means enhances "the happiness of the participants as they perceive that happiness" and "contributes to the most fundamental purposes of ... our nation and, in fact, is the very *raison d'etre* for our nation."[48]

In examining this last argument, we must ask how Kameny can be so sure. History is filled with stories of societies that have endorsed homosexuality in their waning years only to see it hasten their demise. Where has there ever been a society—much less a civilization—that grew strong and expanded without strong taboos favoring the heterosexual family? The heterosexual family is the one social unit no society can endure without. Societies have survived without the protection of strong armies and have endured weak economic conditions, but no society has ever endured, much less thrived, without taboos favoring the formation of heterosexual families.

The social conditions Kameny proposes come from supposing a homosexual utopia that has never before existed. It has no basis in proven reality. In other words, he asks the American people to take a gamble on something that has never yet succeeded and simply accept his personal assurance regardless of the facts. In light of history, Kameny's proposal is not only fraught with risk but also bears the highest of all possible stakes. If it does not succeed as he imagines, and if historical experience is correct, then the survival of American society will be put in serious jeopardy.

The Social Risk of Deconstructing the Family

In the early twentieth century, British social scientist J.D. Unwin conducted a massive study of six major civilizations and 80 lesser societies spanning 5,000 years of history to examine how sexual behavior affects the rise and fall of social groups.[49] In the study, Unwin included every social group for which he could find reliable information. He set out expecting to find evidence supporting Sigmund Freud's theory that civilizations are neurotic and ultimately destroy themselves by restricting sex too much. However, to his surprise, all the evidence pointed exactly the other way.

Freud had said, "It is natural to suppose that under the domination of a *civilized* morality [one that restricts sex] the health and efficiency in life of the individuals may be impaired, and that ultimately this injury to the individual, caused by the sacrifices imposed upon him, may reach such a pitch that the *civilized* aim and end will itself be indirectly endangered."[50] This led Freud to conclude that civilization was unstable and perhaps self-defeating. In fact, as he once wrote to Albert Einstein, he feared that by limiting sex, civilization "may perhaps be leading to the extinction of the human race."[51] Freud especially feared total sexual abstinence outside monogamous marriage. Some restriction might be tolerable, but that was dangerous.

According to Freud, "It is now easy to predict the result which will ensue if sexual freedom is still further circumscribed, and the standard demanded by civilization is raised to the level … which taboos [prohibits] every sexual activity other than that in legitimate matrimony. Under these conditions the number of strong natures who openly rebel will be immensely increased, and likewise the number of weaker natures who take refuge in neurosis…. [When] civilization demands from both sexes abstinence until marriage, and lifelong abstinence for all who do not enter into legal matrimony … we may thus well raise the question whether our *civilized* sexual morality is worth the sacrifice it imposes upon us."[52]

Freud was not a social scientist and never proved his theory, but he did think someone should try. He wrote, "If the evolution of civilization has such a far-reaching similarity with the development of an individual, and if the same methods are employed in both, would not the diagnosis be justified that many systems of civilization have become *neurotic* under the pressure of the civilizing trends? … We should have to be very cautious and not forget that, after all, we are only dealing with analogies…. But in spite of all these difficulties, we may expect that one day someone will venture on this research into the pathology of civilized communities."[53]

Unwin accepted Freud's challenge and set out to study how sexual morality affects civilization. He especially wanted to determine whether Freud was right that restricting sex to monogamous marriage would threaten the survival of societies. He did indeed find strong evidence linking "the cultural condition of any society in any geographical environment … [with] the past and present methods of regulating the relations between the sexes."[54] However, Unwin found in every case that the "expansive energy" of a social group comes from restricting sex to marriage, and that sexual license is always "the immediate cause of cultural decline."[55] All the evidence showed that the survival of a civilization or society depended on keeping people's sexual energy focused on supporting family life and not allowing individuals to have access to sex in ways that did not support family life.

Unwin found, without exception, that if a social group limited sex to marriage, and especially to lifelong monogamous marriage, it would always prosper. There was "no recorded case of a society adopting absolute monogamy without displaying expansive energy." He noted that when sexual standards were high, "Men began to explore new lands ... commerce expanded; foreign settlements [were] established, colonies [were] founded."[56] In contrast, if a social group lowered standards so that sex was no longer limited to marriage, it always lost social energy. Again, Unwin found absolutely no exceptions, saying, "In human records there is no instance of a society retaining its energy after a complete new generation has inherited a tradition which does not insist on pre-nuptial [premarital] and post-nuptial [extramarital] continence."[57] In every verifiable case, once a group became sexually permissive, "the energy of the society ... decreased and finally disappeared."[58]

Unwin found the same pattern again and again. A society would begin with high standards limiting sex to one partner in marriage for life, which would produce social strength and enable that society to flourish. Then a new generation would arise demanding sex on easier terms and would lower the moral standards. When that happened, the society would lose vitality, grow weak, and eventually die. Unwin explained that "in the beginning, each society had the same ideas in regard to sexual regulations. Then the same strengths took place; the same sentiments were expressed; the same changes were made; the same results ensued. Each society reduced its sexual opportunity to a minimum and, displaying great social energy, flourished greatly. Then it extended its sexual opportunity [lowered standards]; its energy decreased, and faded away. The one outstanding feature of the whole story is its unrelieved monotony."[59]

Based on this overwhelming evidence, Unwin decided that "any human society is free to choose either to display great energy or to enjoy sexual freedom; [but] the evidence is that it cannot do both for more than one generation."[60] Not only was Freud wrong, but also he was *dangerously* wrong. No matter how strong a society happened to be, it could not avoid losing social strength once it lowered sexual standards. Once it did, signs of growing weakness would appear within one generation. Freud thought restricting sex to marriage threatened the survival of civilization and could even threaten the human race, but Unwin discovered that restricting sex to the traditional marriage structure made societies strong and that easing sexual standards supporting the traditional family structure always led to social collapse. Unwin's findings reveal that there is no other outcome. If we heed his findings, it means we must realize that deconstructing the family to justify lust will threaten the strength and survival of American society as a whole.

Conclusion

We have taken a close look at the main strategy underlying the movement to normalize homosexual behavior in America and have exposed and criticized the deconstructionist approach to remove social preference for the traditional family structure. After considering steps proposed for deconstructing the family as a defined social institution, we have to conclude that the effort will not only abolish the family as a meaningful social category but will also lead to a level of weakness and instability incompatible with long-run social survival. Should Americans adopt the deconstructionist social agenda presented by activist homosexual leaders such as Franklin Kameny, it will not only jeopardize good government but also threaten the future of American society.

Kameny and other leaders of the homosexual agenda would have Americans believe their vision of sexual relations without social or moral biases—their vision of a nation that encourages an endless variety of family structures—is consistent with historic American ideals. They would have us believe that this vision can be achieved without risk for the benefit of all. However, thinking

Americans must recognize—before it is too late—that this vision is dangerously utopian and does not correlate with social reality. We must not let ourselves be blinded to the realities of social survival. We must realize that social strength depends on restricting individual sexual desires, that the traditional family structure has been proven worthy through millennia of human experience, that objective moral standards do exist and are essential to social order, and that throwing this away will assure the demise of any society who does so.

If Americans are persuaded to gamble on family deconstruction to normalize the idea that (1) gender difference makes no difference, (2) that lust is the ultimate arbiter of institutions essential for social survival, (3) that gender and number are irrelevant to marriage, (4) that parenting is essentially unrelated to the meaning of family, (5) that family is essentially unrelated to the meaning of marriage, and (6) that none of this has any real importance to public life in American society, it will represent a sucker's bet in a game that is impossible to win. For anyone willing to see, the deck is stacked and only those blinded by lust and who ignore sound advice would ever consider risking what we cannot afford to lose.

Notes

1. For a good analysis, see James Davison Hunter, *Culture Wars: The Struggle to Define America: Making Sense of the Battles over the Family, Art, Education, Law, and Politics* (New York: Basic Books, 1991). For an analysis of the deeper moral crisis underlying the culture wars, see Os Guinness, *The American Hour: A Time of Reckoning and the Once and Future Role of Faith* (New York: The Free Press, 1992).

2. *Deconstruction* is the philosophical term applied for this enterprise. For more details, see the highly influential works of French philosophers Michel Foucault (1926–1984) and

Jacques Derrida (1930–2004). See also Franklin E. Kameny, "Deconstructing the Traditional Family," *The World and I* (October 1993), pp. 383-395. (*The World and I* is a quarterly magazine published by *The Washington Times*.)

3. Quoted in Anne Taylor Flemming, *Motherhood Deferred* (New York: Random House, 1996), p. 24.

4. Quoted in Christiana Hoff Sommers, *Who Stole Feminism?* (New York: Simon and Schuster, 1994), pp. 256-257.

5. Robin Morgan, *Sisterhood Is Powerful* (New York: Random House, 1970), p. 537.

6. Shulamith Firestone, *The Dialectic of Sex: The Case for Feminist Revolution* (New York: Bantam Books, 1979), p. 254.

7. Kate Millett, *Sexual Politics* (Garden City, NY: Doubleday, 1970), p. 35.

8. Judith Stacey, *In the Name of the Family: Rethinking Family Values in the Postmodern Age* (Boston, MA: Beacon, 1996), p. 51.

9. Vivian Gornick, *The Daily Illini* (Urbana), April 25, 1981. Also quoted in Francis Beckwith, *Politically Correct Death* (Grand Rapids, MI: Baker, 1993), p. 175.

10. Mary Hunt, "Re-imagining Sexuality—Family," *Re-imagining Conference* (Minneapolis, MN: World Council of Churches, 1993).

11. Linda Gordon, "Functions of the Family," *Women: A Journal of Liberation* (Fall 1969).

12. James B. Nelson, *Body Theology* (Louisville, KY: Westminster/ John Knox, 1992), p. 25.

13. Ibid., p. 91.

14. Michael Swift, "Gay Revolutionary," *Gay Community News* (Washington, DC), February 15, 1987. Reprinted in *The Congressional Record*, 15-21, February 1987, E3081. Swift later dismissed this statement as a joke, but there was no indication he was being insincere when it was published in *Gay Community*

News. Even if Swift meant to be humorous (as he latter claimed), his statement should still be taken seriously. Smith wrote for homosexual activist readers who were most certainly eager to redefine social structures, so any honestly intended *humor* could only be of a sort offered to soften acceptance of a risky proposition.

15. Kameny, "Deconstructing the Traditional Family," p. 384.
16. Ibid.
17. Ibid., p. 385.
18. Ibid., pp. 394-395.
19. I was in Washington, DC, and observed the 1993 March for Lesbian, Gay and Bi Equal Rights in person.
20. This was documented on film by the Traditional Values Coalition. See *Gay Rights/Special Rights: Inside the Homosexual Agenda* (Anaheim, CA: Jeremiah Films, 1993).
21. See "Platform of the 1993 March on Washington for Lesbian, Gay, and Bi Equal Rights and Liberation," printed by march organizers and distributed to congressional staff, the media, march participants, and interested members of the public at large. Copies are available from the Family Research Council, Washington, DC.
22. Firestone, *The Dialectic of Sex: The Case for Feminist Revolution*, p. 254.
23. Marlene Dixon, "Why Women's Liberation? Racism and Male Supremacy," available at edweb.tusd.k12.az.us/uhs/APUSH/2nd%20Sem/Articles%20Semester%202/8%20Dixon.html. See also Marlene Dixon, "Why Women's Liberation? Racism and Male Supremacy" (Chicago: Chicago Women's Liberation Union, 1963), p. 9.
24. Helen Sullinger and Nancy Lehmann, "Declaration on Feminism," originally published November 1971, available at www.spiritone.com/~law/hate quotes.html. Quoted in Francis

Beckwith, *Politically Correct Death* (Grand Rapids, MI: Baker, 1993), p. 175.

25. Paula Ettelbrick, "Since When Is Marriage a Path to Liberation?" in William Rubenstein, ed., *Lesbians, Gay Men and the Law* (New York: The New Press, 1993), pp. 401-405. Quoted in Stanley Kurtz, "Beyond Gay Marriage: The Road to Polyamory," *The Weekly Standard* (4-11, August 2003), p. 29.

26. Ibid.

27. Nancy D. Polikoff, "First Comes Love, then Comes Marriage, then Comes Queers with a Baby Carriage: The Strange Logic of the Hawaii Same-Sex Marriage Trial," *GNC: National Queer Progressive Quarterly*, 22/3 (Winter 1996), pp. 12-14. Quoted in Kurtz, "Beyond Gay Marriage: The Road to Polyamory," p. 29. See also Nancy D. Polikoff, "We Will Get What We Ask For: Why Legalizing Gay and Lesbian Marriage Will Not Dismantle the Legal Structure of Gender in Every Marriage," *Virginia Law Review*, 79 (1993), pp. 1535-1550.

28. Martha A. Fineman, *The Neutered Mother, the Sexual Family, and Other Twentieth Century Tragedies* (New York: Routledge, 1995).

29. See documentation provided in Kurtz, "Beyond Gay Marriage: The Road to Polyamory," pp. 28-30.

30. Reviewed in Kurtz, "Beyond Gay Marriage: The Road to Polyamory," p. 29. See also Martha M. Ertman, "Viva No Difference," *Northwestern University Law Review*, 91/2 (1997), pp. 642-646.

31. David L. Chambers, "What If? The Legal Consequences of Marriage and the Legal Needs of Lesbian and Gay Male Couples," *Michigan Law Review*, 95 (1996), pp. 447-491.

32. Ibid.

33. Andrew Sullivan, "Here Comes the Groom: A Conservative Case for Gay Marriage," *The New Republic*, August 28, 1989.

34. Edward Rothstein, quoted in William A. Borst, "The Meaning of Is," *Mindszenty Report,* 47/1 (January 2005).

35. Jacques Derrida, *Glas,* in *A Derrida Reader: Between the Blinds,* ed. Peggy Kamuf (New York: Columbia University Press, 1991), p. 382.

36. Ibid., pp. 387-388, emphasis mine.

37. Michel Foucault, *Ethics, Subjectivity and Truth* (New York: New Press, 1997), p. 163.

38. Michel Foucault, *The History of Sexuality,* vol. 1, *An Introduction* (New York: Random House, 1990), pp. 7-8.

39. Ibid., p. 395, emphasis in the original.

40. Ibid., pp. 384-385.

41. Ibid., p. 385.

42. Ibid., pp. 387, 389.

43. Ibid., p. 389.

44. Ibid.

45. Ibid.

46. Ibid., p. 392.

47. Ibid., p. 395.

48. Ibid.

49. Joseph Daniel Unwin, *Sex and Culture* (London: Oxford University Press, 1934); *Sexual Regulations and Cultural Behavior* (London: Oxford University Press, 1935); and *Hopousia: Or the Sexual and Economic Foundations of a New Society* (London: George Allen and Unwin, 1940).

50. *Sigmund Freud: Collected Papers,* trans. by Joan Riviere, vol. 2 (New York: Basic, 1959), p. 76.

51. Sigmund Freud, in *The Standard Edition of the Complete Psychological Works of Sigmund Freud,* trans. and ed. by James Strachey in collaboration with Anna Freud (London: Hogarth), vol. 22 (1964), p. 214. See also vol. 11 in the series (1957), pp. 54, 215.

52. Freud, *Collected Papers,* pp. 87-88, 99.

53. Sigmund Freud, *Gesammelte Werks*, vol. 14 (London: Imago, 1940-1952), pp. 504-505. See also Freud, *The Standard Edition of the Complete Psychological Works of Sigmund Freud*, vol. 21 (1961), p. 110; and Ernest Jones, *The Life and Work of Sigmund Freud*, vol. 3 (New York: Basic, 1957), p. 346. My translation follows Ernest Jones.

54. Unwin, *Sex and Culture*, p. 340.

55. Unwin, *Sexual Regulations and Cultural Behavior*, p. 31; and Unwin, *Sex and Culture*, p. 326.

56. Unwin, *Hopousia*, pp. 82-83. See also *Society and Culture*, p. 431; and *Sexual Regulations and Cultural Behavior*, pp. 20, 32.

57. Unwin, *Hopousia*, pp. 84–85.

58. Unwin, *Sex and Culture*, p. 382. See also Ibid., pp. 380, 431; *Sexual Regulations and Cultural Behavior*, pp. 21, 34; *Hopousia*, p. 84.

59. Unwin, *Sex and Culture*, p. 381.

60. Ibid., p. 412.

The reality
is that since 1994 there has
existed solid epidemiologic evidence, now
extensively confirmed and reconfirmed, that the
most common natural course for a young person
who develops a "homosexual identity" is for it to
spontaneously disappear unless that process is
discouraged or interfered with by
extraneous factors.
—Dr. Jeffrey Satinover

HOW THE MENTAL HEALTH ASSOCIATIONS MISREPRESENT SCIENCE

by Jeffrey B. Satinover, M.D., Ph.D.[1]

First published by the title "The Trojan Couch" in
NARTH Conference Reports, 2005.
Revised and republished with permission.

*Call it a sense of contempt toward the mental health
enterprise, radiating vaguely from a variety of quarters
… [a] harsh questioning of the scientific basis of our
professional expertise…. Is not the whole enterprise more
of an illusion—a successful public relations effort, perhaps,
but certainly not the practical and effective application of
a body of scientifically certifiable findings or theories?*

---

[1] Jeffrey Satinover is a psychiatrist and physicist. He is Distinguished Adjunct Professor of Science and Mathematics at The King's College, New York, New York, and is Visiting Scientist at the Swiss Federal Institute of Technology, Zurich. Prior to this, Dr. Jeffrey Satinover practiced psychoanalysis and psychiatry for more than nineteen years, was a Fellow in Psychiatry and Child Psychiatry at Yale University, and served a term as president of the C. G. Jung Foundation. Dr. Satinover holds degrees from MIT, the University of Texas, and Harvard University.

Remarks by John Spiegel, M.D., made during the inaugural address
he gave on assuming the presidency of the American Psychiatric
Association in 1974, which followed one year after the APA
overturned classification of homosexuality as a mental disorder, which
was achieved with his then-secret collusion as a closeted homosexual.

FAIRYTALES REMIND US of those simple truths that, as adults, we no longer wish to accept. "The Emperor's New Robes" shows us that in every generation, on certain matters, a whole society—its experts, its most admired, respected, and trusted leaders and counselors—will adopt as authoritative *a complete illusion.* Some of my psychiatric and psychological colleagues have woven for themselves their own set of illusory robes of authority, and for the past 35 years have been proclaiming doctrines in the public square that depend upon the authority that derives from the public's belief that these robes exist. In particular, they have claimed to the Supreme Court that the scientific data shows that homosexuals form a "class" whose boundaries are defined by a stable "trait." This presumption is false, yet the recent Supreme Court decisions pertaining to same-sex marriage have taken it for granted.

Part I of the paper reviews the history of the diagnostic change that in 1973 removed homosexuality as a formal disorder from the American Psychiatric Association's *Diagnostic and Statistical Manual of Mental Disorders (DSM)*, a change that many now accept as simply indisputable in spite of the fact that it was based wholly on fiction.

Parts II and III analyze the psychiatric guilds' massive misrepresentation of the scientific record in the Supreme Court's *Lawrence v. Texas* and *Romer v. Evans* cases. Part IV examines a key section of the two briefs used to define homosexuality as a "class," a claim which (under precedent jurisprudence) depends upon homosexuality being an innate and immutable trait. (Racial "class" status is dependent upon "race," a parameter that is relatively static with fixed meanings across studies.)

Part I. The APA, the DSM, and Homosexuality. The Campaign Begins

A lifelong hard-left political activist, the psychologist Evelyn Hooker is more than anyone else credited by believers with having demonstrated that homosexuality is normal. Even today, almost 50 years after its publication in 1957 in *Projective Testing*, her "The Adjustment of the Male Overt Homosexual" is the only paper referenced in detail on the main website of the American Psychological Association in its discussion of gay and lesbian issues, as it attempts to make the case that there is no evidence for an association between homosexuality and psycho-pathology.[1] Crucially, her study was one of the two upon which in 1973, the APA decided to remove homosexuality from the list of disorders in the DSM and the one study discussed in the APA's brief in 2003 in the *Lawrence* case. It claims to show that "homosexuals [are] not inherently abnormal and that there [is] no difference between the pathologies of homosexual and heterosexual men."[2]

Eight years after her landmark study, she found herself chair of a newly established National Institute of Mental Health (NIMH) Task Force on Homosexuality, handpicked by Judd Marmor, an influential psychiatrist at UCLA. The only other "mental health" representatives were Alfred Kinsey's close colleagues Paul Gebhard, and John Money, the latter a psychologist from Johns Hopkins and an early (but recently discredited and fired) proponent of transsexual surgery. In 1969 the Task Force issued its report. It claimed, parroting the Kinsey reports almost word-for-word, that sexuality was a continuum from exclusive homosexuality to exclusive heterosexuality, and that some degree of *bisexuality* was the human norm. Without evidence, it stated that any homosexual suffering was caused by societal prejudice. (It avoided mentioning, however, that in Kinsey's view, human sexual taste was almost infinitely malleable.) Thus, there was nothing problematic with homosexuality *per se*.

Within a few years, Marmor, who was active in anti-war, pro-abortion, and other "New Left" causes, became Vice-President of the APA. With Hooker and Marmor in such prominent roles, agitators outside the professions could count on their collaboration in organizing protests aimed at radicalizing an organization which until then held to a tacit ethical creed of professionalism that prohibited them from using the public's trust in their presumed scholarly expertise in circumscribed domains to exercise influence over general matters of civics. One can see the beginnings of a coordinated effort to corrupt this ethos at the APA's 1970 annual meeting, when a most eminent and respected psychiatrist and psychoanalyst (and later a founder of NARTH) presenting a paper on "homosexuality and transsexualism" was interrupted by an outside agitator who had been secretly brought into the meeting.[3] Acceding to pressure, the organizers of the 1971 conference agreed to sponsor a special panel—not *on* homosexuality, but *by* homosexuals. (N.b.: *The state of sexuality constituted their sole purported expertise to speak professionally,* just as though being tall made one an expert in the mechanisms of cell growth, or having cancer.) The program chairman had been warned that if the panel was not approved, homosexual activists would ruin the entire convention. The APA caved. The only psychiatrist at this presentation would be the moderator, Robert Spitzer of Columbia University, a sympathizer in large measure on "civil rights," not scientific grounds, in his later recollection.

After this quick capitulation, the activists decided to seek more. Progressive psychiatrists, gay psychiatrists, and outside activists planned a disruption and sought the services of left-wing activist Frank Kameny, who turned for help to the New Left and non-accomodationist Gay Liberation Front. Kameny's cadre, with forged credentials provided by allies on the inside (some at the very top), broke into a special lifetime service award meeting. They grabbed the microphone, and Kameny declared, "Psychiatry is the enemy incarnate. Psychiatry has waged a relentless war of extermination against us…. We're rejecting you all as our owners. You may take this as our declaration of war." Regardless, a few hours later, the promised panel discussion—presented by the same group of protesters—proceeded without objection by the APA.

The activists soon secured an appearance before the APA's crucial Committee on Nomenclature and Statistics, responsible for publishing the *Diagnostic and Statistical Manual of Mental Disorders*. Loosely coordinated with the international classification of medical diseases, the enormously influential *DSM* had defined homosexuality medically, on a par with many other sexual "deviations" because homosexuals did not have an adult person of the opposite sex as their primary object of sexual interest. The APA was now being pressured—both from within and from without—to change its classification and created a special task force comprised almost entirely of the same people from the Kinsey Institute who had packed the NIMH committee. Judd Marmor was now APA Vice-President, while the President-elect was a homosexual who would keep that fact secret (see below for more details).

Spitzer, who would become the pre-eminent expert in the classification of mental disorders on a statistical basis and the overall director of psychiatry's official classification system, was then a consultant to the Nomenclature Committee. He did not believe homosexuality so intrinsically and self-evidently a "bad thing" that it warranted being listed in a manual of disorders alongside, say, schizophrenia—an evident truth, especially for a profession struggling to find empirical grounding in biological science and turning against the dominance of psychoanalysis and a threatening increase in competing, purely psychological theories and professions. He arranged a meeting between the Committee and a group of outside activists and gay psychiatrists and psychologists.

The Committee was impressed, writes Bayer, by the "sober and professional manner" in which Charles Silverstein, Ph.D. (who would later author *The Joy of Gay Sex* and *The New Joy of Gay Sex*) presented the homosexual case. And, crucially, "Since *none of the Committee members was an expert on homosexuality*, there was considerable interest in the data that had been presented, *much of which was new to those who would have to evaluate the issues* raised by the call for a revised nomenclature" (my emphasis, on the fact that such a crucial decision, affecting so many in society, and so much, was going to be made by so few knowing so little about the subject matter being presented to them, and in so poor a position to judge the scientific quality of the representation).

Silverstein led off with Hooker's work. He also introduced some of Kinsey's arguments—but only some. He emphasized Kinsey's claims about the frequency of homosexuality, but like the NIMH committee before him, he passed over in silence the fact that Kinsey considered sexuality to be mutable. Wardell Pomeroy, co-author of the first Kinsey volume and (like all his male colleagues) one of Kinsey's lovers, argued that the Kinsey data found that homosexuality was not associated with psychopathology and that all *other* studies of homosexuality were intrinsically flawed because they were based on "clinical" samples rather than samples from the regular population—as though this were not precisely what a quantitative comparative pathography would require. Even so, both statements were flat falsehoods, especially outrageous in that the Kinsey data itself—for which he himself was largely responsible— was fraudulently skewed by blatant population sampling biases, and the badgering and even bribing of its imprisoned and largely otherwise institutionalized subjects, which were not reported as such. Pomeroy admitted this in a book published shortly before this very meeting—which even so, he neglected to mention.[4]

Spitzer presented NIMH's official position on homosexuality. According to *Psychiatric News*, it was "essentially upon the rationale of Dr. Spitzer's presentation that the Board made its decision." In it, he argued for normalizing homosexuality because:

1. "Exclusive homosexuality" was a normal part of the human condition, a claim based on Kinsey's data.
2. Homosexuality did not meet the requirements of a psychiatric disorder since it "does not either regularly cause subjective distress or is regularly associated with some generalized impairment in social effectiveness or functioning [sic]."
3. Marcel T. Saghir and Eli Robins' recently published *Male and Female Homosexuality* showed that homosexuality was normal. (Their research—which was astoundingly shoddy—was roundly criticized by colleagues at the time, but no critique was addressed by the presenter or the committee.)[5]

Although Spitzer did not say so then, in later correspondence he has said that another important component of the case was the work of Evelyn Hooker.[6] The APA committee, however, failed to reference critical studies, such as Robins' and Saghir's suicide studies, and their study that found differences in the behavioral patterns and psychology of homosexuals and heterosexuals. These differences would have complicated Hooker's findings—at least in the grossly oversimplified and misrepresented form in which Hooker's findings were presented.

Nonetheless, quickly following the advice of the new homosexual advisors, two-thirds of the APA's Board of Trustees (barely a quorum) voted to remove homosexuality as a psychiatric disorder, with only two abstentions. A few voices formally appealed to the membership at large—scarcely a scientific *modus operandi*, either. Countering this appeal, every psychiatrist (tens of thousands) received a mailing urging them to support the change, purportedly for legitimate data-based reasons and apparently "from" the APA, but in fact surreptitiously financed entirely by the National Gay Task Force. Two-thirds of those members who did subsequently vote, voted to support the change—but only one-third of the membership responded (and far from all psychiatrists belonged to the APA to begin with). Four years later a survey in the journal *Medical Aspects of Human Sexuality* showed that 69 percent of psychiatrists disagreed with the vote, and still considered homosexuality a disorder. Bayer remarks that the APA:

> ... had fallen victim to the disorder of a tumultuous era, when disruptive conflicts threatened to politicize every aspect of American social life. A furious egalitarianism ... had compelled psychiatrists to negotiate the pathological status of homosexuality with homosexuals themselves. The result was not a conclusion based upon an approximation of the scientific truth as dictated by reason, but was instead an action demanded by the ideological temper of the times.[7]

Two years later the American *Psychological* Association—which is three times larger than the APA—voted to follow suit, and soon the National Association of Social Workers did likewise.

The seventh printing of the *DSM* in 1974 placed a special note that announced that the APA had "voted to eliminate Homosexuality *per se* as a mental disorder and to substitute there-fore (sic) a new category titled Sexual Orientation Disturbance."[8] The new entry read as follows:

> **302.0 Sexual Orientation Disturbance [Homosexuality]**. This is for individuals whose sexual interests are directed primarily toward people of the same-sex and who are either disturbed by, in conflict with, or wish to change their sexual orientation. This diagnostic category is distinguished from homosexuality, which

by itself does not constitute a psychiatric disorder. Homosexuality per se is one form of sexual behavior, and with other forms of sexual behavior which are not by themselves psychiatric disorders, are not listed in this nomenclature.[9]

In other words, it had become defined as a disorder for one to wish that the way he expresses his instincts be in concord with the physical organs that do the expressing, as though a fish who thinks itself a bird should be thought ill for hoping one day to be happy in the water. A pure political compromise, this peculiar category would last but a few years before being dispensed with altogether.

What hung in the balance? By the time this struggle ended, "what Frank Kameny had been referring to for years as *the* major ideological prop of society's anti-homosexual bias had been shattered," notes Bayer.[10] Twenty years later all the sodomy statutes in America would be close to being found unconstitutional and five years after that, the Supreme Court of Massachusetts would find marriage itself unconstitutional. Moreover, in 1997, the APA would make a subtle change in how it diagnosed all the paraphilias (the new term for "deviations" like sadomasochism, pedophilia, and fetishism) in a revised edition of *DSM IV*. The Nomenclature Committee rewrote its criteria so that such diagnoses would apply *only if the impulses or activities in question interfered with other functioning or caused distress to the individual himself.* By 2002, the "sexology" community was fiercely debating whether all the "paraphilias" should be removed from the *DSM*, and the American Psychological Association had published an article arguing that pedophilia was not harmful. In 2003 the American Psychiatric Association held a symposium debating the removal of the paraphilias, pedophilia included, from the *DSM*, on the same grounds as homosexuality had been removed.

Part II. Homosexuality as a Disorder in the Guilds' *Lawrence* Brief

The APA's decision to remove homosexuality from the *DSM* was presented to the public as based upon a solid scientific foundation, though this foundation was in fact lacking as we'll see. The APA and others have so often repeated the same falsehoods that the public and even the Supreme Court now take for granted that science has demonstrated that homosexuality is a perfectly normal variant of human sexuality if it is fixed early in life and does not change: that it is a matter of "orientation" or "identity." In political contexts, the bulk of the literature is passed over with a wave of the hand in the form of reviews and reviews of reviews that never characterize the full picture; certain studies, lacking in scientific merit, are presented again and again, no matter how hoary (Hooker in particular, as we will see).

In the *Lawrence* brief, the first point the mental health guild *amici* (friends) make, for example, is that "Decades of research and clinical experience have led all mainstream mental health organizations in this country to the conclusion that homosexuality is a normal form of human sexuality." The footnotes offer no support for this claim. Moreover, the sources they do use do not represent the literature as a whole. For example, although the brief uses the nearly half-century old Hooker study, the only study from which it offers any details, it studiously ignores even the Saghir and Robins studies, which according to Spitzer, were previously presented as crucial.

In fact, however, within the somewhat substantial if scientifi-cally loose literature on homosexuality, few studies on homosexual-ity fail to assert the very strong intrinsic association between homosexuality and psychological distress—far beyond that which could be attributed *solely* to the genuine and additional distress caused by social stigma and prejudice. No literature has succeeded in demonstrating that this excess psychological distress is in fact attributable to stigma and prejudice. Recently, some studies do ask and examine the attribution question carefully, and answer it—but not as the activists assert: Social stigma, bigotry and prejudice *cannot* account for all the increase in psychopathology found in this population. (See below for details).

Before moving to examine some relevant studies, a few other problems with the brief should be noted. A detail-less review monograph by John Gonsiorek forms a major foundation, being cited 17 times in its 63 footnotes, and with no attempt to validate the review's accuracy or to use instead primary sources. The brief's apparent co-author Gregory Herek's own publications are referenced 48 times, making him by far the single largest "authority" to whom the authors as a group "turn" to support their arguments. Indeed, when all the explicit self-referencing is tallied up it amounts to 33% of all cited references (including a substantial percentage of reviews), with Herek himself constituting by far the single largest source of "outside" substantiation of the claims being made (by, *inter alia*, himself).

The authors do refer to a universally respected study by Laumann et al. nine times, calling it (as have many others) "the most comprehensive survey to date of American sexual practices," but do not, as we shall see when discussing the *Romer* brief, admit its real findings.

Study No. 1: The Eli Robins and Marcel Saghir Studies

Eli Robins and Marcel Saghir, whose study "Male and female homosexuality: natural history" was one of the two direct sources upon which the APA seemed to depend upon to reach its conclusion to drop homosexuality from the DSM, have published other studies of both male and female homosexuals. It would have been natural for the authors of the brief to have referenced them, but they did not. Note this, however: While in their book and final research monograph, Robins and Saghir stated as a *conclusion* that between homosexuals and heterosexuals there were no differences in psychopathology, their own studies in fact demonstrate:

- Differences in the behavioral patterns and psychology of homosexual and heterosexual males and females.
- A markedly greater prevalence of alcoholism among female homosexuals as compared to female heterosexuals.[11]
- No difference in completed suicides between homosexuals and heterosexuals, a fact they attributed to the very low percentage of homosexuals in the population, but a markedly greater incidence of suicide *attempts* by male homosexuals compared to male heterosexuals.[12]

But here's the subtlety. The purpose of the particular study presented to the APA was to determine, using a self-administered questionnaire, relative rates of psychopathology in homosexual and heterosexual populations. The problem was the sample. First, the questionnaire was given to male and female homosexuals from so-called "homophile" organizations, including some of the most radical in the "gay liberation movement," and heterosexuals from the general population. An (immediately earlier) 1972 study on homosexuality published by Siegelman found higher levels of "neuroticism" among "joiners" of "homophile" organizations than "non-joiners"—that is, Siegelman was studying the very people who were in the midst of radicalizing the APA.

Second, the authors *chose to study only individuals who had never previously been in a psychiatric hospital*, the population that actually contained the largest proportion of the very condition they claimed to be studying, i.e., psychopathology. 14% of the male and 7% of the female homosexual responders had prior psychiatric hospitalizations. Among the heterosexual responders, none had. All these were excluded in advance from the study! By a very conservative estimate, the number of homosexuals reporting hospitalization is at least five times as high as it should have been, if the hypothesis that there is "no difference" between homosexuals and heterosexuals were true.

In short, the study indicated exactly the opposite of what its authors claimed it did—even ignoring a recruitment bias that worked to suppress such evidence (excluding a-priori any subjects with the strongest indicia for psychopathology—psychiatric hospitalization). It is consistent with other studies they published before and later, all demonstrating a strong association among homosexuality, suicidality, and alcoholism in both males and females, statistically significant and significantly greater than in matched heterosexual populations. And yet, none of these facts were reported or discussed by the authors of the brief—perhaps because to reference them outside of indirect review articles (e.g., Gonsirek's, where the actual data is not just two steps away from potential scrutiny but three or more) might draw attention to its less palatable findings.

Study No. 2: The Evelyn Hooker Study

Evelyn Hooker claimed that her study, "The Adjustment of the Male Overt Homosexual," showed that "homosexuals were not inherently abnormal and that there was no difference between homosexual and heterosexual men in terms of pathology," and that such tests could not distinguish homosexual from heterosexual psychology. In fact, the study was too poorly performed to demonstrate either. It should have (but did not):

- Formulated the hypothesis (purportedly) to be tested, to wit: "Those male homosexuals who do not disproportionately demonstrate any casually observable psychological maladjustment will be indistinguishable in their performance on standard projective tests from a similarly-selected group of male heterosexuals." Even were this hypothesis supported by her research, one may not conclude from it that projective testing would be unable to distinguish homosexual from heterosexual psychology, nor to distinguish a bias in psychopathology (of type or frequency) characteristic of homosexuals, let alone that there *are* no differences in psychopathology between homosexual and heterosexual men. Indeed, such a study could not even *verify its own hypothesis, but merely provide one small bit of evidence for it*, and that meaningless since the hypothesis is on its face trivial.

- Identified a set of projective tests adequate to screen for psychopathology and normative differentiation. If larger, pre-existing controls exist for the tests then the standardized norms can be used as they are vastly superior to ad-hoc or norms based even on control groups of matched size. She rather abandoned the larger standardized norms and invented her own.

- Selected two groups of men, one homosexual, the other heterosexual, and matched them for age and other demographic characteristics.

- Had a group of expert administrators and test interpreters blind to the subjects' sexuality administer the tests to each group.

- Tabulated and scored the results for statistical significance with respect to the original hypotheses.

- Subjected the paper to peer-review and cross-checked for major and minor errors of fact, method, or calculation before publication.

In fact, Hooker failed to follow even the most basic tenets of the scientific method. She *deliberately* had her associates recruit participants to obtain a pool of subjects who understood what the "experiment" was about and how it was to be used to achieve a political goal in transforming society. As she wrote many years later, "I knew the men for whom the ratings were made, and I was certain as a clinician that they were relatively free of psychopathology."[13] In other words, she lacked a random sample and tinkered with the composition of both groups to conform to whatever she defined. Indeed, she selected them in collaboration with "activist" organizations[14]—i.e., the "homophile" groups that in 1972 Seligmann (op. cit.) would identify as having a disproportionate number of "neurotic" members. In addition, individuals with certain signs of "instability" and those in therapy she simply screened out, insuring in advance that, to the best of her ability (as research psychologist of mice, not men, as she was) neither group would display pathological symptoms in projective testing in which she was inexpert. The relative proportion, the presence and relative seriousness of signs of instability in fact remaining in each group were all documented by Hooker but not published in the study—an unacceptable absence, and the data was hastily destroyed by two of her disciples after her death. Nor was information provided on how many unscreened individuals were initially found and subjected to screening, it presumably being much easier to find heterosexual than homosexual individuals, yet Hooker claims finding somehow exactly and only 40 of each.

She asks us to trust that her judgment is accurate and objective even though she had no clinical experience in the field of study, in the experimental measures employed, nor in clinical experimentation; did not have even the qualifications to perform projective testing in a mundane clinical situation beyond her Ph.D., had an obvious bias, and provides no details at all about her procedures. As we will see, the inadequacy of her research was openly acknowledged by the journal that published it.

In performing her experiment, she used the Rorschach test (ROR), the Thematic Apperception Test (TAT), and the Make a Picture Story Test (MAPS). All these tests had national standardized norms—the baseline response of a normal sample—to serve as a control with which to compare the test group. These national standardized norms arise from samples of many thousands of individuals and are vastly more reliable than anything a single researcher, even if an expert, can create if the sample size is small. However, she designed her own heterosexual control group to compare to the homosexual test group on the three standard tests she chose to administer. In other words, "normal" would be defined in her study by how the individuals in her control groups performed rather than by the national standardized norms. Hooker managed to find only 40 adequate heterosexual volunteers and eliminated ten of these, leaving a final control group of thirty (the same as with her homosexual group).

Did Hooker need to create a heterosexual control group? Perhaps she believed the Kinsey data that claimed that more than 1/3 of men had had homosexual experience, so a mere random sample of the "normal" male population would be too heavily weighted by a "homosexual" or bisexual component. The answer is still "no." The sample in the national norms is so huge that any such uncertainty or bias would be a vastly smaller problem than the imprecision and statistical uncertainty—to the point of complete meaninglessness—associated with Hooker's procedure. Hooker simply should have *administered* her tests, in a controlled setting, to a representative sample of homosexuals and compared the results to the pre-existing matched norms for her test group.

But that is not correct either: Someone else, an expert in projective testing, should have done so. Apart from that evident fact, by creating her own norms, she indeed created a counter-factual setting from the outset in which the experimental parameters lacked any objective criteria—other than that the norms of both groups must end up identical—or ought to have unless some difference between the groups was nonetheless so great as to overwhelm the enormous lengths she went to in advance, blur any possibility of the tests' detecting it. One other fatal problem with the study: Hooker did not even maintain the initial experimental procedure she designed herself but altered it when her test (homosexual) group actually *disproved* her hypothesis and did display a difference she hypothesized wouldn't exist.

One of her original hypotheses was that sexual orientation could not be determined by the ROR, TAT and MAPS. But in the course of the established TAT and MAPS test procedures, the homosexual group subjects were unable to refrain from a very high degree of homosexual fantasizing in their imaginary accounts. Not so the heterosexuals. Both the nature and *degree* of sexual fantasy was different in the homosexual group from the heterosexual group, an especially striking fact given that the subjects knew that this "controlled experiment" was supposed to demonstrate that homosexuals were in no way different than heterosexuals. Once it became evident that the TAT and MAPS identified which subjects were homosexual, Hooker dropped these two tests from the experimental design—*post hoc.*

That such a study was considered for publication is bizarre—were one to assume that the peer-review and editorial decision-making process was itself scientific in nature and not purely political. The editors of *Projective Testing* themselves make clear, however, that it was not scientific and they were not acting as scientists. In a footnote on page 18 they explain: "If some of Dr. Hooker's comments, as cautiously presented as they are, seem premature or incompletely documented, the blame must fall on the editors who exercised considerable pressure on her to publish now." In sum, in spite of its being the lynchpin for the APA's decision to de-list homosexuality as a disorder, and the only study offered with any details in the *Lawrence* brief, Evelyn Hooker's 1957 "scientific research" on homosexuality is the American equivalent of Trofim Denisovisch Lysenko's scientific research on the inheritance of acquired characteristics in plant seed left to "germinate" in the Siberian Arctic.[15]

Homosexuality and/as Psychopathology: The Evidence to Date

What is the *actual* scientific status of homosexuality as a "disorder" as provided by the sources used by *amici*? Or, to phrase the question properly, "In the authorities referenced by *amici*, what evidence is there, if any, for an intrinsic association between homosexuality and psychopathology, an association beyond that attributable to stigma, bias, prejudice, 'internalized homophobia,' etc. or any other extrinsic, socially determined factors?" As noted above, judging from the website of the American Psychological Association, the answer is "none," but only a single study is offered to buttress this claim—Evelyn Hooker's, now almost 50 years old. Yet Susan Cochran, apparently also both a co-author (along with Gregory Herek) and self-cited authority of the brief, has performed a linked series of very careful, extensive large-scale controlled field studies addressing precisely this question. (In my judgment, Cochran is herself a careful scientist when acting as a researcher, even if citing herself is inconsistent with the high quality she shows in her research.) Though the *Lawrence* brief references her studies five times, it does not quote them. It is well worth tracking them down in detail.

All the findings of Cochran, et al., were published before the due-date for submission of briefs in the *Lawrence* case. I now cite directly from these articles (the first is taken from Cochran's and May's [2000], the second through sixth from S. E. Gilman et al. [2001], and the last three from Mays and Cochran [2001]):

- "These data provide further evidence of an increased risk for suicide symptoms among homosexually experienced men. Results also hint at a small, increased risk of recurrent depression among gay men, with symptom onset occurring, on average, during early adolescence."
- "Homosexual orientation, defined as having same-sex sexual partners, is associated with a general elevation of risk for anxiety, mood, and substance use disorders and for suicidal thoughts and plans. Further research is needed to replicate and explore the causal mechanisms underlying this association." [N.b., at this point in the research sequence, Cochran et al. indicate that the increased association of "having same-sex partners" with various psychopathologies *cannot* be attributed to extrinsic social factors—rather, the cause is as yet *unknown*.]
- "[Same-sex] respondents had higher 12-month prevalences of anxiety, mood, and substance use disorders and of suicidal thoughts and plans than did respondents with opposite-sex partners only ... elevated same-sex 12-month prevalences were largely due to higher lifetime prevalences."
- "Numerous clinical and community samples have found that lesbians and bisexual women are at greater risk for poor mental health than are other women" (the study cites many other studies).
- "Self-identified lesbians and bisexual women reported significantly lower mental health" (here they are identifying a particularly accurate study).
- "In a more recent study ... bisexuals had the highest scores for anxiety, depression, and a range of mental health risk factors, lesbians fell midway between bisexuals and heterosexuals" (here they are identifying a particularly recent study).

- "Elevated prevalence of psychiatric morbidity in lesbian, gay and bisexual respondents as compared with their heterosexual counterparts (1-9)" (here they are reviewing nine studies with these results).
- "Homosexual and bisexual individuals more frequently (76%) than heterosexual persons (65%) reported both lifetime and day-to-day experiences with discrimination. 42% attributed this to their sexual orientation, in whole or in part."
- "Controlling for differences in perceived discrimination attenuated [but did not eliminate] associations between psychiatric morbidity and sexual orientation." [N.b., following up properly on their earlier findings, the authors now *do* find at least a partial allocation of causal factors, though not an explicit chain of causality: discrimination *alone* does not account for the association between psychopathology and homosexuality.]

In sum, the latest and best conducted research, performed by one of the very authors of the brief, directly, extensively, assert the opposite of what *amici* (among them Cochran herself) claim.

Part III. Homosexuality as a Disorder in the *Romer* Brief

The *Romer* brief presents many of the same problems of the *Lawrence* brief. Its authors make a series of assertions which they try to substantiate by footnoting references—without including damaging direct quotations—to high-quality modern research that contradicts the factual claims they are supposed to support. Moreover, almost one out of every nine of the references from the *Romer* table of authorities consist of the same detail-less Gonsiorek review monograph that forms a major foundation of the *Lawrence* brief.

I will focus on two points. The first is the high value the authors give to a 1994 landmark study, *The Social Organization of Sexuality: Sexual Practices in the United States* (hereafter, "Laumann"), but whose results they misrepresent.[16] The second is the value the authors give, somewhat less visibly, to the work of Alfred Kinsey, and to a cluster of less well known individuals in the field of sex research more or less closely associated with him and/or his ideas: John Money, Wardell Pomeroy, Paul Gebhard, John De Cecco, and Richard Green. These researchers have been engaged in a 30-year process of using the mental health guilds to subvert fundamental societal standards. In particular, many have a long history of advocating the casting aside on principle—that same principle by which homosexuality was originally removed from the *DSM*—traditional restrictions not only on homosexuality, but on pedophilia, sadomasochism, incest, and bestiality.

Study No 1: The Laumann Study

The Laumann study, written by Edward O. Laumann, John H. Gagnon, Robert T. Michael, and Stuart Michaels and published by the University of Chicago Press, was based on a survey of a statistically representative sample of American adults between the ages of 18 and 60, and conducted by the National Opinion Research Center at the University of Chicago. The *Romer* brief refers to it two-thirds as many times as it does Gonsiorek, deems it "renowned," and cites its data—albeit in a most peculiar fashion, carefully avoiding quoting it. Laumann is universally recognized as definitive. Since its publication, numerous large-scale epidemiologic surveys, conducted in all the English-speaking and many other industrialized nations have repeatedly confirmed and strengthened its findings. One of the major points of the Laumann study, which the authors themselves did not expect, is that "homosexuality" as a fixed trait *scarcely even seems to exist.*[17]

"Estimating a single number for the prevalence of homosexuality is a futile exercise," Laumann declares in the first paragraph of an entire chapter devoted to the subject. It is futile not because of bias, underreporting, methodological difficulties, or complexities of behavior, but "because it presupposes assumptions that are patently false: that homosexuality is a uniform attribute across individuals, that it is stable over time, and that it can be easily measured."[18] All the evidence points to the fact that homosexuality is not a "stable trait." Furthermore, the authors found to their surprise that its instability over the course of life was one-directional: declining, and very significantly so. Homosexuality tended *spontaneously* to "convert" into heterosexuality as a cohort of individuals aged, and this was true for both men and women—the pull of the normative, as it were.

So striking and unexpected was this finding that it led researchers all over the world in subsequent years to see if it was really true. Their research involved hundreds of thousands of people and strongly confirmed Laumann. Most of that work had been completed, published, and discussed extensively in the scientific literature long before the *Lawrence* brief experts began their writing, yet they fail to mention any of it. In fact, they claim the scientific literature supports the opposite finding. After making a welter of complex statements about "sexual orientation" admixed with a large number of references and footnotes that appear to sustain each of the individual statements, the authors claim that "sexual orientation" or "identity" is defined well enough to be meaningfully spoken of and in particular used legally to establish homosexuals as a class, following a program laid out years before in a legal paper by Green. They then assert that both Laumann and the other footnoted authorities support the following set of claims (I am paraphrasing sections A through C of the brief):

1. That there are basically three general orientations: hetero-sexual, homosexual, and bisexual, though their boundaries blend somewhat to form a continuum;
2. That such uncertainties as exist in current estimates for the different orientations are due to methodological problems, and in particular the underreporting caused by societal bias;
3. That research has established that "sexual orientation" is comprised of sexual behavior, feelings of attraction to the same or the opposite sex, self-concept, public image, and identity with a community of others;
4. That it is fixed by adolescence; and
5. That it is in significant measure an innate condition.

Looking specifically at point 3, for instance, the brief's references provide sharply limited support. Only sexual behavior, feelings of attraction to the same or the opposite sex, and self-concept (but not public image and identity with a community of others) have proven to be consistent, reliable, and quantifiable measures of "sexual identity." (The support for the claim that public image and identity and community with others help constitute sexual identity comes only from Herek—these are statistically unsupported "dimensions" that he coined and on which he has published extensively. He is, of course, one of the brief's co-authors.)

Furthermore, sexual behavior, feelings of attraction and self-concept have not proven to form a stable, consistent, integrated definition of "sexual identity" or "homosexuality" *per se.* In fact, Laumann's authors were forced by the data to the conclusion that "homosexuality" scarcely exists. To claim to "be gay" is in effect an almost utterly meaningless scientific statement. "Sexual identity" is too unstable to be labeled "identity." Reputable scientific reference provides overwhelming evidence that contradicts the *amici's* claims. The labels "homosexual," "bisexual," and "heterosexual" provide nothing more than convenient shorthand, because the dynamism of sexual "identity" over time frustrates any such static classification system.

Moreover, the authors of the brief allege that "current professional understanding is that the core feelings and attractions that form the basis for adult sexual orientation typically emerge by early adolescence. For some people, adult homosexual orientation is predictable by early childhood." They do not mention the contradictory evidence in Laumann, which provides the most careful and extensive database ever obtained on the childhood experiences of matched homosexual and heterosexual populations. Indeed, later, the authors will cite a paper that Laumann et al. wrote using the same data to analyze the impact of childhood sexual trauma on later life, but will ignore what that study has to say about homosexuality.

They also claim that "Few generalizable estimates exist of the prevalence of homosexual orientation in the United States [their footnote refers to Laumann]. Among existing surveys on sexuality, estimates differ substantially." Laumann actually says: "Overall we find our results remarkably similar to those from other surveys of sexual behavior that have been conducted on national populations using probability sampling methods."[19]

In summary, the meaningful findings about sexual identity in the scientific references *amici* provide are: first, that behavior, reports of attractions and feelings, and/or self-definition can be used alone or in combination, to define sexual identity on a study-by-study basis; second, that sexual identity is not in the least fixed at adolescence but continues to change over the course of life; and third, that there is no evidence whatsoever for its being innate.

Study No. 2: The Kinsey Reports and the Kinsey Associates

The brief's references to Kinsey and his colleagues at the Kinsey Institute as authorities on sexual orientation are striking for a number of reasons: First, because they considered sexual orientation mutable (a point they carefully avoided making out of certain contexts); second, because Laumann gives an extensive, utterly damning critique of Kinsey's' research (though mild by comparison to other critiques in the scientific literature); third, because Laumann's extensive and widely accepted standards for the definition and statistical characterization of sexual orientation have been completely ignored; and fourth, because a reference to Byne and Parsons, the most recent and most scientific review in the lot, completely undercuts the argument.

Kinsey's Colleague: Richard Green

The first of Kinsey's associates cited in the brief that we will consider is Richard Green. One of the three articles of his that the brief cites (alluded to above)—though it is not a scientific article (while referenced as such) and does *not* intelligibly address the scientific validity of any of the arguments—asserts that "growing research evidence exists for an innate origin of homosexuality." But the statement is false. Evidence of any kind was then sparse, but all evidence as of the date he wrote was consistent with the opposite conclusion. Since then, evidence has grown more robust and contrary to the "it's genetic" claim with every passing year. Laumann says in explicit terms: "The recent period of rapid change in sexual practices should be seen, not as a result of unleashed biological proclivities confronting attenuated cultural proclivities, but as an active process of social construction and transformation."

But note how the authors give the opposite idea. They cite two careful reviewers of the scientific literature on the biology of homosexuality, Byne and Parsons, and leave the impression that they claim the opposite of what they actually mean. Byne and Parsons—referenced repeatedly by the authors, but as usual, never quoted—flatly state:

Critical review shows the evidence favoring a biologic theory to be lacking. In an alternative model, temperamental and personality traits interact with the familial and social milieu as the individual's sexuality emerges. Because such traits may be heritable or developmentally influenced by hormones, the model predicts an apparent non-zero heritability for homosexuality without requiring that either genes or hormones directly influence sexual orientation per se.[20]

The *amici* failed to present this information in their brief, nor did they cite Laumann directly. This is rather the brief's summary: "Another study has suggested an 'interactionist' model, under which 'genetic factors can be conceptualized as indirectly influencing the development of sexual orientation.'" (The Byne and Parson's paper is not a study but rather is itself a review of over 100 research studies.)

Kinsey's Colleague: John Money

John Money, referenced three times in *Romer*, was the director of the now defunct "Psycho-hormonal Research Unit" of the Johns Hopkins University School of Medicine and perhaps the world's most effective promoter of "transsexuality" and transsexual surgery. Although Hopkins was once one of the major centers in the world for such surgery, the university abandoned it in 1979, having had the most—and therefore worst—experience with it. The school even stopped performing sex-change surgery on infants with ambiguous genitalia, because they found that psychological sex was clearly determined by chromosomal structure, and that the appropriate treatment was to help the psychology conform to the underlying biology, not the reverse.

Writing in *First Things*, Paul McHugh, Chairman of Psychiatry at Johns Hopkins, noted that scientific studies convinced him and his colleagues:

... that human sexual identity[21] is mostly built into our constitution by the genes we inherit and the embryogenesis we undergo. Male hormones sexualize the brain and the mind.... I have witnessed a great deal of damage from sex-reassignment. The children transformed from their male constitution into female roles suffered prolonged distress and misery as they sensed their natural attitudes.... We have wasted scientific and technical resources and damaged our professional credibility by collaborating with madness rather than trying to study, cure, and ultimately prevent it.[22]

Kinsey's Colleague: Wardell Pomeroy

One of Kinsey's co-authors, referenced with him, was Wardell B. Pomeroy, who had served on the 1973 Nomenclature Task Force. In his book, *Boys and Sex: Wardell B. Pomeroy Co-author of the Kinsey Reports*, he writes that "having sex with the male animal ... whether it is a dog, horse, bull or some other species, may provide considerable erotic excitement for the boy.... Psychically, animal relations may become of considerable significance to the boy who is having regular experience ... [and is] in no point basically different from those that are involved in erotic responses to human situations."[23]

In *Variations* magazine, Pomeroy offers this advice:

We find many beautiful and mutually satisfying [sexual] relationships between fathers and daughters. These may be transient or ongoing, but they have no harmful effects.... Incest between adults and younger children can also prove to be a satisfying and enriching experience.... When there is a mutual and unselfish concern for the other person, rather than a feeling of possessiveness and a selfish concern with one's own sexual gratification, then incestuous relationships can and do work out well. Incest can be a satisfying, non-threatening, and even an enriching emotional experience, as I said earlier.[24]

Kinsey's Colleague: Paul Gebhard

The authors of the amicus brief likewise reference Kinsey's other co-author, Paul Gebhard, another member of the NIMH Homosexuality Task Force, and a presenter at the crucial Nomenclature Committee meeting in 1973. He is also a co-founder of SIECUS and Planned Parenthood, and a former head of the Kinsey Institute. The following is from a transcript of a taped phone conversation in 1992 between Gebhard and J. Gordon Muir, editor of Judith Riesman's *Kinsey, Sex and Fraud*, about the report in the male volume (table 34) supposedly demonstrating multiple orgasms in children and infants as young as six months old. The question as to how this "data" was obtained has been a subject of intense secrecy. Nonetheless:

> Muir: "So, do pedophiles normally go around with stopwatches?"
> Gebhard: "Ah, they do if we tell them we're interested in it!"
> Muir: "And clearly, [the orgasms of] at least 188 children were timed with a stopwatch, according to ..."
> Gebhard: "So, second hand or stopwatch. OK, well, that's, ah, you refreshed my memory. I had no idea that there were that many."
> Muir: "These experiments by pedophiles on children were presumably illegal."
> Gebhard: "Oh yes."

Kinsey's Colleague: John De Cecco

John De Cecco, who teaches at San Francisco State University, is Editor of the *Journal of Homosexuality*, whose articles are often referenced in these briefs as though it were a dispassionately scientific journal with reasonable standards of peer review. It is tendentious, politicized, and self-referential. But, more importantly, De Cecco is a board member of *Paedika: The Journal of Paedophilia*.

In a "Statement of Purpose" published in the journal's first issue, the editors wrote:

> The starting point of *Paedika* is necessarily our consciousness of ourselves as paedophiles ... we understand [paedophilia] to be consensual intergenerational sexual relationships.... Through publication of scholarly studies, thoroughly documented and carefully reasoned, we intend to demonstrate that paedophilia has been, and remains, a legitimate and productive part of the totality of human experience.

De Cecco also was editor of *Journal of Homosexuality's* special 1990 issue devoted to the "debate" over the relationship of homosexuality and pedophilia. This "debate" focuses on two major questions: First, are male homosexuality and paedophilia intrinsically related phenomena, albeit in any given individual they may be differentiated in varying measure, or are they essentially unrelated, even though it is clear that they overlap to a degree that cannot be coincidental? Second, as a matter independent of the first question, is it wise for "the movement" to acknowledge the relationship or overlap between pedophilia and homosexuality, and to seek rights for pedophiles (based on "orientation") similar to those that have been won for homosexuals, or would it be damaging to the gay rights movement to do so, even if it is ultimately the proper thing to do?

Returning to Romer

On its own, of course, the Kinsey associates' support of sexual deviance is not evidence of the falsity of their research on homo-sexuality. Yet the fact that they are activists, promoting such causes as pedophilia and incest, at least undermines their independence and credibility, weakening the basis for their inclusion in the *Romer* brief. Rather than scientists seeking truth, the evidence suggests they are partisans of pedophilia, incest, and the undermining of sexual norms. As I have tried to show, moreover, the authors of the *Romer* brief, in addition to relying on dubious sources of credibility, tried to support their brief with references that contradicted the very claims the brief sought to make. Mixed in with these references are references—though no direct quotations—to high-quality modern research that contradicts the factual claims they are supposed to support.

There are other notable discrepancies in the brief relating to its use and misuse of the Laumann data. For example, the authors cite Laumann directly (a rare instance) in footnote 31 of the brief: "The measurement of same-gender practices and attitudes is crude at best, with unknown levels of underreporting for each...." truncating the citation as shown. However, the full sentence in context is as follows:

> While the measurement of same-gender practices and attitudes is crude at best, with unknown levels of underreporting for each, this preliminary analysis provides unambiguous evidence that no single number can be used to provide an accurate and valid characterization of the incidence and prevalence of homosexuality in the population at large. In sum, homosexuality is fundamentally a multidimensional phenomenon that has manifold meanings and interpretations, depending on context and purpose.

This kind of ambiguity undermines the goal of using "sexual orientation" as a condition to define membership in a well-characterized "suspect class." Hence, this definition is suppressed by the authors of a brief designed to define homosexuality as a class endowed with rights. In fact, on the pages referenced, the Laumann study only incidentally addresses the fact that "sexual orientation" is at best a multi-dimensional construct. And where Laumann does address this fact, it is to make the central point of the study: that homosexuality is so imprecisely multidimensional as to be *essentially meaningless* when understood as a defining "trait." This, of course, is not at all what the authors want the Court to conclude and so they are careful never to mention it.

The un-cited, confounding findings of Laumann and colleagues in these pages are that the great majority of people (both men and women) are exclusively heterosexual throughout their lives. Only a small minority of people ever will consider themselves to be homosexual or will have same-sex experiences, and of these most will eventually change and stop having such experiences. But of those who *do* consider themselves to be homosexual or to have had same-sex experiences, the reciprocal is not true. There is no symmetry. In fact, *just the opposite is true*. For them, the vast majority also has heterosexual experience—less than 1% do not—and the majority undergo a complete transformation.[25]

The point is subtle and powerful, and addresses a confusing false symmetry that activists attempt to create between heterosexuality and homosexuality, as though they were somehow two equivalent poles or ends of a spectrum, the numerically minority status of one being an incidental and trivial fact. In other words, the data illustrates "just how normative heterosexuality is," *even for homosexuals.* The converse—"just how normative homosexuality is, even for heterosexuals"—is false. *Heterosexuality exerts a constant, normative pull throughout the life cycle upon everyone.* (There is no parallel with race: One cannot say, "Findings indicate just how normative whiteness is, but not blackness," nor its converse.) Laumann attributes this reality with regard to "sexual orientation" to "our society," but it's not just our society—it's every society in which it's been studied. A much simpler explanation lies closer at hand: Human physiology, including the physiology of the nervous system, is overwhelmingly sexually dimorphic, that is, heterosexual. It should come as no surprise that the brain self-organizes behavior in large measure in harmony with its own physiological ecology, even if not in wholly deterministic fashion.

Part IV. The Changeability of Homosexuality in *Romer* and *Lawrence*

The authors of both briefs take care to argue that homosexuality is a stable trait, completely ignoring the major finding of Laumann. And so the authors of the *Lawrence* brief argued that "once established, sexual orientation is resistant to change" and specifically, that "there is little evidence that treatment actually changes sexual attractions, as opposed to reducing or eliminating same-sex sexual behavior." But the only references *amici* provide are to two activists, Richard Isay and Douglas Haldeman. Isay, head of the Gay and Lesbian Task Force of the American Psychiatric Association—who spearheaded a failed attempt to make such treatment an ethical violation—has proposed that "homophobia" be classified a mental disorder. Haldeman, an author of the *Lawrence* brief, tacitly acknowledges what the brief as a whole is at such pains otherwise to deny: That homosexuality is not the immutable condition the authors are determined to make it out to be. Nevertheless, the brief makes no mention of the Laumann study's finding, nor of other studies, including those actually conducted under the auspices of the Kinsey Institute itself, that claim very substantial success in reversing homosexuality.[26] The authors did not even bother to critique a study by the Kinsey-developed Masters and Johnson program, published in the *American Journal of Psychiatry* that reported a 65% success rate, but did reference second-hand reviews by non-researchers.

The authors suggest that "conversion" therapy is actually harmful and that programs might even be needed to undo the harm. As evidence they cite "research" on "reparative therapy" sponsored by the National Gay and Lesbian Task Force. The NGLTF used the following advertisement to recruit subjects:

You can be of help in the long process of getting the message out that these conversion therapies do not work and do the opposite of healing by informing your l/g/b communities of our search for participants to be interviewed. Please announce our project in any upcoming lesbian and gay community meetings and spread the word. Help us document the damage!

In contrast, by the time of the *Lawrence* brief, Robert Spitzer had begun to suspect that homosexuality was in fact "not stable" and that the increasingly large number of claims of change he had been hearing might in many cases be true. Upon completion of a pilot study, he presented his findings privately to the Association of Gay and Lesbian Psychiatrists (a group within the APA) expecting his results to be met with scientific objectivity. As he told me, he was urged to suppress his findings on the grounds that, whether true or not, they would harm the civil rights of gays and lesbians. He later received a letter from Wayne Besen, then President of the Human Rights Campaign, warning him not to attempt to perform and publish a full fledged study. As he wrote me: "the intimidation was in the form of telling me that if I did such a study I would be exposed as doing fraudulent research in front of my colleagues."[27]

In spite of Spitzer's reputation as one of the most highly regarded quantitative researchers and bio-statisticians in psychiatry and as the man who had shepherded homosexuality out of the *DSM*, he faced enormous difficulty in getting his study published. Initially presented at the APA annual convention in May, 2001, the results were not published until November, 2003, but the journal of the very organization of which he was the chief editor refused its publication. It was a remarkable slap in the face for someone of his stature, and an indication of the astounding power of political correctness and lack of scientific integrity within the organization.[28] Considering the significance of the study, the numerous comments by eminent names in the field published with it, Spitzer's eminence, and the care he took to approach the Gay and Lesbian interest groups within the APA before proceeding, it is truly remarkable that this study did not even merit a mention in the brief.

The Epidemiology of Change

It would be a mistake to think that the point of this section of the essay is to debate the merits of *therapeutic change of "sexual orientation"* in the fashion of almost all public argument to date. A far more important point was made once again by the authors' own cited authority, Laumann—though they hid it carefully. Laumann concluded that quite apart from therapeutic change, all the evidence points to the fact that homosexuality is not a "stable trait." Furthermore, as was already evident in the data concerning prevalence of homosexuality—however measured, whether by action, feeling, or identity—before age 18 and after age 18, Laumann et al., found to their surprise that its instability over the course of life was one-directional: declining, and very significantly so. "Sexual orientation" was not merely a trait that happened to be *unstable*, rather it was that homosexuality tended *spontaneously* to "convert" into heterosexuality as a cohort of individuals aged; and this was true for both men and women—the pull of the normative, as it were. (See Laumann et al., chapters eight and nine.)

So striking and unexpected was this finding that it led researchers all over the world in subsequent years to see if it was really true by performing even larger scale studies. Their research has so far involved literally hundreds of thousands of people and it only strongly confirms what Laumann et al., had found.

Most of this work had been completed, published and discussed extensively in the scientific literature long before the *Lawrence* brief experts began their writing. Yet, they fail to mention any of it. In fact, they claim the scientific literature supports the exact opposite. A review of portions of that literature now follows, showing the findings of the Laumann study itself as well as some of those that followed in subsequent years. I urge the reader to consult the remainder. To make reading a bit easier, I have provided the main citation once and have added additional individual page numbers only for very lengthy publications in parentheses following the extract proper.

Spontaneous Instability of Sexual Orientation with Age in Laumann et al.[29]

> "The rate for men [having any kind of same gender sexual experience ever] … is 9.1 percent. Men who report same-gender sex only before they turned eighteen, not afterward, constitute 42% of the total number of men who ever report having a same-gender experience. [3.8% of all men have same-gender sexual experience before age eighteen and never again.] Our final measure has the lowest prevalence … only 2.8 percent of the men report identifying with … same-gender sexuality" (pp. 296-297, emphasis added).

> "Overall we find our results remarkably similar to those from other surveys of sexual behavior that have been conducted on national populations using probability sampling methods. In particular two [earlier] very large large-scale surveys in France (20,055 adults) and Britain (18,876 persons)" (p. 297).

Spontaneous Instability of Sexual Orientation with Age in Other (Later) Studies

1. New Zealand Study[30]: The Effect of "Social Influences"

Direct citations with emphasis added in italics:

> "Investigation of prevalence, continuities, and changes over time among young adults growing up in a country with a relatively accepting climate to homosexuality is likely to illuminate this debate."[31]

"10.7% of men and 24.5% of women reported being attracted to their own sex *at some time*."

"This dropped to 5.6% of men and 16.4% of women … report[ing] *some* current same-sex attraction."

"Current attraction *predominantly* to their own sex or equally to both sexes was reported by 1.6% of men and 2.1% of women."

"Occasional same-sex attraction, but not major attraction, was more common among the most educated."

"Between age 21 and 26, slightly more men moved away from an exclusive heterosexual attraction (1.9% of all men) than moved towards it (1.0%)."

"For women, many more moved away (9.5%) than towards (1.3%) exclusive heterosexual attraction."

"These findings show that much same-sex attraction is not exclusive and is unstable in early adulthood, especially among women."

"The proportion of women reporting some same-sex attraction in New Zealand is high compared both to men, and to women in the UK and US."

"These observations, along with the variation with education, are consistent with a large role for the social environment."

This study specifically contradicts *amici's* claim that change might affect *behavior* but not *attraction*. To the contrary, large, dramatic drops in homosexual attraction occur spontaneously for both sexes. Furthermore, not only does this study demonstrate the extraordinary influence of the social and cultural milieu in general, it demonstrates specific effects (e.g., higher education) whose desirability needs to be considered dispassionately and *not* automatically presumed positive, especially as it is being misattributed to biology.

That is, the typical college education in New Zealand almost certainly includes many falsehoods such as, "Homosexuality should be accepted because it is probably innate, which helps explain why it is stable." The above study suggests that such statements—typical of what college students are being erroneously taught here, too, as authors of the briefs are themselves college professors—could plausibly slow the spontaneous decline in homosexual identification in a college-age population, especially among women, thereby increasing its cross-sectional prevalence.[32] Furthermore, the study provides actual evidence for a specific causal mechanism (a social environmental influence) that contributes to its prevalence, whereas no evidence for any biological mechanism exists. Indeed all the present biological evidence points only toward "heritability" levels of roughly 30 to 35%, which geneticists recognize as the signature for behavioral traits in human beings that are essentially *non-genetic* and almost completely determined by environmental influences—to the degree that any human trait enmeshed in a body can be.[33] Hence, if the results of this study were to replace the erroneous explanations provided by the mental health guilds, then without introducing value judgments it could be expected over time to reduce the prevalence of homosexual identification—sans "therapy."

Here's why: The ages between 21 and 26 constitute a distinct demographic group and New Zealand is a country not only with "a relatively accepting climate toward homosexuality," that social climate is merely one component of its well known, social-political atmosphere as a whole. One should not pretend, therefore, that attitudes, including attitudes toward homosexuality, are formed in a vacuum, nor that attitudes have no effect on behavior. Thus, for both men and women *in New Zealand,* more so *for those with higher education* there was a small but statistically significant net movement toward homosexuality and away from heterosexuality (that is, immediately following that education, temporarily). Given that *all* the evidence, when accurately presented, points toward the influence of environment, and the association with education, it is likely that the content of higher education in a politically liberal environment is contributory for the differential effect in this educated cohort of twenty-somethings. This is especially the case given that this *increase* in homosexuality follows a much larger *decrease* that would have had to have taken place in the years before age 21 in order to account for the above numbers. Once the educational effect becomes more temporally remote (wears off), however, the typical decline in homosexual identification resumes.[34]

Second, studies on AIDS in New Zealand show the same hierarchy of risk factors as in the United States. In 2002, the most common transmission risk was male homosexual contact (56%), followed by heterosexual contact (28%),[35] intravenous drug use (3%) and mother to infant transmission (1%).[36] In 1995, of 11 industrialized nations studied and reported on by the International Epidemiological Association, New Zealand had the lowest cumulative AIDS incidence rate—1.4 cases per 100,000 population, versus a U.S. rate of 15.2.[37] At the time, using the figures from that particular study, these cumulative incidence rates would have translated into projected morbidity and mortality rates (at 95% confidence intervals) such that in the U.S. one would have projected that if at age 20 a young man considered himself "gay" then the odds that he would be either HIV+ or dead of AIDS at age 30 would be just under 15% and in New Zealand his odds would be just under 4%. One would have turned out to be mistaken in these odds, since in both cases they turn out to have been severe underestimates. Nonetheless, given the actual instability of homosexual identity, wouldn't it rather make greater ethical sense *to emphasize that fact rather than to misrepresent it as the opposite,* as has universally been done instead? In any event, in 1995 the median age of death for an HIV+ individual in the U.S. was 38; in New Zealand, the same. In Italy it is 29 for men and 28 for women. Of additional note is the fact that an independent study performed in 2003 in New Zealand—a country already remarked upon as having an especially open-minded attitude toward homosexuality—provides evidence of a *"link between increasing degrees of same-sex attraction and higher risks of self-harm in both men and women."* Men who identified themselves as homosexual were 3.1 times more likely and women 2.9 times more likely to have suicidal ideation than were those who did not.[38]

2. *Australia Study[39]: Homosexuality as a Phenomenon of the Epoch*

- Nearly 7,500 Australian adults
- Three five-year wide cohorts at ages 20, 40, 60
- Large, consistent declines in homosexual/bisexual identification for women but not (less marked in) men
- Consistent with other Australian studies
- Inconsistent with other non-Australian studies

This study has a number of subtle implications when understood in the context of the other studies to which its authors compare it, namely (a) other studies on age-cohort variation in sexual orientation conducted in Australia that it confirms and (b) non-Australian studies on age cohort variation in sexual orientation from which it differs.

To make a point, let me first paraphrase their findings, and then quote the research exactly: In their large study, the authors discovered a marked decline with age in homosexual/bisexual identification among women in Australia, consistent with the direct citations of the results from other non-Australian studies, for both women and men. However, the Australian researchers pointedly *do not* express their results in the simple way I have here. They add a rather strikingly different-*sounding* conclusion (I emphasize "sounding"). They do so because their results were apparently found to be true with respect to women only.

I have paraphrased their findings before quoting them directly for two independent reasons. First, merely as a general reminder of *how much critical information can be deliberately added, removed or distorted by an entirely accurate and truthful paraphrase*; second (but more importantly), to draw attention to (at least) *one specific* environmental influence on sexual orientation that is necessarily implied by this differential finding (decline among women, but not men), a specificity that is obfuscated in my otherwise correct paraphrase. I will explain how the specificity involved is likely to be "culture" (what the New Zealand researchers deemed "demographics"). Such terms must take into account not only the *place* one lives (and its effect on a person), but the *epoch* (and its effect) as well. Not only do people age over time, the era ages as well, and people age within an aging era.

This complicates analysis considerably, for it is difficult enough to study a poorly defined behavioral trait that is static in a cohort of individuals. It is more difficult to study a poorly defined behavioral trait in a cohort of individuals that mutates as they age, and yet more difficult when that mutation is variable, inconsistent and itself hard to define. It is then extremely hard to study that trait when the aging cohort is embedded in various location-dependent cultures that clearly have a large—indeed statistically the largest—effect on the age-correlated prevalence of the trait, such that location itself influences prevalence. This was shown to be the case when the erstwhile "gay gene" researcher Dean Hamer was pressed by his fellow scientists and forced to admit, contrary to his sworn testimony in the Colorado "Proposition 2" case that ultimately led to *Romer*, "The relationships among genes and environment probably have a somewhat different effect on someone in Salt Lake City than if that person were growing up in New York City."[40] Matters become extraordinarily tricky when it is found that *only in certain location-dependent cultures, there is a sharp sex-related partitioning* such that for half the individuals in the cohort, one thing is true, and for the other it isn't. Thus, in this Australia study, the authors' findings *and conclusions* in their own words are:

> A strong age cohort difference was found for women, with younger women more frequently reporting a homosexual or bisexual identification. By contrast, no age cohort difference was found for men.... These findings suggest that a heterosexual orientation may have become less common in younger cohorts of Australian women. This finding is consistent with data from other recent studies.

If one has not actually tracked a specific group of individuals over time, checking periodically on their sexual orientations, but, instead, assessed people of different ages, taking a snapshot in time, then indeed, one can legitimately argue that any changes that correlate with age might have nothing to do with individual development, *but instead are caused by the changing culture.* Thus, the process of mutability over time that the authors implicitly point to is taking place not so much in the individual as collectively; in this view, "sexual orientation" is not so much a true characteristic of an individual (like height, weight, sex, or even stable, measurable personality traits—recall the warning of Laumann, et al., that homosexuality is *neither* easily measurable *nor* stable), but rather a collective trend or fashion that waxes or wanes with the times.[41]

Common sense tells us that there is nothing to prevent both processes from occurring at the same time and affecting each other, especially since "the culture" is simply another way of talking about what many interpenetrating cohorts composed of people do. But until such time as a great many carefully designed explicit longitudinal studies are performed, we will be unable to tease out the exact contribution of personal maturation from external cultural fashion in the dramatic decrease over time that is universally confirmed in the prevalence of homosexuality.

Conclusions

In both the *Romer* and *Lawrence* briefs, the mental health guilds take great pains to emphasize that homosexuality is an early established, fixed and stable condition—thus suitable for suspect class status. The authors buttress this claim by footnoting a selected pool of authorities whom they rarely directly quote, and by citing themselves in other places where they have offered the same opinions in different words (and even when their own findings are contradictory). Additionally, they refer to the study of Laumann et al. whose work they completely misrepresent. They do this by extracting portions of his sentences so that his meaning is turned into its opposite, by citing page numbers not relevant to the statements they make, and primarily by simply not reporting the vast bulk of the Laumann study, whose conclusions in *every* area with respect to homosexuality are explicitly opposite to what the authors hold, and also opposite to the formal positions of the mental health guilds with respect to the stability of homosexuality and to its very definition and *definability.*

Furthermore, the briefs' authors completely ignore a very large body of follow-up research that has been conducted since the Laumann study was published, specifically to confirm or disconfirm its findings. This follow-up research has not only repeatedly confirmed the essential findings of the Laumann study, including its conclusion that homosexuality is absolutely *not* a stable trait, but deepened and extended those findings, providing more specific understandings as to the nature and dynamism of that instability. In particular, while a scientist will always approach any statement as a hypothesis and never an absolute truth, to date all the available evidence—the same evidence carefully ignored by the mental health guilds—confirms a view of "sexual orientation" as a trait whose instability has a direction, namely, it tends in general toward normative heterosexuality over the course of life.

Furthermore, the extent to which it does or does not do so, shows clear evidence of being directly influenced by "demographics," and "the environment," even the era one lives in—and no evidence of being directly influenced by genes. To the extent one may be specific about the nature of this "environment," all evidence points towards early and continuing sexual activity and later cultural and demographic reinforcement, even education.

The mental health guilds in their many public pronouncements about "reparative therapy," and the authors of the brief in their selective use of references and in their discussion of change exclusively in a therapeutic setting, appear to want nothing more than to draw the public and the Court into an esoteric debate between which group of psychotherapists is right. But the reality is that since 1994—for 10 years—there has existed solid epidemiologic evidence, now extensively confirmed and reconfirmed, that *the most common natural course for a young person who develops a "homosexual identity" is for it to spontaneously disappear unless that process is discouraged or interfered with by extraneous factors.* We may now say with increasing confidence that those "extraneous" factors are primarily the "social milieu" in which the person finds himself. Ironically, this "social milieu" is the family setting and culture being created by, inter alia, the decisions enforced by the Justices of the Supreme Court of the United States acting in coordination with the misrepresentation of scientific evidence provided to it by the American Psychiatric Association, the American Psychological Association, and the National Association of Social Workers.

"It's a matter of fashion. And fashions keep changing."
John Spiegel, M.D., addressing the diagnosis of homosexuality,
quoted in *Omni Magazine* (November 1986), page 30.

Notes

1. See www.psychologymatters.org/hooker.html.

2. Evelyn Hooker, "The Adjustment of the Male Overt Homosexual," *Journal of Projective Techniques*, 21 (1957), pp. 18-31.

3. Ronald Bayer, *Homosexuality and American Psychiatry: The Politics of Diagnosis* (Princeton, NJ: Princeton University Press, 1987), p. 104.

4. Wardell B. Pomeroy, *Dr. Kinsey and the Institute for Sex Research* (New York: Harper and Row, 1972).

5. Marcel T. Saghir and Eli Robins, "Male and Female Homosexuality: Natural History," *Comprehensive Psychiatry*, 12/6 (November 1971), pp. 503-510.

6. Mentioned in personal email to Kathleen Melonakos, M.A., R.N., dated February 5, 2002.

7. Ibid., pp. 3-4.

8. Ibid.

9. Ibid.

10. Bayer, *Homosexuality and American Psychiatry: The Politics of Diagnosis*, p. 138.

11. C. E. Lewis, Marcel T. Saghir, and Eli Robins, "Drinking Patterns in Homosexual and Heterosexual Women," *Journal of Clinical Psychiatry*, 43/7 (July 1982), pp. 277-279. Their findings have been repeatedly confirmed; see, e.g., Tonda L. Hughes and Sharon C. Wilsnack, "Research on Lesbians and Alcohol," 18/3, *Alcohol Health and Research World* (1994).

12. Lewis, et al, "Drinking Patterns in Homosexual and Heterosexual Women," pp. 277-279; Marcel T. Saghir, Eli Robins, B. Walbran, and K. A. Gentry, *Homosexuality: IV*, "Psychiatric Disorders and Disability in the Female Homosexual," *American Journal of Psychiatry*, 127/2 (August 1970), pp. 147-154; Marcel T. Saghir, Eli Robins, B. Walbran, and K. A. Gentry, *Homosexuality: III*,

"Psychiatric Disorders and Disability in the Male Homosexual, *American Journal of Psychiatry*, 126/8 (February 1970), pp. 1079-1086; Marcel T. Saghir, Eli Robins, and B. Walbran, *Homosexuality: II*, "Sexual Behavior of the Male Homosexual, *Archives of General Psychiatry*, 21/2 (August 1969), pp. 219-229; Marcel T. Saghir and Eli Robins, *Homosexuality: I*, "Sexual Behavior of the Female Homosexual," *Archives of General Psychiatry*, 20/2 (February 1969), pp. 192-201.

13. Evelyn Hooker, "Reflections of a 40-Year Exploration: A Scientific View on Homosexuality," *American Psychologist* 48/4 (April 1993), pp. 450-453.

14. Bruce Shenitz, "The Grande Dame of Gay Liberation," *Los Angeles Times Magazine* (June 10, 1990), pp. 20-34.

15. Hooker, "Reflections of a 40-Year Exploration: A Scientific View on Homosexuality," pp. 450-453. In spite of the title, there is nothing at all scientific in this article's contents. Hooker simply muses as a leftist in the McCarthy era about how she spent her career hoping that someone would eventually find evidence to support the claims she published in her infamous 1957 article. Apart from that she rails at the McCarthy Committee who did terrible things to the gay artistic community in Los Angeles to whom she was personally committed, much of which, between the lines is clearly heartrending even if four decades later. She died three years after this "scientific view" was published.

16. Edward O. Laumann, John H. Gagnon, Robert T. Michael, and Stuart Michaels, *The Social Organization of Sexuality: Sexual Practices in the United States,* (Chicago: University of Chicago Press, 1994).

17. Edward O. Laumann, Robert T. Michael, and John H. Gagnon, "A Political History of the National Sex Survey of Adults," *Family Planning Perspectives*, 26/1 (January-February 1994), pp. 34-38.

18. Ibid., p. 283.

19. Ibid., p. 297.

20. William Byne and Bruce Parsons, "Sexual Orientation: The Biologic Theories Reappraised," *Archives of General Psychiatry*, 50/3 (March 1993), p. 228.

21. The author is using the term "sexual identity" as it was sensibly understood before the term was politically redefined by the gay activist movement. In other words, he is using the term to refer to male and female, not to whether one self-identifies as homosexual and heterosexuality. It is ironic that in the worldview of the modern left, significant differences between homosexuals and heterosexuals (which science shows to be extraordinarily difficult to characterize and wholly unstable) are argued to be innate, while significant differences between men and women (which are enormous, self-evident, and permanent) are alleged to be at once trivial and socially constructed.

22. Paul McHugh, "Surgical Sex," *First Things*, 147 (November 2004), pp. 34-38.

23. Wardell B. Pomeroy, *Boys and Sex* (New York: Delacorte, 1968).

24. Wardell B. Pomeroy, "A New Look at Incest," *Variations Magazine* (1977), pp. 86-88; also in *Penthouse Forum* (November 1976), pp. 9-13.

25. Laumann, et al., "A Political History of the National Sex Survey of Adults," p. 311.

26. Mark E. Schwartz and William H. Masters, "The Masters and Johnson Treatment Program for Dissatisfied Homosexual Men," *American Journal of Psychiatry*, 141/2 (February 1984), pp. 173-181.

27. Wayne Besen is well known for his unrestrained use of invective and distortion. In a recent reference of his to me, for example, reads, "Dr. Jeffrey Satinover, a quack that [sic] says Prozac may 'cure' homosexuals" [sic]. See his column "Anything But Straight," *Falls Church News-Press*, 15/44 (January 5-11).

28. Robert L. Spitzer, "Can Some Gay Men and Lesbians Change Their Sexual Orientation? 200 Participants Reporting a Change from Homosexual to Heterosexual Orientation," *Archives of Sexual Behavior*, 32/5 (October 2003), pp. 403-417.
29. Laumann, et al., "A Political History of the National Sex Survey of Adults," pp. 296-297.
30. Nigel Dickson, Charlotte Paul, and Peter Herbison, "Same-Sex Attraction in a Birth Cohort: Prevalence and Persistence in Early Adulthood," *Social Science and Medicine*, 56/8 (April 2003), pp. 1607-1615.
31. The authors specifically identify New Zealand as a country whose more welcoming attitude toward homosexuality (over against the United States where the Laumann study was conducted and whose findings they are addressing) ought to attenuate or perhaps eliminate the effect found by the Laumann group.
32. In fact, studies done many years ago demonstrated that merely showing people a phonied-up paragraph purporting to offer a biological explanation instantly altered their attitudes. Kurt Ernulf, Sune Innala, and Frederick Whitam, "Biological Explanation, Psychological Explanation, and Tolerance of Homosexuals," *Psychological Reports,* 65/3, part 1 of 3, (December 1989), pp. 1003-1010.
33. This statement does not contradict the presence of "indirect genetic factors" influencing homosexuality. Most people mistakenly presume that an indirect genetic influence refers to a mere technical distinction. In fact, the distinction is crucial. Basketball playing shows a very strong, arguably stronger than homosexuality, indirect genetic influence, but there are no genes for basketball playing—it is a wholly "environmentally" influenced behavior subject to a high degree of choice—much higher than same-sex attraction. The crucial point is that genes that indirectly influence a trait *have nothing at all to do with the trait itself and therefore can't possibly "cause" it.* The genes that

influence the likelihood someone will become a basketball player are self-evident: Those that code for height, athleticism, muscle refresh rate. There are, at present, even strong racial genetic associations to basketball playing. These *associations* are almost entirely socially determined while the genes themselves are biological (and evolved in an era before basketball playing even existed), and the associational degree (i.e., with race) fluctuates over time as basketball spreads across the globe.

34. This phenomenon was actually first recognized not by sociologists, epidemiologists, psychiatrists, psychiatrists, or any other kind of "ist" but by savvy Smith College students who first called themselves SLUGs: Smith Lesbians Until Graduation. Elsewhere, the eponym mutated into Selectively Lesbian Until Graduation.

35. The common pathway of high-risk infection shared by homosexual contact and heterosexual contact is anal sex. Vaginal intercourse has a much lower transmission probability.

36. Graham Mills, et al, "New Zealand's HIV Infected Population under Active Follow-up During 2000," *New Zealand Medical Journal*, 115/1152 (April 26, 2002), pp. 173-176.

37. Katherine V. Heath, et al., "Human Immunodeficiency Virus (HIV)/Acquired Immunodeficiency Syndrome (AIDS) Mortality in Industrialized Nations, 1987-1991, *International Journal of Epidemiology*, 27/4 (1998): 685-90. Even though much of this paper is devoted to an analysis of *trends* in the years stated, the paper also reports static cross-sectional data from later years.

38. Keren Skegg, et al., "Sexual Orientation and Self-Harm in Men and Women," *American Journal of Psychiatry*, 160 (March 2003), pp. 541-546.

39. Anthony F. Jorm, K. B. G. Dear, B. Rogers, and H. Christensen, "Cohort Difference in Sexual Orientation: Results from a Large Age-Stratified Population Sample," 49/6, *Gerontology* (November-December 2003), pp. 392-395.

40. As quoted in an interview by C. Mann, "Genes and Behavior: Behavioral Genetics in Transition," *Science*, 264/5166 (June 17, 1994), pp. 1686-1689.

41. The authors report that the decline for males has a p=.12 which not statistically significant (p<=.05 is the conventional cutoff that is used). To be scrupulous, I have reported everything exactly as the authors have, and it is important to make the point that it impossible wholly to disaggregate "collective mutability" effects from "individual mutability." However, to whatever weight is added to the "collective mutability" component by the possibility that male homosexual identification remained fixed is weakened by the fact that it is far more likely that male homosexual identification did not remain fixed than that it did. This weakening was simply not strong enough—after age 20—to "pass the statistical bar" even though, as the authors do note, the trend is clear. Of greater importance, however, is the fact that in all other studies elsewhere, e.g., in the United States, the greatest drop in male homosexual and bisexual identification occurs *before age 18*. For instance, the Laumann study (p. 296 passim) discusses a drop from 10% of men, possibly well more than that, with some form of homosexual related characteristic before age 18, to 3.8% of men who have had sex with men before age 18, but never again after, to 2.8% with a final homosexual identification. Compare to the above chart that only begins at age 20. Furthermore, it would take very little reduction in error in a larger cohort for the male trend to achieve statistical significance. In any interpretation, additional research of so complex, dynamic and multivariate a subject is clearly warranted prior to major overhauling of fundamental social structures.

THERE'S HELP IF YOU'RE LOOKING

American Center for Law and Justice (ACLJ). A non-government organization that focuses on constitutional and human rights law worldwide. Based in Washington, DC. Chief Counsel: Jay Sekulow. Includes providing advice and assistance to persons dealing with constitutional and human rights issues relating to homosexuality. For questions and petitions for assistance, call 877-989-2255. Internet: http://aclj.org.

Abba's Delight. Address: P.O. Box 991752, Louisville, KY 40269. Phone: 502-939-9269. Email: danielmingo.abbasdelight@insightbb.com.

AboutHOPE. Affiliated with Cross Church. Address: 802 Holiman Street, Springdale, AR 72762. Phone: 479-751-4847. Email: abouthope777@aol.com. Internet: http://www.crosschurch.org/portfolio/about-h-o-p-e/.

Alliance Defending Freedom (ADF). A non-government alliance of Christian attorneys and like-minded organizations that work on protecting and preserving religious liberty, marriage, the family, and the sanctity of human life. This includes providing information, training, and assistance to persons and organizations dealing with legal issues relating to homosexuality. Internet: http://www.telladf.org.

American College of Pediatricians (ACP). A national organization of professional pediatricians and other health professionals that produces sound policy based on the best available research to assist parents and influence society on matters relating to the health and wellbeing of children. It is a reliable source of information on homosexuality as it relates to parenting, health, and wellbeing of children. Phone: 888-376-1877. Internet: http://www.acpeds.org.

Beyond Imagination. Address: P.O. Box 28294, Raleigh, NC 27611. Phone: 919-538-0073. Internet: http://www.beyondimagination.org.

Boundless Treasures Ministries. A Christian ministry focused on helping women find their worth in Jesus Christ. Includes counseling and assistance for women struggling with sexual wounding, sexual confusion, and lesbian attractions. Director: Bekah Mason. Phone: 423-779-7443. Internet: http://www. http://boundlesstreasures.org/.

Bridge of Hope. Address: P.O. Box 23223, Columbus, OH 43223-0223. Phone: 614-228-6129. Internet: http://www. bohcolumbus.com.

Bright Hope Ministries. Address: 5700 Winner Road, Kansas City, MO 64127. Phone: 816-241-4831 ext. 1194. Internet: http:// www.brighthopeofkc.com.

Broken Yoke Ministries. Address: P.O. Box 13906, Milwaukee, WI 53213. Phone: 262-751-1128. Internet: http://www.brokenyoke.org.

Choices Ministry. Address: 75-5851 Kuakini Hwy #240, Kailua-Kona, HI 96740. Phone: 808-960-4833. Internet: http://www. choicesministry.org.

Christian Coalition for Reconciliation. Address: P.O. Box 420437, Houston, TX 77242-0437. Phone: 713-782-7084. Internet: http://www.ccrhouston.org.

Christian Counseling Center. Address: 780 Harry L. Drive, Johnson City, NY 13790. Phone: 607-729-7779. Internet: http://www.christiancounsel.us.

Courage/EnCourage. Companion non-profit Catholic organizations that offer help and support to persons with unwanted same-sex attractions, as well as to parents, pastors, families, and friends who desire to reach out in truth and compassion to such persons. Address: 8 Leonard Street, Norwalk, CT 06850. Phone: 203-803-1564. Internet: http://couragec.net.

Cross Ministry. Address: P.O. Box 1122, Wake Forest, NC 27588. Phone: 919-569-0375. Internet: http://www.crossministry.org.

Cross Power Ministries. Address: 6000 W. Wadley, Midland, TX 79707. Phone: 432-694-5100. Internet: http://www.crosspowerministries.com.

Crossroads Ministries of Charlotte. Address: 6200 Rocky Falls Road, Charlotte, NC 28211-5441. Phone: 704-536-6705. Internet: http://www.charlottecrossroads.com.

Day Seven Ministries. Address: 802 Olde Hickory Road, Lancaster, PA 17601. Phone: 1-866-301-3297. Internet: http://www.dayseven.net.

Eric Garner Set Free. A former homosexual who advises and encourages persons with same-sex attractions seek help with sexual identity issues. Internet: http://www.ericgarnersetfree.com.

Evergreen International. A non-profit Mormon 501(c)(3) organization that assists people who want to overcome homosexual behavior. Address: 307 West 200 South, Suite 3004, Salt Lake City, UT 84101. Phone: 800-391-1000 (toll free). Internet: http://www.evergreeninternational.org.

Face to Face Ministry. Address: 2104 West Louisiana, Midland, TX 79701. Phone: 432-853-4474. Internet: http://www.face2facehope.org.

First Stone Ministries. Address: 1330 N. Classen Blvd., Suite G80, Oklahoma City, OK 73106-6856. Phone: 405-236-4673. Internet: http://www.firststone.org.

Focus on the Family/Pure Intimacy. A source of online information for those struggling with same-sex attraction. Focus on the Family help line: 800-A-FAMILY (800-232-6459). Internet: http://www.pureintimacy.org/homosexuality/.

Free Indeed. Address: P.O. Box 2836, Waterville, ME 04903. Phone: 207-945-3424. Internet: http://www.freeindeedne.com.

Freedom Quest. Address: 6660 Delmonico Drive, Suite D-255, Colorado Springs, CO 80919. Phone: 719-559-1579. Internet: http://www.freedomquestministry.org.

Fresno New Creation Ministries. Address: P.O. Box 5451, Fresno, CA 93755. Phone: 559-227-1066. Internet: http://www.ncmfresno.org.

Genesis Counseling. Address: 176321 Irvine Blvd., Suite #220, Tustin, CA 92780. Director: Joe Dallas. Phone: 714-508-6953. Internet: http://www.joedallas.com.

Genesis Support Group. Address: The Chapel, 135 Fir Hill, Akron, OH 44304. Phone: 330-315-5610. Internet: http://www.the-chapel.org.

Grace in Action. Address: 1290 East Ireland Road, V-100 DMB #205, South Bend, IN 46614. Phone: 574-344-8728. Internet: http://www.graceinaction.us.

Greater Hope Ministry. Address: P.O. Box 772, Harrisonburg, VA 22803. Phone: 540-574-4189. Internet: http://www.greaterhope.org.

Harvest USA. Address: 3901B Main Street, Suite 304, Philadelphia, PA 19127. Phone: 215-482-0111. Internet: http://www.harvestusa.org.

Help 4 Families. Address: P.O. Box 755, Waynesville, NC 28786. Phone: 814-598-4952. Internet: http://www.help4families.com.

His Way Out. Address: 1412 17ᵗʰ Street, Suite 313, Bakersfield, CA 93301. Phone: 661-321-9551. Internet: http://www.hiswayout. com.

Homosexuals Anonymous. A national 14-step recovery group for homosexuals modeled on principles developed for Alcoholics Anonymous. Address: 529 Road 115, Box 113, Houston, TX 77095. Phone: 281-712-2676. Internet: http://www.ha-fs.org.

Hope Quest. Address: P.O. Box 2699, Acworth, GA 30102. Phone: 678-391-5950. Internet: http://www.hopequestgroup.org.

Hope2Turn. Address: P.O. Box 1927, Rockford, IL 61110. Phone: 815-601-6714.

In His Time. Affiliated with Morrison Heights Baptist Church. Address: 3000 Hampstead Blvd, Clinton, MS 39056. Phone: 601-925-6435. Internet: http://www.morrisonheights.org.

Institute for the Study of Sexual Identity. An institute that offers help to persons seeking clarity on matters of sexual identity. Affiliated with Regent University. Address: 1000 Regent University Drive, Virginia Beach, VA 23464. Director: Dr. Mark Yarhouse. Phone: 757-352-4829. Internet: http://www. sexualidentityinstitute.org.

Jews Offering New Alternatives to Homosexuality (JONAH). A Jewish-based organization that assists individuals with unwanted same-sex attractions. Address: P.O. Box 313, Jersey City, NJ 07303. Phone: 201-433-3444. Internet: http://www. jonahweb.org.

Life+Guard Ministries. Address: 6611 Berrywood Lane, Georgetown/Austin, TX 78635. Director: Don Brown. Phone: 512-922-3011. Email: dsloanbrown@aol.com.

LifeMor. Address: P.O. Box 92321, Albuquerque, NM 87199. Phone: 505-503-7961. Internet: http://www.LifeMor.com.

Living Hope Ministries. A non-denominational ministry that serves persons seeking sexual and relational wholeness through Jesus Christ. This ministry specializes in offering online forums on sexual and relational wholeness for adult men, adult women, youth, parents, and mates. Address: P.O. Box 2239, Arlington, TX 76004. Phone: (817) 459-2507. Internet: http://www.livehope.org.

Love and Grace Ministry. Address: 7009 S. Danner Drive, Oklahoma City, OK 73159. Phone: 405-686-1612. Email: lovegrace@cox.net.

Love In Action. Address: P.O. Box 343418, Bartlett, TN 38184. Phone: 901-751-2468. Internet: http://www.loveinaction.org.

National Association for Research and Therapy on Homosexuality (NARTH). A non-profit professional, scientific organization that offers hope to those who struggle with unwanted homosexuality. Disseminates educational information, conducts and collects scientific research, promotes effective therapeutic treatment, and provides referrals to those seeking assistance. Founded in 1992 by Drs. Benjamin Kaufman, Charles Socarides, and Joseph Nicolosi. 2011 President: Dr. Julie Hamilton. Phone: 1-888-364-4744 (toll free). Email: info@narth.com. Internet: http://narth.com.

New Hope Ministries. Address: P.O. Box 10246, San Rafael, CA 94912. Phone: 415-453-6474. Internet: http://www.newhope123.org.

New Pathways. Address: P.O. Box 2516, Springfield, OH 45501. Phone: 937-390-7641. Internet: http://www.newpathwaysohio.org.

New Song. Address: P.O. Box 25564, Columbia, SC 29224-5664. Phone: 803-743-9388. Internet: http://www.carolinanewsong.org.

OneByOne. A non-profit Presbyterian organization that offers to help and assist persons seeking to overcome conflict with their own sexuality. Address: P.O. Box 540119, Orlando, FL 32854. Phone: 407-599-6872. Internet: http://www.oneby1.org.

Portland Fellowship. Address: P.O. Box 14841, Portland, OR 97293. Phone: 503-235-6364. Internet: http://www.portlandfellowship.com.

Positive Alternatives to Homosexuality (PATH). A non-profit coalition of organizations that help persons with unwanted same-sex attractions realize their personal goals for change. President: Arthur Abba Goldberg. Internet: http://www.pathinfo.org.

Prodigal Ministries. Address: P.O. Box 19949, Cincinnati, OH 45219. Phone: 513-861-0011. Internet: http://www.prodical-ministries.com.

ReachTruth.com. An online mentorship program for teens affected by homosexuality. Internet: http://www.reachtruth.com.

Reclamation Resource Center. Address: P.O. Box 1062, Oshkosh, WI 54903. Phone: 920-303-1041. Internet: http://www.reclamationrc.org.

Reconciliation Ministries. Address: 25410 Kelly Road, Roseville, MI 48066. Phone: 586-739-5114. Internet: http://www.recmin.org.

ReCreation Ministries. Address: 54 Eric Drive, Uxbridge, MA 01569. Phone: 603-533-3880. Internet: http://www.ReCreationMinistries.com.

Regeneration. Address: P.O. Box 9830, Baltimore, MD 21284. Phone: 410-661-0284. Internet: http://www.RegenerationMinistries.org.

Restoring Hope. Address: 700 S. Federal Hwy., Daina Beach, FL 33004. Phone: 954-927-5230. Internet: http://www.restoring-hope.net.

River of Life. Address: P.O. Box 125002, San Diego, CA 92112-5002. Phone: 619-502-9484. Email: riveroflife@gmail.com.

Set Free. Address: P.O. Box 14835, Richmond, VA 23221. Phone: 804-358-8150. Internet: http://www.setfreerichmond.org.

Sexual Wholeness Ministry. Address: P.O. Box 580592, Clear Lake, TX 77258. Phone: 281-992-8800. Internet: http://www.grace.tv/swm/index.html.

Sight Ministry. Address: P.O. Box 140808, Nashville, TN 37214. Phone: 615-509-0782. Internet: http://www.thesightministry. org.

Sought Out. Address: P.O. Box 62019, Virginia Beach, VA 23466-2019. Phone: 757-631-0099. Internet: http://www.soughtout. org.

Such Were Some of You. Address: P.O. Box 100133, Pittsburgh, PA 15233. Phone: 312-766-5595. Internet: http://www. suchweresomeofyou.com.

The Way Out Ministries. Address: P.O. Box 292, Columbiana, OH 44408. Phone: 330-921-1120. Internet: http://www. thewayoutministries.com.

The Way Out (SBC). A non-profit Baptist resource service, associated with the Gender Issues Office of the Southern Baptist Convention, that provides speakers, training, and workshops for persons and groups needing honest, compassionate ministry assistance with handling gender issues including homosexuality. Phone: 817-429-9121. Internet: http://www.sbcthewayout.com.

Tower of Light Ministries. Affiliated with Northshore Baptist Church. Address: 10301 NE 145th Street, Kirkland, WA 98034. Phone: 425-216-4443. Email: jeffs@nsb.org.

Transformed Image. Address: P.O. Box 24128, San Jose, CA 95154. Phone: 408-496-9888. Internet: http://www.transformedimage. com.

Truth Ministry. An organization with branch offices in various states. Address: P.O. Box 5781, Spartanburg, SC 29304. Phone: 864-583-7606. Internet: http://truthministry.org.

Waiting Room. Associated with Chandler Christian Church. Address: 1825 S. Alma School Road, Chandler, AZ 85248-1903. Phone: 480-650-9340. Internet: http://WaitingRoomMinistry.org.

You See Me Free. Address: P.O. Box 9120, Waco, TX 76714. Phone: 254-744-8093. Internet: http://www.youseemefree.org.

*Being queer means
pushing the parameters of sex,
sexuality, and family, and in the process,
transforming the very fabric of society ... we
must keep our eyes on the goals of providing
true alternatives to marriage and of
radically reordering society's
view of reality.*

Paula Ettelbrick, Executive Director of the International Gay and Lesbian Human Rights Commission, 2003-2009; Family Policy Director for the National Gay and Lesbian Task Force, 1999-2001; Legal Director for the Lambda Defense Fund, 1988-1993.

Quoted in Paula Ettelbrick, "Since When Is Marriage a Path to Liberation?" in William Rubenstein, ed., *Lesbians, Gay Men and the Law* (New York: The New Press, 1993), pp. 401-405.